Faith Under Scrutiny

Be ready always with an answer
to everyone who asks you
the reason for the "hopeful faith" that you have.
Yet do it with gentleness and reverence . . .

(1 Pet 3, 15—16)

Faith Under Scrutiny

Tibor Horvath S.J.

FIDES PUBLISHERS, INC.
NOTRE DAME, INDIANA

Library of Congress Cataloging in Publication Data
Horváth, Tibor, 1927 (July 28)-
   Faith under scrutiny.

   Includes bibliographical references.
   1. Apologetics—20th century. 2. Catholic Church—
Apologetic works. I. Title.
BT1102.H67   230'.2   75-11797
ISBN 0-8190-0073-6

CONTENTS

VALIDITY OF CHRISTIAN FAITH IN
THE PERSONAL ENTRY OF GOD INTO
HUMAN HISTORY FOR THE SUPER-
CREATURAL BEATITUDE OF MAN

ACKNOWLEDGMENTS

Acknowledgments are made first of all to the following journals for permission to include in this book copyright materials. With some alterations and corrections the following articles have been included in the present book.

"Why was Jesus Brought to Pilate" in: *Novum Testamentum* 11 (1969) 174–184 in Chapter Eight; "A New Argument for the Existence of God?" in: *Revue de l'Université d'Ottawa* 40 (1970) 494–496, "Another New Argument for the Existence and Language of God?" in: *Revue de l'Université d'Ottawa* 41 (1971) 97–99 in Chapter Eleven; "The Early Markan Tradition on the Resurrection (Mk 16, 1–9)" in: *Revue de l'Université d'Ottawa* 43 (1973) 445–448 in Chapter Nine; "Object and Method in Apologetics" in: *Science et Esprit* 24 (1972) 47–76 in Chapter Five.

Acknowledgements are due also to the following publishers for the permission to include quotations from their publications.

Bowes and Bowes, London, for quotations from *Evidence of Tradition,* 1957, by D. J. THERON;

Doubleday and Company, Inc., Garden City, N.Y., for quotations from *Computers and the Human Mind,* 1966, by D. G. FINK;

Faber and Faber, London, for quotations from *The Jewish-Christian Argument,* 1963, by H. J. SCHOEPS;

Farrar, Straus and Giroux, New York, for quotations from *God in Search of Man,* 1955, by A. J. HESCHEL;

Harper and Row, Publishers, New York, for quotations from *Kerygma and Myth: a theological debate,* edited by H. W. BARTSCH.

I want to acknowledge my indebtedness to all the authors mentioned and quoted in this book: alive or gone long ago, they have influenced my reflection upon the faith of the Church. I do hope that the readers will find them as alive in this book as they are in the self-reflective dialogizing dynamism of my faith. The "dialogic" nature of the book reflects the intersubjective nature of faith: there is no encounter with God except in the community of men.

I am indebted to the faculty and students of Regis College for their interest, criticism and help, particularly to Professor M. J. Lapierre, S.J., G. E. Nunan, S.J., J. T. Peck, S.J. and G. P. Schner, S.J. for their assistance in clarifying my writing, to R. P. Finlay, S.J. for editing stenciled copies circulated in class and study groups to substantiate my method, to Maureen Whelan for typing the manuscript and finally to Professor John Adam, S.J. and to the Hungarian Jesuits for their friendship, encouragement and constant support.

INTRODUCTION:

THE RELATIVITY OF APOLOGETICS

Whenever the Church and its faith have been challenged (either from within or from without) there has always flourished a special theological activity called apologetics. Though apologetics became a distinct theological treatise only in 1838, when J. S. Drey published his book *Die Apologetik als wissenschaftliche Nachweisung der Göttlichkeit des Christentums in seiner Erscheinung* (Apologetics as Scientific Demonstration of the Divine Character of Christianity Manifested in its External Appearance),[1] it existed from the earliest times of the Church as the self-reflective dialogizing activity of faith, sometimes dormant, sometimes blooming, but always proportional to the intensity of the challenges.

The different concrete, historical problems of each age demand different approaches to apologetics. However, differences in apologetics are not due exclusively to the different kinds of problems raised but even more to the ever growing self-understanding of the challengers, and consequently of the Church as well. Granted that a problem might endure for centuries, indeed for the life-time of the human race, its understanding and formulation is related to the historical condition of the questioner. The historical condition modifies the nature of the question because it modifies first the self-understanding of the challenger, and this in turn, modifies the self-understanding of the person challenged. The question forces the latter into a new situation upon which he must reflect if he is to understand the challenge. Further, if he seeks not only to understand but also to be understood, he has to express inwardly to himself and outwardly to others precisely this facet of himself which is the most connatural to the historical and logical presuppositions of his challengers.

Dialogue and self-reflection are dialectically conjoined activities. Each challenge in the dialogue conditions a new self-understanding, which, in turn, is directed again to a further dialogue. As a matter of fact, each self-understanding always supposes another understanding of the same person in someone else. In writing, in speaking, and even in his thinking man always directs himself and his understanding to another or to others whose understanding differs from his own. He attempts to clarify this difference, to unify the thought-polarities, by an effort of reconciliation.

Thus, each challenge, each self-defense, discussion, and quarrel reveals a tendency toward unity, and manifests a degree of love between the challenger and the challenged. This love might take either a *childish* form, which manifests itself as "person-devouring," an effort to dominate, destroy, devour the "other" in order to have him completely within oneself, or an *adult* form, which functions as "person-creating" by making the other more aware of himself as "other." However, in either case it is the same fundamental love in man which constantly strives to transform all the surrounding hostile world into a family home. It is more than probable that challenges, discussions, fights, unwillingness to surrender might convey greater love for unity than a silent, peaceful coexistence, or indifferent submission. The commonly formulated principle of freedom, "You do what you want, and I will do what I want," or its negative corollary, "Do not disturb me, and I will not disturb you," is not necessarily the ideal formula for human relations. It means rather the surrender of a love for unity for a dualism of mere coexistence. The transformation of the "You" (do what you want) and the "I" (do what I want) into a "We" (can do what we want) is, indeed, a very difficult and dangerous operation. It is difficult because it implies a series of painful trials of different combinations of "I can do what you want" and "You can do what I want." The transformation is also dangerous, for during the trial, the love for unity, because of its shortcomings, might be defeated, and by its defeat the righteousness of "cool" justice apparently vindicated. Indeed, it may happen that love passionately seeking unity may commit more sins against the same unity, than the "prudent" justice of not interfering with the business of others.

Perhaps in the light of this consideration the exclusivity, universalism, and sometimes intransigent tendency of Christianity as well as the tenacious constancy of its challengers might be understood as the actuation of man's all-embracing love for real unity, even though manifested in an ambiguous form. Both the constant self-defense and the pertinacious attack express a fundamental conviction that the real unity of the "We do what we want" is of greater value than the pure coexistence of the "You do" and "I do," each in his own way.

Within the context of these considerations it is clear why the history of apologetics has always been connected with the missionary function of the Church. The Church, in addition to its care for the eternal salvation of souls has mainly been nourished by the conviction that no real, permanent human love and unity between men is possible without a unity concerning Ultimate Reality and Meaning.

Further, it is clear in this context why in the life of the Church, when external challenges were lacking, internal challenges could not be absent. The dialogue of challenge seems to be so necessary for the growth of self-understanding that in times of external peace in order to foster development in self-understanding and to cement further unity, faith itself provided an atmosphere of internal turmoil within the Church. Thus, it is not strange that in our day when external attacks on the Church have largely ceased, Christians themselves have started to criticize their own Church.

Since the challenges which fostered the Church's self-understanding and unity were also the cause of the theological treatises of apologetics, the history of apologetics is, indeed, nothing else but the history of the different challenges (external and internal) which the Church has had to face since its beginning.

PART ONE

THE HISTORY OF
THE SELF-REFLECTIVE DIALOGIZING
ACTIVITY OF CHRISTIAN FAITH

CHAPTER ONE

THE HISTORY OF APOLOGETICS FROM THE 1ST CENTURY TO THE 18TH CENTURY

1. JESUS' APOLOGETICS ACCORDING TO THE GOSPELS

Christian apologetics first began, according to the synoptic gospels, when, on account of his friendship with sinners and of his neglect of ritual purification, Jesus' righteousness was challenged. To meet this challenge, Jesus proclaimed a new and different justice and righteousness exceeding that of the Scribes and Pharisees. A new standard of love, and of justice, became the light revealing to the world that Jesus, and, through him, his disciples, had indeed been sent by God. This holiness, manifested in the mighty miracles of this active charity, in curing the sick, feeding the hungry, relieving the poor and depressed, etc., served to express the meaning of Jesus' existence as well as that of his disciples, and to legitimatize their faith and mission before all challengers (cf Mk 6,7-13; Mt 9,35-10,42; Mt 5,20-48; Lk 6,27-36; Mt 7,15-29; Lk 6,43-49; Mt 5,16; Mt 25,31-46; Lk 9,1-6; Mk 16,20).

This "general principle of apologetics," common to most of the books of the New Testament, is further specified in Jn 17, 23. The fact of complete unity among the disciples is the witness wherein the world can recognize that God sent Jesus and that God loves the world. If we compare the synoptic presentation with the

Johannine one, we seem to discover that the Jesus of the synoptics is really more an apologist than the one in John. The Jesus of the latter appears rather like a theologian, who constantly refers to the invisible authority of God, his Father, witnessing to all that he has said, while repeating his sayings again and again without explicitly helping his challengers towards a better understanding (cf Jn 5,19-47; 6,30-71; 8,13-59; 10,24-39). On the other hand, the Jesus of the former seems to be a successful debater (Mk 12,28) and controversialist (Mk 8,11), who silences his challengers (cf Mt 19,1-12; 21,23-27; 22,15-46), masterfully bypasses their traps (Mk 12,13-17; Mt 22,15-22; Lk 20,20-26), and puzzles them with extremely clever riddles (Mk 12,35-37; Mt 22,41-46; Lk 20,21-44).

2. THE APOSTLES IN JUDEA

But the Church faced its first real significant challenge when the apostles began to preach the resurrection of Jesus. The Acts of the Apostles, confirms this with the introduction of a new vocabulary which indicates explicit apologetical activity. According to the author, Stephen and Paul do not only preach (κηρύσσω, εὐαγγελίζομαι καταγγέλλω), teach (διδάσκω) and bear witness (μαρτυρέω), but also discuss (συζητέω, Acts 6,9; 9,29) and reason (διαλέγομαί, Acts 17,2; 18,19; 19,8-9) with the Jews. They try to refute them (διακατελέγχομαι, Acts 18,28) and to demonstrate (ἐπιδείκνυμι, Acts 18,28), and to prove (συμβιβάζω, Acts 9,22) that Jesus is Christ by persuading and convincing (πείθω: Acts 18,4; 19,8; 28,23-24) them about Jesus and urging them to become Christians (Acts 26,28).

The apostles' demonstration was probably a sort of simple argument of literal fulfillment based upon an uncritical accommodative interpretation of scripture, the authoritative source of truth for their Jewish challengers. Nevertheless, it is interesting enough because it shows the first self-reflective dialogizing activity of faith.[2]

3. THE GRAECO-ROMAN WORLD

When Christians left Palestine, they met new unexpected challenges. This encounter produced another rather nonbiblical apologetics. In Rome not only their faith in God, but also their moral conduct was challenged. Christians refusing to worship pagan gods were accused of being atheists. Their eucharistic celebrations led to charges of eating human flesh, the flesh of a child (the body of Jesus, son of his Father). The kiss of peace seemed incestuous. To refute these calumnious accusations, the great theologians of the second century, especially Justin and Tertullian, wrote their Apologies. They not only refuted the accusations, but they defended the meaning and usefulness of Christianity. Though Christians are not distinguished from the rest of the world by their language or eccentric mode of life, explains the author of the *Epistle to Diognetus* (an imaginary representative of the contemporary pagan world), their way of living is extraordinary and worthy of admiration. They are needed in the world, as the soul is needed for the body. "What the soul is in the body, that the Christians are in the world."[3]

Before Romans, for whom the Roman Law was the final word, Tertullian defended the existence of Christian communities as legal according to Roman Law, and not guilty of the accusations brought against them.[4] For the Roman philosophers, who liked arguments from etymology, the same Tertullian elaborated another apologetics based upon the use of human language and experience.[5] Perhaps he was the first to appeal to the human conscience in favor of Christianity. In spontaneous expressions, such as, for example, "God sees," "God will judge," "May the departed soul rest in peace," etc. the soul proclaims the unity of God, survival after death, and the existence of eternal justice, realities which Christianity proclaimed. Thus, the soul, though it is not born Christian, during its lifetime develops a taste for Christianity, so that it becomes Christian without being aware of it (*Christianum nomen sapiebas*).

It would be difficult to know what influence these arguments exercised upon the Romans. But, as a matter of fact, the Romans seemed to have listened to the voice of their consciences and became Christians.

4. THE BARBARIANS

Contrary to the expectations of many,[6] the Constantine peace did not end challenges for the Church. In the fifth century Alaric took Rome. The efficiency of the Christian God was challenged by many Romans who believed that the old pagan gods had avenged themselves for being abandoned. To answer the new challenge Augustine wrote his *De civitate Dei,* explaining that the victory of the pagans was in fact their defeat by Christ. Both victory and defeat served to clarify the meaning of history: that everything must be submitted to Christ according to the great plan of Providence.[7]

And, indeed, it was so. The barbarians who took Rome were, in turn, taken by the Christians, and the apologetical activity of the Church seemed about to be replaced by the more quiet work of teaching. But the events did not correspond to expectation. Though the external challenges disappeared, new internal vicissitudes were forming in the sixth century which reached their climax in the great schism of East and West in the ninth and eleventh centuries. Since then internal conflicts have not ceased to foster the dialogizing self-understanding activity in the life of the Church.

5. SCHOLASTICISM AND REFORMATION

At the beginning of the second millennium the external challenge arose again. This time it came from the Aristotelian rationalism of the Arab philosophers. The fruit of this confrontation was a philosophical apologetics, which, as exemplified in the *Summa Contra Gentiles* of St. Thomas, tried to apply the basic requirements of reason to the fundamental mysteries of Christianity. The Church made a serious effort to bring itself up to date and to prove its reasonableness to Aristotelian thinkers. It succeeded, but its success became the cause of new internal challenges. Thinkers of the sixteenth century, under the inspiration of Luther, questioned the adequateness of the new development and the updatings which were taking place in the Roman Church. To regain the vision of its relation to Christ, the Church had to make a new retrospective self-inquiry. If Christ's work was once and for all completed, was there any role for the Church as a visible society in continuing and implementing that finished work? The first fruits of the Church's self-reflection, v.g. Bellarmine's *Controversiae,* led to many others. Indeed the great challenges of the 16th century continue to foster a better self-understanding and love for unity in the life of the Church even to our own day.

6. THE ENLIGHTENMENT

In the following century the newly developing natural and historical sciences more and more replaced the methods and certitudes of ancient physics. The new certitudes of positive science were based more upon an accumulation of independent and convergent probabilities than upon an a priori *intellectus principiorum.* To help the scientist of his age in his search not only for discoveries, but also for God and infinite happiness, Pascal[8] tried to construct an up-to-date apologetics based not upon metaphysical arguments, but upon natural and historical proofs. After applying the theory of probability to apologetics, he tried to show that the risk of faith can be justified from a logical point of view. Since there is such a convergence of independent witnesses to Christian revelation, God, as the origin of Christianity, can be known by means of convergent probability. The passage, however, from probability to the certitude of faith can be made only by the *l'esprit de finesse,* a sort of insight similar to the *instinctum fidei* of Thomas Aquinas, or later, to the illative sense of Newman. Because the chances to be taken are minimal, whereas the happiness to be gained is infinite, it can appear logical and worthwhile for the heart to venture through faith to God. Thus, by applying the method and certitudes of the new sciences, Pascal seems to have constructed for the first time a real science of apologetics among other contemporary sciences.

But the most radical challenge was yet to come. The results of the quickly developing sciences, especially in the area of archeological and historical research, made it clear that scripture contained many statements which were historically and scientifically untenable. Scripture, previously accepted as the Word of God, now seemed to contain as many errors as the other writings of its own time. Therefore, since the bible looked like any other human work, the divine origin of Christianity was radically questioned. The Church's claim of being founded by God could not be justified. Even if it were founded by Jesus of Nazareth, something which is questionable in itself, this would not be conclusive, for

Jesus was not God but a fallible man, a victim of his ideas. The self-reflective dialogizing activity of faith from now on was directed to the problem of the origin of Christianity, and the "golden age" of apologetics was inaugurated. It lasted over 180 years: from the appearance of Reimarus' book in 1774 until the beginning of the second Vatican Council in 1962, when Christian apologetics finally took another direction.

CHAPTER TWO

APOLOGETIC CONCERN
FOR THE ORIGIN OF CHRISTIANITY
(1774-1962)

1. THE LIBERAL-RATIONALISTIC CHALLENGE AND THE RESPONSE

A. The Challenge

As scientific discoveries and historico-critical research increasingly manifested the considerable gap between the doctrine of faith and the conclusion of reason about the origin of Christianity, it became a scientific task to discover the purely scientific facts, free from any religious interpretation about the cradle of Christianity. Historical elements were to be separated from the dogmatic elements. Since history was defined as a description of past facts detached from any contemporary interpretation,[9] historians' main concern became the effort to write a biography of Jesus (*Leben-Jesu-Forschung*) which would reveal Jesus in the manner of a photograph, free from any interpretation. Indeed an increasing number of authors tried to discover what really happened to Jesus and to describe the events of his life as they might have been seen by any neutral observer.

1) Reimarus

The first man who undertook this task was H. S. Reimarus (1694-1768), professor of oriental languages at the University of

Hamburg in Germany. His book *Apologie* was released only after his death, during the years 1774-1778.[10] Reimarus' basic insight was that a man cannot be known and understood except by his intentions and desires. Therefore, to understand Jesus meant to understand what he desired and intended to do. Reading the gospels in a neutral frame of mind it became evident to Reimarus that Jesus' intention was to found a this-worldly political, messianic kingdom in exactly that form which his contemporaries expected. However, like many others, Jesus could not realize his dream, and was executed on unsound charges.

Only after Jesus' death did Christianity really begin to exist. His followers or disciples first hid themselves for fear of persecution. Noticing however, that they were no longer being persecuted, they became bolder, and, as rabbis, began to preach that Jesus was the Messiah. The main obstacle to their success was evidently the unfortunate and scandalous crucifixion of Jesus. In order to explain it, the disciples invented the theory of the double coming of the Messiah, first in a lowly form (cf Is 42,1-4), and secondly, with glory in the clouds of heaven (cf Dan 9,20-27). They proclaimed that though Jesus died for the salvation of men, he would come again with glory in the final, imminent parousia.

Now, such an interpretation logically required the resurrection. The disciples, therefore, stole the body of Jesus and buried it in some hidden place. After some time the corpse disintegrated, and no trace remained of it. This was why, said Reimarus, that there were such great contradictions in the narration of the resurrection (firstly, about the places in which the apparitions occurred and, secondly, in the fact that Jesus appeared only to his own followers, and never publicly in Jerusalem to the Jewish people or to his enemies). The resurrection of Jesus as well as Christianity, was therefore the fruit of the great messianic expectations of Jesus' followers. With this theory Reimarus became the precursor of the eschatological school and the author of the so-called theory of fraud, in which the origin of faith in the resurrection is seen in a fraud committed by Jesus' disciples.

Reimarus' theory was accepted by E. Renan,[11] more fully explained by A. Schweitzer[12] and modified somewhat by J. Carmichael.[13] E. Renan suggested that it was not the disciples, but rather Magdalene who stole the body of Jesus.

2) Paulus

H. E. G. Paulus (1761-1851) could not agree with Reimarus' theory. The origin of Christianity was due rather to the appearance of Jesus to his disciples after his death.[14] According to Paulus' view, which later was called "the theory of apparent death," Christ did not die on the cross, but underwent so strong a syncope that he seemed to be dead. When he was placed in a cool tomb under the influence of a massage with ointment, his youthful energies woke him from his lethargy. He then left the tomb, and for some days afterwards appeared and showed himself to his disciples. Later he withdrew and concealed himself in a hidden place, where he ended his life in peace, while his disciples preached about him as risen and alive. Paulus' ideas were echoed later by W. Sand,[15] P. Calluaud[16] and Prosper Dor[17]. However, neither Paulus nor Reimarus was as influential as D. F. Strauss. His book, *The Life of Jesus* reached twelve editions in a rather short time.[18]

3) Strauss

Both Reimarus and Paulus tried to demonstrate the validity of their theory from the gospels, and so implicitly admitted their historical value. D. F. Strauss (1808-1874) was much more radical. Since the gospels, contrary to the opinions of Reimarus and Paulus, did affirm miracles and resurrection, anyone who admitted their historicity had to admit the historicity of the miracles, resurrection and all the supernatural happenings narrated in the gospels. But, since all these, like any other supernatural happenings, were impossible, the historicity of the gospels had to be denied. They were only tales, myths containing some philosophical and religious ideas under a mythical covering. All were anonymous creations of the first Christians who wanted to glorify their Christ at any price, and through their imaginings and hallucinations made Jesus rise from the dead. Now, since a long time is needed for a collective elaboration of a myth originated in hallucinations, the gospels, as we have them now, could not have been written until the second century A.D.

4) Harnack

But the most outstanding representative of the older liberal quest, and the most prominent member of the Tübingen School founded by C. Baur[19] was A. Harnack (1851-1930). His book on *The Essence of Christianity,* more of a popularization than a scholarly work, appeared from 1900 to 1927 in thirteen languages with more than 70,000 copies.

According to Harnack, Jesus was not an eschatological dreamer, as Reimarus thought, but a great moral teacher. His teaching could be reduced to three main subjects: the coming of the kingdom of God; God, the Father of mankind, and the great commandment of love. Jesus himself lived in the conviction that he was under the special providence of God, the Father, and thus had a special relation to God as his beloved son. This living faith later was transformed into a belief in Jesus himself as the unique Son of the Father in a transcendental sense, and the Easter fact (*Osterglaube*) was transformed into the Easter message (*Osterbotschaft*). The difference between Easter fact and Easter message was indicated in the gospels themselves. We read the following in Luke 24,22-23: ". . . and some women from our group have astounded us: they went to the tomb in the early morning, and when they did not find the body, they came back to tell us they had seen a vision of angels who said that he was alive." There was the fact: his body was not found. And here was the belief: angels said that he is alive. John 20,29 betrays a similar difference (by praising faith without seeing).

5) Schweitzer

A. Schweitzer strongly criticized A. Harnack's view of Jesus. In his *The Quest of the Historical Jesus* he shows that not the ethical but the eschatological view of Jesus is the basis of Christianity. Jesus' view was essentially an eschatological world view. He believed that an imminent cataclysm would end the world, and this eschatological world view was the common element which joined Jesus and his Church. In this view faith and history coincided. Dogmatic faith and historical reality were one since the Church believed what Jesus historically believed. Therefore, according to Schweitzer the historical origin of Christianity was nothing else but Jesus' erroneous belief in the proximate end of the world.[20]

6) Fideism

The liberal critics attempted to solve the problem of faith and history in favor of history. Faith was reduced to reason and history, and real knowledge of Christianity became the monopoly of historical research. In order to escape from the menacing claims of this rationalism, fideism[21] as a counter position maintained that faith was absolutely invulnerable to the results of historical research. Faith was, above all, supernatural. It was revealed by God to men, and as such was immune from any proof or disproof. Thus, while rationalism defended the rationality of faith at the price of its supernaturality, fideism extolled the supernaturality of faith but at the expense of its reasonableness.

7) Vatican I

In 1870 the first Vatican Council, in an effort to keep a balance between the two tendencies, urged that Christian faith was supernatural as well as reasonable. As supernatural it was the gift of God and could not be reduced to any scientific proof or demonstration. Being reasonable, it could not be reduced to a blind movement of the mind, but ought to be consonant with reason. Consequently, faith was not only mere belief, because in some sense it could be helped by way of demonstration,[22] reasoning,[23] and by the evidence of credibility.[24]

Within this framework of the self-reflecting, dialogizing activity of faith outlined by Vatican I, it was up to the Catholic apologists to work out more concretely the harmony of faith with the results of historical research.

8) Kähler

But before we give a general summary of the different positions concerning the origins of Christianity at the end of the 19th century, we have to mention the name of M. Kähler. In order to liberate Christian faith from its dependence on scholars and the uncertainties of criticism, Kähler, in his book *Der sogenannte historische Jesus und der geschichtliche, biblische Christus*[25] (The so-called historical Jesus and the historical, biblical Christ), made a distinction between the notion of *historisch* (historical) and *geschichtlich* (historic) which Bultmann was to utilize in its full sense. Kähler felt that the notion of history used by the liberal rationalist school was not adequate. He associated historicity not so much with the actuality of a past event, but rather with its impact upon the coming ages. Faith in Christ is historically valid because of its impact on the centuries that followed Jesus.

9) Conclusion

In conclusion we can see that in spite of the losses the 19th century was extremely fruitful for the self-reflecting dialogizing activities of faith. The pros and cons of the challengers and the challenged took a very definitive form. The divine origin of Christianity was challenged in a double way: on the basis of historical fact which the Church asserted as the basis of her faith, and on the basis of new indisputable data which seemed to contradict that same faith. To be more specific, the points of challenge on historical fact were:

a) Jesus' resurrection (Reimarus)

b) Jesus's death (Paulus)

c) the historicity of the gospels (Strauss)

d) the faith of the Apostles (C. Baur)

e) the apparitions which were considered as mere

(1) illusions and hallucinations (Strauss) or

(2) vivid pathological imaginings and the desire to see Jesus (E. Renan), or

(3) memories of the past, imagination of the resurrection (Goguel),[26] or

(4) a reaction of trust in Jesus following the first depression; (Guignebert)[27], or

(5) internal mystical experience, either subjective, as, e.g., when Paul saw Jesus on the way to Damascus (R. Otto),[28] or objective by the special intervention of the soul of Jesus or of God himself, but without corporeal resurrection (E. Dobschütz, K. Lake)[29]

The points of challenge arising from new indisputable data were:

a) A twofold tradition of apparitions:

(1) One tradition, that of Mark, Matthew and the apocryphal gospel of Peter, spoke only of the apparitions in Galilee, and had nothing about those in Jerusalem.

(2) The other tradition affirmed apparitions on the third day in Jerusalem (cf Luke, John, Mark 16,9-20), and ignored the apparitions in Galilee.

(3) That one tradition really ignored the other was further confirmed by the following results of textual criticism.

b) It seems that Mark's conclusion, 16,9-20, which speaks about the apparitions in Jerusalem is not authentic. The style is different and the episode is missing in the manuscripts of greater importance. The gospel of Mark ends with verse 8, where only the apparition in Galilee is indicated. According to P. Rohrback,[30] the last part of Mark was added by the preachers of Ephesus so that they could make Mark agree with the tradition of John concerning the apparitions at Jerusalem.

c) John chapter 21 is also a later addition. It contains particular characteristics and a style which indicate that it could not have been written by the same author. John ends his gospel in chapter 20, after which there begins a new narration. It is evident, therefore, that this chapter dealing with the apparition in Galilee was added later so that the tradition of John might be made to agree with the tradition of Mark.

d) Matthew, who belongs to the Galilean tradition, seems to commemorate in 28,9 the apparitions in Jerusalem. But this unique verse is an interpolation.

e) Paul himself supports the Galilean tradition. 1 Cor 15 recalls neither the apparitions of Emmaus, nor the apparitions to the women, nor the empty tomb. All of these were unknown to Paul. Otherwise he would have mentioned them, since he proposed a critical series of apparitions in which each held a determinate place and time.

f) Moreover, in the term "according to the scriptures" Paul himself gives the exegetical basis and the source of faith concerning the resurrection. The resurrection is not based on the apparitions as historical facts, but it is a scriptural creation and gets its basis from the prophetic messianic texts.

In accordance with the results of textual criticism the origin of Christianity can be described as follows. After the death of Jesus his disciples went into Galilee. In Galilee everything recalled Jesus to them. Places where they were together with him, homes, the countryside, indeed all spoke to them of Jesus. The scripture reading gave them faith. If he was the Messiah he could not remain in the tomb according to Psalm 16,10.

Such faith provoked visions. The first to have such is Peter, then after him others. Strengthened by visions, they return to Jerusalem. There the idea of spiritual resurrection is transformed little by little into a belief in the corporeal resurrection. Compelled now from apologetic necessity, they posit the first apparitions in Jerusalem in the neighborhood of the tomb. From this necessity comes the report about the empty tomb. Afterwards Luke and John, in their narrations, elaborate the nature of these visions in order to overcome doubts and unbelief.

Similarly according to text criticism there is no evidence that Jesus in his earthly life ever claimed for himself divine sonship in an exclusive sense, i.e. elevating himself above creatures. According to the synoptics, Jesus is only the revealer of the fatherhood of God, and of the duty of charity to men as brothers. He is the Son of God in a common religious sense. Thus the fundamental truth about the Christian religion is nothing but this: Jesus, even after his death, lives in the hearts of his disciples.

B. The Response

This was the challenge which created the so-called "classical apologists," of the 19th century such as H. Hurter, C. Mazella, P. W. Devivier, J. Forget, C. Pesch, A. Tanquerey, S. Schiffini, etc.[31]

Their demonstrations had four stages:

(1) Demonstration of the *a priori* possibility and knowability of revelation, conceived as a speaking of God to man.

(2) Demonstration of the historical value of the gospels.

(3) Demonstration of the testimony of Jesus and the veracity of this testimony. This demonstration included two moments:

   a) Jesus knew, and testified indeed, that he was God.

   b) The veracity of his testimony he proved through prophecies, miracles and mainly through his historical resurrection. Since these events demand divine intervention; God himself testified through them that what Jesus said was true. The historicity of the resurrection was proved through a threefold testimony:

   aa) from the testimony of the disciples,

      (i) who had not been deceived,
         —because in spite of their difference of age, of sex, of character and of education they agreed in this belief:
         —because they ate with him, they touched him, and

they did not believe easily, for the doubt of Thomas demonstrated the doubts of the other apostles.

(ii) nor did they wish to deceive others, for
— there was no reason why they should; their persecution indicated what they could expect from the preaching of the resurrection;
— their good faith, their ingenuousness, their discouragement, their dispersion and sufferings disprove such a supposition;
— and even if they had wished to lead others into error this was not possible; they could not have hidden the body because of the guard, nor was it an easy task to persuade the world that Jesus rose.

bb) from the testimony of the enemies of Christ,

— the strange attitude of the Sanhedrin and
— the silence imposed by the Jews in Jerusalem after the event and before the preaching of the apostles, confirmed the truth of the resurrection.

cc) from the testimony of history; the rapid expansion of the Christian Church, the conversions, the constancy of the martyrs, the miracles performed by the apostles, were all inexplicable facts without the resurrection.

Thus Catholic apologists held up three contrary facts in opposition to the three theses of the rationalists:

— to fraud (Reimarus)—the moral transformation of the apostles
— to apparent death (Paulus)—the subtle and accurate description of the evangelists
— to hallucination (Strauss)—the normal state of the apostles.

(4) Having demonstrated the veracity of the testimony of Jesus, the apologists went on to respond to the difficulties posited by the rationalists.

a) To the first difficulty that Jesus did not manifest himself to his enemies they responded that it was due to the mystery of the providential plan of God that through faith and not through knowledge the world should be saved.

b) To the second, namely, that there are great incoherences and contradictions in the narrations, they answered that the same incoherences are found in all the writings of the time.

The substance of the fact is the same among all the evangelists. The difference in circumstances is intelligible from the extraordinary nature of the paschal event. Moreover, incoherence itself is a sign of authenticity. It indicates that the apostles did not have a previous agreement in deceit and fraud to relate the affair in the same manner, so that they could prove with unanimity the historicity of something nonexistent.

The literal contradiction is apparent, and coordination is possible. The narrations are fragmentary and incomplete. Each of the evangelists has his own personal preoccupations, according to which he orders the material in a different way. Thus, for example, Matthew wishes to show the triumph of the Messiah, which was promised to Israel. Mark wrote the gospel of the Son of God, and of the Lord elevated to the right hand of the Father. Luke showed Jesus as the Son of God and as the Son of Man, and that because of this twofold title he was the redeemer of humanity. John followed the exact succession of events, while the synoptics have more dogmatic and less chronological preoccupations. Nevertheless, this preoccupation does not alter the substance of the story, but only circumstantial facts.

The main deficiency of the classical apologists was that they did not concern themselves enough with the arguments of Strauss. The challengers had already introduced the method of historical criticism and wished to detect the sources of the gospels in legendary tales of popular tradition. According to Strauss, one could not simply argue from the gospels, but ought to analyze what role the fable-generating action of tradition played and how it transformed the facts.

Many Catholics saw the problem and reacted in different ways. The historical method so increased the difficulties that many sought to free themselves from the pressure of the problem by simply denying its legitimacy. Nevertheless, there were others who tried to defend the ancient faith by the new methods. Invading the camp of the adversaries, they used the very methods of the latter to show the falsity of their conclusions, and in this way to demonstrate the veracity of the faith. Such an apologist was Vincent Rose.

1) Rose

By admitting the hypothesis of the historical method in his book, *Études sur les Évangiles*,[32] Rose made perhaps the first attempt to give a solution to the double tradition. According to him, Paul in 1 Cor 15 testified to the apparitions at Jerusalem, and not, as the adversaries said, to the apparitions in Galilee. For Paul and Luke were the only ones who mentioned the apparition made to Peter. Now, since Luke belonged to the Jerusalem tradition, so, Paul, too, favored that tradition.

The difference in the selection of apparitions in Luke and in Paul must be explained from their different forms of argument. Each wished to demonstrate the physical resurrection of Jesus. For Paul, Jesus rose in the flesh, because he appeared, whereas for Luke, Jesus rose because he was eating with the disciples, who touched him, and observed his wounds.

We can understand Matthew's selection from the fact that he centered his resurrection narrative on the theft calumny of the Jews. His purpose was to show the incredulity of the Jews, who rejected the messianic gifts. Since for Matthew the salvation refused by the Jews passed to the Gentiles symbolized by Galilee, he recounted only the apparitions in Galilee.

Other Catholic studies also appeared in the same vein, v.g., those of A. Allini, H. Lesêtre, F. Tillmann, etc.[33] They were a good start. A better solution to the problem, however, required more time.

Although they found no satisfactory solution to the rationalist challenge Catholic apologists were now forced to direct their attention to a new challenge. In 1902 a book appeared by A. Loisy, *L'Évangile et l'Église,* and shortly afterwards another, A. Meyer's *Die Auferstehung Christi* (The Resurrection of Christ) in Tübingen in 1905. These two books inaugurated the era of modernism.

But before we turn to modernism, the new challenge to faith in Christ, we must mention John Henry Newman and M. Blondel.[34] Though not classed among the "classical apologists" of the 19th century their defense of Christianity is a most important contribution to the self-reflecting activity of faith in the 19th century. Both were more sensitive to the challenges of speculative thought than to the results of the biblico-historical research of their age.

2) Newman

Newman wanted to trace the origin and development of Christian faith in order to help men accept Christianity. His main concern was the "illative sense," the power of understanding by which man can pass from probability to certitude. Since Newman considered probability to be related to truth and certainty, his illative sense resembled more the *phronesis* of Aristotle than the Pascalian intuition of heart looking for happiness. It was conceived as inward light which directed the mind from one statement to another and connected them with the concrete. Its function was to help the mind to accept the propositions of faith with absolute certitude.

Newman then, like most theologians of that time, considered faith in its relation to the noetic aspect of revelation rather than in its relation to the existential aspect. He admitted that the fact of revelation could be known and, indeed, was known by reason. The function of the illative sense was therefore reduced to the intellectual apprehension of the content of revelation and not the recognition of God in faith as the Revealer. He did not consider sufficiently enough that the divine testimony to revelation is very different from shared human testimony. In human conversation the witnessing is not believed but known. Not the fact of witness, but the content of the witness is the object of human faith. But in the case of God's revelation not so much the content as the fact of the divine witnessing, i.e. that God is the One who reveals himself and not somebody else, is the central problem of faith.

3) Blondel

Like Newman, Blondel also tried to answer the new challenges of scientific research and justify for the speculative mind the obligation to receive Christianity. If such an obligation existed, a trace or echo of it should be manifest in the nature of human existence. Otherwise, the obligation could hardly be reasonable.

Blondel found this trace in the self-transcending nature of every action.[35] Each human action transcended itself and aimed at the absolute, i.e. at what seemed absolutely necessary, and at the same time, was absolutely impossible. Each action showed that man could be satisfied with no less than the absolute. Indeed, all the reasoning power of man led to the same conclusion: he must not and could not be satisfied with any given action. Since Christianity offered and made it possible to reach this absolute, it must be seen as absolutely necessary for man to fulfill his exigencies. Thus Christianity is nothing else but the historical determination of the general human exigence for the absolute. Listening to this argument of Blondel, one cannot help recalling Tertullian's apologetics based upon the witness of the human soul to Christianity.

As often happens, Blondel's apologetics, which was supposed to answer challenges, raised more problems than it solved. If Christianity were really so necessary for human existence, the gratuity of the supernatural becomes questionable. This is always a great problem in apologetics: if someone proves nothing at all, he invalidates reason; and if he proves too much, he invalidates faith. Further, if apologetics is conceived not as the self-reflecting activity of faith, but a propaedeutic activity of reason, it may do more harm than good to the faith. Modernism, our next focus of attention, is a good illustration of how a poor defense can distort the very faith it wants to defend.

2. MODERNISM AND THE CHURCH'S RESPONSE

Basically modernism is a Christian apologetics for the defense of the Christian faith. To relieve Christian faith from the pressure of the difficulties raised by scientific discoveries, modernism wished to radically separate faith from science. Truth and faith were conceived as two different layers, one having no relation to the other. Truth, the proper concern of science, was irrelevant to belief. For belief did not rest upon the verification of sensible experience, but upon the life of the human spirit. Therefore, it was not usual that affirmations of faith seem to science as incompatible with truth.

A. Modernist Solution

1) Loisy

The main exponent of modernism was A. Loisy. His basic insight was that Christianity could not escape the law of life: the

continual movement and effort to bring about perpetually changing, new conditions. The present Church resembled the early
community as an adult resembles the child. The Church of this
latter period was a legitimate outcome of the early Church but did
not have much in common with it.

Loisy, like other modernists, refuted Harnack's thesis: the main
concern of Jesus was that God is father. Jesus made messianism
the core of his preaching although he did not have the same
messianic awareness from the beginning of his life. Only after the
acclamation of John the Baptist and the people, did he begin to
believe that he was the Messiah and to speak about the messianic
eschatological reign. Later, however, when he saw that the people
and leaders of Israel did not accept his ideas, and threatened him
with death, he realized that he had erred, and began to speak
about his passion and future death, in an attempt to transform his
national mission into a universal one.

As regards the Easter event, Loisy admitted Harnack's distinction between Easter fact and Easter message. According to him,
however, the distinction was not founded in the gospels, as Harnack thought, but in reason. Since the resurrection was supra-
historical, it did not pertain to sensible experience, and, therefore,
could not be shown historically. No historical argument proved
the resurrection. The argument of the empty tomb did not prove
it because the absence of the body could be explained in another
way. Nor did the apparitions, for the historian does not have the
means for analyzing the nature and meaning of these phenomena.
The resurrection was nothing else but the entry into immortal life.
Therefore, no one could observe it. At the most, all that could be
observed was the return of the dead into mortal life. But this
return would have been a mere revival and not a resurrection.
Accordingly, says Loisy, the primitive preaching and early faith
did not insist on the historical circumstances of the resurrection,
but on the glorification of Jesus at the right hand of the Father.

Since, according to Christian tradition, history and faith, as well
as science and faith, could not be completely separated, the
modernists' solution to the problems seemed insufficient to the
Catholic apologists.

B. Response

1) Palmieri

D. Palmieri[36] argued that history and faith complemented one another. A historical fact must have its proper time and place. Now, the resurrection had its proper time and place in history, therefore, it is an historical fact and as such is accessible to scientific investigation.

2) Disteldorf

J. B. Disteldorf in 1906 used a new argument in reply to a book by Arnold Meyer. Meyer thought that all apparitions not mentioned in 1 Cor 15 ought to be eliminated from the gospel account. The remaining five were reducible to the vision of Paul on the road to Damascus. Now, since this vision was merely a spiritual vision, these other apparitions too were to be taken as internal religious experiences and not as external apparitions.

In defense of the true nature of the apparitions in 1 Cor 15, Disteldorf made use of an argument which he had borrowed from A. Seeberg.[37] Seeberg claimed that after the death of Christ, the Christians composed a catechism based in large measure on the words of the Lord. The teaching of this catechism was already universally preached in the apostolic age. Seeberg wanted to rediscover parts of this catechism to shed new light on the period 30-50 A.D., a period whose significance was so greatly disputed. Focusing his attention on the phrase "for I handed on what I had received," he thought he found fragments of this primitive catechism in 1 Cor 15. By doing this, Seeberg anticipated form criticism.

Disteldorf accepted this method of argument, and extended it to Acts, the historical antiquity of which had been reestablished that very year by Harnack.[38] Using various texts of Acts, Disteldorf showed that the object of the primitive preaching was not only the glorification, but also the real resurrection of Jesus (Acts 2,24; 3,15; 4,33; especially 2,31 and 10,41). But if the resurrection according to the flesh was already the object of the primitive preaching one might ask what could give rise to this preaching. After one examined all the evidence, only one probable explanation remained, the fact of the miracle of the resurrection.

3) Lamentabili

In 1907, after the publication of D. Palmieri and J. B. Distel-dorf, the decree *Lamentabili* was issued by the Holy Office. It contains two condemnations of special interest for us.[39]

> No. 36 The resurrection of the Savior is not a true fact in the order of history, but only a fact in the supernatural order and is neither proved nor probable, but something that the Christian conscience gradually developed from other facts.

In the proposition two statements were criticised:

a) the resurrection is not a fact of the historical order, and hence it is not proven and it cannot be proven historically.

b) the resurrection was developed gradually by the Christian conscience.

The term 'historical' can be understood in two senses: firstly, it can signify a fact which truly happened and as such is opposed to the unreal, the non-existent, the mythological or legendary; and secondly, it can signify that this fact can be established by the science of history. These two meanings can, but do not necessarily coincide. Thus, for example, original sin might be historical in the first sense, but not in the second sense, since it does not belong to the science of history, but exclusively to revelation.

According to the decree *Lamentabili,* resurrection as an histori-cal event is understood in both senses, whereas the Creeds of the various ecumenical Councils[40] generally mean the resurrection in the first sense. Therefore, if someone said that he admitted Christ's true resurrection according to flesh, but not as a possible question for historical research, such a man would accept the Creed, but not the decree *Lamentabili* which considered the resur-rection as historical in both senses.

> No. 37 Belief in the resurrection of Christ was not at the beginning a belief in the actual fact of resurrection, but in the immortal life of Christ with God.

This proposition is found in the works of Loisy.[41] The formula itself does not exclude a belief in the bodily resurrection of Jesus. It is not impossible that the primitive faith contemplated the glory of Christ more readily than it contemplated the paschal event. But Loisy meant something more. He thought that the early faith, abstracting from the resurrection of the body, gave its attention primarily to the immortal life of Christ. The bodily resurrection was only an image of a concrete expression of the basically spiritual idea of the resurrection. Thus, the early apostles did not wish to witness to the bodily resurrection of Jesus, but only to his spiritual glorification in heaven. The proposition so understood was evidently erroneous, since it contradicts the analysis of later form criticism.[42]

Scarcely two years had passed after the condemnation of modernism when a new aspect of the problem of Jesus appeared. In 1909 a book, *Histoire générale des religions,* appeared in which S. Reinach intended to show that all religions could be reduced to myths. Christianity, a recapitulation of ancient pagan religions, was not excluded from this schema. Thus with Reinach, a new movement, the history-of-religions-school, began.

3. THE HISTORY-OF-RELIGIONS-SCHOOL AND THE RESPONSE OF THE APOLOGISTS

The rationalistic and modernistic hypotheses about the origin of Christianity raised a serious difficulty. If Christianity was basically a Jewish messianic faith in the coming Kingdom of Yahweh, how could the Gentiles so rapidly accept a faith based on a Jewish faith, foreign to the hellenistic mind?

For such a problem only the comparative study of religions offered a solution. Since Christianity seemed, especially in its faith in the resurrection, to have taken its definitive form from the myths of dying-rising gods in the hellenistic world, the Greeks could easily accept Christianity as consonant with their own patterns of thought.

A. Reitzenstein

In 1910 R. Reitzenstein[43] systematized these ideas. He asserted that Paul transformed Christianity by hellenizing it. Paul, to be a Greek to the Greeks, had studied Greek mythology and introduced its basic ideas (e.g. spirit, gnosis, a savior god who passes through suffering to glory, etc.) into the primitive Christian tradition.

Though the main idea of Reitzenstein seemed to be very plausible, his method of argumentation was not accepted. Loisy[44] in his review of Reitzenstein confessed that he found it difficult to imagine Paul studying the writings of mystery cults. In place of a direct influence he proposed an indirect influence. At the beginning the gospel of Christ was not a mystery in the sense of the pagan religions, for it was a messianic evangelization within Judaism. But when the messianic proclamation was preached to the Greek world, Christianity had to conform and adapt itself to the new cultural atmosphere. The Judaic, messianic expectation was changed into the mystery of universal salvation. The real human death of Christ became the death of the divinity which spread its saving influence over the whole world for all times. Thus through the pagan mysteries Christianity intentionally evolved into a mythic religion in which salvation was achieved by efficacious rites, e.g., the rite of baptism and of the eucharist through which the believer realized his spiritual union with Christ.

The divinization of Jesus took place only gradually. The mere human Messianism had been transformed into a transcendental one in the Palestinian church's Christology concerning the Son of Man, the heavenly Man, introduced into messianic Judaism by gnosticism. The Christology of the Son of Man later gave birth in the hellenic churches to the cult of the Lord Jesus, the divine King, or Son of God in the transcendent sense. This came about under the influence of the cult of emperors and kings as well as under the influence of the hellenistic mysteries and gnosticism. These are the principal instances of the so-called "hellenized Christology" whose principal proponents were R. Reitzenstein, W. Bousset and R. Bultmann.[45]

The influence of the new history-of-religions-school drew apologetics from the study of the sacred scripture to the study of religions. Three myths, that of Attis, that of Adonis, and that of Dionysius were of special interest, since these three gods were said to have died and risen again.

B. Lagrange

In their response, Catholic apologists agreed with the new school that ritual was at the basis of myth and, therefore, that myth ought to be explained in terms of its rites and not vice-versa. The myth and the syncretistic fusion of cults were late developments. Scholars, accordingly, should have striven to determine to what extent fusion existed. In his study M. J. Lagrange found that there was a radical difference between Christ and the dying-rising gods of Greek mythology.

1)The Myth of Attis

Attis in his mystery rites was represented in two ways: as a god who died, and as a god who was castrated. Now which of these two was primary and original, and which was the later addition? [46] Did Attis truly die or was he only wounded? According to Lagrange the fundamental theme in the Attis mysteries up to the 2nd century A.D. was that of castration. The death of the hero was introduced only under the influence of the mystery of Adonis. The primitive underlying rite consisted in the castration of roosters who were consecrated to the cult of the goddess Cybele, just as royal eunuchs were castrated for the service of the queen. In this context one could not speak of the death or of the resurrection of Attis. Consequently, the Attis mystery was not the origin of the death and resurrection of Jesus.

But what could be said about the feast of Hilaria, celebrated after the day of blood (castration) during the vernal equinox? Was not this the origin of the Christian triduum of Holy Week? Here is the program of the week-long celebration:

March 15   Day of the entrance of cane. Procession of trumpets. Sacrifice of six year old bulls.

March 22   Day of the entrance of the pine tree: a pine tree was cut in the sacred forest, decked with violets, and carried to the Palatine.

March 22-3   Days of chastity and abstinence: meat of swine, grapes and fish were forbidden.

March 24   Day of blood: dances to the accompaniment of cymbals before the pine tree; priests of Cybele sprinkled the pine and the altar with their own blood and some castrated themselves in fanatical orgies.

March 25   The feast of Hilaria: a "free love" masquerade.

March 26   A day of rest.

March 27   The sacred rock, i.e., Cybele was washed in the Almo river.

Lagrange pointed out that, from these facts, one could not argue to the death and resurrection of Christ. The feast of Hilaria was never called the feast of Attis, but the feast of his mother, Cybele. On March 27, which is the high point, Attis had no part. If this had been a feast of death and resurrection, why was the day of rest placed after the resurrection and why not between the death and Hilaria? Stoic and Neo-Platonic exegesis, which saw in Attis the eternal god, did not know about death or resurrection in the Attis cult.

In the third and fourth centuries A.D., the Attis and Cybelline mysteries were interpreted as rites of the death and resurrection of the god. Only at this late date was the cult of Attis assimilated into the cult of the dying god. A picture or statue of Attis was tied to a pine tree, placed funerealwise in a litter and wept over. It seems very likely that this took place under Christian and gnostic influence. That Attis rose again was only found in the book of a Christian convert, J. Firmicus Maternus, *De errore profanarum religionum*, written c. 346. Consequently, it seems that not pagans, but rather Christians under the influence of their faith saw a proper resurrection in the Attis rites.[47]

The underlying theme of the myth of Attis is the gods' envy of man's procreative powers. It was believed that because of their envy the gods might do harm to the human race. To avoid this men tried to placate their gods by castrating themselves voluntarily.

2) The Myth of Adonis

According to the myth, Adonis certainly died and was mourned with tears and funeral rites. Babylonian poems speak of his return from the nether world. He was certainly a living god among the shades, but he did not really rise again.[48] The myth did not speak of resurrection.

3) The Myth of Osiris

The Osiris myth was, perhaps, the only rite in which "resurrection" was celebrated. However, Loisy himself noted that the Osiridian resurrection was merely the symbol of the new germination of grain.[49] The sense of the mystery, therefore, was clear.

The Osiridian death and resurrection meant the "death" and "resurrection" of the crops. According to the ancient legend, Osiris, the king of lower Egypt was killed by his brother Set, king of upper Egypt, and his body cut up into pieces. Isis, his wife, gathered up the scattered pieces and put the body together again with the help of Amybis, a herald sent by the Sun. Then Isis had intercourse with the dead body and from this union Horus was born. Horus, the son of Osiris, ruled, henceforth in Egypt, whereas, Osiris, enjoying another life, ruled in the nether world. Osiris, therefore, lived again only in Hades and was reborn in his son who took the place he had held on earth. But life in Hades should not be confused with resurrection from the dead. As a matter of fact, not Osiris' immortal life in Hades, but the grief of Isis burying the body of her brother-husband was the object of the ritual celebration.

4) Dionysus-Zagreus

Loisy thought that in Dionysus one could find an analogate of the Christian paschal mystery. Dionysus, son of Zeus and his daughter Persephone, was still a young man when the Titans tried to kill him. In his flight he assumed various animal forms to avoid capture, but this did not prevent the Titans from discovering him in the form of a bull and devouring him. Only his heart was left. Athene, his sister found it and carried it to her father, Zeus, who took it and ate it. Thus Zagreus was reborn in Dionysus of Thebes, newly born son of Zeus and Semele. The rite, however, did not mention resurrection but rather indicated how the divine life-principle was transformed. Only one version spoke of the resurrection of Dionysus, viz., that found in St. Justin. Here again we have an instance of how the Christian imagination attributed resurrection to the pagan gods.

C. The Direct Influence

J. Lagrange refuted in summary fashion the direct influence as follows.

One cannot argue in defense of the direct influence that Bacchus was wine or the vine, and that the vine rose again; but rather that Bacchus was a god who died and rose again in person. Now such an argument seems impossible.

Nor can one affirm that primitive religions joyfully celebrated the return of divinities from the nether world (in any case this cannot be considered as true death or true resurrection) but rather the changes of summer and winter.

Although there might be some similarity between Christianity and Orphism, an essential difference still remained. While Orphism wished to be freed from the body, Christianity sought to find the body again. Life after death was one thing, resurrection was another. Moreover, the Greek gods were immortal and hence did not need resurrection according to the Greeks. Therefore, the direct causal influence of the pagan mysteries on Christianity was to be excluded.

Since the thirties the theory of the direct influence of the pagan mysteries on Christianity had become obsolete.[50] From that time a new tendency was prevailed in the studies of religions. The phenomenological method, instead of trying to deduce one religion from any other by the principle of causality, attempted rather to describe and define the specific uniqueness of each religion. There were differences among religions. Why should these differences not also exist between the pagan mysteries and Christianity? Each religion was unique, so was Christianity.

In the coming decades only one particular question remains: if a difference does exist between Christian and non-Christian religions, is this difference so antipodal that Christianity supplants all other religions?[51]

D. The Indirect Influence

The indirect influence of the pagan religions on Christianity is twofold. Firstly, the Christian religion, for missionary purposes, so conformed itself to the sentiments of pagan religions that it gradually became essentially different from the apostolic faith (indirect transforming influence). Secondly, Christianity borrowed expressions, formulas, and even ideas, from the surrounding religions and gave to the old terminology and ideas new sense and meaning (indirect contributory influence).

1) Transforming Influence

The indirect transforming influence of pagan religions was rejected by K. Prümm in 1935.[52] Christianity for Prümm never completely conformed to pagan mysteries, for the fundamental difference between Christianity and the pagan religions existed from the very beginning and still exists. This essential difference consists in the fact that the apostles placed the decisive historical experience of Easter at the basis of their faith. The apostles' faith did not come from deductive speculation, but from the historical event of the resurrection. This historicity was altogether special to Christianity, for other religions never alluded to historical events for proof of their positions. Christianity placed at its center a historical person: the God-man in his bodily resurrection. Mythology had no historical, but only literary protagonists. If the meaning of a doctrine determines the meaning of its parts, then, Christianity is completely different from other religions in its totality. The parts can not be understood apart from their relation to the whole. Christianity was never a religion in the common sense of the word.

There was evident reason for saying this. If Christianity, in its essentials, could be traced back to pagan elements, then it was no longer a divine revelation in which God revealed himself to man (as Christianity claimed to be) but a human revelation in which man revealed God to man. The divine origin of Christianity had to be manifested somehow in its uniqueness and original novelty.

This assumed uniqueness and original novelty was at stake once again in the fifties after the Qumran discoveries.

Edmund Wilson in his book, *The Scrolls from the Dead Sea,* wrote that the monastery of the Qumran sect, more than Bethlehem or Nazareth, was the cradle of Christianity.[53] The Scrolls "are really God's Gift to the Humanists," said C. F. Potter, "for every unrolling reveals further indications that Jesus was, as he said, 'The Son of Man,' rather than the deity, 'Son of God,' his followers later claimed."[54] Since Jesus carried out into the world the principles of the Qumran sect, Christianity was nothing but one of numerous Essene sects. The similarities and points of contact (organization and practices, sacred meal, the bishop as head of communities, communal possessions, baptism, angelology, eschatology, opposition between sons of light and sons of darkness, Holy Spirit, the Teacher of Righteousness, the Messiah, etc.) led A. Dupont-Sommer[55] to suggest that it was "from the womb of this spiritual ferment," of which the Qumran community was part, that Christianity emerged.

However, direct causal influence was, again, quickly ruled out. Christianity did not in any sense owe its origin either to the Qumran sect or to hellenism. G. Graystone argued that "the uniqueness of Christianity is not at stake. The careful reading of the scrolls side by side with the New Testament brings into greater relief the uniqueness of Christ and transcendence of the religion which he founded."[56] There were many substantial differences between the primitive Church and the Qumran group. E. Stauffer pointed out eight.

(1) In Qumran the priests played even a larger role than in any other Jewish groups. In the message of Jesus we cannot find this kind of clericalism. (2) The ceremonial ritualism of Qumran is completely unknown to the writers of the New Testament. (3) The Qumran people had to hate the children of darkness, while Jesus commanded that his followers love their enemies. (4) Qumran proclaimed militarism, Jesus rejected violence. (5) Qumran people were calendar specialists. Jesus never addressed himself to calendrical problems. (6) The teaching of the Qumran sect was a secret teaching; Jesus denied expressly that he taught anything which was not public knowledge. (7) The wilderness sect believed in the Messiah of the house of Aaron, to which there was no parallel in the New Testament. (8) The Qumran group rejected the Jerusalem priesthood, its Temple and cult. Jesus celebrated Jewish festivals and did not repudiate the Temple. The members of the primitive Church prayed and worshiped in the Temple (Lk 24,53; Acts 3,1).[57]

Moreover, Qumran was exclusively for Jews and not for all mankind. In the Scrolls there was no explicit reference either to the resurrection of the dead, or to the punishment of the evil man after death. The essence of Christianity, explained J. Coppens, might be conceived as God's tender love for the individual human soul combined with divine Fatherhood, or as universal fraternity, the presence of the kingdom of God on earth. There was, however, no parallel to these ideas in the Qumran writings.[58]

But the most radical difference, the fundamental antithesis between Qumran and Jesus, consisted in the relation of each to the Mosaic Law. The Qumran sect based itself on the Mosaic Law, and was contained within the framework of the Sinaitic Covenant. The Christian faith abrogated the Sinaitic Covenant and terminated the regime of Mosaic Law. Jesus more than once failed to observe the Sabbath (Mk 2,28; Jn 5,10-12; 9,14) and allowed his followers to depart from it. The wilderness sectarians of Qumran would have had to condemn Jesus to death as a rebel against the Sabbath just as others had done in Jerusalem. The Jewish sect was "deprived of revelation flowing from the divine source and, therefore, nourished itself instead upon a fantastic exegesis of texts from the law and prophets. Contrary to this, Christianity appeared from the beginning as a new dynamic religion in which the presence and experience of the Spirit shows forth a vitality that is unique." If the first Christians did borrow from the sectaries some expressions and ideas, as they did in fact (cf the later books of the New Testament) the "breath that now flows through them is that of the life-giving Spirit, the Holy Spirit, the Spirit of Jesus."[59]

2) Contributing Influence

The fact that Christianity did not owe its origin to Qumran or to other religions does not mean that it did not borrow expressions and ideas, investing them with new and fuller meaning. Thus, the indirect contributory influence of Qumran as well as of the pagan religions was admitted, since many elements of the NT could be traced back to Qumran or hellenic origin.

The indirect contributory influence of pagan religions was not only admitted by the apologists, but it was considered an essential condition of the very nature of Christianity. The religion of God was born into a world which was the product of a collision between hellenic and Jewish cultures. These two cultures mingled many centuries before Christianity. By this mutual interaction God prepared both for the Incarnation: through *Dichtung,* the hellenic world, and through *Wahrheit,* Judaism. Using this distinction, A. J. Toynbee in 1939[60] confirmed the distinction between hellenism and Christianity made by K. Prümm. According to A. J. Toynbee, Christianity could borrow ideas from the hellenistic world, since the hellenistic world itself was one of the tributaries of Christianity which played a great part in catching and transmitting the word of God. God prepared the hellenistic world for Jesus' coming by folklore. The Greek mysteries could have predisposed the Greeks to accept Christianity as a religion of intimacy with divinity. The Greek spirit passionately sought encounters with the gods and thus accepted a religion of Incarnation more readily. The correspondence between the story of Jesus and the stories of certain hellenic Saviors might be superficial and trivial;[61] however, the hellenic spirit had been moving towards the stream of Christianity. This longing was all the more intense because the Syriac wing of hellenic society had inherited from the prophets of Israel (who had risen in their midst in the time of exile) the saving truth, the native awakening to a sense of sin [62] and of salvation.

Thus, on account of a confrontation with the comparative study of religions apologetics was further developed. It became above all a historical study. In place of a theoretic and speculative method, literary and historical method became the proper method in apologetics. The function of the apologist from then on was to investigate and to establish the "facts." A further consequence of historical method was that apologetics, centering itself on the person of Christ, became the apologetics of Christ and not an apologetics of religions. If an apologetics did not speculate but rather sought the true facts, then it had to find Jesus Christ as the principal and overriding historical event of Christian religion. In one word, Christian apologetics had to become Christocentric. In the confrontation with other religions Christianity was to become aware of its specific essence and uniqueness, i.e., the uniqueness of Jesus, the Incarnated God.

4. FORM CRITICISM: HISTORY OF THE FORMATION OF THE GOSPEL TRADITION

A. The Origin of Form Criticism

From the start of the 20th century the characteristics of ancient writings and their differences from modern literary works have been the object of study.[63] But now, the history of religions, having placed Christianity among the oriental and hellenistic religions, the next logical step was to apply the conclusions of these linguistic studies to holy scripture. H. Gunkel was the first to do this, but he only worked with the Old Testament, especially with the books of Genesis and the psalms.[64] Before long the same method was also applied to the gospels. Independently, but almost contemporaneously, numerous works were published on this sub-ject: M. Dibelius, *Die Formgeschichte des Evangeliums* (Form Criticism of the Gospel) Tübingen, 1919: K. L. Schmidt, *Der Rahmen der Geschichte Jesu* (The Structure of Jesus' History) Berlin, 1919; R. Bultmann, *Die Geschichte der Synoptischen Tradition,* Göttingen, 1921, Eng. trans. *The History of Synoptic Tradition,* Oxford, 1963; M. Albertz, *Die Synoptischen Streits-gespräche* (The Synoptic Controversial Discourses) Berlin, 1921; G. Bertram *Die Leidensgeschichte Jesu und der Christus-Kult* (The History of Jesus' Passion and Christ's Cult) Göttingen, 1922.

The common intention of these authors was to explain the origin of the gospels, and thus to find some satisfactory solution to the synoptic problem by tracing the genesis of the small literary units or forms in which the gospel message was presented and transmitted until it was definitively fixed in the present text. The new method was called *Formgeschichte,* a term taken from philol-ogy. O. Cullman preferred the name "history of gospel tradition," while in English, V. Taylor called it "form criticism."

B. Procedures and Tenets of Form Criticism

According to proponents of the new method the gospels were not literary works endowed with an organic unity written by eyewitnesses or by a historian. Rather they were compilations, consisting of small literary units of popular writings with the characteristics of the contemporary rabbinic and hellenistic popu-lar literature. The characteristics of this popular literature were approximately the following:

The compiler depended mostly on tradition and received his material from this source.

The work was anonymously presented. References to time and place were arbitrary, yielding to the purpose of the story and the theme.

The written or oral tradition, on which the anonymous editor depended, consisted, in its primitive state, of diverse pericopes, which were circulated orally independent of one another, prior to compilation. To understand and classify these small units, the later external frame had to be broken down and the autonomy of the different pieces of the gospel mosaic restored.

All these traits of popular writings were also found in the gospel writings. Thus to understand the real meaning of the literary forms of the gospels, the artificial form which the evangelists imposed, had to be removed and these subliterary units examined in themselves. This phase of analysis was called the static moment of form criticism.

1) The Static Moment

The basic division of the gospel units, based on the analogy of Jewish and Greek literature, was a division into sayings and deeds. Regarding the sayings, all critics accepted pretty much the same nomenclature as Bultmann.

a) Wisdom sayings (exhortations, sapiential words, etc.).
b) Prophetic and apocalyptic sayings (the preaching, threats, eschatological exhortation, apocalyptic prophecy).
c) Legalistic sayings and disciplinary rules.
d) "I" words ("I say to you").
e) Parables and allegories.

Dibelius distinguished the deeds as follows:

a) Paradigms (or pronouncement stories): short narratives whose origin was a phrase or gesture of Jesus which was afterwards dramatized. Such narratives were especially useful in preaching by way of example.

b) Stories: more developed accounts where an action was described more fully. Ordinarily, the miracles were described in this fashion; hence the name *Wundererzahlung*, miracle story.

c) Legends: i.e. stories which did not belong to any of the above categories, e.g. references to the biography of Jesus, his infancy, baptism, temptation, transfiguration, passion and resurrection—the biography of the disciples, their vocation, Peter's confession. (Notice, in this context, legend does not necessarily mean fiction, but rather pious and edifying accounts apart from any questions of historicity.)

2) The Dynamic Moment

Classification by unit was followed by the dynamic moment of form criticism. The different literary forms were then placed in their *Sitz im Leben,* in their original milieu. Since the community expressed, through these literary forms, its problems, its needs and existential tendencies, form critics by analyzing the purposes of these literary units tried to reconstruct the milieu the community lived in. What purpose did these forms serve in the life of the primitive community? What was their function? What were the motives for composing them? These were the questions which the second phase of form criticism attempted to answer.

According to Dibelius this existential need could be determined *a priori* as the kerygma. The origin and motive of the gospels were the necessity of preaching. The gospels were written as an aid to preaching; therefore, they were always to be understood and interpreted in the light of preaching.

Bertram thought that the motive for the written tradition was not the necessity of preaching, but the need and desire of adoring Christ. The gospels had not so much a kerygmatic as a liturgical function in the primitive church. Their purpose was to foster the adoration of Christ among the faithful.

According to M. Goguel[65] the principal motive for the written gospels was to be found in the eschatological expectations of the early Christians. For E. Hirsch[66] two crises in the early church were of great moment in the formation of the paschal legend and the consequent written tradition. The first arose around the year 50 A.D. and concerned the lot of the faithful who died before the advent of Christ; the second was the crisis of gnosticism which reached its climax in the second century. The church reacted to these crises with the antipodal doctrine of the bodily resurrection.

In contrast, O. Cullmann, using the same method of form criticism, arrived at the very opposite of Hirsch's position. According to Cullmann, the paschal faith was not born of an eschatological faith as Goguel and Hirsch had supposed, but rather the paschal faith gave birth to the eschatological expectation. The resurrection of Jesus, not the eschatological expectation, was the central theme of the primitive preaching.[67]

According to R. Bultmann there were a great number of motives which produced the constituent parts of the gospels. Some were primary and some were secondary, but all influenced the formation of one or other pericope. Besides the problems of preaching and adoration, the community had other problems and duties: the task of education, the formation of preachers, legislation, etc. It had controversies within its own ranks and debates with outsiders. These were exterior trials to which interior difficulties or psychological problems, common among men, have to be added. But from all of these preoccupations, one was missing: the concern about history.

A common characteristic of primitive man, lacking a sense of objectivity of dedication to scientific history, is to measure everything through feeling and thinking. He dramatizes and concretizes theories since he does not have the capacity of abstracting universals from particulars.

And so it was with the gospels. The Christian community, like primitive man, with his natural tendency to mythologize, placed itself as a screen between its members and Christ. Hence it gave us some image of Christ, not that of a flawless mirror but rather that of a prism which refracted and resolved the light of objective reality into different colors distinct from the original. The Christian community through its tradition gave us only certain aspects under which it interpreted and represented Christ to itself. To preach Christ in his true form, the gospel is to be separated from this mythologizing of the primitive church. To do this, Bultmann proposed a process which he called demythologizing.

a) Bultmann's Demythologizing through Existential Interpretation.

Bultmann's fundamental insight, the stimulus to all his thinking, was the irreducible opposition he saw between the ancient mythical conception of the New Testament and the views of modern science.[68] The mythical world of the New Testament is unacceptable to modern technical man. Man cannot use electric lights, radio, have recourse to modern hospitals, and at the same time believe in a world of evil spirits and the miracles of the New Testament. For the use of electricity and the curative methods of modern hospitals implies one view of the world in which productive activity and creative power is completely assigned to man. Scientific man certainly knows that he is subject to unknown influences, but all these elements constitute a certain unique world in which responsibility, liberty, intelligible motivation and activity lie on man in the last analysis, and not on other-worldly forces. Man's free responsibility excludes all other-worldly elements as unintelligible explanations.

In a mythical world, by contrast, every feeling, thought, and act of the will is subordinate to external forces which exercise a magical constraint on man. The mythically orientated man seeks an explanation in other-worldly elements, such as diabolic or divine intervention. He lives his life passively because he lives in a world open to all sorts of interventions which can disrupt the daily experienced cosmic order. A mythic world is not a place of law but of arbitrary and uncontrollable wills which *de facto* and *de jure* defy human control. This is the reason why modern man repudiates the New Testament's world as unintelligible. He cannot understand death as a punishment for sin because he knows that he is destined to die long before he has incurred any personal guilt. Nor can he accept the doctrine of original sin, a punishment for the sin of another transmitted like a sort of hereditary sickness. Such a belief would be an infra-moral and irresponsible act. It would lack liberty, and hence even the character of sin. In like manner, he rejects the mythic conception that a divine being expiated the sin of man by the shedding of his blood. He also finds distasteful the notion of the resurrection of Christ as a salvific event imbued with the power of granting life which man obtains for himself through the sacraments. Is not this to confuse the action of God procuring life for man with some event of nature? It is almost impossible that modern man could really see divine activity in such action.

But there is further contradiction in the gospels. In the gospels man is seen as a mythic, passive and cosmic being who acts deterministically, and at the same time as a free agent who can lift himself up or destroy himself. Because these alternatives are mutually exclusive, one of them has to be rejected. Bultmann wanted to eliminate the passive, deterministic view because it is precisely this passivity which is proper to myth, and, therefore, incompatible with the thought of modern man.[69] For myth is that which represents something other-worldly, *unweltlich,* divine as if it is of this world. Myth acts through the material world on man, by subjecting him passively to the influence of material factors. So Bultmann's meaning of myth is very different from the modern meaning of this term.

Myth is here used in the sense popuarlized by the "History of Religions" school. Mythology is the use of imagery to express the other-worldly in terms of this world and the divine in terms of human life, the other side in terms of this side. For instance, divine transcendence is expressed as spatial distance. It is a mode of expression which makes it easy to understand the cultus as an action in which material means are used to convey immaterial power. Myth is not used in that modern sense, according to which it is practically equivalent to ideology. [70]

Such terrestrial influence of other-worldly elements has to be denied, according to Bultmann, because it takes away the active liberty of man which is affirmed before all. The elimination of the passive element is precisely the demythologizing effected by means of existential interpretation. After existential interpretation only that part of the New Testament is accepted as authentic which looks to action, to decision, to responsibility and liberty.

b) The Existential Interpretation of Bultmann

Existential analysis does not lead so much to knowledge of God, as to knowledge of the self. It illuminates individual existence, as living in the future, through decision and liberty. This knowledge of self is the only meaningful theme of existential analysis. Man cannot speak of God as an object. If he speaks of God as an object, he already speaks of him as someone outside of man, whom he considers as a spectator. Thus he does not really speak of God any more, for man lives and exists in God who is in him the Reality which has determined his existence. [71] God cannot be known as an object about which man can speak, but only as a subject who speaks. Therefore, he who rightly wants to speak of God can necessarily only speak about man inasmuch as he is limited by God (in creation), or called (back to creatureliness in the revelation) by the word of God.

Consequently, the revelation of the New Testament did not introduce a new knowledge of God. It did not mediate a self-understanding, a new world-view, or any kind of communication of supernatural knowledge, but an occurrence in which the original relation of creation, refused by sin, was reestablished. [72]

If this is true, it follows that sin is nothing but a "rebellion against God, forgetting that man is a creature, misunderstanding himself and putting himself in God's place." [73] The world, immersed in sin, does not know that it is limited by God. The forgiveness of sin consists, therefore, in a new eschatological eon in which the world comes to an end, since the original relation of man's creatureliness is reproduced.[74] Man understands himself again as a creature and does not attempt to secure his existence by means of what he himself has established. Sin takes as secure what is really insecure, as definitive what is provisional; therefore, in the forgiveness of sin (which is not remission of moral failures), everything wordly or provisional once again acquires the character of being provisional.[75]

In the new eon of the revelation of Christ, man's creatureliness is to be acknowledged in the "that" of being called and addressed now by God in Christ. The revelation in the New Testament was not a cosmic process which took place outside of man, and of which the world could merely make report, but an occurrence that took place in man himself. There was no content in it, there was no "what" and "how" since God could not be the object of revelation, but only be the "that" of revelation, namely, that God was he (the subject) who was speaking to us, who was addressing us in the preaching. Revelation always took place in preaching, in the proclamation which did not make the revelation present by a communication of knowledge but by a presentation in the form of an address of love directed to man here and now.

This address of God directed to man by the word of preaching became the revelation of Christ. "Christ is revelation and that revelation is the word; these two are one and the same."[76] Revelation in Christ meant revelation in word. Therefore, "the Christ of the kerygma is not a historical figure."[77] He was not even a divine person beside God as later dogmatic formulations might suggest, but he was the word, the word of God, the action of God in which he addressed man here and now.[78] To believe in Christ meant to believe in God's creative operation in the world, which was not confined to the historical personality, Jesus of Nazareth. There is no question of believing in Jesus, but of believing in Christ through Jesus.[79] Thus Paul himself could become "Christ for his hearers—not because he is deified and is gazed upon by them as a pneumatic, but because he preaches to them" in such a way that God made his appeal through him and encountered Paul's hearer in the eschatological now of the revelation.[80] The novelty and the specific essence of Christianity consisted not of *what*, but of *that* God addresses to men here and now and not in the past.[81]

This existential theology focused all of its attention on the act of revelation, the actual meeting with the transcendent God. In the gospel the historical Jesus and his life were presented, but it was not the historical life, not the circumstances of the life of Jesus that God wished to reveal to us, but only the one unique fact that God himself had spoken to us. Jesus himself did not overly stress his historical life, but laid stress on the "here and now" intervention of God, and salvation was not ultimately founded in a historical event but in man's free decision to bear the cross and make it his own. The cross was not a salvific event, because it was the cross of Christ, but because it was a salvific event, therefore it was the cross of Christ.[82] The faithful had to interiorize the cross of Christ just as he must interiorize revelation. This interiorization was not a rationalistic process, but was ever open to a new and a constantly reiterated free acceptance of the cross at every moment of time. In this free acceptance of the cross at every moment consisted the eschatological moment of the proclamation of Christ. Through this eschatological dimension *Historie* (the facts of the past established by the historian) received their historic character and became *Geschichte* (facts of the past having a vital existential impact on man's present life).

c) The Difference between the Historical Jesus and the Christ-Kerygma

Following Kähler, Bultmann made a distinction between the *historisch* (historical) and the *geschichtlich* (historic). A historical fact could be considered, first, simply as a thing of the past without any personal relation to the viewer. Thus, for example, the death of Christ, inasmuch as it means nothing to men, was a historical fact. But historical facts could also be considered in their relation to the person considering them. Such a consideration of historical facts was called by Bultmann *geschichtlich* (historic). In the concrete case of the death of Christ, the cross of Christ was not only historical, but historic, i.e. through its new significance there was communicated to men the fact that God looks upon men in Christ with mercy.

Corresponding to this consideration in Bultmann's view, the cross and death of Christ was historical and at the same time historic. Whereas the resurrection was historic but not historical; it was not an event found in space and time, but rather the expression of the value of the cross of Christ for man. The basis of the faith of the apostles in the resurrection was not a historical fact. It was uniquely caused by divine action without apparitions or visions. It was not caused passively by the perception of some fact, but by the free decision of man, who willed to believe that God, in the cross of Christ, was indeed merciful towards him. When man confessed that Jesus had risen, he affirmed the death of Jesus with its message of divine grace and forgiveness, but not that Jesus in some moment of space and time rose bodily.

The historical Jesus was not God, not even Christian, but a Jewish man standing within Judaism who died like anybody else. The primitive Christian kerygma mythologized this Jewish man, inasmuch as it maintained that God had made the historical Jesus "the Christ," and proclaimed that he died vicariously on the cross for the sins of men and was miraculously raised by God for man's salvation. The kerygma, therefore, presupposed the historical Jesus since without him there would be no kerygma. In other words, the historical existence, the "that" of Jesus, is presupposed by kerygma. However, it does not presuppose at all the "what" or the "how" of the historical Jesus. The Christ of kerygma was absolutely different from the historical Jesus. The Christ of kerygma was not a historical person, but an action of God, the demythologized reality of the presence of God in the Christian faith. The gospels were evidently a combination of historical report and kerygmatical Christology. This combination, however, was not for the purpose of giving historical legitimacy to the Christ-kerygma but for the purpose of giving legitimacy to the history of Jesus. The kerygma did not ask for the objective historicity of the person and work of Jesus but required faith in the crucified and risen Lord. The life of the historical Jesus, the Jesus according to the flesh, was irrelevant.

d) Discussion Between Bultmann and his Disciples

It is remarkable that, in spite of his influential teaching, R. Bultmann aroused a special interest in the historical Jesus among his students. Reacting to their professor, most of them tried to elaborate the unity of the historical Jesus and the Christ of the kerygma and to show that kerygma presupposed not only the "that," but also the "what" and the "how" of the historical Jesus as a requirement of the kerygma in order to be understood as well as believed.

One group of Bultmann's students attempted to show that Jesus' personality and activity were implicit in the kerygma. [83] Another group attempted to show that Jesus' activity, words and deeds were already kerygmatical[84] and his understanding of existence demanded our eschatological self-understanding.[85] But R. Bultmann always rejected all attempts of his students as unsuccessful[86] because they did not succeed in legitimizing the kerygma by historical-critical research. The kerygmatic faith could not be mediated historically. The historian could not lead his hearers or readers to a situation where they had to decide for or against Jesus, since then the Christ-kerygma would lose its meaning and become superfluous. If it could be shown historically that the historical Jesus urged his claim of demanding faith in him as the coming Son of Man, or as Christ, then the validity of his claim still would not be established by historical proofs. Historical-critical research includes the subject-object relation, i.e. the historian as subject who stands over against history as his object. Now, in faith this subject-object scheme does not exist at all. In fact there was no continuity at all between Christ-kerygma and the kerygma of the historical Jesus. The faith that Jesus might have asked for was a faith in him who promised salvation, meanwhile the kerygma demanded faith in Jesus who actually had already brought salvation. The "once" of the historical Jesus had been changed by the kerygma into "once-for-all," not by reproducing the past but rather by a unique contemporizing of the word of God here and now. And this evidently could not be done by any historical research.

e) Bultmann and his Critics

All of Bultmann's critics admit that he has been one of the most influential as well as one of the most discussed theologians of the 20th century. His greatest contribution to theology and Christian life was the contemporizing of the call of the revealing God by stressing that God did not speak to men only in the past, but also speaks today, here and now. There is a personal dialogue between the believer and the calling God.[87] It is true that Bultmann did not want to admit the divinity of Jesus for pastoral reasons, nevertheless, he believed many things about Jesus, e.g., that God spoke his final word to him in Jesus, and that Jesus freed him from condemnation, etc. These things could be admitted only if Jesus was what the Christian faith proclaimed him to be, God.

In spite of the general recognition given Bultmann he has been seriously criticized for falling into a methodological error and of making an illegitimate transition from the literary order to the historical order.[88] He made the same mistake with which he charged primitive and mythological man. The method of form criticism is not necessarily a historical method which can pass judgment on the value of the authenticity of a form.

Moreover, several of Bultmann's presuppositions were questioned. Was the incompatibility between the biblical conception and the mode of thought of modern man all that evident? The opposite might be true. Perhaps modern man was more likely to admit mysteries of life and limits to his science than nineteenth century man and hence was closer to the New Testament mentality than his immediate predecessors. Modern man knew that he could grasp only certain phenomena and not the inner and ultimate secrets of reality. So was it not a question of the incompatibility between Bultmannian and the modern concept, rather than between the modern concept and New Testament modes of thought? Karl Jaspers especially criticized Bultmann for this.[89]

K. Barth objected that Bultmann's theory destroyed Christianity's historicalness and made of it pure ideology like any other religion.

The main criticism of Bultmann, however, was that in defending his personal insight he overlooked the complexity of reality. This one-sided simplicity was due to the life of the community in which Bultmann lived. He shared the philosophical view of his age as well as the professional interest of his family. Like the idealist of the nineteenth century he could not see that man was necessarily a man in the world who could not achieve his fulfillment without the appropriation of historical, cosmic reality. Similarly, he could not achieve a faith which did not have any historical, cosmic traces. For him the freedom of man was a pure act of the subject and not an act of a subject in the world about the world. Evidently freedom is not conditioned by the world, nevertheless it is about the visible historical, cosmic world, which man can recognize as his own. The "I" according to Bultmann was still the encysted "I" of Descartes, and not the "I" necessarily inserted into the world of modern man.[90] A faith without cosmic repercussions was therefore nonsense for modern man, since he felt himself as a spiritual-historical-cosmic unity. The historico-cosmic aspect of faith was not required for the purpose of legitimizing, of proving, and hence of diluting the faith, as Bultmann feared. It was rather an essential part of the word of the calling God, who had to be the Lord of history and cosmos as well as of ideas if he wanted to address the spiritual-historical-cosmic man. Therefore, the word of God could not be reduced to an internal, invisible action; nor could faith be reduced to verbal preaching. Bultmann, as a son of a Protestant preacher, might have wanted to defend the value of preaching and to propagate the faith. However, he did not succeed because modern man stayed closer to the complex faith of the first Christians whose Christ was *Pantocrator,* the Lord of the cosmos as well as of history, than to the simple faith of Bultmann. The modern time, indeed, is Teilhardian rather than Bultmannian time.

f) *Pannenberg's Reaction*

There was no better indication of this change of time than the considerable success of W. Pannenberg's theology. Among the Protestant theologians Pannenberg and his circle[91] forms probably the most radical reaction to Bultmann's demythologizing program. According to Pannenberg if what happened to Jesus of Nazareth can only be seen by faith and is completely inaccessible to rational research, it is impossible to think of faith otherwise than as pure illusion and arbitrariness. Since God is revealed and known in the Old Testament not by his words, but by the deeds he performed in history, Bultmannian theology of the word has to be replaced by the theology of history. Christianity can not retreat from world history into pious subjectivity and the safe harbor of superhistoricity. To be able to believe in Jesus one presupposes that the message about him is true. And this includes the facts that Jesus really proclaimed the coming of God's reign, and that he really rose from the dead. Therefore, the resurrection of Jesus as well as the revelation of God in him is a historical question which can be answered only by historical arguments.

But how can the resurrection of Jesus be historically demonstrated? Pannenberg thinks that man can gain a knowledge of Jesus' resurrection and of God's revelation in him, if the historically verifiable facts are not considered in isolation, but in the context of historical tradition, more precisely in the context of the apocalyptic expectation of the general resurrection from the dead that speaks of God in an intelligible way.

If the disciples knew that the Jewish messianic expectation included the cosmic transformation of the whole world, indicated since the time of Isaiah (26,19) by the image of the resurrection from the dead (cf Ez 37,1-14; Dan 12,2; 2 Mach, 7,9), and if they believed that the end of history appeared in Jesus, the historian has to conclude that Jesus could not remain dead since in the context of this tradition the bodily resurrection was an absolute, irreplaceable metaphor. It was only the raising action of God which could lead the disciples to refer to Jesus as the final revelation of God in whom the end of history appeared.

Pannenberg stressed the context of the general tradition as the principle of historical verification, instead of analogical comparison in determining the historicity of an event. If the analogy is taken as the exclusive criterion for evaluating events, the historian cannot but admit the historicity of those events which he somehow experienced previously. Thus the resurrection of Jesus can be understood as a final revelation not in the analogy of the experience of resurrection from the dead which no one ever experienced, but only in connection with the whole history mediated by the course of Israel. Through the knowledge of Jesus as the risen One and the final revelation of God, man can be led to faith which is nothing else than trust in the promised future. This faith, or trust in the future, unites man to God and imparts salvation. But without previous knowledge this trust in God will be but blind superstition.

Pannenberg may have gone to the other extreme in opposing Bultmann. Some even felt it necessary to bring back a "little of the supernatural" into his system.[92] Faith in Jesus was replaced by trust in the future of God based upon the knowledge of Jesus. Nevertheless, Pannenberg's theology of history made it clear once more that the immanent forces of faith cannot be reduced to an internal, personal encounter with God. They, themselves demand rather a challenging confrontation with the history of the world as known by historical science. Faith and history can not be separated if faith in the incarnation is to be taken seriously.

C. Evaluation of Form Criticism In the Nineteen Sixties

Since the new method seemed to provide solutions for contradictions which the rationalists had discovered in the gospels, form criticism was soon applied to the problem of the resurrection. [93] Among the Catholics, H. Dickmann was perhaps the first to recognize that form criticism provided a new insight into the problem of Jesus.[94] According to the new method, the liberal distinction of the two periods of tradition, sc., Jesus of the first century as moral teacher, and Jesus of the second and third century as Savior-God, proved to be untenable. In the tradition there is not the slightest trace of such a difference. The primitive tradition, as well as the modern belief, attested to the adoration of Jesus as God and Savior. Thus form criticism restored and vindicated Christian tradition. It demonstrated that the cradle of Christian belief did not originate either in the faith of the late post-apostolic Church (as rationalism assumed), or in the pagan mythic religions (as the history-of-religions-school claimed) but in the primitive community almost contemporary with the historical Jesus.

Besides the traditional signs (miracles, prophecies, etc.) a new miracle was discovered: the primitive Christian community, whose wondrous life captivated the inquiring mind. Who they were, what they were, why they believed, and why they behaved as they did became the urgent questions requiring answers (immanent or transcendent) as the miracles did in the previous eras. The primitive Christian community became the only sign worthy of study.

As a matter of fact, form criticism as a literary method was admitted almost unanimously by Catholic theologians, and since Vatican II is proposed as the doctrine of the Church.[95]

The acceptance of form criticism as a literary method, however, did not mean necessarily its acceptance as a historical method. Whether from these literary forms the historical life of Christianity could be reconstructed with some historical certitude was, and still is, under discussion. The fact that the authors could not even agree on a definitive listing of the literary forms indicated that there was not enough evidence to discover and observe the function that each pericope had in the life of the community. A conclusion affirming that not only the literary composition of the gospels but also the historical reality of faith was a composition and creation of the primitive Christian community was not justified. There were found many facts which invalidated form criticism as a historical method.[96]

First of all, the primitive Christian community was not an anonymous community. It was guided by the apostles as authorized eyewitnesses, and we know many members of this community. That the apostles and the community had a genuine interest in history was indicated by the notion of "witness" and "testimony" which in their different forms occurs over one hundred and fifty times in the New Testament.[97] The creative power of the Christian community was overestimated by reason of some philosophico-sociological theories, which are now far less self-evident than they once were. On the contrary, there was evidence that the characteristic feature of the community, as well as of its leaders, was the faithful transmission of a tradition constantly defended against any innovation. The primitive Christian community rather lacked imagination and creative initiative, (Rom 6,17; 1 Cor 11,2.23; 15,1-3; Gal 1,8-9; Gal 2,2; Phil 4,9; Col 2,6-8; 1 Thess 2,13; 2 Thess 2,15; 3,6 etc.). The power of the community in general was more stimulating than creative in function, rather suggestive than decisive. The Christian community, as any community, received its determination from its preeminent individuals.[98] Further it was not logical, as many believed, to deduce from literary form the character and general properties of a people. The great difference between apocryphal accounts of the miracles of Jesus and the gospels indicated that the community under the guidance of the apostles did not completely lack a sense of history.

CHAPTER THREE

APOLOGETIC CONCERN
FOR THE MEANING OF CHRISTIANITY
(1963-1972)

The second half of the 20th century brought a new challenge to the Christian faith. There was a considerable shift from questions about Christian origins to the meaning and usefulness of the Christian message. The main concern was no longer whether God founded the Church but what the Church is really for. What could it offer that modern man really needs and cannot get better and more speedily elsewhere? Most of the activities and functions of the Church, like teaching, social charitable work, psychological care, counseling, and so forth, are done in modern society by trained personnel and apparently with greater success. What can a man really get through faith? When the Church asks this question from the neophyte who wants to become a member, the answer is "eternal life." But if eternal life is given to those who do not enter into the Church through the baptismal rite, and non-Christian religions can as well be a means of salvation,[99] is the Christian faith as we know it now really necessary for that purpose?

The most simple, and at the same time best answer to the question "What is the faith for?" was, evidently, and is still, "To help men to encounter and understand God." But another question arises: "What is God for?" "Does modern man need God?" "If so, why?" He does not need him as he did before, to find food and prey, to control the wind and rain, to influence favorably the

growth of crops and cattle. This is done now by scientific research and technology. Moreover, God is not needed either to
keep order in the big cities or to win a war or to put a missile into
orbit. For mental troubles, psychological care seems to offer a
faster and more reliable service than prayer. If it is difficult to see
what God is for, it is even harder to understand what faith is for.

Indeed, in these times faith has to face a most unique challenge,
the challenge of uselessness and of inferiority, the challenge of
disillusionment and bitter disappointments; in one word, the
anxiety of decay and death.

1. BONHOEFFER

Faith's agony for survival is manifested in the theology of one
of the most influential theologians of the sixties, D. Bonhoeffer. [100] During the apparent triumph of the enemies of his
faith, he bitterly criticized Barth's and Bultmann's theology of
God "up-there" and transformed God into the God in the world,
the incarnated God in Jesus, the man for others. Since the God of
religions is irrelevant, even nonexistent, Christianity, in order to
survive, has to cease being a religion looking "up there" for the
divinization of men; it must be a life of grace strengthened by
suffering and self-sacrifice for others.

Faith cannot survive except by realizing these values which are
the real interest and concern of the modern world. Christian faith
has to take these values into itself in order to be appreciated or at
least tolerated by the world.

2. DEATH-OF-GOD THEOLOGY

The same vital self-affirmation of faith in face of challenge is
manifested also in the Death-of-God theology. [101] If the notion of
God has lost its meaning and relevance for modern man, in order
to keep itself alive, faith has to be detheologized. If modern man
does not understand other values aside from the values of the
world, faith must put on all the characteristics of the secular
values, the only ones with a future. Through the forward moving
kenosis, faith has to be incarnated into the world and die in order

to transmit all its properties to the world in which and with which it can survive. "While the Oriental mystic," said T. J. J. Altizer, "knows an incarnational process whereby the sacred totally annihilates or transfigurates the profane," it is only the Christian faith that is capable of descending into the profane to progressively abandon or negate "its particular and given expressions, thereby emptying them of their original power and actuality." Therefore, the death of faith in the totality of experience is the natural continuation of the forward movement of the divine process which by negating itself becomes actualized and real in history as an all-encompassing, immanent "kingdom of God."[102]

3. MOLTMANN

Though in Protestant theology the incarnational process of faith as described by Bonhoeffer and by the death-of-God theologians already signifies a considerable break from the transcendental-eschatological Augustinian-Lutheran concept of the world, it is Moltmann's theology [103] which shows a definitive overcoming of the cross-death as the general horizon of the search for the meaning of faith. Though in the death-of-God theology, the secularized world does not seem to have self-sacrificing death as its final moment of grace, concerning the religious values, Luther's insight of the cross as the central point of salvation is still reflected there. The immanent optimism of the death-of-God theologians concerning the secularized world becomes more explicit in Moltmann's theology of hope, where the resurrection-hope and not the cross becomes the context of theological understanding. Though Moltmann does not necessarily admit the metaphor of resurrection as a definitive and unambiguous concept of reality, world history is seen as heading towards the process of a hopeful event which biblically has been understood as resurrection. By giving a positive, hopeful, optimistic future to the world, faith becomes useful and able to survive. Since its concern becomes the fundamental concern of modern man, the future of the world, it can survive with the world and for the world.

After the incarnation Jesus is to be seen as a man of the future who can be properly described not by what he is, but by what he is hoping for. He is considered not as eternal God but rather as a man living for promises to be actualized and revealed only when the world of faith and world of the universe achieve their common end and become definitively identified.

4. THEOLOGY OF REVOLUTION AND OF POLITICS

Moltmann's theology of hope prompted the theology of revolution and of politics. "In order to practice Christian hope for the world," wrote C. E. Braaten, "we must reflect on whether or how God may be active in revolutionary situations. . . . Christians need a theology of revolution. Without it we will be at a total loss about what to do for the rest of the century." [104] Once the two kingdoms, that of heaven where man is expected to live after death, and that of the world where man lives at the present time, are brought close together, it is necessary that the Church find a "new job" in this world. If it wants to stay relevant and meaningful, in addition to its skill recognized in the "other world," it has to make itself useful here and now. Like anyone else on earth, it must have a plan, a project and make its living.

J. B. Metz one of the representatives of the theology of revolution defined the Church's new role as "criticizing the world with a liberating task to it." [105] Its task is not so much to elaborate systems of social solutions, but challenge the existing political systems.

The idea of the Church's role as criticizing the existing political systems found good reception in North and South America. As a result two theologies came forth: the black theology in the North[106] and revolution theology in the South.[107]

For both, language was not just a tool of communication, or way of understanding, but above all a tool for changing history.

5. RENEWAL OF GOD-LANGUAGE

The concern for finding meaning in the Church's faith-experience urged also the rethinking of the difficulties raised by linguistic analysts as well as the finding of a new language which the world in which the Church lives can understand.

It was some time ago that A. J. Ayer [108] announced that

religious language being unverifiable is unreasonable and meaning-less. Now F. Ferré [109] answered that the linguistic analysts failed to realize that the language has a threefold functional meaning: factual, emotive and conative. The factual meaning contains the knowledge of the "matter of fact" verifiable by observation. The logical positivist admitted this use of language in an exclusive sense. The function of the emotive meaning is to move and direct moods and feelings. God-language has such a function. Its verifica-tion is the measurement of the impact made on the listener. And finally there is the conative function of the language. Its purpose is to change situations, to adapt new ways of life by accepting new values. Such a function of language is adequate if it has valuational adequacy (including all the values and the desire to make life full) as well as valuational coherence and effectiveness.

John Macquarrie, [110] following Heidegger's understanding of language, tried to legitimize God-talk by leading his reader from the language of existence to the language of being in which the being is expected to disclose itself. The language of being is force where a new world is called into being. It is an encounter with being, the coming alive to the mystery that there is a real Other, and not just nothing.

L. Gilkey saw the meaning of God-language verified in "man's experience of ultimacy, in relation to which he finds himself in all facets of his being." [111] God-language has meaning since there is an area where "the creature experiences his own limits, and in experiencing precisely these limits, he asks the question which reaches beyond the creaturely—a question about an ultimacy that the creaturely cannot itself provide." But since these questions are the questions of man's existence they belong to the analysis of secular experience. By their relevance to the deepest problems of the ordinary secular life, the symbolic forms of the Christian existence interpret and illumine the secular human experience. Thus such a language is intelligible as a coherent and relevant answer to the questions that existence raises in all men every-where. [112]

The future of religious language is seen as intimately interwoven with that of faith. On adequate language depends the Church's ability to maintain unity and solidarity with her members in the struggle of life as well as with the society in which she lives. [113]

6. VATICAN II

The same vital forces of faith at work in the renewal of God-language enlivened the discussions of Vatican II. The purpose of the Vatican Council was precisely to face new challenges, to define the Church's place in the modern world, and to present to contemporaries the doctrine of faith concerning God, man, and the world "in a manner better suited to them, with the result that they will receive it more willingly."[114]

Now, in order to explain to the world what the Church is, the Council stated that although the Church communicates divine life, with a saving eschatological purpose to be fulfilled only in a future world, it is, nevertheless, at the same time, the soul of humanity. Paul VI in his closing speech expressed this idea much in the spirit of Bonhoeffer. The Church is the *servant of humanity*.

But in what does this service consist? Is this a service which humanity really needs? Can the world not find this service somewhere else?

In answer to these questions, the Council continued to say that on account of the divine life communicated to it, the Church can heal, elevate the dignity of the person by strengthening the seams of human society and imbue the everyday activity of men with *deeper meaning and importance.* [115] According to this, the great contribution of the Church to the world consists in making the family of man and its history more human, especially by giving deeper meaning and importance to human life.

Since man is never satisfied by what the world has to offer and he always wants God, it follows that if man follows Jesus Christ, the perfect man, he himself will become more of a man. He will, as Christ did, safeguard personal dignity and liberty, repudiate all bondage, promote the dignity of conscience, freedom of choice, the employment of human talents (culture), and charity for all.

Moreover, the Church has something to offer not only to individuals but also to humanity as a whole. It promotes and fortifies the unity of the human family by a unity founded on Christ, as the family of God's sons. [116] However, the Church's contribution to the unity of the world is not fundamentally political, economic or social, but mostly religious. Since the external unity results from a unity of mind and heart, namely, from that faith and charity by which any unity is unbreakably rooted in the Holy Spirit, the Church projects into modern society a force (i.e. faith and charity put in practice) which is an indispensable condition of unity among all men. More particularly, by giving light and energy, it fosters the nobility of marriage, the development of culture, economic development, by giving useful guidelines, political freedom, peace and unity among all nations. [117] Indeed, the Church purifies, strengthens, elevates and ennobles all that is true, good and beautiful.[118]

The promotion of the unity described above can not be considered as some external, temporarily accepted task of the Church. It belongs to its innermost nature since in its relationship to Christ it is a sacrament, i.e. a sign and instrument of intimate union with God, and of the unity of the whole human race.[119]

This is the most explicit answer Vatican II gave to the question about the usefulness of the Church and Christian faith in the modern world. Vatican II believed that this is precisely what the world most deeply needs and can find nowhere else.

But the challenges remain. Is the Church indispensable for achieving that unity? Is the Church an exclusive instrument of man's union with God and with the whole human race? Are not other religions, also, signs and instruments of man's union with God? Are not the Church, and other religions too, with their intransigent claims rather a hindrance than a help to the unity of mankind? Cannot humanity be more easily united without religion than through it? After two thousand years are Jesus and his Church still trustworthy? Can the Church of Jesus validate itself before the man of today by raising ever new hope in him?

These are the questions the post-Vatican II apologetics was concerned with. Its tendency was less scriptural and resembled somewhat the classical theodicies. In search of a new language, more adapted to the mind of the present secular man, it tried to give some guidelines concerning the origin of man, that of evil, the role of Christianity in social revolution, etc.[120]

Its way of proceeding had been conditioned by some concrete crises experienced individually or collectively. The framework was the human existence and not the God-given Christ event, the only ever-lasting context in which revelation-faith dialogue can take place. The apologetics of the revelation-faith event is to demonstrate that context in which an authentic encounter of Jesus Christ with man and man's participation in the creation of the God-given Christ-sign-event are possible. Only this way will apologetics be able to face the challenges of the final part of the 20th century.

CHAPTER FOUR

APOLOGETICS AND THE NEW SET OF ABSTRACTIONS OF THE COMPUTER AGE (1973-)

As the first three, so the last quarter of the 20th century will not fail to bring about new challenges for the faith in Christ. The future challenge, however, probably will not come from the possibility of constructing some sort of machine-man, superior to man. [121] The concern about how to explain the uniqueness and the superiority of man in regard to the computer is an obsolete problem. The real problem rather will be concentrated around a man-computer symbiosis, which for apologetics will create the problem of the believer-computer symbiosis and its consequences for the future of belief. This challenge will be similar to that which religious belief experienced at the time of the discovery of writing.

1. "HOLY COMPUTER"

Modern man likes to think of himself not so much as contemplator but as creator of his world, which, unlike that of his classic forefathers, is not a world at rest but a world within worlds in progress. The purpose of a distinctively human existence is not contemplation but tool-making—tools to be fitted into a world of tools. True enough, tools must be made to transform what at first seems an unmanageable environment into something manageable, which can answer man's needs and desires. But tools are also needed by man as means of self-expression and communication with others.

In the history of tool-making there are two which have the greatest importance—language and writing. The invention of language did not mean just some improvement in human living, it probably marks its very beginning. Once the sound uttered by hominoids was no longer just the outer expression of some basic biological urge that might trigger common movements of the herd, but became a tool for remembering, wondering, thinking and guessing, the threshold between infra-human and human existence had been crossed over once and for all. By use of such a tool man was at once differentiated from all other animals.

It is not surprising, then, that language was considered by early man as something sacred and the source of a mystical power. Indeed the discovery of language meant also the beginning of religious beliefs and assumptions. That is why there is hardly a religion that lacks the notion of a "holy language" or of "words of god" that are means not only of evoking religious belief but also of renewing and transforming it.

Another important tool that man has for remembering, wondering, thinking and conjecturing is writing. It brought further changes in communication and self-expression which would necessarily affect man's religious belief. Once a considerable part of a group could use not only words but letters for communication and self-realization, neither reluctance nor fear could stop a further development that would lead from "holy words" to "holy scripture." From this time on the gods could not only speak to man, but also complete or replace their words by handing over to man inscriptions on tables of stone (cf Ex 24,12), or books written in heaven.

The introduction of writing into the life of religion gave rise to the problem about the relationship between sacred words and sacred writings. In certain cases sacred scripture took over completely the place of sacred words. In other cases, long-lasting discussion led eventually to the idea of either parallel status, or of subordination of one to the other, or of mutual determination.

Today a third tool is being added to language and writing, for remembering, wondering, thinking and conjecturing—the computer, which, it is believed, will have a similar or even greater impact on man and his world than language and writing had. The speaker and writer will in great measure be replaced by some sort of man-computer symbiosis. In the preface of their book E. E. David and J. G. Truxal [122] foresee the 21st century as the beginning of such a symbiosis, in which, by man's brain being electrically connected with a computer, the capabilities of man and computer will be combined to remember and to perform routine calculations; and this use of the computer will transform not only outwardly but inwardly man's habitual way of talking and writing and undoubtedly, too, his way of believing.

If one believes that religion will survive, and if he takes seriously the claim of some computer engineers that the dual language-scripture tool is now to be extended into the tool-triad of language-scripture-computer, the idea of the "holy computer" as a development of the old "holy word" and the "holy scripture" comes spontaneously to mind. Perhaps today the idea of the "holy computer" may sound quite ridiculous, but one might well wonder whether it sounds much more fantastic than did the idea of "holy books" at the time of the transition from speech to writing. One cannot help asking oneself whether there will not be someone in the 21st century who will feel himself inspired to found a new religion and who will try to make a similar use of computers that sacred writers made of scripture. Just as once voice was replaced by papyrus, pen and ink, so now letters will give way to electronic currents, switches and magnetic fields. The inspiration once given to men for writing will be extended to computer programming. This idea of God's handing over not books or tables of stone, but a sort of heavenly computer to an inspired computer engineer, may be somewhat strange, but it is certainly not incompatible with the modern notion of inspiration, according to which the holy writings are the expression of a community's faith to which God claims special ownership.

Until today no one indeed has ventured to talk about "holy computer," yet given the development that has taken place in the computer's history, one can perceive that after the example of the holy books the idea of the "holy computer" is already on the way.

2. PRE- AND POST-1962 SYSTEMS

Since 1945 when the first automatic computer was built, men have tried to use the machine to do not only physical but mental work. W. McPhee, H. Simon, A. Newell, I. Pool, R. Abelson and others were among the first to try computer simulation of social and political systems. During the following 25 years computer scientists have endeavored to build mental processes into the machine, and consequently to make it more and more a model of human behavior and mental activity. Especially after 1962 the great concern was not so much how to establish an "a priori" logical pattern, but how to represent human knowledge in the computer. Breaking with the idea that only logical sequences can be represented in the computer, scientists broke through the limitations of the pre-1962 systems and were able to program into machine language human operations such as finding analogies between different ambiguities in word meaning, recognition as perceptional, decisional attainment, consciousness, translation, question-answering, proving theorems, playing a game of checkers, and so on.[123]

From that time not only physicists and mathematicians, but also psychologists, biologists, sociologists, economists and political theorists have successfully used the computer as a model of mental behavior, and with varying results they have been able to create semantic models of their subject matter. Donald Fink has even ventured to predict that the computer with its new features will be able to imitate man's creative artistic endeavor and not merely assist in it, as is the case today.[124]

3. BELIEVER-COMPUTER SYMBIOSIS

The ambition of programming all human behavior will certainly not stop short of man's religious behavior. For the believer also appears as a tool-maker. Faith, like any other human activity, creates symbols to help man towards an understanding of himself. As in most cases of programming human behavior, however, the macro-flow chart, i.e. the description of the situation to be pro-grammed, will be much more difficult to prepare than the programming itself, i.e. the micro-flow chart. Religious belief requires sharp analysis and a firm grasp of the nature of human behavior with all its implications or subroutines. The age-old questions— what is understanding?; what is artistic creation?; what is consciousness?; what is faith?; etc.—must be asked again, to permit the machine to represent all these functions symbolically, i.e. not in human but in its own machine-language. Since there can be no question of a replica or facsimile of human behavior, which would reproduce perfectly all its characteristics and operative features, but one that would express all its components and interconnections by formal models or symbols, one who is to program human behavior—and especially, religious behavior—will need not only a sharp analytical mind but also a gift for analogies. It will be from such a mind, analytical and analogical, that some further technical development is to be expected and the first contribution made towards a man-believer-computer symbiosis that is capable of detecting a higher level of insight, now beyond man's present mental powers, but perhaps already functioning in all human behavior.

Perhaps no one has yet come so close to such an attempt as Donald G. Fink in the last chapter, "A Long Look," of his *Computers and the Human Mind.* [125] It is not difficult to recognize there a system of thought similar to that which is found in John's gospel, when he describes the Logos as the unique revelation of the Father to men who have never seen God (cf Jn 1,18).

According to Fink, the computer, like speech and writing, is a tool of thought, which provides man with a new set of abstractions and extrapolations which lead the human mind into an unknown echelon of thought beyond the highest echelon of natural thought so far known.

> Just as we can visualize the concept of infinity . . . so can we visualize a machine and program whose hierarchy of abstraction contains one echelon above the highest echelon of natural thought. Further, we may conceive that this extra echelon need not be "thought out" by man (who, by definition, does not possess the mental equipment for the task). It *might* be produced by extrapolation from previous designs. In this sense, intelligent machines may forge into the unknown. . . . It will not matter that man cannot conceive, by definition, of what processes would be employed by the machine in this higher-than-human set of abstractions. It will be sufficient that the machine, *dropping down to the level at which it can*

communicate with man, can reveal [italics are added]   verifiable truths obtainable in no other way.[126]

Fink is sure that the attempt will be made sooner or later, and that man will experience an intellectual evolution which was withheld for thousands of centuries.

It is not likely, however, that Christianity, after the fashion of some such futuristic religion of the 21st century, will extend its age-old problem of word-scripture into that of a word-scripture-computer complex. For revelation was closed with the first generation of the Church, which did use scripture but knew nothing of computers, as a tool of self-expression and communication, and it is quite unlikely that Christian faith will ever rely on holy computers as it relies on the holy words and holy scriptures transmitted to it by the first believers. Nevertheless, it is inevitable that the computer as a new tool of self-expression and self-realization will effect changes in Christian belief. For in a world of man-computer symbiosis the creation of a believer-computer symbiosis is also imperative.

4. PROGRAMMING FORMS VS. LITERARY FORMS

To avoid a simple misunderstanding of this conclusion a word of explanation is necessary. The believer-computer symbiosis does not mean some sort of computerizing the scriptures or patristic writings to make them accessible to the believer after the fashion of a catalogue-index. Such computerizing most likely will be done, but this is not what we have in mind.

Computer science, or, in more general terms, information science, is based on the fact that we represent all that we know by means of pictures, logical statements and symbolic models. [127] The believer-computer symbiosis would, then, mean nothing else than the creation of new symbols and formal models that would make possible a dialogue between man and the computer on religious experience. Since the believer operates with symbols and the computer can be called a symbol-manipulating machine, the believer-computer symbiosis would mean only a successful communication in symbols through the translation of one's symbolism into the others.

In such a dialogue man will be engaged in expressing and translating into machine language all the internal network of relations which he perceives in his behavior as a believer. The computer, then, having read this account, will retrieve all man's ideas and their structural connections in a way that can be verified, and so manifest "objectively," without any personal color, all immanent inconsistencies never observed before. Like any dialogue and like any confrontation with new symbols, the dialogue with the computer will bring about a new insight into the real nature of what man thinks about his faith. In the believer-computer symbiosis the computer will fulfill a function similar to that of myth in ancient religions, or to the *"species expressa"* of medieval thought, but with unprecedented effects with which those of its predecessors just mentioned, cannot be compared.

The invention of new presentations or models, or, in simpler terms, the production of new tools, is an indispensable condition for progress in man's thinking or communicative self-realization. Corresponding to the second law of thermodynamics, the production of new presentations or models brings about an increase in tension between the model and the object modeled, and consequently an increase in energy available, and with it the possibility of action and life. Contrariwise, the lack of a model means an increase in entropy, i.e. decrease in differentiation, which at its lowest point would mean the end of movement and life. Accordingly any change in knowledge, communication or self-realization must cause a change in the symbolic model or result in a new model. Otherwise man would be converted from an open into a closed system, without inflow or outflow of information; and this would lead inevitably to an increase of entropy, the measure of unavailable energy.

Faith and religious behavior, like all human conduct, needs its own model, and has to make its own tools for self-realization and communication. It needs the continuous interactivity of input and output if it is to function and help man to progress. If the older theology forgot the first of these two elements, some more recent theologies have disregarded the second. A believer-computer symbiosis would aim at keeping both input and output active and at producing the most appropriate tool or model for further progress in man's thinking, self-realization and self-communication.

The development of semantic models, or presentations of religious behavior, will, as we have already noted, contain two steps:

first, the making of the macro-chart, i.e. a clear description of the problem; secondly, the programming itself, i.e. shaping the symbols that the machine will understand. The new apologist might get some help here from his colleagues in the information sciences, who have already made progress in expressing human behavior in machine activity. Like the writers of the sacred books who learned to use the *literary forms* of their times, the theologian who is to contribute to the believer-computer symbiosis must learn the new *programming forms* and see whether his understanding of the faith can be expressed in these forms. Here are some sample problems:

A. If the apologist working towards a believer-computer symbiosis finds that faith is in a way a discovery of analogies between sets, he might find a programming form in the article of T. G. Evans. [128] To get a clear idea of the problem of analogy there is no better way than to construct a program by which a computer can recognize analogy. With this end in view, Evans first developed a system for describing complex objects in terms of certain relations between their most basic parts. He then constructed another system for comparing objects according to the relations between their descriptions. Finally, he worked out a scheme for assessing the similarities and differences discovered. Although Evans worked mostly on geometric analogies, his procedure might also be helpful in the religious sphere where analogy, i.e. comparison of relations in similitude and dissimilitude, is a permanent set of structure.

B. In faith, again, as in any dialogue between persons, the problem of *ambiguities in word meanings* occurs. With Bertram Raphael's program [129] we can get an insight into how one can solve ambiguities in information meanings. On the supposition that no new information is available, Raphael seeks to solve ambiguities on the basis of previous unambiguous sentences. He proposed word association models which represent objects and the specific association which exists between these objects. He distinguishes set-inclusion, set-membership, part and whole relationship, left to right or right to left relationship, ownership-relation, etc. After collecting all nouns and verbs he then forms a noun tree and a verb tree, where all the possible relationships of each verb and each other term within the system are represented.

Since faith-experience involves many elements together with

their functions and set-relations, Raphael's method would make clear to the apologist how set-inclusion, set-relationship, set-part and whole-relationship, set of subset and superset, functioning in faith can be expressed in machine language. A like method applied to faith would be enormously complicated and perhaps impossible today. For the apologist first must have a very clear idea of how he conceives his faith experience; secondly, the technical and financial means needed are not yet available. It is not certain, however, that these difficulties will persist throughout the 2000's. At present it will be useful to watch the analysis of the information scientists, for they are the "philosophers" of our times who now define how human activities, such as recognition, heuristic understanding, consciousness, etc. are grasped today.

C. If, however, the apologist, instead of expressing his faith-experience by process verbs, i.e., action verbs, such as gazing, looking and seeing, would prefer to use for this purpose *attainment* verbs (attaining something or someone) and *decisional* verbs (deliberate activity through consideration and action), then K. M. Sayre could give help in modeling faith-experience. [130] Sayre claims that every mental function, such that its input and output can be specified with precision and the transformation performed, and can be expressed by equations which indicate a determinate relationship between input and output, can also be modeled with some degree of adequacy. If, however, there is no adequate understanding of input and output (and how difficult to formulate this in faith!), then there is no way to achieve an adequate model of the function. It is not certain that the apologist is now able to answer the questions asked by information scientists about human behavior. A consideration, however, of the questions and an attempt to translate them into the domain of faith can be rewarding. A new and better understanding of the faith will follow, even though the apologist is not able at the present time to write a program for the machine. For the information process is basically a kind of communication which passess from X to Y, and such a process cannot be overlooked by an apologist who likes to describe his faith-experience as communication.

D. In his book, *Consciousness*, K. M. Sayre makes another attempt to describe consciousness in terms of information-process. To be conscious, he says, is to produce patterned, i.e. structured or unified, responses to sensory stimulation, [131] whereas to lose consciousness is to experience a gradual loss of coherence. Such a description, it is evident, would be preferred by an apologist who stresses faith-experience as unity of meaning and conceives its loss as a loss of coherence (cf. e.g. H. R. Niebuhr).

Sayre's book on *Consciousness* is an example of the first preparatory step in programming. It is a descriptive analysis of what is to be programmed and not a claim that the time has come to propose a micro-flow-chart. Perhaps, this is also the case for faith-experience. The time for programming is far away, but its description and its analysis in the light of information science is undoubtedly already here.

5. CONCLUSION OF PART ONE

These are the new challenges which imperatively demand the renewed self-reflecting, dialogizing activity of faith. An uncritical faith which claims the old privilege of immunity from any scientific research and which refuses to face the challenges of reason is inadmissible both to the mentality of modern man and to the nature of faith. Modern man does not accept religious or theoretical premises uncritically. He wants to acquire a reasonable conviction of their belonging to the reality of existence.

To ask for a complete engagement without reason or sign of workability is not only inhuman [132] but also against the nature of faith itself. The history of apologetics manifests, indeed, the inner tendency of faith to be challenged into a dialogue with reason. This aspect of the nature of faith explains why theories defending the dichotomy between reason and faith (or in modern terms, between the historical Jesus and kerygmatic Christ) are always quickly suppressed by a synthetic trial. The Old Quest had to be replaced by a New Quest, which certainly is going to be replaced by another Newer Quest, since Christian faith is essentially incarnation-faith, having an internal tendency to be incarnated more and more. For this reason Christian faith becomes automatically vulnerable to scientific research. Perhaps this vulnerability of Christian faith may explain why Christianity seems to be a better cradle of atheism than any other religion. According to statistics, the doubt and unbelief of most Christians is admittedly due not to a desire for unlimited freedom but to the seeming contradictions between science and faith, facts and beliefs.

Now before undertaking a fresh apologetics to meet the challenges just described, we think it is proper to make some concluding reflections upon the history of apologetics.

In reviewing the history of apologetics a striking fact stands out. In contrast to the constant and permanent vitality of Christian faith in facing its challenges, there is a great variety of opposing opinions succeeding one another as insufficient and inadmissible in the light of the progress in history. Many theories which appear one day to be scientifically irrefutable become the next day inadequate to explain the origin of Christianity. Moreover, by the permanent elimination of different opinions, several tenets of belief become vindicated.

Thus, for example, as we will see very soon, the existence of the historical Jesus is no longer questioned. The date of the composition of the gospels is no longer placed in the second century, but in the period 65-95 A.D., as the Church always held. After the discovery of Papyrus 52 (in the year 1935), dating probably from about 130 A.D., [133] and of the Egerton papyrus (in the year 1934) with the Gospel of Truth (in the year 1945), [134] the views of D. F. Strauss (in the year 1835) and C. Baur (in the year 1847) on the time of composition of the gospels (150 and 130 A.D. respectively) were definitely improved. The distance between the autographs and the actually possessed copies is notably reduced.

After D. F. Strauss it was generally admitted that the gospels attested to the faith of the Church, i.e. from the gospels one could prove what the Church believed concerning miracles, the resurrection and divinity of Jesus. The gospels were in complete accord with the faith.

The theory of the direct influence of pagan religions and of mystery rites on Christianity has been given up by most of the challengers since 1930.

Form criticism removed the cradle of Christianity from the post-apostolic Church, as well as from the pagan mystery religions and the Qumran sects, to the primitive Christian community and thus brought it very close to the time and milieu of the historical Jesus.

By the same form criticism the pre-gospel tradition was discovered, and its consonance with the later gospel tradition admitted. The gospels and pre-gospel tradition witnessed to what the Church believed. The time of faith in the divinity of Jesus had been traced from the present time not only to the second century, as held in the 19th century, but to within a few years of the death of Jesus.

The constant changes which took place especially during the last two centuries in the critical effort to explain the origin of Christian faith, were more pro than contra faith. The trend of the changes may be outlined as follows:

1.1 The Church finds in the gospels that its faith about Jesus is true.

1.2 The first challenge wishes to demonstrate through literary criticism that what the Church believes cannot be proved from the gospel.

1.3 Apologetics shows through literary criticism that what the Church believes according to the gospels is true from these very gospels.

2.1 The second challenge, by admitting the conformity of the faith of the Church to the testimony of the gospels, wishes through historical criticism to demonstrate that the primitive Church did not believe those historical events which the Church later transposed from the ideological order into the historical order.

2.2 Apologetics shows through historical and literary criticism that the first tradition of the Church affirms the same historical events which the modern Church accepts as historical.

3.1 The third challenge admits that not only the gospels but also the primitive tradition affirms the same thing as the Church today believes about Jesus Christ, but maintains that neither the gospels nor tradition testify to the historical Jesus, since each is a creation of the community. Each attests to the faith of the community, but not to historical truth. The Christ of faith is the same as the Jesus of the gospels and tradition, but is distinct from the Jesus of history.

3.2 Apologetics wants to show now that the Christ of faith is not evidently distinct from the historical Jesus. The Church is not evidently mistaken since Jesus was not evidently otherwise than the Church believes him to be.

In other words, apologetics seeks to show now that besides the Holy Spirit also the historical Jesus is the revealer of the fact that in him God has personally entered human history, and is therefore, together with the Holy Spirit, the source of Christian faith in his divinity.

Evidently one must ask, why do Catholic apologists not like to accept that it was the Christian community and not the historical Jesus that discovered he was God? If this early Christian community, under the inspiration of the Holy Spirit, had realized the fact that Jesus is God, the divine origin of the Christian faith could not be questioned since it came from the Holy Spirit. What would be wrong then with saying that the historical Jesus did not know that he was united with God in an unique way and died like anybody else, and that the Holy Spirit alone revealed this to the Christians? Or still more simply, could it not be that the historical Jesus knew who he was but did not give any sign of it, leaving everything to the Holy Spirit? What is wrong with this way of thinking or believing? Why does the divine origin of Christian belief include, besides the testimony of the Holy Spirit, the testimony of the second divine person as incarnated in Jesus of Nazareth? Why is the double testimony needed? Does the divine origin of Christian faith necessarily require that the historical Jesus as man knew and revealed who he was, and that he rose from the dead? Why are these two instances with equal consequences denied by one side, and defended by the other side?

Then, there is a further question. Would the admission of the historical Jesus' conscious affirmation that he was God joined with the fact of his resurrection necessarily mean, as the old apologetics supposed, the acceptance of belief in him and the obligation to accept him as God? Why can it not be true that in spite of his sayings and of his resurrection, Jesus is still no more than a man? If someone were to tell me, for example, that he is supercreatural (God), and if I were to meet him again on the street after his death, would I believe in him as God or would I think of some other explanation for the event, even if no other were left but statistical fluctuations of natural forces, which would not exclude absolutely the possibility of rising from the dead? Where is the force of this old Christian apologetic argument? Is there any logical necessity in saying that if a man is aware of himself as above all creatures as is God, and then rises from real death, then this man cannot but be God? Is this statement really so evident?

The presupposition of the apologists is that if man as historian cannot say anything about the supercreatural claims of the historical Jesus and his resurrection, as well as about the historical and cosmic traces of the presence of God, the Lord of history and cosmos in Jesus, then, the Church must confess that its faith is merely "faith." The kingdom of God grounded upon faith in Christ would be a pure spiritual kingdom and after its coming nothing would be changed except the mind of the believers. The faith of Christians would be no more historical and reasonable than the faith of non-Christians, and the divinity of Christ would not stand any better before human understanding and historical investigation than the divinity of Buddha, or of any pagan god. Thus, indeed, Christian belief in the divinity of Christ would be no more due to the historical Jesus, than the divinization of Buddha to Guatama Siddhartha.

The Church evidently does not want to admit all this. It claims that its faith is true, unique and different from all others. But is it really different? Was Jesus historically more than a religious man, a good teacher who wished to lead all men to God? Was he really more than any other founder of religion? Did he really know that he was a unique instrument of God, or did he pass away unaware of his divine redemptive mission like any sacramental instrument, "matter and form," or channel of graces? In one word, is faith in him really something different from faith in other religious founders?

To answer these questions about the way God can be recognized in Jesus as well as about the "usefulness" of Christianity and the meaning of its language, will be the task of the two following chapters.

We hope that this survey of the history of the self-reflective dialogizing activity of faith, was useful to our readers for two reasons:

First, we hope that they may be able to draw from it a more exact understanding of the problem as it is posed today. Second, having seen the evolution and the transitory historical relativity of many opinions about Chrisitan faith we hope that they may avoid proposing again an old and long surpassed historically insufficient solution.

Finally, corresponding to the challenges of the late part of the 20th century, the present essay might be seen as the first step in programming the believing behavior of man. By describing exactly all the elements involved in an authentic faith-experience, the possibility of making the first macro- and micro-flow chart for the faith-attitude may become less remote.

PART TWO

OBJECT AND METHOD

CHAPTER FIVE

"THEOLOGICO-HISTORICAL" DEMONSTRATION OF THE VALIDITY OF FAITH

If there is any doctrine which is ill-defined and whose object is problematic for theologians, it is certainly apologetics, wrote A. Gardeil at the beginning of this century. [135] Midway through the century J. Levie and A. Liége felt the same. [136] The last decades did not change the situation very much. [137] Many suggestions have been made concerning the constitution of a new apologetics, [138] but no author has dared to publish a comprehensive work on the subject.

The problem of apologetics involved was this: Is the divinity of Jesus a legitimate question for apologetics? Does the divinity of Jesus come within the range of apologetics or not? If the divinity of Jesus is included in the reach of apologetics, then the apologist has to presuppose what he wants to demonstrate, i.e., the faith, and he is asking the partner of his apologetical dialogue to admit notions like incarnation, hypostatical union, etc. in a dogmatic sense. And so he has already left the proper domain of scientific apologetics since these notions are not to be found in the sources which apologetics can adduce.

But if, on the contrary, the divinity of Jesus is excluded from the range of apologetics, the apologist would cut asunder the testimony of the apostles and lessen Jesus, since he would reduce him to a simple prophet, to a divine legate like any religious man.

But is Jesus only a man sent by God endowed with thaumaturgic powers as were many other holy men, founders of religions?

There was the dilemma: what should be the proper object of apologetics: Jesus as religious teacher, or Jesus Christ, the Incarnate Word?[139]

Corresponding to these possible objects there were two ways of proceeding in apologetics: *a priori* (philosophical) and *a posteriori* (historical).

The *a priori* way of proceeding began with a general consideration of religion and from this theoretical starting point, derived the religion of Christ as the best religion. The primary object of study was religion in general. The investigation started from a common philosophical notion of religion and once this general notion had been grasped, a comparison of religions was made by asking the question: Which one of any given religions is most in conformity with the general notion of religion?

This method was called *a priori* since it proceeded from the universal to the particular, from the abstract to the concrete. Its principles were taken from a philosophy of fundamental experience and not from faith. It was based on the belief that man can proceed from reason to faith by means of some sort of syllogism, in which the major is a rational principle admitted, or at least admissible, by all believers and nonbelievers. Its presupposition was that one can secure a common philosophical ground for the believer and the nonbeliever. A more recently revised example of this *a priori* pattern of thought is proposed by H. Bouillard[140] and K. Rahner.[141] Their starting point is man's experience and Christian faith introduced as the historical definition of man's *a priori* transcendental relation to the Absolute.

The inadequacy of such a procedure stems from the supposition that the norm of true religion is human reason. The abstract human religion is conceived as a general form or genus to which the Christian religion is subordinated as a minor species.

Now the *a posteriori* procedure began not with speculative considerations but with the fact of faith, sc. with the phenomenological data that many people actually believe. It then asked for the scientific value of that belief. It did not start from the philosophical notion of human existence and religion, nor did it predetermine which philosophy or religion is the correct one. The main question was whether Christian faith is reasonably credible.

But since the Christian faith, as it exists now, includes in its contents a great complex of articles of faith, the authors could not agree on the specific object of apologetics.

After long discussion the most obvious solution of the *aporia* seemed to many the radical sublation of the problem itself. If faith cannot be proved, apologetical activity is useless and nonsensical. Precisely its immunity from proof would secure the divine origin of Christian faith. But again the same immunity from proof was called nonsense by others. [142] Thus, to the doubt of the object and method of apologetics a new doubt was added, sc. doubt of its usefulness.

Though in such a state the future of apologetical theology does not look too promising, a trial can still be in order. Failure in the past is not the infallible negation of future success. It is true that life influences theology, but theology can change life, for it reflects faith which demands apologetics as its self-reflective dialogizing life-activity. And the following is an attempt to let this self-reflective dialogizing activity of faith be thematized and expressed in language.

1. THE OBJECT OF APOLOGETICS

Evidently the object of Christian apologetics cannot be anything but the most basic and distinctive characteristic of Christianity. Now it seems that all Christians accept the personal entry of God into human history in Jesus of Nazareth as the real cornerstone of the Christian faith.[143]

Admitting this we can describe the object of apologetics as *"the theologico-historical" demonstration of the validity of faith in the personal entry of God into human history in Jesus of Nazareth for the supercreatural beatitude of man.*

There are many reasons which demand such a determination of the object of apologetics.

One reason is the proper relation of apologetics to its general context, i.e. to fundamental theology. Since the object and method of fundamental theology is equally problematic in our days, we have to sum up here its notion as well as its structure. A rightly defined and structured fundamental theology projects a proper determination of apologetics, object and method.

A. The Notion and Structure of Fundamental Theology

Fundamental theology is called fundamental because of its themes, the evidence which it uses, and its method. According to this threefold meaning, fundamental theology includes the formal theology of the revelation of Christ, the apologetics of the revelation of Christ, and the methodological foundation of theology as a particular science.

1) Fundamental theology as a formal theology of revelation deals with revelation, which is indeed the foundation of every theological treatise. But, while the other dogmatical treatises explain the material content, the "what" of revelation, fundamental formal theology tries to study the "how" of revelation, i.e. the ways and forms in which God revealed himself. Thus the fundamental formal theology of revelation is opposed to the dogmatic theology of revelation like the "how" (form) to the "what" (matter) of revelation. [144] This separation of fundamental theology from dogmatic theology is, however, rather methodological than real. Fundamental theology is not fundamental in an absolute sense. It supposes dogmatic theology insofar as it supposes a complete knowledge of dogmatic theology on faith, or the Church, or grace, or Word Incarnate. [145]

Since revelation includes two subjects, namely, God who is revealing and man to whom he reveals, the fundamental formal theology of revelation must include the theological as well as the anthropological formal principles of the "how" of revelation.

The theological, i.e. the granting, divine aspect of revelation must be worked out descriptively from the faith of the Church. [146] From scripture and from the doctrine of the Church the specifically distinctive characteristics (by which Christian revelation differs from any other revelation claimed by non-Christian religions such as Vedism, Zoroastrianism, Islamism, etc.) have to be explained as well as the ways in which the Christian revelation occurred.

The anthropological, i.e. the receiving, human side of revelation must be developed from the anthropological sciences (history, history of religion, psychology, sociology, philosophy, etc.) which consider man particularly as a religious being, i.e. man in his limitless reference to the infinite, in his openness to infinite being, to the fullness of reality. Thus Christian revelation will appear as the greatest chance for man, the greatest fulfillment of values, which man really needs and which only Christian revelation can give to him.

2) Besides the formal theology of revelation, fundamental theology includes the apologetics of Christian revelation. After the "how" of revelation it asks the "that" of revelation, that is, it asks whether it did happen in the way the Church believes it did. Apologetics can be called fundamental because of the natural evidence it uses; the historical or "empirical" traces of revelation function like nature in regard to grace (cf *gratia supponit naturam*).

3) Fundamental theology also includes the method of theology, i.e. the methodological foundation of theology as a particular science. Since revelation opened a new field and new form of human knowledge, it has also increased the number of human sciences. Therefore, theology as the science of this new field must have its own principles, method and technical language validated in the world of sciences. Consequently, fundamental theology as the method of theology carries out the claims and demands of revelation on the world of science. It sets theology before the exigencies of scientific method, asking whether theological conclusions might be regarded as scientific in the world of human sciences. It includes not only the question of the knowability of supernatural revelation, but also of progress in knowing it more profoundly, either by different functional expressions of the same experienced event (catechetical, kerygmatical, speculative functions) or by systematical confrontation of one revealed datum with the others, or of the revealed data with scientific data.[147]

Using this notion of fundamental theology we can sketch a well-defined outline of fundamental theology.

B. Outline of Fundamental Theology

Part One: Revelation of God in its original form
  The granting side: from the side of the granting God
    — preparatively in Israel: theophanies, dreams, oracles, the Spirit of God, the word of God, wondrous deeds and signs of God in history, etc.
    — definitively: Jesus the fulfillment of the revelation of God
  From the side of the believing Church

— revelation in its receiving subject: faith as the response of the believer to the revealing God

The wanting side: openness of man to God

— the fact of religion: its diversity and historical continuity (history and archeology)
— the meaning of religion: the phenomenology of religion, psychology of religion, sociology of religion, the common notion of religion
— the truth of religion: philosophy of religion, experience of God in the thought of modern thinkers, psychedelic experience, atheism[148], theology of religion[149]

Confrontation of the revelation of God with man's fundamental need

— the values of Christianity and mankind's need of these values
— human and Christian freedom and the responsibility of seeking and communicating the value of Christian revelation[150]

Part Two: Apologetics of the revelation of Christ in its original form

Part Three: Revelation of God in its contemporizing (transmitting) form

From the side of the communicating Church

— in the form of scripture which is human testimony to the revelation (testimony of the tradition concerning Scripture, literary forms, the history-, pre-history of composition, time, theological purpose, etc.) as well as divine testimony to the revelation (inspiration, inerrancy, bread of life for the Church, etc.).
— in the form of the tradition of the Church which as the mystical body of Christ, is the sacramental continuation of Christ's presence among men.

From the side of progressing humanity (by new discoveries and progress and by the consecutive extension of the redemptive revelation of Christ to it, the latent virtual potentialities of God's revelation become more evident till the end of time culminating in the beatific vision of God)

From this outline it is clear that our definition is a logical demand of total fundamental theology. Since the definitive revelation of God took place in Jesus, so that Jesus' coming is believed to be God's coming into the world, the object of the apologetics of Christian revelation cannot but be the personal entrance of God into human history through Christ. Such a determination also corresponds exactly to the specifically appropriate aim of apologetics itself.

In addition to the reason taken from the proper relation of apologetics to the whole of theology, there are other reasons which support the proposed determination of the object of apologetics.

1) Apologetics conceived in this way will be wholly theological since its object is taken from theology. It not only leads to theology but is itself theology. It will show the reasonableness of faith—not the reasonableness of faith in general, but the reasonableness of faith in Jesus Christ.

2) It also will be wholly Christological. It will concern itself exclusively with Christ who is not brought in as just a corollary to apologetics but made its very center.

3) Moreover, such a determination of objects brings about unity in apologetics. All questions and solutions are directed uniquely to Christ in order to demonstrate and understand him.[151]

4) Apologetics will be, further, a vital science (a science with life) because it deals with a concrete person. Hence it will be understandable, even to contemporary man, who does not care much for abstraction but is greatly interested in the person.

5) Apologetics with its object so determined becomes effective apologetics in an eminent sense, i.e. it becomes what it ought to be, namely, a "defense" of the faith. For God's entrance into the world is especially questioned by those who challenge the Christian faith. The final root of all difficulty is ultimately the fact that it cannot be reasonably admitted that God entered the world and was made man. All the other objections of the challengers are merely proofs of this central thesis. It seems to be more effective, therefore, not to fret over such difficulties and objections put forward to defend this fundamental thesis, but to discuss directly that question which supports all questions and from which all difficulties arise, namely, the problem of God's entry into human history.

6) Again, apologetics if so conceived will be really ecumenical, since it follows a way on which all men can gather together the

most easily. It is meant primarily not to defend or spread the faith, but to find God more consciously through a better understanding of the one faith which offers unheard possibilities of encountering God. For it does not discuss whether this or that religion is true according to speculative norms in regard to which there is always a very great difficulty in achieving unanimity. Neither does it suppose a common philosophical formation concerning values and human nature nor the recognition of the personal character of ultimate reality. It supposes solely that all men in some way wish to come into contact with the ultimate reality and the ultimate meaning of human existence. Men are apparently one in being interested in ultimate reality and meaning, but they are divided in finding a way to attain it. Conceiving ultimate reality as transcending human existence, philosophers have proposed diverse abstract methods of going "out" to it. But experience shows that abstraction makes it extremely difficult, if not impossible, for men to find a common way of seeking ultimate reality.

But there is a religious tradition of humanity which affirms that God entered the world and that man is able to meet him in this world. Now if anyone sincerely wishes to find ultimate reality, he should investigate and examine whether it is true or not that God can be encountered in this world. For if God meets man in the order of experiential fact and not in the order of abstraction, then a common way of finding God is more available. The way of finding God present in the world, not through abstraction but through history, is without doubt a simpler way, and as such it should be thoroughly investigated and examined.

7) By determining the object of apologetics as the personal entry of God into human history, apologetics not only becomes efficacious and ecumenical, but at the same time the apologetics of a "divine" religion. For the *phenomenological* difference between a divine and human religion can be given descriptively by assuming that in a divine religion God came to man, while in a human religion, man seeks God. In divine religion the initiative comes from the willingness of God, whereas in human religions man begins to act so that he may acquire for himself a God who is indifferent. With this phenomenological description we can classify religions into two classes: human and divine. Human religion is

that in which man seeks God. Divine religion is that in which God seeks man.

The active initiative of God in meeting with man shows the divine character of the religion, while the moving out of man from the world to God, i.e. human activity joined with a certain indifferent divine passivity, is the property of human religion. This human tendency of going out from the material world to God through proper natural forces is found in Gnosticism, Manicheism, Pelagianism and all hellenistic-latin religions. According to these religions, gods are indifferent toward men either in an absolute way, so that they do not think anything at all about this world or man, just as the gods of the philosophers, or in a relative way, so that the gods remain indifferent, but man is able through his own natural strength to change the indifference of the gods and to bring them to his assistance. The initiative and the seeking always remain with man if he wishes his own salvation.

The idea of God seeking man is known in some non-Judeo-Christian religions also. But there is no religion which extols God's activity among men so much as the Judeo-Christian faith which is completely and *par excellence* the religion of God seeking man.

As a matter of fact, in the gospels there is never a question of man's search for God. In all the parables it is Christ who seeks man. If somebody seeks God, he does so because he is first sought by him. [152]   In the Christian religion God saves man [153] and the doctrine of the Church on grace is based definitely upon this fundamental initiative of God. [154]

Even the Jews themselves believe that through this note the Jewish religion differs from all other religions. Abraham Joshua Heschel expresses this idea in his book *God in Search of Man:*

> Israel's experience of God has not evolved from search. Israel did not discover God. Israel was discovered by God. Judaism is *God's quest for man.* The Bible is a record of God's approach to his people. More statements are found in the Bible about God's love for Israel than about Israel's love for God. We have not chosen God; He has chosen us. There is no concept of a chosen God but there is the idea of a chosen people. The idea of a chosen people does not suggest the preference for a people based upon a discrimination among a number of peoples. We do not say that we are a superior people. The "chosen people" means a people approached and chosen by God. [155]

And this is all the more remarkable since the God of Israel is an entirely transcendent God, who does not have flesh or bones, as the pagan gods. He is spirit, who cannot be represented in a picture or a statue without sin. This transcendent God seeks man not for himself (he does not need man) but for the beatitude of man, i.e. for man's happiness.

Hence there is no phenomenological likeness between the entry of the transcendent God of the Christians into the world of man and the Greek mythological narration. The Greek gods are said to intervene in human affairs. According to Herodotus they seem to determine the end of wars, and consequently, human history. It must be noted, nevertheless, that the Greek gods and men are found in the same species, and there is no essential difference between them, only a qualitative one. The Greek gods do not enter the world because they are from the world they are in the world always from the beginning. They are sons of the earth just as men are, [156] both under the necessity of fate.

Hence, one cannot speak of the entry of God into history among the Greeks because that which holds the place of God and to which the Greeks (gods and men) are subordinated is fate, the transcendental and the inscrutable fury of necessity. Greek gods indeed might help men, but always at the request of men. They have their favorites among men, but in moments of crises they desert them, as Apollo deserted Hector when he was faced by Achilles.[157]

It is likewise in the holy book of Bhagavad-Gita, one of the Upanishads, compiled about the 2nd century B.C. The divine Lord Shri Krishna apparently entered into the world at the request of the noble soldier, Arjuna. [158] But Krishna came into the world to free man from the world, encouraging him in his tendency to escape the world, in order to find God.

That man may depart this world and thus become a god is in line with the religions of the ancients. But that God could become man to encourage man to be a man of God in this world did not make sense for the ancient mystic religions.[159]

This phenomenological difference (which is not meant to be necessarily identical with the difference between Christian and non-Christian religions) seems to be confirmed by the way that ultimate reality is perceived in psychedelic experience. The psychedelic experience of ultimate reality caused by LSD, or similar chemical means, is described by the authors as an expansion, reaching outward to encompass a wealth of phenomena, a sort of crossing over into the integral, the eternal and the absolute, where the sense of self, subject-object relationship, as well as other dualities are lost. [160] Not the absolute, but man has to reach the integral one. In opposition to such an experience Christian faith is described as an experience of another "I" who seeks man, loves him and makes demands upon him by sending him on a mission into the world. On the grounds of these differences our phenomenological distinction between "human" and "divine" religion seems to be valid and so can be adduced in support of the manner that we described the object of the science of apologetics.

8) In virtue of its properly defined object, apologetics will further be more, not only Christian, but also "catholic," i.e. involving spiritual as well as historic and cosmic realities. In Catholic theology there has always been an interest in the visible aspect of God's presence in the world, e.g. the visible Church, sacraments as visible signs, the transformation by sanctifying grace of man's whole being. The visible Church, the sacraments, the internal justification of man are in a real sense the extension and continuation of the incarnation of Christ and of his presence in the world.

9) Finally, such an apologetics will be well suited to modern man, who is not irreligious but areligious. He does not want to bother about God because the earth suffices for him. He does not want to depart this world to find God, because he does not seek God. He persecutes no one who desires and seeks God, but he does not intend to commit himself. A French writer best expressed this mentality, when in a play he replied to Satan who was trying to tempt him: "Lord Serpent, you have made a mistake; I do not wish to be like God; I do not need your solicitation; I want to be as I am, man and nothing more." This attitude is legitimate if God is to be sought outside the world. According to this position, if someone wants to find God, let him depart from this world. But if someone does not want to search for God, let him remain in this world without God, for God is outside the world.

But after the entry of God into the world this position will be peremptorily challenged. If God has, indeed, personally entered into human history (without the invitation of man, though not without his consent) it is no longer a question whether man wishes heaven with God or the world without God. A world without God would not exist, and so no one is able to live in a world without God. In such a world the presence of God occurs as a definite reality which cannot be denied without warping human history. Once God has entered into human history man is "condemned" to live in a world where God is really and historically present.

After the entry of God into the world there cannot be a happy world without God, nor can human beatitude exist without God. There is only one beatitude, i.e. that with God, because the world in which God lives, is the only real world. No true beatitude can prescind from the existing world.

The whole of human existence is implanted in a divine world, and in such a world, to prescind from God is the same as to prescind from and to discount the sun in the equatorial regions or the cold in the northern regions.

Once God has entered human history in person, the whole tragedy of human history consists in this, that man wishes to escape from God into another world where God does not exist. Man has to contrive new ideal worlds, new conceptions, new schemes, new methods, in which he thinks no place remains for God and where he could proclaim the death of God. But after a time it becomes apparent that God is present even there; the man who does not want God must flee still further, and again devise another "Weltanschauung" where again God seems to be condemned to death and nonexistence.

Since this is so, an authentic apologetics has to demonstrate that God has entered into the world, not indeed to prove his divinity, but to make man happy by communicating his own divine happiness. His intention is to make man happy, not with created goods but directly with himself, through his personal presence. This is the idea which the term "supercreatural beatitude" conveys. This notion of supercreatural beatitude will explain the meaning of the obligation of believing in God. If there is an obligation for man to strive for supreme happiness (beatitude), then there is an obligation to accept the happiness offered by God. After God's entry into human history, to reach happiness means to accept God as man's supreme happiness. If, therefore, modern man asks what Christ is saving man from (not from death, certainly, because men still have to die after Christ's redemption, nor from sin, because men might sin again), the only answer is that

Christ saves men from a world where there is no God, no divine beatitude. Neither sin nor death is a matter for despair, if in spite of sin and death, men are still able to be with God and find supreme happiness.

All the above-mentioned reasons suggest that the proposed definition of the object of apologetics is promising. The urgent question now is: what method must apologetics use to fulfill its task?

2. THE METHOD OF APOLOGETICS

It is a generally admitted principle of modern methodology that the same method cannot be applied to different objects of investigation. Since the purpose of method is above all to give the object the opportunity to manifest or reveal itself, determination of the object already predetermines the method. In order to find the method corresponding to the object investigated, it is convenient to address oneself to the given intentionalities of the object and observe more closely all its actuations.

Now since the object of apologetics as we have defined it is to demonstrate theologico-historically the validity of faith in God's personal entry into human history as man's supercreatural beatitude, the nature of Christian faith must first be described. An inadequate understanding of its nature might lead to an inadequate method which could jeopardize the proper outcome of our research.

A. The Nature of Christian Faith in Jesus Christ

The main task of apologetics is not to justify, in a missionary sense, to those outside the faith, the self-communicative thrust of faith, but through internal and external challenges to present the self-reflection of faith as a dialogue. The fundamental question of faith will not be how I can convince some people that Jesus is God, but how can I, the believer, believe that Jesus is God. Am I right in accepting such a hard saying? How do I know, or how can I know, that Jesus of Nazareth, a man and a contemporary of Tiberius Caesar, the Roman Emperor, and of Pontius Pilate, the Roman Procurator, is truly God?

1) Faith is Supernatural-ecclesial

The answer to the question, why do we believe that Jesus is God, is, from the viewpoint of faith, obvious. We believe that Jesus is God *because* (and not *on account of,* for we believe on account of the witnessing authority of the revealing God [161]) the grace of supernatural faith is given to us by the Father through the Church of Christ. Neither flesh nor blood, but the heavenly Father has revealed to us that Jesus is the Christ, the Son of God (Mt 16,17). "No one can say, 'Jesus is Lord' except by the Holy Spirit" (1 Cor 12,3). Therefore, the ultimate "reason" or justification of our faith is the grace of God [162] which we have received through the Church.

This mediation of the Church in the acquisition of our faith is twofold: internal and external; the Church teaches that Jesus of Nazareth is God, and simultaneously communicates the grace of faith for believing this. Our faith is, therefore, at once supernatural and ecclesial, based upon the knowledge of the revealing God. Since by the free supernatural gift of faith the knowledge of God himself is communicated to us, faith is not based upon something else, e.g. human reason, but upon God, because God (whose knowledge is communicated to us) cannot be explained by something outside of himself. The ultimate motive of supernatural faith must be God's own knowledge of himself.

The divine life of grace is communicated to the believer in order to actuate in him the knowledge and love of God in virtue of which the believer becomes in some sense like an "eye-witness" to the actually revealing God. He will, consequently, believe that Jesus is God, not because, he *knows* through the mediation of the created world that God has revealed it, [163] nor because he *sees* in the signs that God is the one who had revealed it, [164] nor because he *wills* to believe it. [165] He will believe only because he perceives and recognizes God as revealing himself in the Church and witnessing to him in the attracting grace of faith that Jesus is God. [166] Consequently, the man of faith does not believe in God on account of the Church, but rather he believes the Church on account of God. The question of belief in "God as the one who reveals Jesus' divinity to me" cannot be reduced to human knowledge on the grounds of external evidence, because man would then be believing on account of his own knowledge, and not on account of the testimony of the revealing God. Because of an inward illumination of grace the believer is able to perceive God's uncreated testifying word which, being the ultimate and unique foundation of its own credibility, does not receive its credibility from another. The divine uncreated testifying word not only affirms that Jesus is God, but also that it is precisely God who reveals Jesus' divinity. Faith, therefore, because it is a supernatural sharing in the knowledge of God, cannot spring from any process of reasoning.[167]

2) Faith is Reasonable.

The same supernatural and ecclesial faith, however, which tells us that Jesus is God, teaches us also that this belief is reasonable. [168]   Faith is at once supernatural and in agreement with reason, so much so that our intellect is able to give a reason consistent with its own nature for its inclination to assent to God in faith. Faith is not a blind movement of the mind. [169]   There is something in faith which is not only believed, but also "seen" by way of "demonstration." [170]   According to the faith and doctrine of the Church, if one of the faithful is asked why he believes, he is able to bring forward not only the grace of faith, but also other reasons to show that his faith is reasonable.[171]

According to the first Vatican Council, the reasonableness of faith means not only that: (a) faith cannot be simply a blind movement of the mind and thus (b) there can never be any real (definitive) disagreement between faith and reason, [172] but also that (c) between faith and reason there is mutual dependence and help [173]   and so (d) faith being consonant with reason [174]   (e) has its own proper evidence. [175]   But the evidence of faith certainly cannot be the evidence of truth (which would be incompatible with the nature of supernatural faith). It is rather the evidence of credibility. [176]   Without the evidence of credibility no man could believe sinlessly, since an evidently incredible faith would lead him away from reality, which would mean self-destruction and self-annihilation. In every reasonable faith, therefore, there must be a real act of - understanding, a recognition of evident credibility.[177]

The recognition of evident credibility is effected through external, visible and understandable signs [178] —that is, through revelatory constellations in which created testimony, both external (e.g. history of Israel, Jesus' life, resurrection, his Church, the scripture, the great deeds of mercy, etc.) and internal (the created, enlightening grace of faith), as well as uncreated testimony (the actually revealing God) constitute the ground of faith. Since supernatural Christian faith in God is based on the witnessing, revealing God, the external testimony or revelatory constellation is like a visible, external sound in which God's voice resounds, or like a mirror in which the faithful look at God.[179]

Although the light of faith, with external testimony as the revelatory constellation, effects a supernatural as well as a reasonable faith, it cannot effect an absolutely compelling certitude and evidence. Faith must be free. [180] The antinomy between the believing mind's certitude and the freedom of faith can however be explained, for the function of the light of faith is not the same as the function of natural evidence in general knowledge. In the case of natural evidence man sees with equal certitude that A is A and also that A cannot be B. In the case of faith the believer, by virtue of the divine knowledge communicated to him, perceives with absolute and infallible certitude that A is A (for example, Jesus is God), but he does not *see* with equal certitude that A is not B—that is, that the predicate "not-God" is absolutely excluded in the case of Jesus. In other words, he does not see at one and the same time as absolutely impossible that Jesus be not God. The exclusion of "not-God" is reductive, not direct, therefore only verisimilar. Thus in faith the possibility of error is not excluded.

Thus the life of faith is a constant confrontation and wrestling of reason and faith over the possibility of error. Since this struggle will not cease until the final synthetical elevation of reason and faith into the beatific vision, there will be a constant fight to purify faith from errors as well as preserve it from them. On account of this dualism, a man can be said to be at once a believer and a nonbeliever. The believer lives in faith and at the same time is always approaching it (Mk 9,24).

In correspondence with this double nature of faith, external testimony, the revelatory constellation, has a permanent double function. In the life of faith it is like a mirror or a language. In its introductory function to the life of faith, it is like a puzzling dilemma, a mysterious incomprehensibility *through* which man is invited to think, ask questions, to wonder and ponder. In its other function it is like a beam of light from a house, flooding objects outside, inviting an outsider into the house to see and understand things more clearly and distinctly. Each of the faithful, as a believer, lives the life of faith, but as an unbeliever, he lives like one who is always being invited once more from outside into the life of faith.

Thus the external revelatory constellation, which we will call the theologico-historical event (or Christ event), like any clue given to human understanding for responsible decisions, will not affect the freedom of man more than any other challenging and attractive possibility of a new way of life, which man accepts reasonably without any paralyzing hesitation. Like a good scientific hypothesis, the external testimony will not overpower man, but only invite man to follow its lead towards an encounter with God.

Christian faith, therefore, is always essentially both supernatural and reasonable, reflecting the life of Jesus Christ, who is real God and real man, present to everybody, "in" and "through" his Church-sign at once visible and invisible.

Thus a total response to the question whether Jesus is God will be given neither by faith alone (fideism) nor by reason alone (rationalism), but only by a reasonable faith (Christianism).

3) Faith is Historical

Furthermore, there is another special aspect of Christian faith in Jesus Christ. Faith in Jesus is a supernatural and reasonable faith, which proclaims historical events. Historical events, which are supposed to have their place in the profane history of the world, are accepted by faith. Therefore, it can be asked whether those events which are believed to be historical, can be established as such. Can the facts held by faith be the objects of historical science so that they can be judged not only by faith, but also at least to a certain degree by the science of history? Can the truth of our faith concerning Jesus be somehow historically established? How and to what extent can I establish historically that Jesus of Nazareth, who lived in the time of Tiberius Caesar and the governor Pontius Pilate, is "God"?

According to the twofold aspect of faith (supernatural and ecclesial, on the one hand, and reasonable and historical on the other) the total response to our question necessarily includes a

twofold understanding of our faith in Jesus. This twofold understanding is gained by a twofold science of faith, namely, by
dogmatic theology and by the fundamental theology of apologetics. The first deals with the supernatural (that is superhistorical)
and ecclesial, the second with the historical and reasonable aspect
of the faith. The complete answer to our question, therefore, has
to include both dogmatic and apologetical considerations.

B. The Nature of the Demonstration of the Validity of Christian Faith in Jesus Christ.

1) The Question-Raising Function of Apologetics and the Theologico-Historical Sign-Event of Christ.

From what we have said about the nature of faith, it follows
that the demonstration of Christian faith cannot be understood as
a proof in the form of a syllogism founded on mathematical
evidence. Demonstration is taken here in the original sense as
"de-monstration," a showing or manifesting of something. Demonstration of the validity of faith means to manifest or set forth
sign-events or revelatory constellations which cannot simply be
broken down, for even by the standards of right reason alone, they
still have in themselves sufficient objective force to invite man to
open himself up freely and reasonably with the help of grace to
the life of faith.

Consequently, the theologico-historical demonstration of the
validity of Christian faith in the personal entry of God into human
history means bringing to light the real *Sitz im Leben* of the
sign-events. In proper context they will show themselves puzzling
enough to surpass any easy human solution and provoke a series of
questions. The first question: *"Is this possible?"* (addressed in the
form of a doubt to the inquirer himself), through further inquiry
will be replaced by another question: *"Is he really acting as he is
believed to be acting?"* This again will lead to a further question
(addressed directly to God): *"Are you the one who has done all
this and so is here present acting thus to me?"* And when through
the mediation of conscience man perceives the divine "Yes" as
answer, the personal dialogue of faith between revealing God and
believing man has been realized in its full sense. In this moment of
the dialogue of faith, the believer becomes like an "eye-witness"

to the actually-revealing God and recognizes God as giving witness to him in the Church about Jesus, his Son.

Such a self-reflecting, questioning process is conditioned by man's basic intention to come to terms with himself as scientist, as philosopher, as historian, as psychologist, as sociologist, as ethician, as artist, as religious and, after the Christ event, as believer. The different branches of science are simply the skillful, methodological execution of each man's various intentionality-types or strata.

Man as scientist wants to consider particular objects in their time and space correlations.

Man as philosopher is eager to see the complexity of the different scientific objects pointing to their totality as such.

Man as historian wishes to consider man in his relatedness to the complexity and wholeness of objects and events both as their conditioner (creator) and their conditional (creature).

Man as psychologist tries to see man as person, i.e. as submerged not in the world of objects and events, but as a time-space transcending presence to himself who is able to react freely to the unity and complexity of the meaning of objects and events.

Man as sociologist looks at man not as isolated in his own world, but in the intersubjective community of men both as creator and at the same time as being-conditioned by the intersubjective community.

Man as ethician is searching in the complexity and unity of objects and events in their relatedness to man as creator and creature of his intersubjective community for something which is good for the whole man as well as for every human being.

Man as artist sees the complexity and unity of reality in particular ecstatic and fascinating intensity as embodied in space or time constellations.

Man as religious sees the complexity and unity of reality as a saving process on account of a definitive commitment to the Numen.

After the religious experience of Jesus of Nazareth there is to be added to these previous strata a ninth: man as believer characterized by the revelation-faith experience. The revelation-faith experience reverses the questioning process by a twofold awareness of being invited. In this invitation during revelation-awareness in the complexity of the wholeness, a new personal force appears who as completely unconditioned from the context, transcending the given wholeness of the reality of the previous strata, invites man to accept his absolutely free unrestricted self-giving to man; and during the faith-awareness (which forms an essential part of revelation-awareness, as another aspect of it) the new inviting personal force is understood as answering affirmatively man's question about the possibility and the reality of man's acceptance of God's self-giving.

Now on account of the internal dynamic relationship existing between the different intentionality types, each man wants to be not only scientist, philosopher, historian and so on, but the scientist in each tends to reach the philosopher who again turns to the historian, who again wants to meet the psychologist, sociologist, who again will analyze the religious, the ethician, the artist, and the religious in its turn challenges the believer. In a certain sense human life consists in a constant trial to face these challenges and actualize both the more intensive realization of each type and a more penetrating confrontation of each.

Now each intentionality type has a more intensive tendency to penetrate the stratum above than the one below. Thus for example man as a philosopher is more interested in science than man as scientist in philosophy. Or, for example, the ethician is more interested in sociology than the sociologist in ethics.

That revelation-faith experience and its systematic reflection, theology, is a deeper stratum than any previous one appears from the fact that whereas the other strata can proceed in the realization of their end quite independently from faith and its interpretation, revelation-faith experience in its progress cannot prescind from their function and result. Precisely because it transcends them it is in its turn effected by them and thus in its progressive fulfillment has to include the progressive fulfillment of science, philosophy, history, and so on. Science can be independent from faith because its aim is delimited and does not and need not include faith. But because the end of faith transcends the various intentionalities, it necessarily includes the aim of all previous strata.

In other words, this means that a historian can be a good historian without having the revelation-faith experience. A believer, however, cannot be a good believer without knowing history and the other strata. This is demanded by the universal redemptive dynamics of the revelation-faith experience.

Now the saving impact of revelation-faith does not mean that by itself it makes the scientist, historian, and so on, a better scientist, historian, and so on. Its redeeming impact consists in its power to open up for every stratum the possibility of a new stratum. The new opening is not just another system of the infinite. The nature of the human spirit includes the openness to the infinite. But this openness is a finite human system of the infinite. Now this finite system of the infinity will be transformed by revelation-faith into the infinite system of the finite and infinite. The finite limited system of the infinite becomes not just a system *of* infinite but an infinite system. Revelation-faith experience is not just a system of infinitude, but rather an infinite system of the finitude. The difference between this experience and any other experience is not so much in what the experience is approaching, but in the way the object is approached: the infinite becomes a possibility everywhere. In other words, God can appear as revealer in any stratum or intentionality and invite man to accept his free unrestricted self-giving to man.

The justification of this kind of structuralization is a fascinating study. Here it should be enough to appeal to the common observing experience which forms the basis of the above mentioned process. Admitting this, it follows that the most subjacent intentionality type, the revelation-faith experience has the more powerful self-transcending tendency. Faith as a self-fulfilling thrust looks for the realization of man as religious, artist, ethician, sociologist, psychologist, historian, philosopher and scientist. Thus in a certain sense faith includes as its constitutive element the various kinds of human knowledge, scientific, philosophical, historical, psychological, sociological, ethical, aesthetic, and religious, but at the same time it must be noted that it cannot be reduced to any of them.

That faith as self-reflecting intentionality includes all kinds of human knowledge without being identified with any of them, is based on two grounds: first, the "believer" and "man" form one subject, sc. the believing man; second, the Christ event is inserted into the real world of man with all the consequences of such an insertion. Consequently the Christ event will have specifically proper objectives and intentionalities which can be targets of the different critical analyses.

As the object of scientific investigation the Christ event will point to the concrete objects and events in time and space related to Jesus of Nazareth and to the Christian community.

As the object of philosophical knowledge it points to the complexity and wholeness of the events and the possibility of their being expressed in one human being, s.c. Jesus.

As the object of historical knowledge the Christ event points to Jesus and the early Church in their relatedness to the complexity and wholeness of the objects and events as their conditioner as well as their conditional.

As the object of psychological studies it appears as a case of personal transcendence of time and space and of absolutely free reaction to the unity and complexity of the meaning of objects and events.

As the object of sociological science, the Christ event is seen not isolated in the world, but in the intersubjective community of men.

As the object of ethical consideration, the complexity and the meaning of objects and events related to Jesus and Christian community appears as the saving and redeeming good not only for one man, but for everyone.

As object of aesthetic experience, the Christ event appears in its particular ecstatic fascinating intensity as embodied in space or time constellations.

As object of study of religion, the Christ event appears as the saving process in the definitive commitment of men to the community of Christ.

Finally, as object of revelation-faith knowledge (theology) the Christ event manifests its authenticity in its specifically unique intentionality.

Revelational-faith knowledge cannot be called knowledge except in a transferred sense. The verb "to know" has a meaning here which it does not have anywhere else. The possibility of transferring the verb "know" to "revelation-faith" knowledge is grounded not on a structure common to faith and knowledge as activity, but on the unity of the person who is wholly believing and wholly understanding. His faith as well as his understanding thoroughly penetrates him. Thus the Christ event, indeed, opens up a new level of "understanding" in which the unity of meaning and saving activity is recognized as an authentic invitation by God for men to accept his beatifying, unrestricted self-giving. Faith-knowledge is perceived as God's answering the question of man about Christ. Therefore the whole uniqueness of the revelation-faith stratum consists in the mysterious awareness that God's self-offering and his answering loses all its mythological appearance and forms; it becomes the most true reality which demands in turn a sort of demythologization of the previous strata.

Our question process described above embraces all the knowledge intentionalities just mentioned.

The first *"Is this possible?"* implies scientific, philosophical, historical, psychological, sociological and ethical knowledge.

The second *"Is it possible that it is really he? Is he really acting as he is believed to be acting?"* includes aesthetic and religious consciousness.

And the third *"Are you the one who has done all this and is here present acting and offering yourself to me?"* indicates the beginning of revelation-faith knowledge. Here the self-questioning process begins to be transformed into prayer, the only place where revelation-faith knowledge can take place. This is necessarily so, once faith is described, not as a form of knowing, seeing, or willing but as dialogue with God offering himself unrestrictedly to man. Consequently once the word "Yes" of the answering God is perceived in the consciousness of man, the revelation-faith knowledge reaches its fulfillment. Revelation-faith knowledge starts with man's questioning the word of God that is proposed to him first as word (of the eighth stratum) then passes through man's questioning God and himself and ends in the answering Word of God perceived by man as such.

This is possible because the theologico-historical events (or signs) are so grouped that they let men ask questions about God, and address him. In this way, and only in this way, can he and man freely enter into a dialogue which is, indeed, a dialogue of faith.

These events can truly be called really historical because they are a temporal and spatial embodiment, a tangible medium of personal self-expression. They are theologico-historical because they have the power of raising questions concerning God and his personal presence in history. [181] These theologico-historical events—the pre-Christian Jewish tradition of Yahweh's special active presence among his people, the self-and-God revelation of the historical Jesus, his death and resurrection, as well as his sacramental presence after his resurrection (i.e. the Church)—are complex enough and perplexing enough to defy any easy human explanation, and convincing enough to make man come to a definite decision: either simply to bypass them, or to yield to their forceful appeal. Impregnated with God's special presence, they point beyond themselves to the higher goal of human existence, the goal given in Christian faith.

Since these events are meant to provoke in the human mind a question which initiates a dialogue with God, they must have in themselves something unusual, critically inexplicable. They do not let human understanding simplify or overlook their complexity. They aim to challenge man and constantly force him to address questions about Jesus to God, which he himself has implanted in man's mind. There can be no dialogue between revealing God and believing man unless man freely wills to bring these questions before God and to await his answer.

The principal task of demonstration will be to make manifest the very complex nature of these events in order to exclude any short circuit in understanding them by simply overlooking their complexity. Since the human mind is prone to simplify events in order to give a satisfying explanation of them, apologetics' main role is to expose these events in all their complexity, and so forestall the too facile interpretation that the human reason will strive to give them. It is only when they are rescued from the pseudo-context in which an inept historical interpretation has located these events, and are placed in their proper, original context (or horizon) of understanding that their real intentionality, viz. their being utterances of God's self-communicative presence, will be perceptible.

2) The Context-Creating Function of Apologetics and Supreme Love.

Now, in our view, the proper and original context (or analogy) of the historical understanding of these theologico-historical events cannot be either an assemblage of factual data of the past which prescinds from any personal contemporary interpretation, as the liberal positivistic historiography claims, [182] or the actual self-understanding of the historian, as e.g. W. Dilthey, E. Troeltsch, M. Weber, M. Heidegger, etc. propose. It cannot even be the sacred history of Israel as O. Cullman, in particular, has argued, [183] or an apocalyptic expectation of the general resurrection as W. Pannenberg has claimed. In order to understand the meaning and to admit the validity of the history of salvation or of the resurrection from the dead, all of these must be first placed in a different horizon or context of understanding. Another analogy, another context of historical understanding, is needed for the historian to be able to accept the resurrection from the dead as a historical possibility. And this analogy, or context of historical understanding, is the context of supreme love (charity). Charity, understood as the communication of the fullness of being, with its perfect unity of knowing and loving, [184] is the only analogy or context of historical understanding in which all the theologico-historical events can perfectly manifest all their intentionalities, i.e. as signs of God's presence communicating this plenitude of being. It is only in this context of infinite charity that these Christ events find their final intelligibility and meaning.

Consequently, only the historian who admits the possibility of supreme love (the communication of the plenitude of being in its perfect unity of knowing and loving), as the valid analogy or context (horizon) of historical understanding, will be able to see and recognize the validity of these theologico-historical events. The question whether the resurrection of Jesus, or God's entry into the world in Jesus of Nazareth, can be considered as a historical event depends finally upon the question whether supreme love, as we have defined it, can be admitted by the historian as a principle of historical investigation and accepted as the general context (or horizon) of historical understanding.

Since the theologico-historical Christ events find their final intelligibility and meaning in supreme love, the function of apologetics cannot be reduced merely to raising questions concerning the sign-event itself and urging man to strive to put his life and the world in the right context, viz. that of supreme love. It must extend to creating the proper context of understanding, sc. of supreme love, in which the theologico-historical events of Christ can become the transparent manifestations and the understandable language of the revealing God who addresses man and invites him to the dialogue of faith. Apologetics, then, has as its function to let infinite love emerge as the horizon in which this dialogue between the aroused-questioning man and the arousing-answering God can take place.[185]

Since supreme love has its own necessary conditions the creation of its context implies the projection and realization of the same conditions. Now since supreme love is fullness of being with perfect unity of knowing and loving, the context-creating function of apologetics will be threefold.

The first function will be to help man to *want and desire* everything which belongs to the plenitude of being and to save him from his constant tendency of absolutizing the limited particular. The desires of man must be enlarged, and he must be saved from supinely resigning himself to not willing the wholeness of existence and the fullness of being. In other words, man is to be freed from sin, which is the progressive limitation of existence to an attainable now instead of the unlimited newness of tomorrow. Apologetics has to try to free man from the restrictedness of the presently knowable and lovable existence, or in one word, from being satisfied with himself. Since supreme love includes the plenitude of being, there will be no place, no area of life where apologetics should not be active and help man to know and love everything.

The second function is to help man *know and love* the wholeness and fullness of being. To this end, apologetics must stimulate his mental curiosity and increase his loving capacity by convincing him that the plenitude of being with all its possibilities is both knowable and lovable.

The third function of the context-creating function of apologetics is to help man *to recognize* the fullness of being with its perfect unity of knowing and loving *as a total and unrestricted giving of self.* Apologetics has to bring about the conviction that plenitude of being is essentially a communication of itself, and therefore, the possession of the supreme happiness is not possible without the total and unrestricted self-giving for the beatitude of the other as for one's own beatitude.

These are the functional conditions of supreme love without which all the intentionalities of the Christ event cannot be fully and explicitly realized. Once apologetics has established supreme love as the proper context of understanding, men can be drawn by the light of faith to acknowledge the personification and representation of the universal milieu of infinite love in one being who is able to address man as a person and invite him to share in the communicative life of his being. In the same context, man can also be able to admit that the personal incarnation of God in Jesus is the necessary condition for the perfect communion and union of all men in one and the same beatitude, as well as the necessary condition for the visible manifestation of the personality of supreme love.

The two functions, the question-raising and context-creating, are inseparable. Indeed, apologetics as a science relates to apologetics as life in the same way as language does to being.

Now if such a description of apologetics is correct, the lack of apologetics in the life of the Church would be a symptom not only of weakness, but above all of lack of charity, since it would be refusing to create that atmosphere of the supreme love in which the Christ event can become meaningful words of God speaking to men in the voice of conscience.

After having expounded the object and method in apologetics, in the following chapters we try to describe in a concrete way the question-raising and context-creating functions of apologetics. We will go into the analysis of the different theologico-historical events and, after having placed them in their proper historical context we will see their validity for man in provoking questions concerning God's personal, loving presence in history. We will examine successively the pre-Christian Jewish tradition concerning Yahweh's special active presence among his people, Jesus' self-and-God-revelational life, his death, resurrection, the purpose of his whole personality, and the Church as the sacramental presence of the risen Christ.

PART THREE

THEOLOGICO-HISTORICAL EVENTS DEMONSTRATING THE VALIDITY OF CHRISTIAN FAITH IN THE PERSONAL ENTRY OF GOD INTO HUMAN HISTORY FOR THE SUPERCREATURAL BEATITUDE OF MAN

CHAPTER SIX

PRE-CHRISTIAN JEWISH TRADITION CONCERNING YAHWEH'S SPECIAL ACTIVE PRESENCE AMONG HIS PEOPLE

According to Christian belief before the historical realization of God's entry into human history in Jesus of Nazareth, there was a tradition which witnessed not to the general tendency of man to God, but to God seeking man. Though it cannot be excluded with absolute certitude that such a tradition was not known outside the Jewish tradition, it is certain that the books of the Old Testament are the most consistent and the most explicit in revealing God as the incessant initiator who in spite of negligence and indifference on the part of men, again and again takes on new initiatives, new undertakings, in order to be with man.

If we suppose the date of composition of the earliest parts of these books to be about 1,000 B.C., for 1,000 years it was stated and believed that some divine interventions began with the dawn of time and continued down to the time of the composition of these books.

Though these interventions of God were described differently, all converged in one conviction: through this intervention man would be better off because God approached him and was with him. Moreover, all these interventions were interrelated, successively complementing one another. They did not have a meaning only for the here and now; they were preparations for a future intervention and consequently for a happiness to come. They were at once gift and promise. They had a meaning for the present and a meaning for the future. This divine intervention created the belief that man would be better, but always in relation to a future happiness to be given through a further intervention.

Thus each intervention was a preparation for one supreme intervention, which would exceed all others, the final messianic age. [186] But the different interventions of Yahweh not only prepared for God's final great intervention of the messianic age, but also obscurely prefigured it. A common meaning was seen to evolve successively through each intervention. Upon analysis of these interventions their common meaning indeed seems to be a certain coming of God to men, some kind of "being of God with man" manifested in the special presence of Yahweh in the midst of Israel. Thus the essence of messianism was the idea of a special presence of God among the Hebrews. Messianism might be described either as the material abundance of all earthly goods, or as the fullness of national ambition achieved in the subordination of all peoples to the worship of Yahweh in Jerusalem. However, the essential condition and cause without which the messianic good could not have been conceived, was always the special "being of Yahweh with Israel." According to the faith of the Old Testament this special presence of God with Israel was going to be realized in an excellent way through a definitely final intervention, intended to inaugurate the messianic age. The early Christians interpreted this final intervention as the personal entry of God into history in human form, sc. in Jesus of Nazareth, in order to be with his people and communicate his beatifying presence to them. All previous interventions signified in an obscure way this presence of the incarnate God, as all the interventions signified some presence of God in Israel. Thus Jesus was recognized by his disciples as the new Israel, the fulfillment of the destiny of Israel, the fulfillment of the dwelling of God among his people. Evidently the Jews neither considered nor could consider that God would come in human form and that in this human form he would live among men. Such an interpretation cannot be deduced from the Old Testament. What the Jews could and did believe was that the Lord would come to be with them in a special way, and that his presence would mean salvation for Israel and through Israel, salvation for the whole human race.

The messianic meaning of the Old Testament, defined as the special presence of God in Israel can be seen as a "prediction" in the light of modern historical criticism, since the human author, in spite of his special interest in messianic goods, could and did indeed know this presence.[187]

Such an idea of messianism is the literary and historical meaning of the Old Testament, which, prescinding from its eventual historical realization, as a religious conception can be admitted without any belief. The existence of books written before the historical realization of God's entry into the world and witnessing to this religious belief, are a historical fact. Prescinding from many questions, they clearly attest to a faith in God's activity towards man to achieve this happiness. This attestation is constant through many centuries, and in spite of many different authors and human religious tendencies, these books remain free from the notions of merely human religions (man seeking God), and constantly describe God as seeking man.

This is the only historical fact that one can affirm here: these books tell us that God seeks man.

The value of this datum is twofold: on the one hand it will be clear that the followers of Christ could not have invented this idea because of its greater antiquity, and on the other hand, within the context of the relativity and historicalness of all human ideas, the constancy of this idea demands some special explanation.

Now, this idea, of God's special being with Israel, as we will see, is not only consistent with Jesus but also in a marvelous way is fulfilled in him. According to the criterion of prophecy of Deut 18,22 (cf Jer 28,9 and Deut 13,1-3) the historicity of the previous interventions will be definitively established by the realization of the ultimate intervention of God in Jesus. Thus, following our method, from the historicity of the personal entry of God in Jesus, we will conclude that those interventions must be thought of, not only as a special concept of religious belief, as we consider them in this chapter, but also as historical reality, as an embodied, verifiable means of the supreme charity of God recognized in Jesus. The historical truth of the Old Testament is founded finally on the truth of the New Testament. But the truth of the New Testament is not complete without the confirmation of the Old Testament, since a realization cannot be recognized as a realization without the recognition of its preparation. The possibility of recognizing some events as a temporal spatial embodiment of supreme love supposes the admittance of supreme love as a rationally acceptable, general context of historical understanding. This seems to be precisely the purpose of the time before Christ.

After this introduction, let us now recount the various interventions of God in the Old Testament, and see how all of these interventions describe God as seeking men in order to be with them and communicate to them his supreme happiness.

1. THE FIRST INTERVENTION: ADAM, WHERE ARE YOU?

According to the narration of Genesis, the world which God created was good. About the works of each day it is singly announced that they were good (Gen 1,4; 1,10; 1,12; 1,18; 1,25), and afterwards in summary fashion it is reaffirmed again that the things that he had made (1,31) were indeed good things.

After the creation of the world, God does not seem to have the intention of intervening in the world as a creator. The world of Yahweh is perfect, unlike the world of other religions, whose perfection is completed only by its return to its principle. According to the Book of Genesis, God completes his work on the seventh day; and he rests on the seventh day from the entire work that he had prepared (Gen 2,2-3). Unlike the "demiurges" of the Greeks, he seems to establish this good and perfect world not for himself but for man. For without exception the other things that he made, he handed over to Adam and placed at his disposition (Gen 1, 28-31) that Adam himself might impose names on the rest of the creatures, which God created, and thereby possess them as his own (Gen 2,19).

In distinterested fashion, whatever God does he does for the good of man. So, also, he notices that it is not good for man to be alone (Gen 2,18) and he gives man a help-mate similar to himself, so excellent a divine gift, that on account of this man leaves father and mother that he may cling to her (Gen 2,24).

In the new world created by God only three things were not found: evil, suffering and death. And Adam was to learn this. God himself informed Adam that these three, evil, suffering and death, were placed in his power (Gen 2,16-17).

This reveals all the more God's love for man. Not only did he hand over to him everything that he made, but he handed them over with the power of good and evil, with the power of life and death. Yahweh, God, not only wishes that man live, but that he live with freedom and indeed with the freedom of creating death. Man is able, if he wishes, to create death. And man indeed did create and give to the world death, suffering and evil. By eating from the tree of the knowledge of good and evil, he gave the history of the world a direction other than God wished. And from that moment the meaning of the history of the world became life and death.

But Yahweh, the lover of man, seemingly at rest from his work as creator, does not cease to be the Lord of history. He does not allow man created out of love to die. He does not intervene to destroy what man fashioned, namely, death, but to lead man through death to life again. And by this "through death to life" a new history of the world is founded, a history at once human and divine. Human, because man will die, divine, because man through death will come to life. In this dialectic of death and life a sense of history is constituted in which God and man interact with each other; God for life and man for death. Man wishes to extend the dominion of death (which is in his power) right up to God, and God wishes to extend the dominion of life (which is in his power) right down to man. Man wishes the death of God, and God wishes the life and salvation of man.

This is the reason for the first intervention of God into the new world of man. In this three moments are to be noted:

a) *God seeks man.* "Where are you?" (Gen 3,9). After the fall of man God immediately began to seek him. And from now on his own activity will be nothing else than the pursuit of man who flees from him. The whole divine history is summed up in this: God pursuing man. Man tended to the higher, to the divine; he wished to be like God; now, God tends to man, and seeks man. But man, hides himself from God who seeks him and does not wish to meet God walking in the world (Gen 3,8-9).

b) *God seeks man not to destroy but to reorient the direction which man gave to history.* i.e. *the grief, sorrow, and labor, sweat and death.* (Gen 3,19). The world remains as man "re-created" it and God does not deny or destroy that liberty and power which he himself gave to man. With the intervention of God the sense of history does not cease to be human. The human sense of the history is rather reaffirmed and deepened. (Once he personally enters into human history, he does submit himself to the new creation of man and dies as every man does after Adam. His death shows that he really appropriates and assures the human sense of the history of the world.)

c) *The seed of woman, man, conquers death.* With God's assistance victory is promised to man. God places himself on the side of man, and they together will overcome death, evil and suffering. The sense of God's new activity is therefore victory of the seed of woman on account of the visitation of God among men.

2. THE SECOND INTERVENTION: WHERE IS YOUR BROTHER?

With the history of Cain and Abel the creative human freedom to destroy began. Man brings about death but God defends even the life of the murderer. After the death of Abel, God again came without being called in search of Cain. He did not intervene to prevent the assassination of Abel with whom he was well pleased, but he did to defend the fratricide Cain, against all (Gen 4,15).

3. THE THIRD INTERVENTION: NOAH—COVENANT

When man does not care for God, God again takes the initiative and comes again to him. He chooses and calls a few men to join with him in an eternal pact and so saves the earth.

After the deluge, for the first time, he sets up his own pact with men and with their descendants and places his own sign in the *clouds* as a seal that his treaty will be recorded forever with man and with the living spirit (Gen 9,16). Through his intervention, therefore, God wishes to establish a stable relation, a covenant, with man. He wants to join himself with man in a constant, and not merely transitory manner (Gen 9, 8-13). He chooses a few men who, if they obey and receive him, they, and through them others, will be saved. All those who do not receive him can never come through death to life; they remain in death. Hence the intervention of God will have a double aspect: purification—death, and covenant—the union of God with man.

4. THE FOURTH INTERVENTION: THE TOWER OF BABEL: LET US GO DOWN

Though man wishes to reach God (Gen 11,4) God comes to man and enters into a covenant with him, not in heaven as man wishes, but here on earth (Gen 11, 5-7).

5. THE FIFTH INTERVENTION: ABRAHAM "I SHALL ESTABLISH MY COVENANT BETWEEN YOU AND ME . . . THAT I MAY BE YOUR GOD" (Gen 17,7).

God again approached man through his own proper initiative and joined himself through an eternal covenant with him whose sign is in the flesh of Abraham. He leads him out of Haran (Gen 12,1-5) and seals a covenant with him (Gen 17, 1-25).

The result of the covenant of God with Abraham will be that Abraham receives Canaan, and becomes the Father of many nations. But the most fundamental result is that Yahweh himself becomes the God of Abraham, and Abraham with his descendants the people of God (Gen 17,7-8). All the nations will be blessed in Abraham's descendants because Abraham obeyed the voice of God (Gen 22,18).

6. THE SIXTH INTERVENTION: ISAAC "I SHALL BE WITH YOU" (Gen 26,24).

After Abraham's death, God took care that his covenant made with man should not be forgotten. He recalls it to the mind of Isaac whom he leads (Gen 26, 2-5), as he led his father, by being with him (Gen 26,24).

By reason of the covenant made with Abraham, God is specially with Isaac. This being of God with Isaac is essential, because possession of the earth and a multitude of children is owed to this union (Gen 26,3-4). Abimelech and Ahuzzath were aware of this, and so they wished to enter into a covenant with Isaac (Gen 26,28).

7. THE SEVENTH INTERVENTION: JACOB, THE LORD IS IN THIS VERY PLACE, THE HOUSE OF GOD

The Lord comes also to Jacob and recalls his covenant by reiterating his promises. He will be with Jacob and guard him wherever he goes. He will not forsake Jacob, until he has done what he promised. Jacob understands that these blessings are due to that special presence of Yahweh, which because of its duration can be called the dwelling of God, the "house of God" (Gen 28,16-22; 35,7). Yahweh remains with Jacob and accompanies him in his wanderings. His presence is not confined to the land of Canaan, since he goes along with Jacob even into the land of Egypt (Gen 46,3-4).

8. THE EIGHTH INTERVENTION: ISRAEL THE ONLY BEGOTTEN SON—THE PASCH.

God does not cease to bind himself to man more and more. He calls Moses, as he called Adam (Ex 3,3-4.7-12; 6,2-8) to make Israel his people and his firstborn son (Ex 4,23). After having afflicted the Egyptians with many plagues he makes the Pasch, the passover of the Lord, i.e. the day on which God in passing over Egypt leads Israel out of Egypt (Ex 12,12-14; 13,2-16). The liberation of Israel from Egypt is due again to the fact that God was with Israel all its days.

God now wanders with his people and leads them to Mount Sinai.

> The Lord went before them, by day in the form of a pillar of cloud to lead them along the road, and by night in the form of a pillar of fire to give them light, that they might travel by day and by night; the pillar of cloud by day and the pillar of fire by night did not move from the head of the people (Ex 13,21-22; Num 9,15-16)

The Lord carried Israel, " . . . as a man carries his son, all the way of his journey" (Deut 1, 31-33).

9. THE NINTH INTERVENTION: THE SINAITIC COVENANT THE PEOPLE AS PERSONAL PROPERTY OF YAHWEH.

Further, God wishes to bind Israel to himself in a special way, and so he leads him to Mt. Sinai to ratify there his covenant with him as a people. The covenant will be a bilateral one. God desires man's free acceptance of that which he himself initiates.

The people indeed accept it and agree upon the covenant and ratify the union of God with man (Ex 24,7-8). Through the Sinaitic covenant the people of Israel become the property of God, the most precious and beloved One of Yahweh, the people whom Yahweh has taken for his own.

As a consequence of this covenant God places a tabernacle in the midst of Israel and walks among them.

> I will set up my dwelling among you, and will not contemn you, but will walk among you, and will be your God and you shall be my people (Lev 26,11-12; cf Ex 25,8).

Because of God's presence and dwelling in Israel's midst day and night (Ex 40, 34-38) the camp must be kept pure and all uncleaness must be cast out (Num 5,3). For the same reason if anyone not called approaches the holy place, he dies (Lev 10,1-3; Num 17,11-13;18,7).

The one who does not believe in this special presence of God in the midst of Israel will be punished. Indeed none of the explorers of the land of Canaan lacking in confidence entered the promised land. Only Caleb and Joshua took possession of the land which they trod with their feet because they believed that the Lord was with them and they did not fear the people of Canaan (Num 14, 6-9; Deut 1, 34-36).

God dwells with Israel and takes her as his own because he loves her; not for any merit or excellence on the part of Israel, but through his own free choice (Deut 7, 6-8).

10. THE TENTH INTERVENTION: JOSHUA AND JUDGES

After Moses God chose Joshua (Num 27, 18-23; Deut 1, 37-38), for Joshua believed that God was with Israel (Num 14, 9). As with Moses, so the Lord was with Joshua (Josh 1, 5-9) in order to bring what was already begun to a successful conclusion. In dying Joshua impresses once more upon Israel the fact that God will remain with her, and that she must only take care to love Yahweh (Josh 23, 3-11).

After Joshua God also raised up Judges in order to free his people from their enemies (Judg 2,16,cf 3,9). After Gideon God raised up Samson and the spirit of God began to be with him (Judg 13,24-25).

The spirit of the Lord rushed upon him, that he might overcome the lion (Judg 14,6) as well as the thirty men (Judg 14,19). And only then, when the spirit of the Lord had withdrawn from him, was he captured (Judg 16,20). The Judges, like Joshua, indeed, owe everything to this special presence of God who, as Deborah sang, truly went out and passed over with Israel (Judg 5,4-5).

11. THE ELEVENTH INTERVENTION: DAVID—SOLOMON— KINGS

God called Samuel, just as he called Adam and Moses (1 Sam 3,1-14). Since the Lord was with Samuel (1 Sam 3,19), he grew and was the faithful prophet of the Lord.

The people too knew that they owed everything, even victory, to the presence of God in their midst. That is why they carried the Ark of the Covenant into their camp against the Philistines (1 Sam 4,3-7). The ark, however, signified the presence of God who cannot be constrained. God comes and dwells in the midst of Israel when and how he pleases. Therefore no one should wonder that Israel fell and the ark was captured. For this was the way in which God wanted to strike the Philistines and their god Dagon, not only in their camp, but also in their very homes (cf 1 Sam 4,1-6,12).

Later when Saul becomes the king of Israel, he was given a triple sign that God was with him (1 Sam 10,1-7). Through anointing the Lord was with Saul and had let him succeed (1 Sam 14,47-48) until Saul committed a sin on account of which God withdrew from him (1 Sam 13,11-12; 15,22-23) and chose David in his place. From that day Saul was afraid of David because the Lord was with David and had departed from him (1 Sam 18.12).

After David the Lord chose Solomon and through him built the temple wherein he dwelt in the midst of the children of Israel (1 Kings 6,13-14). When the temple was built, God came down to it, just as to the tent in the desert, and filled his house with his presence.

> ... A cloud filled the house of the Lord, so that the priests could not stand to minister because of the clouds; for the glory of the Lord filled the house of the Lord (1 Kings 8,10-11).

The Lord sanctified the house; he put his name there and remained in it, but only conditionally, that is, on condition that Israel keep the commandments and the covenant of the Lord. If she did not, the temple was to be destroyed and to be made an example for the whole world. The existence of this temple, then, and the presence of God in it was conditional, whereas God's promise was certain and independent of Israel's infidelity. Therefore, neither God's presence nor his dwelling in the midst of Israel through the temple was definitive. God was preparing another presence for which this was only the sign.

12. THE TWELFTH INTERVENTION: THE PROPHETS—THE DAY OF YAHWEH

A. Isaiah.

Israel had forgotten the Lord and spurned him (Is 1,2 ff.), but God did not forget his covenant. He visited his people Israel, because he wished to complete his work, to be with man. This visitation of the Lord (Is 6,8-10) "the Day of the Lord," when God visits his people, is a day of salvation and a day of judgment (Is 2,6-43). Its ultimate purpose, however, is to rebuild God's temple in the midst of Israel (Is 4,4-6). Just as on Sion God was present in his tent, and through his presence was a refuge and a shelter for the people, so also now, when he visits his people, he wishes to save them through his presence, and to make them happy. He does not guard Israel from afar, but comes to her, and through his nearness works out the salvation of Israel.

Therefore the sign which God gives to Achaz through Isaiah is of a young woman conceiving and bearing a son, whose name is Emmanuel, that is, "God with us" (Is 7,14). God spreads out his wings and covers all the land, which is the land of Emmanuel, i.e., the land where God is with us (Is 8,8-10).

This new day, when God comes to man and becomes "Emmanuel," that is, "God with us," is described in a way very like the day on which God led his people out of Egypt (Is 11,11-16). Once again he will come down upon Sion, because his fire is there, and his furnace is in Jerusalem (Is 31,4-9). He will come to save his people (Is 35,4), and Israel has to prepare herself since God is coming (Is 40,4-11) to be with her (Is 43,1-5.15).

God's presence, i.e. the fact that he is with Israel, effects both freedom from sin and holiness. God is the creator of Israel and her redeemer as well (Is 44,24), and by his many interventions becomes so present to Israel, that even the Gentiles and other peoples recognize it (Is 45,14). From now on the new intervention is indicated as close at hand. God has brought his righteousness near and his salvation will not be delayed any longer (Is 46,13; 51,5; 56,1; 60,1-2).

B. Jeremiah

God also chooses Jeremiah. Jeremiah whom God chose must again proclaim the same thing as the other prophets, namely, that God wishes to dwell with Israel (Jer 3,17) and that the land was given to Israel that Yahweh might dwell there with men and be their God (Jer 7,23; 11,4; 24,7; 30,22; 31,1; 32,38-41; Bar 2,35). For God is so bound to Israel and Israel to God, that they are one externally, and internally too. God makes the whole house of Israel cling to him, "as a waistcloth clings to the skin of a man" (Jer 13,11).

C. Ezekiel

Ezekiel is likewise sent (Ez 2,1-3) to proclaim: Israel is God's flock, and God visits his sheep as a pastor visits his flock. He toils for Israel (Ez 34,11-17). In giving them a new heart and a new spirit, he removes their heart of stone and substitutes a heart of flesh (Ez 11,19-20; 36,27-28). As the bridegroom takes the abandoned bride, the merciful man the abandoned child, so God will take Israel to himself (Ez 23,1ff) that she may be his (Ez 16,1ff). God becomes their God, and they become his people, because he pitches his tent in their midst and lives among them (Ez 37,27). The temple of God will be rebuilt and the house of the Lord filled with glory (Ez 43,2-5), will become the place of Yahweh's throne. He will dwell in the midst of the children of Israel forever (Ez 43,7). From that day on the name of the city will be "The Lord is there" (Ez 48,35).

D. The Other Prophets

The message of other prophets is no different. They proclaim God's coming and dwelling in the midst of Israel. Joel (3,17-21), Zephaniah (3,17), Haggai (1,13), Zechariah (2,5.10-13), Malachi (3,1-2) made sure that the idea of God's special dwelling in the midst of Israel should not be forgotten by Israel.

E. Daniel—The Son of Man Coming With the Clouds of Heaven

In addition to the usual symbols of Yahweh's special presence in the midst of Israel, such as the column of cloud, the pillar of fire (in which the Lord used to go in front of Israel in the desert), the glory of the Lord (resting on Mount Sinai and filling Solomon's temple) and the tabernacle (where he dwelt among Israel) there is a new symbol in the book of Daniel.

> . . . And behold, with the cloud of heaven there came one like a son of man, and he advanced toward the Ancient One, and was brought near his presence. To him was given dominion, and glory, and kingly power, that all peoples, and nations, and tongues should serve him; his dominion was to be an everlasting dominion, that should not pass away (Dan 7,13-14).

Daniel's theophany is a sort of prophetic and apocalyptic literary work of the 2nd century B.C. The Son of Man (Aram. 'bar nasa' or Heb. 'ben adam') as well as the description recalls the first chapter of Genesis about the creation of the world.

The vision happened to be by night, when the four winds of heaven were stirring up the great sea (Dan 7,2). The narration of Genesis is a very likely model: ". . . it was darkness and the Spirit of God was moving over the face of the waters" (Gen 1,2). As in Genesis the waters brought forth swarms of living creatures, sea monsters, likewise in Daniel four great beasts came out of the sea each different from the other (Gen 1,20-21; Dan 7,3). The beasts of Daniel, however, are really monsters with four heads, mixtures of animals, birds and man, symbols of the powers dominated by sin and rebellious to Yahweh.

There is, however, a considerable difference between Genesis and Daniel in regard to the introduction of the Son of Man into the scenery. In Genesis the creation of man is in the framework of six days followed by the seventh, when Yahweh takes his rest, symbolized by sitting. Now in Daniel, the Ancient One takes his seat before the introduction of the Son of Man. The Venerable One takes his throne of fire on earth, where the beasts are judged after having risen out of the sea. Heaven is not mentioned. When the fourth beast is judged and his dominion is taken away and the lives of the four beasts are prolonged "to harass the Saints of the Most High" (see vv 21.25), then only is the Son of Man introduced. He does not come out of the sea (cf Gen 2,6-7) but with the clouds of heaven. Heaven is brought into the scenery for the first time by the Son of Man who approaches the Ancient One sitting on his throne of fire on earth. When he is brought near the presence of the Ancient One, dominion, glory, everlasting kingdom is given to him and all peoples, nations and languages to serve him (Dan 7,14-27; Gen 1,28-30; 2,19-20).

As a prophetic and apocalyptic literary work Dan 7 poses several problems for the exegete. The first is whether the Son of Man in Daniel means an individual or a group. The author seems to explain him in a collective sense, since there is an immediate reference to the people as the Saints of the Most High (vv 18.27). The later apocalyptic literature takes him as an individual. It is very probable that it means both, since prophetic thought easily moves from the representative individual to the group represented, and vice versa.

The other problem about the Son of Man of Daniel is the much discussed question whether he is an ascending or a descending figure? Is he a human being elevated by God, the fulfillment of the Adam of Genesis who finally receives and possesses all the authority given to him by Yahweh? [188] Or is he rather a superhuman and even someone mysteriously divine?

It seems that the Son of Man stays closer to God than to the beasts, symbols of earthly human power. [189] Some authors consider the Son of Man as an ascending figure coming up to God who is supposed to be in heaven. [190] However, in the vision of Daniel, God took his throne on the earth, since the beasts are not taken into heaven for judgment. Now the Son of Man comes down to the Ancient One during the judgments with the clouds of heaven. [191] He comes not only with clouds, but with the clouds of heaven which are always signs accompanying a theophany of Yahweh. The clouds are mentioned in the Old Testament about 100 times, in 30 of which they are descriptions of natural phenomena. The other 70 times they are always visible signs of the presence of Yahweh. If the Son of Man were only a symbol of man, like any other, without the special presence of Yahweh in him, this would be the only case where a man came with the clouds. [192]

Moreover, it is interesting to observe how the two visible signs of the presence of Yahweh, the fire by night and cloud by day (cf Ex 40,34-38) are divided in Daniel's vision. The fire accompanies the Ancient One (v 10) and the cloud the Son of Man (v 13).

Further, there is another consideration which may indicate that the Son of Man in Daniel cannot be an ascending figure coming to God. According to the prophets, a man like the king of Babylon or the prince of Tyre, who tries to ascend into heaven and scale the heights of the clouds, will be rebuked down to Sheol, to "the recess of its Pit" (Is 14,14-15; Ez 28,1-8; cf Gen 11,4-9). But the Son of Man in Daniel, unlike the king of Babylon, is favored by God and his kingdom will endure forever.

In conclusion we can say that the Son of Man in Daniel is no one else but the prophetic expression of that presence in the midst of Israel which from the time of Exodus was foreshadowed in the various descriptions of the descent of God. He is a symbolic figure of God's ruling presence in the world. He may be taken in a collective or in an individual sense, but it must be admitted that in him and through him God once again visits mankind and establishes his kingdom on earth (v. 13-14), which is nothing else than the presence of God among men, manifested by his power and glory. The Son of Man, like the column of cloud or fire in which the Lord used to go in front of Israel in the desert, or like the

Šekinah, the glory of God which rested on Mount Sinai and filled Solomon's temple, is the visible sign of the presence of God who dwells among men.

Like the temple previously from now on the Son of Man, type of the new Israel, the new people of God, becomes the prophetic image of Yahweh's final presence and his special being with Israel foreshadowed from the time of Exodus by his numerous interventions. On account of Yahweh's special presence, the Son of Man becomes "holy," somehow divinized, like the temple was, through the indwelling God. In the Son of Man and through him, God seeks man and establishes his kingdom on earth definitively, so that the Son of Man is a sign and summation of all that was believed about the activity of God seeking man. The Son of Man as symbol of God's activity in pursuit of man, is indeed the conclusion of the Old as well as the introduction to the New Testament. It is like a climax in which the preparation of the time before Christ culminates, and the realization of the time of Christ is inaugurated.

13. CONCLUSION

The essential and fundamental idea of the Old Testament is that God himself, the one and only Creator, seeks man, actively intervenes in history in order to be with his people and to share with them the supreme happiness of his presence. The belief of God's being with his people, his active dwelling among his people in order to make them supremely happy in his presence is an element common to the New and Old Testament. God's loving presence communicating his beatitude to men is introduced in the Old Testament as a general horizon or a general context of revelation and for an understanding of the whole world of history. It is proposed as the only principle of historical understanding which can make every event understandable, credible. This new principle of historical understanding, introduced and proposed in the Old Testament, reaches its final historical realization, its factual embodiment in the New Testament. The general context of understanding becomes reality (cf Col 2,17) in Christ in whom the twofold structure of historical understanding, personal intentionality and its objective embodiment become completely one.

CHAPTER SEVEN

JESUS' SELF-AND-GOD REVELATIONAL LIFE

After our overview of the preparatory time before Christ, we will now analyze the different theologico-historical events which demonstrate the validity of Christian faith in the personal entry of God into human history for the supercreatural beatitude of man. The first of these will be Jesus' revelational life. According to our method we will ask whether Jesus' consciousness and words could create theologico-historical situations in which man could feel reasonably invited to an affirmation of faith, i.e. "My God you are present here." Or in other words we will see whether the historical Jesus was a man who could lead others to find in him the mystery of God. We will examine successively the sayings concerning the kingdom of God, the Son of Man, and the Son, and ask whether the historical Jesus could with these sayings succeed in bringing his followers into a puzzling dilemma or mysterious incomprehensibility in which they could feel invited to raise a question about God's supreme active presence in him?

But before examining these points of inquiry, we have to say something about Jesus' historical existence and historical research. It is natural for man to be interested in knowing whether a person really existed before he spends his time finding out who he was and what he wanted to do.

1. THE HISTORICAL EXISTENCE OF JESUS

It is true that the problem of Jesus today does not principally concern his historical existence. The doubt, says R. Bultmann, as to whether Jesus really existed is "unfounded and not worth refutation. No sane person can doubt that Jesus stands as founder behind the historical movement whose first distinct stage is represented by the oldest Palestinian community." [193] However, this was not so evident in the last century.

A. History

Those who denied the historical existence of Jesus were mostly from among the liberal rationalists of the 19th and the early 20th centuries. The first seems to be C. F. Volney in the year 1791, [194] followed immediately by C. F. Dupuis in 1794. [195] Both conceived Jesus as an astral or solar myth, like the Persian Mithra, god of light, without any real historical existence. The idea was defended later on, with slight nuances, by J. M. Robertson, [196] A. Drews, [197] W. Erbt [198] and by P. Jensen who considered Jesus as a new variant of the Babylonian numen, Gilgamesh. [199] In the year 1850-51, B. Bauer assumed that Jesus was nothing else than a late personification of early Christian ideas. [200] Bauer's view was further specified by A. Kalthoff, [201] proclaiming Jesus as a symbolic figure of a revolutionary social movement. Twenty years later P. L. Couchoud, with A. Bayet, one of the last of the deniers of the historical existence of Jesus in our time, considered Jesus as a great eternal dream of man derived from Christian consciousness. [202] Before P. L. Couchoud, B. Smith proposed an original idea by holding that Christianity was in fact a pre-Christian sect, since it already existed before our Christian era as a Jewish Nazarene sect which adored some kind of god, called Jesus. [203]

The main argument brought up by the liberal school of rationalism against the historical existence of Jesus was the absence of non-Christian testimony concerning Jesus and the mythologico-kerygmatic character of the gospels from which it seems to be impossible to demythologize the real human historical Jesus. A. Drews denied Jesus' historical existence because of his conception of the very nature of religion. According to him, religion necessarily originated from ideas, since only ideas could have the absolute and universal values that religion requires. Therefore, the religious "materialism" which tried to attach religion to a historical concrete existence, had to be fought and rejected as contrary to the very nature of true religion.

This argument, however, could not resist for long the criticism of the coming historical school. The historical criticism accused the rationalists of an ignorance of history. C. Guignebert, a prominent representative of historical criticism, in no way wished to admit the divinity of Jesus; nevertheless, in his book, *Jesus,* he made the following judgment about the rationalist school's denial of the historical existence of Jesus:

> Opened up at the end of the 18th century by French "philosophers," in particular Dupuis and Volney, the debate has been going on ever since, alternating between crises and slumbering periods. It is quite obvious that if the person and initiative of Jesus were to disappear from history, the birth of Christianity would still remain to be explained, and this is what the deniers are actually concerning themselves about, with a conviction which equals only the divergence of their thesis and the weakness of their reasons . . . Deniers are almost all "amateurs" and mythologists. The former are naive and blocked on surface information whose deplorable state they do not even suspect; the latter are instructed, sometimes even erudite, but just as foreign or refractory to the modest and patient discipline of exegesis, and are ready to turn a text upside down or to do violence to it, instead of accepting it with circumspection and humility; they are ready to impose with authority the conclusions which their own convictions need, instead of resigning themselves within the limits which a critical and historical sense would impose upon them. To add a construction that is without foundation is not to serve science, which, in order to live on hypotheses, cannot be satisfied with paradoxes without risk.[204]

It is remarkable that the representatives of the school of historical criticism prove the historical existence of Jesus not from the existent profane and pagan documents, but from the gospels themselves, which, after their demythologization, demonstrate the historical existence of Jesus with historical certitude. The reason is that the pagan documents witness rather to the existence of Christians than to the historical existence of Jesus.

The pagan testimony was handed down to us mostly by Cornelius Tacitus, G. Suetonius Tranquillus, C. Plinius Secundus Minor and by Mara bar Serapion, probably a Syrian Stoic of the first or second century.

Tacitus in his work *Annalium,* 15, 44 which he wrote during the rule of Trajan (A.D. 98-117) narrates that:

> . . . In order to disprove the rumor, [205] Nero falsely accused culprits and subjected to most unusual punishments those whom, hated for their shameful deeds, the populace called Christians. The author of this name, Christ, was put to death by the procurator, Pontius Pilate, while Tiberius was emperor; but the dangerous superstition, though suppressed for this moment, broke out again not only in Judea, the origin of this evil, but even in the city, where all atrocious and shameful things flow together from all sides and are practised. First, therefore those were seized who confessed (that they were Christians); then, upon their information, a great multitude was convicted not so much upon the charge of setting fire (to the city) as for hatred of the human race.

Thus Tacitus doubtless testifies that Christians lived in Rome at the time of Trajan and they were said to have been founded by Christ.

Suetonius around 120 said, in *The Life of Claudius,* cap. 25, that Claudius "expelled from Rome the Jews who were constantly stirring up a tumult under the leadership of Chrestus." Similarly, in *The Life of Nero,* cap. 16, he indicates that Christians, a sect of men of a recent and wicked superstition, were put to death.

Pliny in his *Epistles* 10, 96-97, which he wrote to the ruler Trajan around the year 111-113, refers to the manner in which he dealt with Christians who were deferred to him:

> I interrogated them whether they were Christians. . . . if they . . . persevered, I ordered them to be executed. . . . Those who denied they were, or had ever been, Christians . . . and who finally cursed Christ . . . these I thought it proper to discharge. . . . the whole of their guilt, or their error, was that they were in the habit of meeting on a certain fixed day before it was light, when they sang in alternate verses a hymn to Christ, as to a god. . . .

From Pliny's testimony no more can be established than that in the time 111-113 after Christ, the Christians already adored Jesus as God.

Another very interesting document of gentile source is the letter of a Syrian Stoic, Mara bar Serapion to his son, Serapion:

> For what else have we to say, when wise men are forcibly dragged by the hands of tyrants, and their wisdom is taken captive by calumny, and they are oppressed in their intelligence without defense? For what advantage

did the Athenians gain by the murder of Socrates, the recompense of which they received in famine and pestilence? Or the people of Samos by the burning of Pythagoras, because in one hour their country was entirely covered with sand? Or the Jews by the death of their wise king, because from that time their kingdom was taken away? For with justice did God make recompense to the wisdom of these three: for the Athenians died of famine; and the Samians were overwhelmed by the sea without remedy; and the Jews, desolate and driven from their own kingdom, are scattered through every country. Socrates is not dead, because of Plato, neither Pythagoras, because of the statue of Juno; nor the Wise King, because of the laws which he promulgated.[206]

According to historical criticism none of these documents could be accepted in favor of the historicity of Jesus. The Roman historians, Tacitus, Suetonius, and Pliny, testify only that Christians existed at Rome. Concerning their origin, they relate only what the people held about the Christians, repeating probably what the Christians themselves said about themselves, viz. that they were founded by Christ crucified in the time of Tiberius. Roman historians could not have known that Jesus existed unless they had learned it from the Christians, for they could not have had any other historical document concerning him. On this point, let us hear once again C. Guignebert:

... If the composition of the Annals is situated about 115, it is quite obvious that the elements of Christian tradition about the life of Christ should then be vulgarized so that the information of Tacitus only echoes a commonly accepted bit of hearsay. It suffices that this be possible in order that the value of our text fall to nothing. The authority of Suetonius is worth even less. ... The letter that Pliny the Younger ... wrote is well known. It would certainly take a good and fearless will to count this assertion among the number of testimonies which could be received in favor of the historicity of Jesus.[207]

Thus historical criticism rejected the rationalistic opinion, and thought that Jesus' existence can be historically demonstrated, not on the basis of profane non-Christian sources, but on the basis of the gospels, the "ideology" of Paul manifested in his letters and the attitude of contemporary Jews.

B. The Gospel Evidence

From the gospels' way of narrating, it can be seen that the writers of these documents did not invent and construct the image

of Jesus in their imaginations, but were writing under the impell-
ing influence of a really living man, whose rude reality was only
troublesome to them. The incoherencies and contradictions which
are to be found in their writings, indicate that they were not
absolutely free in their accounts, but were influenced by the crude
"humanity" of an existing real man into whose human existence
they wove their legendary tales. Jesus normally appears in the
gospels with trivial manners, inferior properties, and characteristics
absolutely opposed to the tendency of divinization, which the
writers projected. Jesus, as the hero of the gospels, appears in
contrast to the heroes of that time, for those heroes experienced
no incertitude, no fear, no humiliation. The evangelists, in fact,
did not employ the literary form of legend so popular in their
times which would have been of great utility and would have
made their work easier. Why, then, did they choose this more
difficult approach? The reason can be only one: they could not
yet get rid of the real existence of this man whom they knew and
whom they precisely wished to divinize.

Why are so many incoherencies and gaps left in the legend of god if it was
constructed outside of all reality? Why is this legend loaded with traits of
vile humanity which are perfectly useless, even scandalous? Why go to the
trouble of speaking of the brothers and sisters of god and even give them
names (Mk 6,3)? Why does his family consider him out of his mind (Mk
3,21)? Why does he get angry? Why does he sorrow and cry over himself
and others? Why does he not allow that he should be called good (Mk
10,18) and proclaim that God only is good? Why does he, who has come
down to announce and determine salvation, declare that he does not know
when the supreme day will come (Mk 13,32)—the day called "his day" in
the Pauline perspective? Why is his last cry (Mk 15,34) one of despair (My
God, why hast thou abandoned me), at the moment when he has just
consummated the great mystery of the cross? Why? To make it more
likely? That would be to attribute a great deal of method and consistencies
to men who ordinarily are lacking so much of it. Why is there so much
uncertitude in a teaching whose aim even today we don't always see
clearly? Above all, why did those who drew up the legend, let the hero of
their time live contrary to the customs followed by all religions without
trying to assure themselves of the profitable benefits of antiquity?—To all
these questions, and it would be easy to extend the list, the deniers give no
satisfying answers. It is sufficient to read the gospels to see that . . . they
(the redactors) experienced his humanity (of Jesus); their narrative is made
up of legendary variations upon a reality which bothers them, and with
which they would not have been cheerfully burdened themselves.[208]

C. Paul

However, the best witness to the historicity of Jesus is Paul, whom some pretend to be the principal supporter of the myth theory. Certainly Paul's Christ is a divine being. Paul, who was in a sense the creator of the myth and who placed the importance of the Christian life in spiritual knowledge of Christ, does not deny the privilege of the twelve apostles arising from the fact of having known Jesus in the flesh, but only tried to reestablish the legitimacy of his mission in face of the prestige of the Twelve by proposing his spiritual knowledge of Jesus. This clearly shows that Paul was certain that Jesus lived in the flesh, although this fact added very little confirmation to his so-called Pauline doctrine.

The mystic Paul's certitude concerning the historical earthly life of Jesus is further maintained by the fact that a fundamental schema of events of the life of Jesus of Nazareth is found in the Pauline letters written 15-20 years before the gospels. Thus Paul says that Jesus was the offspring of Abraham (Gal 3,16), descendant of David (Rom 1,3), born of a woman under the law (Gal 4,4). He had brothers (1 Cor 9,5), one of them was called James (Gal 1,19) and three of his apostles were Peter, John and James (Gal 1,18; 2,9). He was betrayed (1 Cor 11,23), and gave his testimony under Pilate (1 Tim 6,13), was condemned to death by the Jews (1 Thess 2,15) and crucified (Gal 3,1; 1 Cor 2,2). He died and was buried (1 Cor 15,3-4; Rom 6,4). After his resurrection (1 Cor 15,4,14; Rom 4,25) he appeared to the Twelve (1 Cor 15,5) and to many brethren (1 Cor 15,5-8), then ascended into heaven (Eph 4,9-10), he is seated at God's right hand (Col 3,1) from where he will come again (1 Thess 1,10; 4,16). This fundamental schema of the events of the life of Jesus, used also in the early kerygmatic sermons (cf, Acts 10, 37-42), was the core of the later gospel narratives.

D. Jews

That Jesus lived can be demonstrated further from the attitude of the contemporary Jews. Why did the Jews, in their struggles with Jesus' followers, not cut short all discussion by proclaiming simply that he did not even exist? The rabbinic literature, Talmud, Toledoth Yeshu, try to degrade Jesus, but they never deny his

existence. [209]   Baraita of the *Babylonian Talmud* (Sanhedrin 43a)
narrates that Yeshu was hanged on the eve of the Passover because
he had practiced sorcery and enticed Israel to apostasy. [210]

Beside the Talmud tradition there is Josephus, the Jewish historian (37?-100), who in his *The Antiquities of the Jews* gives
another extra-biblical reference to Jesus. The text of *Antiquities,*
18,3,3, very likely has undergone some Christian interpolation;
however the following sentence is regarded as original by the
majority of modern critics: "And when, upon accusation of the
leading men among us, Pilate had condemned him to the cross,
those who had loved (him) at the first did not cease." [211]

Thus, although the non-Christian references to Jesus tell us little
about Jesus, they are not absolutely silent. Moreover, in spite of
the kerygmatic character of the gospels it can be established with
historical certitude, by means of the method of form criticism,
that behind the gospel narrative there indeed existed the man,
Jesus of Nazareth. Today all historians, non-Christian as well as
Christian, admit the historical existence of Jesus. R. Bultman may
be right when he says that the doubt whether Jesus really existed
is unfounded and not worth refutation. However, the question
about the historical existence of Jesus is not entirely irrelevant.

For although we live in the 20th century, there might be not a
few "contemporaries" who pose questions of the 19th century.
For centuries coexist in the mentality of men. It is possible that
some people hold and believe a theory which science has already
abandoned as inadmissible.

2. THE ORIGIN OF FAITH IN THE DIVINITY OF JESUS AND THE HISTORICAL RESEARCH

After describing the existence of faith in the divinity of Jesus,
the next task of historical research is to ask whether there is any
relation between actual faith in the divinity of Jesus and his
historical existence some two thousand years ago. To answer this
question it is necessary to look for the time when the actual faith
in the divinity of Jesus really began. It is evident that if this faith
cannot be traced to the time of Jesus, it is hard to admit that the
faith in his divinity could have been originated by the historical
Jesus, and that his life was a powerful revelatory event able to

create situations in which his fellowmen could feel the supreme presence of God in him.

Looking for the historical moment of the origin of faith in the divinity of Jesus, we can start from the testimony of the fourth gospel and move from the time of the writing of the synoptic gospels to the prior history, to discover the earliest time we have written documents testifying to the Church's faith in the divinity of Jesus Christ. Thus, we shall see the testimony of the evangelists, as well as the testimony of the early Church prior to the written gospels. We will then be able to ask the question whether Jesus could have been the originator of the Church's faith in his divinity and how he did succeed in raising questions concerning God's presence in him and leading men to recognize through faith the same God's presence in him. Our intention is, therefore, not to establish whether Jesus knew, or whether he expressed in the same terms what the gospels say that he knew and expressed in certain words, [212] but rather to establish the historical possibility of his raising faith in himself as Yahweh raised faith in himself through Old Testament prophets.

A. The Testimony of the Evangelists

1) About 100 A.D. John's Gospel Testified that Jesus was God.

The discovery of the Rylands Papyrus 457 (p^{52}) and that of the Egerton Papyrus 2 supplied certain evidence that the fourth gospel was written about 100 A.D. At this time the author of the fourth gospel testifies that Jesus was believed to be God. In his Prologue he says: "The Word was God" (Jn 1,1). Similarly, at the end of his gospel, he confesses that he wrote it so that his addressees might believe that Jesus is the Christ, the Son of God (Jn 20,31). The thesis of his gospel is to demonstrate the identity of the Logos of faith and of Jesus in the flesh. Thomas, after putting his hand into Jesus' side, confesses, "My Lord and my God" (Jn 20,28).[213]

The same author testifies also that Jesus and the Father are one (Jn 10,30). Jesus was the Son of God in a real sense (5,17-26; 8,35), who proceeded from the Father (6,33; 6,38; 11,42; 17,8) and was equal with God the Father in acting (5,17; 8,18; 14,10), in knowing (10,15) and in being (5,18; 10,30.33.36; 14,7.10.20; 17,21).

It should be noted that, according to our author, the Jews well understood the meaning of Jesus' words even before the resurrection, though even the apostles did not have a confirmed belief in Jesus until after Jesus' resurrection, when they received the Holy Spirit. These same Jews sought to kill him because he made himself equal to God (Jn 5,18), and wanted to stone him. They said: "We are not stoning you for doing anything good, but for your impious talk, and because you, a mere man, make yourself out to be God" (Jn 10,33).

The testimony of the fourth gospel is important for it shows that belief concerning Christ's divinity has been unchanged at least from the year 100 A.D. to the present day. Moreover, it seems that the author intended his gospel to be received as real history on account of events which actually happened, and of the discourses which actually took place.[214]

2) About 70 A.D. the Synoptic Evangelists Testified that Jesus Was Equal to God.

Since there is very little indication in the synoptic gospels concerning their dates of origin, we cannot know the exact years of their composition. Evidently they are earlier compositions than John's gospel. Ignatius of Antioch, and especially the Didache (from the nineties of the first century) appear to have quoted Matthew's gospel.[215] The most critical view dates Matthew in 80-90 A.D. and Luke between 78-85 A.D. Mark must be dated still earlier than 70 A.D., that is, around 65-70.

Mk 13,14 mentions the siege and fall of Jerusalem as the abomination of desolation. This obscure description in contrast with that of Lk 21,20 (Jerusalem will be surrounded by armies) supplies an internal evidence that Mark must have written before the fall of Jerusalem in 70 A.D. There are some arguments for earlier dates of the composition of the synoptic gospels;[216] however we take the seventies as a median period witnessed by the synoptic evangelists.

The synoptic evangelists did not, in fact, call Jesus "God." However, they did not hestitate to transfer to Jesus what the Jews said about Yahweh.[217]

In Luke Jesus frequently is called Lord (7,13; 10,1.17.39.41; 11,1.39, etc.) i.e. Kyrios,[218] the Greek name of Yahweh in the Septuagint.

Mark's gospel is to show in all events from the very first verse (1,1) through the revelation of the Father (1,11; 9,7) and the confession of demons (5,7; 3,11) to the faith of the Roman centurion (15,39) that Jesus is the Son of God. [219] The author attributes to the Son of God, to the Lord of the Sabbath (Mk 2,28) the power of forgiving sins (Mk 2,1-12), of calming the sea and the winds (Mk 4,41) and of sending angels (Mk 13,27) which were all, according to the Jews, exclusive powers of Yahweh.

Matthew's Greek gospel testifies also that Jesus placed himself above the level of creatures by putting himself on a divine level equal to God.

> No one understands the Son except the Father, nor does anyone understand the Father except the Son, and anyone to whom the Son chooses to reveal him (Mt 11,27).

The object of the mutual knowledge is not merely the fact that God is Jesus' Father in a general sense. For the people of Israel, apart from this special revelation of Jesus, recognized already that Yahweh was to be considered as Father. Here is a case of another type of knowledge, which concerns the intimate character and life of the Son as related to the Father. According to Matthew, Jesus affirms a mutual correlation in the same order of the Son with the Father. From the parallel positions (cf v 27b with v 27c) the Son is on the same level as the Father, both by reason of his power of knowing, and by reason of the object known. No one knows the real Within of the Son except the Father, and no one knows the real Within of the Father except the Son. The Father and Son are set up as two ineffable terms in the same order. Their relationship to each other in the same order is suggested by the absolute exclusion of anybody else (No one . . . but . . . Son/Father . . . No one . . . but . . . Father/Son) and by the parallelism of a relationship uniquely reserved to these two persons, and of mutual knowledge which does not suppose revelation, because it is connatural to both. The saying in Mt 11,27 suggests Jesus' experiences of his oneness with the Father and logically demands the consciousness of his preexistence. [220]

In Matthew 16,16, the author, unlike Mark (8,30) or Luke (9,20), gives us a profession of belief in the divinity of Jesus through Peter's confession.

Jesus praises Peter's answer and attributes it to a knowledge that is not merely natural, but is a revelation specially given by the Father (cf 11,27). Now, if it were a question of recognizing Jesus' role of Messiah or his sonship in a general sense, there would be no need of such a special revelation, since such a recognition was already spoken of previously, but Matthew now presents Peter's confession as something new.

The question is what did Peter himself understand when he spoke those words. Did he speak them as they are given in Matthew, since Mark and Luke mention only the words about the messianic character of Jesus without any special praise of Peter on the part of Christ?

The mind of Matthew himself is clear, for he also includes in his gospel the clear answer of Jesus before the high priests and his condemnation for blasphemy, a passage which illustrates the same thing as Peter's confession.

> ... "Tell us whether you are the Christ, the son of God." Jesus said to them, "It is true." ... "He has uttered blasphemy. ... He deserves death" (Mt 26,63-67).[221]

The synoptic evangelists, therefore, witness to the belief that Jesus was like God and that Jesus declared himself to be equal with the Father. The following sections will show that the gospels in this aspect faithfully attest to the historical Jesus.

B. Testimony of the Early Church Before the Gospels

1) In the Fifties, A.D., Paul Testified to the Divinity of Christ.

In Tit 2,13, Rom 9,5 (cf also Heb 1,8-9 and 2 Pet 1,1, 1 Jn 5,20) Jesus is called God. Since many critics (and with them R. Bultmann) consider these passages as deutero-pauline texts, it is not certain that Paul actually called Jesus θεός, and if he did, he did so only as an exception. These texts, however, reflect the belief of the early Church. Even if the letter to the Hebrews is only indirectly Paul's work, it must have been written before 67, and so before the gospels. It bears witness to the Christological paradox that Jesus is at the same time with God and yet is himself God, not in the sense of a king, cf Ps 45,7, but in the sense of God, the Creator, since the author transfers to him what the Old Testament said about God, namely the creation of heaven and earth (1,8-12).

For Paul Jesus is the Lord, the Lord of Lords (1 Tim 6,15), in whom the whole fullness of God's nature lives embodied (Col 2,9). He sits at the right hand of God (Col 3,1; Eph 1,20) and so Paul prays to him as to his Lord (2 Cor 12,8; 1 Thess 3,12; 2 Thess 3,2). In 1 Cor 8,6 the preexistent activity of Christ in the creation is mentioned and in 1 Cor 16,22 he is expected to come back again as the Lord (cf Rev 22,20). Paul therefore confessed Christ's preexistence in the form of God and believed in the divinity of Christ [222] in the fifties, A.D.

It is certain that Paul did not invent this belief in Christ's divinity, since he quotes confessional formulas (Rom 10,9; 1 Cor 12,3; 1 Tim 3,16 with Eph 5,14, etc.) which were already in liturgical use in the Church before Paul. Faith in the "Kyrios" had started before Paul who learned it from the tradition handed on to him by the earlier Church.[223]

2) About 40 A.D. Christological Hymns of the Primitive Church Testified that Jesus Had Been Worshiped as God

Although we find these hymns in the letters of St. Paul, they are more ancient than the letters themselves. They are most likely hymns of the primitive Church of Palestine and Antioch. Paul takes them up into his own letters in the form of previously composed literary units. We wish to examine two of these hymns which provide an amazingly concrete description of the mysterious union of the incarnation. One of these is found in Phil 2,6-11 and the other in 1 Tim 3,16. There is a third Christological hymn in Col 1,15-20, which stresses that Christ is the Creator of all the heavenly powers and the head of the Church having primacy over all things, since the pleroma, the fullness of God, dwells within him. This latter, however, is more probably a hymn composed by Paul himself, therefore we will not consider it here.

a. *Phil 2,6-11*

6   Though he possessed the nature of God ($\mu o \rho \varphi \acute{\eta}$)
       he did not grasp at the equality with God,
7a   but emptied himself ($\dot{\epsilon} \chi \acute{\epsilon} \nu \omega \sigma \epsilon \nu$)
       to assume the nature of a slave, ($\mu o \rho \varphi \acute{\eta} \ \delta o \acute{\upsilon} \lambda o \upsilon$)
7b   became like other men ($\dot{\epsilon} \nu \ \dot{o} \mu o \iota \acute{\omega} \mu a \tau \iota$)
       and in external appearances ($\sigma \chi \acute{\eta} \mu a \tau \iota$) he was found as a man;

8   he humbled himself
and became obedient unto death,
death on the cross.

9   Therefore God has so greatly exalted him,
and given him the name above all other names,

10   so that at the name of Jesus everyone should kneel,
in heaven and on earth and in the underworld,

11   and everyone should acknowledge
Jesus Christ as Lord,
in the glory of God the Father.

In this passage we can discover the characteristic marks of a hymn. The division into stanzas, the rhythm, parallel structure and use of ideas and words found in other hymns, etc. indicate that this is truly a hymn. Further, there is a noticeable difference between these verses and the other parts of the letter. In these verses we find a type of dogmatic summary of the redemptive work of Christ, whereas the letter in itself is not dogmatic. It does not deal with any problem of faith, but has an entirely personal character. Paul is writing to his favorite community recommending humility to them. In a letter of this sort, it is difficult to explain why one passage contains a brief, highly condensed dogmatic formula, unless it is a citation of some text very familiar to the readers. [224] Although only verses 6-8 support the lesson on humility, Paul added the other three verses probably because he did not want to destroy the unity of the hymn.

The author of this hymn does not seem to be Paul, since Paul never speaks of Jesus as the servant of God, although he sometimes refers to himself as such. The terms ἁρπαγμός, χαταχθόνιος are hapax legomena in the New Testament. Εὑρεθεὶς with ὡς is neither a Pauline nor a Greek construction. Εἶναι ἴσα Θεῷ has only one parallel case in the NT, namely in Jn 5,18. Similarly, χενόω and μορφή have an uncommon sense in Phil 2,6-7. [225]

How can we know now that this hymn is a very ancient, pre-Pauline hymn? Its Christology is an ancient Palestinian Christology, very different from the later Christology found in the teachings of Paul and John who were probably influenced by hellenistic thinking. Here the incarnation is considered as a humiliation, an "emptying out," whereas in later writings the taking on of a human nature by the Son of God is considered as a glorifica-

tion and exaltation of human nature and of the whole of humanity. Further, the death of Christ is not yet considered as a source
of salvation with its expiatory effect for the remission of our sins
(the core of Paul's Christology, cf., 1 Cor 15,3-5; 1 Thess 5,10; Gal
1,4; 2,20; 3,13; Rom 8,3.32; 14,15; Col 1,24; Eph 5,2.25, etc.)
but only as a source of the exaltation of Christ as Lord. This
theology is similar to the one which appears in the early kerygmatic sermons (Acts 2,23-24; 3,13-14; 4,10; 5,30). Christ is the
Lord not only of the faithful Church, but of the whole cosmos,
divided into three different levels: heaven, earth and the underworld. Finally, the exaltation of Christ is expressed by giving Jesus
the name above all others. This theology of giving names is typical
Hebrew thinking and it is not found elsewhere in Paul's writings.
Instead of "in the name of Jesus" he used to say "in the name of
Christ" (cf 2 Thess 3,6; I Cor 5,4; 6,11; Col 3,17; Eph 5,20).
Therefore, the hymn may have been composed in Palestine or
Syrian Antioch by a predominantly Jewish community in the
early forties.

Meaning of the Hymn

The same noun μορφή is used in each phrase: μορφή Θεοῦ,
μορφή δούλου. It means the internal foundation, the basic source of
the external manifestation of a thing. From a study of the terms
σχῆμα and its derivates (e.g. 1 Cor 7,31; Rom 12,2; 1 Pet 1,14)
and μορφή (Rom 8,29; Phil 3,10; 2 Cor 3,18) as well as of their
distinction (e.g. Rom 12,2; Phil 3,21), J. R. Lightfoot concluded
that "in the passage under consideration the μορφή is contrasted
with the σχῆμα as that which is intrinsic and essential with that
which is accidental and outward. And the three clauses imply
respectively the true divine nature of our Lord (μορφή Θεοῦ), the
true human nature (μορφή δούλου), and the externals of human
nature (σχήατι ὡς ἄνθρωπος). [226] The meaning of μορφή is very
close to the meaning of "nature," as many translators put it.
Μορφή in Koine Greek, under the influence of philosophy, took
on the meaning of nature.

However, we do not need to assume that the hymn derived
from any philosophical consideration. It seems more likely that it
was derived from the biblical tradition on man created in the
image (εἶδος) of God on *kabôd*, the glory of God, and on the Song
of the Servant of Yahweh. [227] As *kabôd*, the glory of God, so

μορφή refers to divine holiness and power, or something intrinsic to God, i.e. what makes God to be God, but manifested externally. That Jesus possessed (ὑπάρχων) the μορφή Θεοῦ, means that he had what makes God to be God and consequently the right to be manifested as such. Indeed he did not and could not consider his divine status, to which the divine cult of adoration is due, as something foreign (*res rapta* or *rapienda*),[228] but as something justly belonging to him. He nevertheless did not wish to manifest his divinity in the manner of the divine majesty but rather his humanity in the manner of a slave, the condition of human existence after sin. This latter, however, was σχῆμα, something transitory (see the frame of this world in 1 Cor 7,31) since after his death, Jesus is glorified and given the name "Lord" and the adoration of all creatures.

The origin of the hymn is disputable. Its teaching, however, seems to be clear: those who used the hymn believed in the divinity of Jesus.

b. 1 Tim 3,16

This hymn describes faith in the divinity of Jesus in terms of a ceremonial enthronement of a king:

> Obviously great is the mystery
> of our religion!
>> He was revealed in flesh,
>> vindicated by the Spirit,
>> seen by the angels,
>> proclaimed among the pagans,
>> believed in throughout the world,
>> taken up into glory.

The structure of the hymn follows as a model the enthronement rite used in Egypt and Mesopotamia. [229] The ceremony consisted of three parts: (1) Elevation of the new monarch to divine dignity; (2) his presentation among the gods of the national pantheon; (3) enthronement or accession to the supreme power of the state. A similar structure can be found even in the first chapter of the letter to the Hebrews.

This hymn probably is later than that in Philippians 2,6, and comes from the Antioch church. It does not contain Hebraic theology about the name of God. It speaks of nations, the universal extension of faith, and Jesus' divinity in profane rather than biblical terms.

The meaning of the hymn is that through the mediation of his holy humanity, especially through his death and resurrection, Jesus' divinity is revealed to all mankind. Following the structure of the enthronement rite the divinization of Jesus is progressively described by three steps.

(1) *Elevation of Jesus* is expressed by his being "revealed in flesh" and "vindicated by the Spirit." His revelation in flesh implies his death. Thus in Mark's gospel Jesus is revealed through his death: "This man surely was the Son of God" (Mk 15,39). According to John his glorification takes place in his being raised up on the cross (Jn 8,28; 12,32.34). As his revelation in flesh indicates his death, so his vindication by the spirit means his resurrection. The Paraclete is the one who does convince the world concerning Jesus' going to the Father (Jn 16,10).

(2) *Christ's presentation* is described by his being seen through the angels and by his proclamation among the pagans through the preaching of the apostles.

(3) Finally *his enthronement* as God is described first in terms of a faith-acceptance of the universal Christian belief among both Jews and Gentiles, second in terms of Christ's entrance into heaven: "believed throughout the world, taken up in glory."

This hymn was most likely a baptismal hymn. The first section of it is found in Eph 5,14. Thus, the newly baptized will be introduced into the mystery of Christ. Through the following hymn he confesses his belief in the exaltation of Jesus to the right hand of the Father, in his assumption into the *"kabôd"* Yahweh, the glory of the Father.[230]

From these two hymns we can conclude that before Paul's letters about 40 A.D. belief in Christ's divinity was found already present in the widely scattered churches. The belief was expressed in a formulation that was fixed, but with variation according to the practice and character of individual churches, as their creeds and liturgical cults [231] reflect it.

As a result of our analysis we can say that the Church's present faith in the divinity of Jesus can be traced back to within ten years after Jesus' death, an extremely short time for the divinization process of a hero. The question is now, how did this faith in the divinity of Jesus witnessed to by the gospels, the letters of Paul, and the ancient hymns of the pre-Pauline Church begin? Who did start this belief? Some nameless, anonymous community? Or did the historical Jesus have something to do with it? Did he express something similar concerning himself to his friends?

3. THE HISTORICAL JESUS' AWARENESS OF GOD'S RELATION TO HIM

Before we begin our analysis, we must clarify one point. When we confess that Jesus is God, grammatically we do nothing else than apply a metaphysical notion of God, or perhaps only the technical term "God" or *theos,* to Jesus. Now we have to realize that this was impossible for Jesus. By reflecting upon the mystery of his being he could not conceive and express God's relation to himself by joining the Greek term *theos* to his "I." He could not do this for the evident reason that he was neither thinking and speaking in Greek, nor could he translate the sentence, *ego eimi theos,* into Hebrew for his interlocutors.

Since "Yahweh" was not a specific name of the divinity, like *theos* for the Greeks, but the personal name of the Father, Jesus could neither think nor say that he was Yahweh since he was not the Father. In Hebrew it was unthinkable to use the term "Yahweh" as a predicate in a composition with other subjects, like the Greek *theos,* which could be equally predicated of different subjects like Zeus, Apollo, Hermes, Hades, etc.

To explain his mysterious Within, the historical Jesus could not use either *El* or *Elohim,* originally specific names of the divine species. For although in earlier terminology *El* had been used as a personal name of Yahweh, later, in the time of Jesus, it had already a pagan idolatrous implication. In addition to Yahweh, other pagan gods were called *Elohim,* and as such were non-existent, which Jesus could not suggest about himself by using this name. Since the name *Elohim* recalled so much idolatry, the Jews themselves tried to suppress the use of this term in regard to their true God, Yahweh, beginning from the third century B.C.

Moreover, by saying that he was *Elohim,* Jesus would not have revealed very much about himself. In the sense of a proverb of the Talmud, "Man's šeliah is, as it were, himself." Thus the emissary or representative of Yahweh was considered as if he were Yahweh, himself, and so sometimes called by the name of Elohim. Not only judges (Ps 58,1; Ex 21,6; 22,6-8) but kings also could be addressed as god: "Your throne, O god, is forever . . . therefore has God, your God anointed you" (Ps 45,6-7). In the same sense the Messiah is called god (*El*) by Isaiah (9,6) as are the priests and judges by the author of Deuteronomy (19,17). This meaning is used in the NT too. According to Jn 10,34-35 all those to whom God's message was addressed were called gods. Similarly Moses acted the part of God in regard to Aaron and to Pharaoh, because he inspired and commanded what Aaron and Pharaoh had to say or to do (Ex 4,16-Yahweh; 7,1-Elohim). In the messianic time, the house of David would be like God, because it would act like the angel of the Lord before the inhabitants of Jerusalem (Zech 12,8; cf also 2 Sam 14,17; 1 Sam 28,13).

Thus, by saying he is El or Elohim, Jesus would have revealed nothing unusual in his personality.[232]

Besides these linguistic difficulties there was also the characteristic Jewish social mentality which made Jesus' situation much more difficult than that of his early Church if he were to manifest his personality's exclusively unique and irreducible greatness and novelty.

If he is not Yahweh, and yet he is a descendant of the Patriarchs, the Fathers of Israel, Jesus, like any Jew, could not expect to be recognized by his people in any other way than as someone inferior to any of his forefathers. The prevailing social view of the historical milieu could not but inspire in Jesus a role necessarily subordinate to that of the great men of Israel. It is more than probable that the Jews also acknowledged the persuasion of most archaic peoples, according to which the older one is, the greater he is, since he is thus closer to the Beginning, to God, who is called usually the most Ancient, the Ancient One (Dan 7,9.13.22; cf the One who lives in the beginning: Gen. 1,1-2; Jn 1,1—and for ever: Rev 4,8.10; 1,8). It seems therefore, that if the historical Jesus wanted to announce the irreducible unique greatness of his Within, he had to question not only the fatherhood of his father, Joseph, but that of all great men of Israel and to extol Yahweh as his only Father. He had to react and rebel against his forefathers and somehow emancipate himself from the hindering genealogical consequences. If he wanted to be really unique, he had to put himself somehow over all great men of the Old Testament. He had to be more than Jonah (Mt 12,41-42), more than David (Mt 22,43-45), more than Moses (Mt 5,21ff Jn 5,46), more than Abraham (Jn 8,56-58) and even more than any created being who ever lived and thus to come to the idea of preexistence before all created beings (Jn 8,58). Genealogical ascendence as a measure of personal greatness explains why some heroes are presented without geneology and why primitive peoples thought of their God through the idea of preexistence, i.e. as the most ancient of all, and not through the more sophisticated notion of "pure actuality" or that of "absolute consciousness", etc.

All this supposition is further confirmed by the NT (cf Mt 13,54-58; Mk 6,1-6; Lk 4,16-30) when the Jews, especially Jesus' own townfolk, presume that they know him, since they know his father, mother, brothers and sisters. To know someone in their view was equal to knowing his ancestors. And this was so true that the knowledge of the fathers already gave some sort of superiority in regard to all of their descendants, who had to respect and submit themselves not only to their fathers, but to all who knew their fathers. Thus it seems that the only escape from the corresponding subordination was the negation of the fatherhood of that man who was known as father and to acclaim a father who was not known to the interlocutor (cf Mt 11,27; Lk 10,22). If Jesus was to save his exclusive uniqueness, in his discussion with the Jews, he must have been forced to affirm the unique fatherhood of God and an unique sonship for himself, since any brotherhood would have jeopardized the uniqueness of his personality.

In this historical context the use of the term "Son" was fitting for Jesus but not for his followers, who could not call him simply "Son" without indicating that Jesus was their son. To avoid this kind of misunderstanding the best way seemed to be to transform Jesus' term "Son" into "Son of God." This was the only possible rendering of Jesus' idea, if it was to be pronounced by somebody other than Jesus.

Thus, the historical situation had to influence the awareness of Jesus so much that in a different social and historical milieu he would have expressed his uniqueness in another way. Similarly the difference in the situation had to bring about a different Christology for the Church. The pre-paschal *ipsissima verba* had to be transformed by the Church in order to communicate faithfully

Jesus' self-understanding and to avoid misunderstanding prompted by changing times.

Thus the absence of a metaphysical notion of God in Jewish tradition can be considered as an inspiring incentive as well as a hindrance to the human mind of Jesus in his quest to indicate the uniqueness and everlasting originality of his role and personality. It can be considered a hindrance because it seemed impossible for him to express his exclusive greatness among men in a way understandable to everybody. But at the same time it can be considered as an inspiring incentive for Jesus to invent a notion which would provoke in the Jewish mind a similar reaction to the one provoked by the term Θεός in the Greek mind.

This is the complexity of the situation in which the historical Jesus had to find himself if he wanted to express that he was something more than any of his predecessors. But did the historical Jesus think that he had an irreducible uniqueness? Was he aware of the everlasting originality of his role and of his personality? We have seen the way he would have proceeded had he had this awareness. But did he have it? Did he really have the problem which we have just outlined? Did he solve it? And how? Now by studying Jesus' message about the kingdom of God, and his sayings concerning the Son of Man and the Son, we will be able to see that it was not historically impossible that Jesus did think and act the way the early Church believed that he did think and act.[233]

A. The Historical Jesus' Message: The Kingdom of God is at Hand

In the synoptic gospels there is a proclamation which implies Jesus' awareness of his exclusive uniqueness. This proclamation is the "kingdom of God is at hand."

According to the synoptic gospels the kingdom of God was the theme of Jesus' preaching (Mk 1,15; Mt 4,17; Lk 4,43; 16,16) as well as that of his deeds (Lk 11,20; Mt 11,5; 12,28; cf 9,35).[234]

1) The Use of the Term "Basileia" and its Authenticity

"The kingdom of God" as an expression occurs 139 times in the NT books.[235] One hundred and four of these 139 occurrences are in the synoptic gospels and 35 in the rest of the New Testament. Its distribution is just the opposite of the distribution of the term "ecclesia" which occurs only three times in the synoptics (Mt 16,18; 18,17 a.b.) and 111 times in the other books of the New Testament. The kingdom of God is, therefore, evidently a synoptic notion. It is interesting that besides general nouns and names like "man," "Jesus," "son," "God," "Lord," "Father," "heaven," "disciples" and "crowd," the "kingdom" is the term most frequently used by the synoptics. It seems that all that was brought by Jesus is summoned up in the synoptics in the concept of the kingdom of God. What "gospel," "faith" or "life" is for Paul and John, the "kingdom of God" is for the synoptic gospels.

The statistical divergency which exists between the usage of the term Church and "kingdom of God" might suggest already that the kingdom of God is rather a pre-paschal term. The early post-paschal Christians preferred such terms as "Church", "community" or "faithful" to "basileia."

But there is another line of evidence which indicates that the kingdom of God is not a post-paschal belief. After the death of Jesus the paschal preaching moved from the topic of "kingdom of God" to the proclamation of Jesus' resurrection. The great preaching theme of the post-paschal community was not any longer the kingdom of God, but Christ and his resurrection, a theme which seems to be identified with the kingdom of God.

The pre-gospel tradition already shows the identification of the kingdom of God with Jesus' personality. [236] There are several passages where Jesus' name is used in place of the kingdom of God. For example, Mk 11,10 says that blessed is the kingdom of David. Meanwhile, in the parallel passage of Mt 21,9, the kingdom of David is replaced by the Son of David and in Lk 19,38 by the term "King." [237] Furthermore, the expressions "on account of me" "on account of the kingdom of God" and "for the name of Christ" are interchangeable (Mk 10,29; Lk 18,29). In passages where Mark and Luke speak of the kingdom of God, Matthew speaks of the Son of Man (Mk 9,1; Lk 9,27; Mt 16,28). The people who are waiting for the kingdom of God are waiting for the Son of Man (Lk 12,40; Mk 15,43). Finally, sayings referring to the messianic kingdom were said to be fulfilled in the person of Christ (Mt 11,5; Lk 4,21; 7,22).

The transition from the kingdom of God to the identification of the kingdom of God with Jesus appears especially in the primitive preaching related in the Acts of the Apostles. According to some passages of Acts the theme of the preaching of Philip as well as that of Paul still seems to be double: the kingdom of God and the Lord Jesus Christ (Acts 8,12; 28,23.31). But this double feature of the kerygmatic preaching is not too general. Most passages give only one topic, namely Jesus Christ (2,32-36; 4,10; 5,42; 8,5; 9,22; 10,36; 13,33; 14,22; 19,8; 20,25). This identification might have been promoted by two considerations: 1) the kingdom of God was believed to have been inaugurated in the life of Jesus; 2) after the paschal event the first Christians had to realize that the kingdom after all was not restored to Israel (cf Acts 1,6).

In view of these changes in the preaching's central theme, we have to admit that the kingdom of God is pre-paschal and, as such, goes back to the Christology of the historical Jesus himself. As a matter of fact, it is generally admitted by the critics that Jesus preached the kingdom of God. [238] A further consideration, however, perhaps will be not entirely superfluous. For the analysis of the different sayings concerning the kingdom of God in NT will further confirm that the kingdom of God belongs to a pre-paschal Christology.

2) The Sayings Concerning the Kingdom of God and Their Authenticity

a) Basileia Sayings Outside the Synoptic Gospels

As we have said there are 35 occurrences outside the synoptic gospels. In the letters of Paul we have 14 instances. Ten of the 14 refer to the eschatological kingdom of God which as connected with the second coming of Jesus (1 Cor 15,20; Eph 5,5; 2 Tim 4,1; 4,18) cannot be inherited by the unrighteous, by the impure, or by doers of the works of flesh (1 Cor 6,9.10; 15,24; Gal 5,21; 1 Thess 2,12; 2 Thess 1,5). The kingdom of God and the kingdom of Christ is the same one kingdom (Eph 5,5).

There are only four instances which indicate the kingdom of God is already present. The kingdom of God does not mean food and drink but righteousness and peace, joy and the Holy Spirit (Rom 14,17). It consists not in talk, but in power (1 Cor 4,20). It is forgiveness of sins and redemption (Col 1,13) and gospel (Col 4,11 with Phil 4,3, Rom 16,12 and Eph 6,21).

In the letter to the Hebrews it occurs twice and means the eschatological future kingdom (Heb 1,8 with Ps 45,6-7; 12,28).

The same future eschatological kingdom is meant also in James 2,5 and 2 Pet 1,11.

In the book of Revelation the future eschatological kingdom occurs three times (1,9; 11,15; 12,10); the idea of the kingdom of God as present occurs twice with an unexpected development, i.e., the identification of the kingdom with the believing Christians (1,6; 5,10; cf Ex 19,6 with 1 Pet 2,9). In John's gospel there are three instances of the eschatological kingdom (18,36 a.b.c.) and two cases of the presence of the kingdom which Jesus' followers have to enter (3,3.5).

In the Acts of the Apostles the kingdom of God occurs always as a theme of preaching, either with (8,12; 28,23.31) or without (14,22; 19,8; 20,25) an explicit parallelism to Jesus, the risen Christ. At the beginning of the Acts, as in the synoptics, Jesus is presented before the resurrection as preaching about the kingdom of God (1,3). Thus, the continuity between the risen Christ and the Galilean Jesus is expressed by Luke in a literary way. In the Acts there is no reference to the coming kingdom.

b) Basileia Sayings in the Synoptic Gospels

We can divide all the basileia sayings which occur in the synoptic gospels into six categories: (1) sayings concerning the actual presence of the kingdom of God; (2) sayings concerning the actual preaching of the kingdom of God; (3) sayings concerning the entry into the kingdom of God; (4) sayings concerning the parables about the kingdom of God; (5) sayings concerning the imminent coming of the kingdom of God; (6) sayings concerning the future final eschatological fulfillment of the kingdom of God.

(1) Sayings Concerning the Actual Presence of the Kingdom of God

There are 12 occurrences: 5 in Matthew, 6 in Luke and 1 in Mark. The "here and now" of the kingdom of God is expressed in four different ways:

i)   by the aor. ἤγγικεν (Mk 1,15; Mt 3,2; 4,17; 10,7; Lk 10,9) which means that the kingdom of God has already arrived and it is here;

ii) by the aor. ἔφθασεν (Mt 12,28; Lk 11,20) which means that it has come upon those who are talking with Jesus;

iii) by ἐντός ὑμῶν (Lk 17,21 see ibid 20 a.b.) i.e. the kingdom is already among Jesus' listeners;

iv) by "since the time of John the Baptist;" before him the law and the prophets were preached but after him the kingdom of God (Lk 16,16; Mt 11,12; notice also the ἕως ἄρτι "until now" of Mt 11,12 and the Elias ἤδη ἦλθεν "has already" come in Mt 17,12 with Mal 3,23).

(2) Sayings Concerning the Actual Preaching of the Kingdom of God

We have 11 cases: 5 in Matthew and 6 in Luke. All these occurrences indicate the presence of the kingdom of God. The kingdom is to be preached because it is here. It is preached by Jesus (Mt 4,23; Lk 4,43; Mt 9,35; Lk 8,1; Lk 9,11), by the disciples (Mt 10,7; Lk 9,2), by Jesus' followers (Lk 9,60). It is to be preached in general now (Lk 16,16) and everywhere (Mt 24,14). For this reason it has been given to the disciples to know the secrets of the kingdom of God (Mt 13,11).

(3) Sayings Concerning the Entry into the Kingdom of God

These sayings are the most numerous; half of Mark's basileia sayings belong to this group. There are 38 cases altogether: 21 in Mt, 7 in Mk and 10 in Lk. Since entry was required of those who were listening to the preaching of Jesus and his disciples, these sayings are also related to the presence of the kingdom of God. Most of these sayings indicate the conditions for being admitted, or the kind of people who are to be allowed to enter the kingdom of God.

The kingdom of God belongs: to those who are like children (Mt 19,14; Mk 10,14.15; Lk 18,16.17; Mt 18,1.4); to the poor (Mt 5,3; Lk 6,20); to the little flock (Lk 12,32); to those who are persecuted for it (Mt 5,10) as well as to the men of violence (Mt 11,12b); to those who love God and their neighbor (Mk 12,34) and whose justice exceeds that of the scribes and pharisees (Mt 5,20); to those who do the will of the Father (Mt 7,21a.21b) and produce fruit of it (Mt 21,43); and finally to those scribes who bring out of their treasure what is new and old (Mt 13,52) by teaching the commandments but especially by observing them (Mt 5,19a.19b). Tax collectors and harlots will go in (Mt 22,31) while the pharisees will not enter and will even hinder others from entering (Mt 23,13). The real power of loosing and binding is given to Peter, who has the keys of the kingdom (Mt 16,19). For the rich man it is difficult to enter (Mt 19,23.24; Mk 10,23.24.25; Lk 18,24.25). It demands sacrifices (Mk 9,47; cf Mt 18,9) as well as an unhesitating decision (Lk 9,62). Sacrifice for the kingdom, however, will be well rewarded (Lk 18,29; cf Mt 19,29, where Jesus and in Mk 10,29, where the gospel takes the place of the kingdom of Mt). The kingdom of God has to be sought as the first thing (Mt 6,33; Lk 12,31). Continence is of no value except in view of the kingdom (Mt 21,12), where the least is greater than John the Baptist, the greatest among those born of women (Mt 11,11; Lk 7,28).

(4) Sayings Concerning the Parables about the Kingdom of God
There are 22 sayings concerning the parables about the kingdom of God: 13 in Matthew, 3 in Mark and 6 in Luke. The basic idea of all of these parables is that the kingdom has begun already but is still growing towards its complete fulfillment. These sayings stand midway between the sayings concerning the actual presence of the kingdom and the sayings concerning its future coming. Nevertheless, they are to be counted more properly among the sayings concerning the present kingdom, since they indicate without doubt the inauguration of the kingdom, which has taken place already and has begun to develop.
There are 14 parables of the kingdom of God: the sower (Mt 13,19; Mk 4,11; Lk 8,10), the mustard seed (Mt 13,31; Mk 4,30; Lk 18,13), the leaven (Mt 13,33; Lk 13,20), the wedding feast (Mt 22,2) and the great banquet (Lk 14,15), the weed (Mt 13,24.38.41), the treasure (Mt 13,34), the pearl (Mt 13,44), the net (Mt 13,47), the unforgiving debtor (Mt 18,23), the vineyard laborers (Mt 20,1), the talents (Lk 19,11), the fig tree (Lk 21,31.32), the seed growing by itself (Mk 4,26), and, finally, the wise waiting bridesmaids (Mt 25,1).

(5) Sayings Concerning the Imminent Coming of the Kingdom of God
We have seven sayings in this group: 1 in Matthew, 2 in Mark and 4 in Luke. These sayings seem to indicate that the final eschatological fulfillment of the kingdom will take place, at the

latest, during the lifetime of Jesus' contemporaries. Jesus' listeners will see the kingdom of God with power (Mk 9,1; Mt 16,28; notice that Mt 16,28 has there the Son of Man coming in his kingdom). Jesus' generation will not pass away till the kingdom of God will take place (Lk 21,31.32; the "Son of Man" has replaced the "kingdom of God" in Mk 13,30 and Mt 24,34). People believed that the kingdom was to appear immediately (Lk 9,11) and seemingly Joseph of Arimathea was also hoping to see it (Mk 15,43; Lk 21,31; the parallel text in Mt 27,57 says of Joseph that he was a disciple of Jesus). Finally, the angel Gabriel announced to Mary that Jesus was to reign over the house of Jacob and that of his kingdom there would be no end (Lk 1,33).

(6) Sayings Concerning the Eschatological Fulfillment of the Kingdom of God

We list here the prayers for the kingdom to come (Mat 6,20; Lk 11,2), the imminent banquet near at hand for Jesus (Mt 26,29; Mk 14,25; Lk 22,18) in which the disciples will also share with him (Lk 22,29.30) as well as the two sons of Zebedee (Mt 20,21; Mk 10,37 gives "glory" instead of the "kingdom") and the good thief (Lk 23,42). Besides these, there will also come many others from east and west to participate in the same banquet (Mt 8,11.12; Lk 13,28.29). But above all we have to list here the final judgment at the end of the world (Mt 25,34). Thus we have 14 instances: 6 in Matthew, 1 in Mark and 7 in Luke.

The purpose of the classification we have just made was evidently not to establish the authenticity of each single saying. As a matter of fact, it would be very difficult and in the most cases impossible to distinguish between the redactional use of the basileia and the original use on Jesus' lips. There is only one point which we wanted to show, namely, that in the synoptic gospels the sayings concerning the presence of the kingdom of God outnumber the sayings concerning the future final coming of the kingdom of God by 83 to 21 (in Mt by 44 to 7, in Mk by 11 to 3 and in Lk by 28 to 11). Meanwhile outside the synoptic gospels the sayings concerning the future coming of the kingdom outnumber the others by 19 to 16.

As a result we can say that the Church did reinterpret the idea of the kingdom of God as far as the post-paschal community discovered the double coming of Jesus. But precisely in the light of this happening it seems that there is a close relationship between the historical Jesus' own personal presence and activity on the one hand, and the inauguration of the kingdom of God on the other. It seems clear enough that the pre-paschal community lived much more with the idea of the presence of the kingdom of God than the post-pachal Church. Therefore, we can say that the actual establishment of the kingdom of God was the basic idea of the historical Jesus and with this term he wanted to manifest his own role as well as the mystery of his Within. For it meant the purpose and the meaning of his life.

If this is true, the main question to ask is what Jesus could have understood and meant by saying that the kingdom of God was at hand? What kind of relation between himself and Yahweh did this idea provoke in Jesus' awareness? Or in other words, what kind of awareness impelled Jesus to formulate his message, and how could he have thought that the kingdom of God had been established with him and through him?

3) The Historical Jesus' Awareness Involved in His Message, 'The Kingdom of God is at Hand.'

a) The Notion of the Kingdom of God in the Old Testament

The kingdom of God in itself is not a new term of the NT. Although the God of the patriarchs is never presented as king, the title had been applied to Yahweh already in the period of the judges (Judg 8,23; Deut 33,5). Most of the references to Yahweh as king, naturally, are from the period of the kingdom. From the postexilic period we have even the expression, kingdom of the Lord (1 Chron 28,5; 2 Chron 13,8), and the kingdom of God (Wis 10,10).

Now, the Hebrew *malkut* had two meanings: reign (kingship, sovereignty) and realm (kingdom in a territorial sense). The Jewish tradition admitted God's kingdom in Israel in both senses. [239] By virtue of the covenant Israel became Yahweh's people, Yahweh's personal property (cf Ex 6,6) defended and guided by the Lord. From this idea it followed that the final definitive form of the kingdom of Israel would be established not by men, but by a divine intervention, which might shake the very foundations of the world (cf Is 24,18-23; Zech 14,1-21, etc).

In the sixth chapter we saw that the fundamental idea and meaning of Yahweh's different interventions was that he would come to dwell among Israel in a special way and that his presence would mean salvation for Israel and through Israel, the whole human race (cf Jer 3,17ff). All interventions aimed at this final supreme intervention, which being final, would surpass all other previous interventions and would never be surpassed by any new intervention, since it was definitively final. In a different fashion, after the new covenant, Israel will have no need of any other intervention since God will forever dwell in the midst of Israel. This will be the consummation of the history begun by Adam's sin. Though it might be exposed to hardship for awhile (cf Dan 7,21,25), it will, nevertheless, endure forever.

b) The Historical Jesus' Understanding of the Kingdom of God.

In this historical context the proclamation of the kingdom of God now at hand has a special relevance and depth. If the historical Jesus, after having known the books of the Old Testament, dared to proclaim the kingdom of God as present, it implies the presumption and, consequently, the awareness that in him and through him Yahweh visited his people in a supreme way and Yahweh's supreme presence among Israel was realized. When Jesus said that the kingdom of heaven had arrived with him, he announced that there was a time when God visited his people in such a manner and dwelled in the midst of Israel in so intimate a way, that it surpassed all previous presences and was a way in fact never to be surpassed. In other words the proclamation of the presence of the kingdom of God could imply in Jesus' human mind an awareness that through him God had come to Israel and was present in its midst in an absolutely unique and irreducible way. Thus, through the expression, "the kingdom of God is at hand" he could affirm not only his messianic character, but first of all the absolutely unique and irreducible union of God and himself. If the historical Jesus proclaimed the presence of the kingdom of God, he had to have a consciousness that God was united with him in a way which he had never been with any other man. The union of God with him surpassed all other types of union between God and men in history.

Since God's mysterious union with him eminently surpassed all judaic figures and symbols of Yahweh's dwelling among the Israelites, Jesus had to acknowledge his superiority to Abraham, Moses, David, Solomon, Elias, John the Baptist, and all great men of the Old Testament, and even the temple. And this might be the most ancient Christology, the Christology of the historical Jesus himself which offered the most simple and most Jewish way of manifesting who he was. This idea could lead Jesus' human mind to the idea of his preexistence as well as that of his unique sonship to the Father. This may be the explanation of why he always relates himself to the Son of Man of Daniel, the last and final symbol of the establishment of the kingdom of God in the Old Testament. Since he could not identify himself with the other antecedent symbols of Yahweh's presence in Israel, he took up the symbolic figure of the Son of Man surrounded by the cloud, symbol of Yahweh's presence in the desert leading his people during the day. This symbol indicated the final and definitive establishment of Yahweh's final and supreme engagement with Israel much more than any other previous symbol. From here it can also be understood that when people were asking for the messianic goods, Jesus insisted always upon the fundamental meaning of his Messianism, i.e. the special presence of Yahweh which he brought to Israel. And again this is why to the historian he always appears a very religious man filled with God, who speaks of God as God *the* Father.

Thus the historical situation and his interlocutor's connatural terminology could lead Jesus to formulate the mystery of this Within by the term "the kingdom of God." By this formulation he could provoke in the mind of his contemporaries the same reaction which the term *theos* would have provoked in the Greek mind. His followers indeed related him to God in the most intimate and absolutely unique way of applying to him the terms "Son of God," *kyrios* and *Theos,* and later in the Council of Chalcedon by calling this relation the hypostatic union.

The concept "kingdom of God," the confrontation with the great men of Israel, and superiority to them, indicated by an exclusively unique sonship and by the symbol of the Son of Man, were very fitting in the social, historical situation of the historical Jesus, though they were inadequate for the Christology of a post-paschal community. For the post-paschal community these concepts did not seem to indicate the exclusively unique union of God with Jesus sufficiently enough. The Church had to construct a new Christology with new terms to express adequately for a people in a new historical situation the exclusively unique and irreducible union of God and Jesus.

B. The Historical Jesus' Sayings Concerning the Son of Man

The title "Son of Man" is one of the most debated topics of the New Testament. [240] We will examine its uses and meanings in the New Testament as well as its authenticity.

1) Uses of the Title "Son of Man" and its Authenticity

Ὁ υἱός τοῦ ἀνθρώπου, the Greek expression of the Aramaic *bar nasa,* occurs 82 times in the New Testament. Eighty-one of these occurrences are in the gospels, and only one is in Acts (Acts 7,56). In the gospels Mark uses this title 14 times, [241] Matthew 30 times, [242] Luke 25 times, [243] and John 12 times. [244] Removing all merely parallel passages, the title is used 52 different times. In the book of Revelation the expression, "one like to a man's son," an evident reference to the Old Testament, occurs twice (1,13; 14,14) but the characteristic expression ὁ υἱός τοῦ ἀνθρώπου of the Aramaic tradition is missing there. The author of the letter to the Hebrews applies the term 'υἱὸς' ἀνθρώπου (the article τοῦ is missing) to Jesus in the fuller sense of Ps 8.4 where the literal sense means man in general (Heb 2,6).

Moreover, the occurrences of the title, "Son of Man," are distributed in such a way that they are represented in the triple tradition (i.e. in Mark's gospel with parallel verses from Matthew's and Luke's) as well as in the non-Markan material common to Matthew and Luke (Q) and in the verses belonging exclusively to Luke, Matthew or John. Both the large number of these passages and their wide distribution among the various traditions suggests the authenticity of the title.

That Jesus himself used this phrase is suggested by a remarkable threefold fact.

(a) "Son of Man" is frequently used in the gospels, but is lacking in the rest of the New Testament.

(b) In the gospels it is heard, except in one case, exclusively on the lips of Jesus. The exception however, really proves the normal usage since it is actually a repetition by others, in question form, of what Jesus himself said (Jn 12,34).

(c) Jesus uses the title "Christ" with great circumspection, whereas he frequently and openly throughout his entire life uses the title "Son of Man."

(a) The first fact cannot be explained either by Pauline innovation, for Paul does not use the title,[245] nor by the Christology of the post-paschal community. For the post-paschal Christology is found in the kerygmatic sermons, in the epistles, and in the ancient formulas of faith, or liturgical invocations. In all of these places Jesus is never called "Son of Man" but "Christ," "Lord," "Servant of Yahweh," the "Just One," "the Holy One," "Prince of Life," etc. Only Stephen calls him Son of Man in an evident allusion to Daniel at the end of his long apology before the Sanhedrin (Acts 7,56) for Jesus' Messianism. This might be a literary construction introduced by Luke in his effort to adapt the trial and condemnation of Stephen, the first martyr of the Church, to Jesus' trial before the Sanhedrin (Mk 14,62; Mt 26,64; Lk 22,69). For it is a well-known fact that Luke tried to show in Acts the similarity of the suffering and persecution of the Church to those of Jesus (cf e.g. Acts 9,5; 22,8; 26,15). Now the question arises: Why is this title to be found in the later gospel narrative of the early church and not in the earlier and yet more developed Christological writings? Why did the Church preserve this phrase, if, in the beginning, it did not make use of it? If the title came from the community, in all probability the community would have used it in at least some professions of faith. But it did not happen that way. Why not? The only reason can be that the title, "Son of Man," was no longer useful either for preaching or for liturgical purposes. However, the Church preserved it in the gospel narrative, and only in the gospel narrative, as a historical record of Jesus' sayings.

A. J. B. Higgins and H. M. Teeple, following R. Bultmann,[246] have tried to demonstrate that the saying "Jesus is the Son of Man" originated in the Church independently of the historical Jesus. They suppose that besides "the Jesus is the Lord" Christology there existed in the primitive Church a "Son of Man" Christology. The gospel authors probably attempted to convince readers through the repetitions and through the authority of Jesus (by the use of the saying on the lips of Jesus) that Jesus was the Son of Man. By this title they could easily teach the divine preexistence of Jesus, reminding the readers of the concept of "Son of Man" known from 1 Enoch (chapters 37-71) as a supernatural being existing in heaven with God from before the creation of the world (chap. 48,6; 62,7). By calling Jesus, therefore, the "Son of Man" the Church could indicate his preexistence and his supernatural being as opposed to the time-bound, human qualities of the "sons of men."

However, we have to notice that the "Son of Man" Messiah of the parables of Enoch was not a very well known idea among the Jews. The "Son of Man" was not a judean belief. The Book of Similitudes seems to have been unknown even to the Qumran community. Fragments of every chapter of the Ethiopic Enoch have been found in Qumran, except of the chapters of the Book of the Similitudes. Although this fact does not mean necessarily that the Book of Similitudes was written after Jesus' time and incorporated only into the Ethiopic version (since the Greek versions do not contain the Book of Similitudes), it does prove that the Son of Man Messianism was very little known in the time of Jesus.

Now, considering the catechetical purpose of the gospels and their sources it is difficult to understand why their authors, writing to such diverse peoples, want to demonstrate the truth by an idea which is absolutely irrelevant to most of them. Why do all four (Matthew directed to Palestine Jews, Mark to a predominantly Gentile community, Luke to the Graeco-Roman world, and John to Greek-speaking Diaspora Judaism) use the same unpopular and unknown title without any allusion to the apocalyptical notion of the Son of Man? The notion of "preexistence" concerning the "Son of Man" of the Similitudes [247] is absent in the synoptic gospels. John, himself, indicates the preexistence of Jesus by the term *logos,* rather than by the term Son of Man used by Enoch.

The purpose, moreover, of the gospel authors is evidently not to demonstrate that Jesus is the Son of Man, but that he is the Christ, the Son of God (Mk 1,1; 1,11; 9,7; 15,39; Mt 16,16; Jn 20,31, etc.). If anyone (e.g. R. Bultmann, W. Bousset, or H. M. Teeple) were to maintain that because of Acts 7,56 the idea came from the Hellenistic-Jewish Christians, he would be opposing the historicity of one case outside the gospels to 81 cases in the gospels. It seems more logical to ascribe the one case of Acts 7,56 to Luke's method of literary composition.

Finally, if neither Jesus nor Paul, nor the authors of the gospels (since their sources had it already) introduced this title, the man who conceived the idea of applying the apocalyptical Son of Man concept to Jesus must have been some unknown, obscure anonymous figure of the primitive Church. But how could he remain in complete anonymity and why should one assume the existence of an unknown pioneer of the primitive Church based upon authority of well-known men, when we already know of Jesus of Nazareth? Furthermore, why should one postulate such an unknown pioneer when this would make it more difficult to explain the other two uses of this title in the historical situation of the primitive Church?

(b) The second fact confirming the authenticity of the title is that the phrase "Son of Man" is used almost exclusively on the lips of Jesus and not on those of other men. If the messianic use of the title "Son of Man" had come from Christian usage that usage should have been very popular. Otherwise, the large number of passages employing the title would not have been understood. But if the title were so popular, why did no one except Jesus use the phrase in the gospels? Moreover, since the composers of the gospels wrote down what a large community of the believing Church communicated to them, how could all of these contributors have agreed to put this phrase only on the lips of Jesus? On the other hand it is very understandable that people, not aware of the full meaning of the title, were reluctant to confess Jesus as "Son of Man," and they preferred to use titles like "Son of David," "Master," "Chief" (cf Lk 5,5; 8.24, etc.), "Prophet," "Son of God," etc. which were more common and more apt to express the mystery of Jesus according to their own personal grasp and notion of it.

(c) Finally, there is a third aspect of the title "Son of Man" which also demands an explanation. Why is it that according to the New Testament while Jesus used the title "Christ" with great circumspection yet frequently employed the title "Son of Man," the early Church, on the contrary, used the title "Christ" very frequently and the title "Son of Man" not at all? Χριστός, the Greek version of the Hebrew word "messiah" is used in the New Testament 56 times in the gospels and about 328 times outside the gospels. [248] In the gospels Jesus is called Christ by others (evangelists, Peter, Caiphas, etc.) several times and he seems to agree with it. However, there are only eight occurrences [249] in the gospels where Jesus designates himself by this title. Since these instances reflect the early Christian manner of speaking, it remains uncertain whether Jesus directly designated himself even once by calling himself the Christ. But this is not the point at present. The interesting fact is that even according to the gospels Jesus seems to use the title "Christ" very rarely.

This is worth noting, especially since the gospels were written, as is commonly admitted, to generate belief in Jesus as the Christ and as "Son of God." However, despite this semantic evolution, the gospels still show Jesus not only as "Christ" but also as "Son of Man." This seems to confirm the archaic character of the title.

The gradual increase in the use of the title "Christ" and the gradual decrease in the use of "Son of Man" fits with the changing historical situation. The title "Christ" was inappropriate during Jesus' public preaching because of the connection of that title with Israel's political ambitions, but this problem ceased after the events of the resurrection when the primitive preaching began. If Jesus wanted to reveal the nonnationalistic character of his messiahship in a progressive process and, thereby an unexpected mystery, he could use the title "Son of Man" as a very appropriate means for this special revelation of himself. The title could signify the "I" of Jesus with a certain amount of solemnity. It was also able to suggest in an enigmatic way the supercreatural messianic meaning of Jesus' personality. Yet the title in no way called into question the historical earthly reality of the "I" of Jesus.

But after Jesus' death the situation was changed altogether. The title "Son of Man" with its ambiguous meaning, which had previously served to keep his mysterious self-revelation progressive, was now less appropriate. In fact, it was not useful at all for preaching Christian doctrine. A more appropriate title for preaching was "Christ" or "Lord." The disciples had already understood what Jesus wished to say, and they said it clearly and directly, although Jesus had revealed it to them over a rather long period of time in different words. After his death and resurrection, there was no longer a danger that Jesus' Messianism would be understood in a nationalistic sense. It was appropriate therefore to give testimony to his divinity with various clear unambiguous titles and terms.

Summing up, there can be no serious doubt that the historical Jesus could use this title and that it could originate in the usage of Jesus himself. Since the evidence for Jesus' use of this title does not exclude the possibility that the gospel tradition did not make a more extensive and, for the life of the Church, more suitable use of it than Jesus himself, we have to examine the different sayings concerning the Son of Man in the gospels and to challenge their authenticity.

2) Sayings Concerning the Son of Man and Their Authenticity

In the usual Semitic manner the mysterious being of the Son of Man is described in the gospels not by abstract attributes, in the manner of the Greek philosophers, but more dynamically by actions and offices. Some of these activities of the Son of Man are performed on earth, and some of them in heaven. The sayings concerning the activities of the Son of Man in the gospels can be grouped under the five following categories:

i) Sayings concerning the Son of Man's human condition;
ii) Sayings concerning the Son of Man's divine power;
iii) Sayings concerning the Son of Man's kerygmatical apostolic mission;
iv) Sayings concerning the Son of Man's redemptive suffering and resurrection;
v) Sayings concerning the Son of Man's eschatological glorification in his equality to God.

The first three of these occur before, and the last two after the confession at Caesarea Philippi, seemingly a central turning point in the life of Jesus as presented by the synoptics. It coincides approximately with the end of his preaching in Galilee, and is at the same time both an end of his previous manifestations to his disciples and a beginning of new and more difficult manifestations that demand a stronger faith. Since we have demonstrated that Jesus himself could use the title of Son of Man, it will be easier to show the authenticity of the eschatological sayings than of the others since these suggest some references to Dan 7,13 ff. Therefore, we will start with the fifth series of "Son of Man" sayings, proceeding in reverse order to the first.

a) *Sayings Concerning the Son of Man's Eschatological Glorification in his Equality to God.*

The eschatological "Son of Man" sayings are perhaps the largest group. They are present in the triple tradition. According to the solemn declaration before the Sanhedrin the Son of Man "seated at the right of the Almighty is coming upon the clouds of Heaven" (Mk 14,62; Mt 26,64; Lk 22,69). He is seated already at the right hand of God, which indicates that he shares in divine power; he is equal to God. He is not only coming with the clouds, like Yahweh himself (Ex 24,16; Lev 16,2; Num 11,25) and the Son of Man of Daniel (Dan 7,13), but he is also sitting at the right hand of God, a characteristic not found in Daniel or Enoch or 4 Ezra. This text, therefore, is not derived from Enoch's Son of Man, but from Ps 110,1 so familiar to the early Church (Acts 2,34; Rom 8,34; 1 Cor 15,25; Eph 1,20; 1 Pet 3,22; Heb 1,12.13; 8,1; 10,12; 12,2). The Son of Man in 1 Enoch either stands before the Lord of Spirits (49,2) or sits on the throne of the Lord of Spirits (51,3), on the throne of his glory (61,8; 62,2.5; 69,29); he is never said to be sitting at the right hand of God. When, in the second century, Aquiba, interpreting Dan 7,9 "thrones were placed," explained that one throne was placed for the Venerable One and the other for David (the Messiah), R. Yosé replied with indignation that Aquiba profaned Šekinah. In the light of Is 66,1, R. Eléasar ben Azaria interpreted one of the thrones as the footstool of the other (Hagiga, 13a; see also Is 14, 14-15).

That Jesus could cite and apply to himself Ps 110 is confirmed from the episode reported by the three synoptic gospels, when Jesus asked the puzzling question about David's Son (Mk 12,36-37; Mt 22,44-45; Lk 20,42-44). The fact that the evangelists themselves do not seem to know how to answer the question indicates the originality of Jesus' saying. Ps 110 was an enigma for the Jews because they could not reconcile the davidic sonship of the Messiah with his Lordship over his father, David. [250] Jesus, however, by combining Dan 7,13 with Ps 110 could form a creative synthesis, which on the one hand transcends the meaning of Daniel's "Son of Man," since he is equal to Yahweh, and on the other hand shows the connections with the Old Testament, since according to Dan 7,14 an everlasting ruling power has been given to the Son of Man.

The other eschatological saying concerning the Son of Man in the triple tradition indicates again, that the power, which the Son of Man has, is not limited to earth, but extended to heaven. In the apocalypse of the synoptics (Mk 13,1-37; Mt 24,1-51, Lk 17,22-37; 21,5-36) the Son of Man is coming with great power (Mk

13,26; Mt 24,30; Lk 21,27) and he sends the angels like his servants to gather all things (Mk 13,27; Mt 24,31; cf Mt 13,41 and Lk 12,8-9). The sending of an angel-like servant was a power belonging properly to Yahweh. Jesus does not only share the power with God in the eschatological final judgment, like the Son of Man in 1 Enoch (49,2-4; 61,8-9; 69,29) or like the apostles judging the twelve tribes of Israel (Lk 22,30), but he judges alone on his own and the Father does not seem to be present at the final judgment at all. Meanwhile, in 1 Enoch in the final judgment there is a constant changing of the names of the judges (61,8; 62,2; 62,10; 63,1-12), in the gospels the Son of Man comes alone to judge in the glory of his Father (Mk 8,38; cf Lk 9,26; Mt 25,31).

Besides these the triple tradition has in addition a third eschatological saying concerning the coming of the Son of Man, found in Mk 8. 38-9,1; Mt 16, 27-28; Lk 9,26-27.

Furthermore, the eschatological sayings are present in the material common to Matthew and Luke in the so-called Q. The day of the Son of Man will come like lightning flashes shining from one end of the sky to the other (Lk 17,24; Mt 24,27) at a time when no one expects him (Lk 12,40; Mt 24,44), as it happened in the time of Noah (Lk 17,26; Mt 24,37).

Finally, there are some eschatological sayings which are peculiar to Luke (Lk 17,22; 18,8b; 21,36) and to Matthew (10,23; 19,28— although 19,28 might belong rather to Q—;25,31). Luke relates that the disciples will sit on thrones and judge the twelve tribes of Israel (22,30); however, he does not mention the title Son of Man as Mt 19,28 does (cf 25,31). In Luke, Jesus uses the "I" instead of the Matthean Son of Man. This instance indicates that the sayings concerning the Son of Man were identified with Jesus in the Q texts already, and the originator of the synoptic tradition might have freely introduced some editorial usage of the title, "Son of Man," in place of the "I" of Jesus. A similar identification is to be found in Mt 10,32 where the "I" replaces the "Son of Man" of Lk (9,26) and in Mk (8,38), where once again, the Son of Man is identified with the kingdom of God (see Mk 9,1 and Lk 9,27). Mark and Luke agree on this against Mt (16,28). This fact has not been sufficiently considered by those who, while admitting the authenticity of the eschatological sayings, believe that Jesus never identified himself with the glorious Son of Man. A. J. B. Higgins, at the end of his study on *Jesus and the Son of Man* said that Jesus "could hardly have regarded himself, a man on earth, as the Son of Man and have been sane. His references to the Son of Man must all have been directed as if to another—not himself." [251] Similarly, in his book *The Son of Man in the Synoptic Tradition,* H. E. Tödt [252] assumes that it is a sign of authenticity when the Son of Man seems to be other than Jesus himself. According to him, the identification came from the Palestine community, in opposition to R. Bultmann who assigns it to the hellenistic Church. In fact, A. J. B. Higgins and H. E. Tödt follow R. Bultmann who also denied that Jesus could have thought of such heavenly glory as that of the Son of Man in connection with his own condition. [253] W. Bousset, [254] in the year 1913, admitted that several passages referring to the Son of Man as an eschatological king, cannot be rejected by merely historical criticism, but he did not think that they can be attributed to Jesus himself. Nevertheless, after his historical criticism he honestly asked the question: Could it be possible that Jesus would truly have wanted to create a myth out of his own personality by use of an expression of this sort?[255]

Jesus' historical usage of the title, the large number and the wide distribution among various traditions, show the historical authenticity of the eschatological sayings. The hypothesis of Bousset, Bultmann, Tödt and Higgins that Jesus did not, or more precisely could not, identify himself with the glorious Son of Man seems unfounded. The identification was certainly made at the time of the composition of Q, in the early teaching material of the Church. But who, then, made the first identification? If, according to Tödt, the Church had such reverence for those texts which seem to represent the Son of Man as other than Jesus (the only texts the authenticity of which Tödt admits, e.g. Mt 24,27 - Lk 17,24; Mt 24,37.39 - Lk 17,26; Mt 24,44 - Lk 12,40; Mt 10,32 - Lk 12,8; cf Mk 8,38 - Lk 11,30 - Lk 17,30) that it did not dare to modify them, how did it dare to take the liberty of changing them in other instances, and to ascribe its own creation to Jesus himself? The free interchange of "I" with the "Son of Man" in Q and the fact that the editorial usage does not coincide necessarily with Jesus' own historical usage of the title in the same eschatological sayings, confirms that the Son of Man was identified with Jesus in the teaching material of that early Church. There is no evidence that either the Church or the historical Jesus expected someone else to come. In Jesus' teaching, indeed, there is no room for another Son of Man greater than himself. The eternal destiny of man depends upon man's response to him. That Jesus applied the title "Son of Man" to himself appears also from the fact that the Son of Man of the gospels, in contrast to the Enoch's Son of Man, shares in the human weakness and helplessness of the Suffering Servant of Yahweh. With this in mind we can pass now to an examination of the suffering-sayings.

b) Sayings Concerning the Son of Man's Redemptive Suffering and Resurrection.

The sayings concerning the suffering of the Son of Man are predictions connected mostly with the idea of resurrection. They occur in about 33 passages of the gospels, all after the confession of Peter, with the exception of one verse in Mt 12,40, which is parallel to the passage of Lk 11,30 following Peter's confession.

According to the triple tradition, after Peter's confession Jesus three times announces the passion and the subsequent resurrection of the Son of Man: Mk 8,31-32; Mt 16,21; Lk 9,22 - Mk 9,30-32; Mt 17,22-23; Lk 9,43b-45 - Mk 10,32-34; Mt 20,17-19; Lk 18,31-34. After hearing this, according to Matthew and Luke, the disciples became worried, sad, and puzzled. In Mt 16,21 we again have the "I" of Jesus instead of the "Son of Man" in Mark's and Luke's parallel passages. Neither Daniel nor Enoch mention directly that the Son of Man must suffer. However, it is suggested by Dan 7,25 that the saints of the Most High will be delivered for a few years to the last king of the fourth kingdom who "shall harass the saints of the Most High." Again, this might be a case of Jesus' creative synthesis which on the one hand transcends, and on the other hand remains connected with the Old Testament. Therefore, using the title Son of Man, on account of Dan 7,25-27, Jesus could think about the temporary suffering followed by his everlasting kingdom.

In the triple tradition there is a fourth prediction of suffering without making mention of the resurrection. The veiled form recommends its authenticity. The Son of Man is to "go away" as the scripture says of him because he will be betrayed (Mk 14,21; Mt 26,24; Lk 22,22).

In the material common to Matthew and to Luke, in the Q, there is another veiled prediction under the sign of Jonah. Like Jonah in the stomach of the whale, so the Son of Man will be three days in the heart of the earth (Mt 12,40; Lk 11,30; cf. Mt

16,1-4; Mk 8,11-13). Therefore it cannot be said with certainty, as A. J. B. Higgins [256] and R. Bultmann [257] suggest, that Q does not contain suffering sayings referring to the Son of Man. In the double tradition common to Mark and Matthew there is still another prediction of suffering and resurrection (Mk 9,9.12; Mt 17,9.12) as well as the betrayal into the hands of sinners (Mk 14,41; Mt 26,45). It is interesting that the earliest form of prediction speaks of death and not of crucifixion. The ambiguous form indicates the archaic age of these sayings.

There are also some suffering sayings peculiar to Matthew (26,2) and to Luke (17,25; 22,28; 24,7).

In a passage common to Mark and Matthew the Son of Man willingly gives his life for men, to ransom and free them (Mk 10,45; Mt 20,28). According to the gospels Jesus never explicitly calls himself the Servant of Yahweh, but he clearly attributes to himself the redemptive task of the suffering servant in Isaiah (Is 42,1-9; 49,1-6; 50,4-11; 52,13-53,12). At one point, Jesus is said explicitly to cite the passage from the canticle of the Servant of Yahweh (Lk 22,37; cf Is 53,12). Sometimes the words of Jesus, as they are formulated in the gospels, contain certain reminiscences of the same canticle.

The Son of Man	*The Servant of Yahweh*
". . . does not the Scripture say of the Son of Man that he will	"He
(a) suffer much	(b) was despised and rejected by men,
	(a) a man of sorrows, and acquainted with pain,
(b) and be refused?" (Mk 9,12; cf Mt 17,12)	(b) and like one from whom men hid their face, he was despised, and we esteemed him not" (Is 53,3)
"For the Son of Man himself has not come to be waited upon, but to	". . . .
(a) wait on other people,	(b) he makes himself
(b) and to give his life	(c) a guilt offering. . . .
(c) to free	(a) My servant shall
(d) many others" (Mk 10,45; Mt 20,28)	(d) bring righteousness to many" (Is 53,10-11)

Therefore, the passages which say that the Son of Man has to go away according to the scriptures, (Mk 14,21; Mt 26,24; Lk 12,22) seem to have special reference to the fourth canticle of the Servant of Yahweh.

Besides Isaiah, Ps 22,1 (used by Mt 27,46; Mk 15,34), Ps

118,22-23 (cited in Mk 12,10-11; Mt 21,42; Lk 20,17), the term "ben adam" of Ezekiel, and Ps 8 could remind Jesus that the Son of Man idea includes humiliation, suffering and death, as well as the subsequent glorification promised by Yahweh. If Jesus was able to think of the Servant of Yahweh, he was able also to think of the Servant's glorification. Furthermore, many passages in which Jesus is concerned with his death offer special signs of authenticity. One example is the passage where the apostles receive the predictions too irritatedly or cowardly. As e.g., Peter scolds Jesus for announcing his death, Jesus replies: "Get out of my sight, Satan" (Mk 8,33; Mt 16,23). Another example is when John and James without shame seek the first places in the kingdom of the Messiah (Mk 10,35-41; Mt 20,20-24). The authors in the early doctrinal tradition would not have made up such details. In other passages, the allusion to death remains obscure (Mt 12,39-40; Lk 11,30). Finally, it is difficult to deny that Mk 10,39 (Mt 20,23) is a real prediction. The Christian community could not report the martyrdom of John in such an early tradition as that of Mark (notice the significance of v. 41). Thus the historical authenticity of the suffering sayings concerning the Son of Man cannot be denied without raising much more embarrassing difficulties.

c) Sayings Concerning the Son of Man's Kerygmatical Apostolic Mission

The kerygmatical missionary sayings are mostly in the double tradition of Matthew and Luke. The Son of Man is the sower of the word of God (Mt 13,37) who came to serve (Mt 20,28) and to seek what was lost (Lk 19,10). His role is a soteriological one. Those who confess Jesus and accept his doctrine (Mk 8,38; Mt 10,32-33; Lk 9,26; 12,8-9) will be saved, since they will be acknowledged by the Son of Man before the angels of God (Lk 12,8-9), Jesus' Father in heaven (Mt 10,32). All who disown Jesus, will be disowned by Jesus before his Father (Mt 10,33; Lk 12,9; Mk 8,38). Matthew again has the "I" of Jesus instead of the Son of Man of Luke. The disciples, therefore, must suffer for Jesus (Mt 5,11), for the Son of Man (Lk 6,22).

The absolute demand of Jesus to acknowledge and follow him at the risk of eternal salvation is repeated without the title Son of Man in other passages of the gospels (Mk 8,34-35; Mt 16,24-25; Lk 9,23-24 - Mt 10,37-39; Lk 14,26-27 - Mt 8,21-22; Lk 9,61-62 - Mk

10,29-30; Mt 19,29; Lk 18, 29-30 - Jn 3,17-21; Jn 12,47-48). That
Jesus made himself the center of religious life so that salvation and
eternal happiness depended on faith in him is more than historically probable. [258] A question which has always puzzled the
historian is, how could the disciples believe in Jesus before the
paschal experience. The existence of a pre-paschal community
must be admitted. [259] Post-paschal faith was not based only on
the experience of the resurrection of some unknown man, but of a
man in whom the members of the community had already had
some kind of expectation before his death.

Now the nature of a community depends always upon the
relation which exists between the leader and the other members of
the community. The teacher and his students form a school, the
master and his disciples a disciplehood, the prophet and his followers a group of prophets, the Messiah and his believers a
messianic community, the priest and the worshipers a liturgical
community. In the tradition of the Q there are some indications
which suggest that Jesus and his pre-paschal community formed
none of these communities. The pre-paschal community seems to
be unique in the history of religion. According to the gospel
tradition Jesus, as he appears in his miracle-performances as well as
in his calling of [260] the disciples, is a man who urged the necessity
of a personal and absolute adherence to himself. He asked for faith
not in God but in himself.

Moreover, in his demand for faith he does not allude to some
vision as the prophets or the apocalyptical writers do, but to
himself. He puts himself as the foundation of this faith. Indeed,
the center of the pre-paschal community is nothing else but the
words and the person of Jesus. The object of the preaching of the
pre-paschal community (limited to Israel, Mt 10,5) was already the
demand of accepting the word of Jesus (Mt 10,5b-14; Lk 10,8-12)
and adhesion to Christ. Since preaching about the kingdom could
not have been without any reference to Jesus, the pre-paschal
preaching had already some kind of "Christology" (cf, e.g. Mt
16,13-18; Lk 7,18-23; 10,22-24).

Evidently, there was a great difference between the adherence
of the pre-paschal community to Jesus, the Son of Man, and the
adherence of the post-paschal community to Jesus as the risen
Lord, because of the testimony of the Holy Spirit. The sin of
those who rejected Jesus during his lifetime can be forgiven, as the

early Church preached to the Jews who crucified Jesus (Acts 2,22-24.36-39; 3,13-15.17-20; 4,9-12), but the sin of those who reject him after the resurrection testified to by the Holy Spirit, will not be forgiven (Mt 12,32; Lk 12,10; cf also Acts 5,3-9; 7.51).

Thus, although Jesus' claim on the absolute adherence to him of all those who want to be saved seems to be certain, not all the sayings concerning the Son of Man's missionary activities must be admitted as historical. In these sayings Jesus' own historical use of this title does not coincide necessarily with the usage which is found in the gospels. Thus, for example, the sayings in Mt 12,32 and Lk 12,10 about the sin against the Son of Man might be easily admitted as a creation of the Church explaining her missionary activity and interest amongst the Jews who explicitly rejected Jesus. [261] In spite of Jesus' sayings (Mt 10,32-33; Lk 12,8-9; Mk 8,38; Lk 9,26) the Jews who rejected Jesus as the Son of Man, might still expect the acknowledgement of Jesus, the Lord, before his Father. Similarly, the confession of the blind man that Jesus is the Son of Man in Jn 9,35 shows a very developed ecclesiastical construction (adoration, exclusion from the synagogues, unknown in Jesus' time). In this environment it seems to be a little archaic to use the title of Son of Man. Since the intention of the fourth gospel was to demonstrate precisely the identity of the Logos of faith and of Jesus in the flesh, the author might have increased the use of the title, Son of Man.

In addition to the salvific kerygmatical office there is never attributed to the Son of Man of the gospels any cosmogonic office. The Son of Man differs essentially from the mythical figure of the "Anthropos" of Hermetic, Gnostic, and Manichean writings, a transcendant exemplar of humanity, a half-divine *Urmensch*, "primal man," whose elements are spread among good men, and which ought to be collected and brought back to the original innocent stage. [262] Jesus' soteriological function does not consist in collecting scattered elements spread in the cosmos, but in calling everyone (not only the good man, but more emphatically the sinner, a fact unique again in the history of religions) who wants to believe in him.

d) Sayings Concerning the Son of Man's Divine Power

Before Peter's confession of faith, according to the triple tradition, Jesus attributed to himself, as to the Son of Man, the power to forgive sins (Mk 2,10; Mt 9,6; Lk 5,24). The Jews, well aware that God alone is able to forgive sins, murmured: "This is a blasphemy. Who can forgive sins but God alone?" (Mk 2,7; Mt 9,3; Lk 5,21). In this passage it is stressed especially that the Son of Man has authority to forgive sins on earth (Mk 2,10; Mt 9,6; Lk 5,24) in contrast to his power in heaven exercised in the eschatological time (Mt 25,31-46; Mt 10,40-42; Mk 9,37-41; Lk 12,8-9).

Because of the disunity of the Markan narrative [263] and of its contrast with the authentic parousia sayings, it had been assumed that the saying was formed by the community and, therefore, Mk 2,10 should not be regarded as an authentic saying of Jesus. [264] However, the contrast with the eschatological sayings is not so evident. The power and dominion given to the Son of Man in Daniel as well as Jesus' absolute demand of fellowship with himself as a guarantee of salvation, is in accord with the power of forgiving sins of Mk 2,10.

A much more serious difficulty against the historicity of Mk 2,10 is the disunity of the narrative. The whole narrative can be divided into two stories: the miracle story (5a.11-12) and the pronouncement story (5b-10), which is seen as an ecclesiological interpolation to support the Church's claim in exercising the right to forgive sins.

On account of the ecclesiological reinterpretation and literary construction of the passage, the editorial usage of the "Son of Man" title in Mk 2,10 is very probable. However, since the early Church's consciousness of having the right to forgive sins is attested to from the very beginning (Acts 2,38; 5,31; 10,43; 13,38; Mt 16,19; 18,15-18; 28,18-20), it can be admitted that the power of forgiving sins on earth is to be ascribed to Jesus. Such an innovation can hardly be introduced by a community which continued steadfastly in the teaching of the apostles (Acts 2,42) who were with Jesus during his earthly life (Acts 1,21 ff.). Furthermore, the Church could have been led to this consciousness by Jesus himself. As soon as Jesus could apply the Son of Man concept to his earthly life by means of the suffering sayings and make his followers conscious of their indispensable solidarity with the humiliation of the Son of Man he could also communicate to them the consciousness of the power promised to the saints of the Most High (Dan 7,27). If Jesus regarded himself as the Son of Man, he could recognize himself as being charged with bringing into being on earth the everlasting kingdom of the saints of the Most High. He could not apply to himself the first part of Daniel without the second part, inseparably united with the first part. If there was, therefore, anyone who could persuade the Church that it had the earthly as well as the heavenly power to forgive sins, then he could only be the man who recognized and called himself the "Son of Man." Therefore, in spite of the literary ecclesiological redaction, we can admit that Jesus as Son of Man could attribute to himself the power of forgiving sin.

Besides Mk 2,10 there is another passage which ascribes divine power to the Son of Man, namely, the story of the calming of the sea and the winds. The Son of Man (Mt 8,20), when a great storm came up on the sea, so that the waves broke over the boat, commanded the winds and the sea, so that there was a great calm (Mt 8,26; Mk 4,39; Lk 8,24). The historicity of this story is recommended by the fact that it had not been used by the Church to support any of its liturgical or kerygmatical practices.

Another saying concerning the Son of Man's divine power is the saying about the Lord of the Sabbath (Mk 2,28; Mt 12,8; Lk 6,5). Yahweh was the Lord of the Sabbath, and now Jesus is told to give himself the same title, again indicating his equality with God. The text, however, has its difficulties. According to the evangelist's interpretation not man (which occurs in v 27) but the Son of Man (v 28) is the Lord of the Sabbath. However, there is the possibility that Jesus did not refer to himself in the second sentence as the Son of Man, but to man in general, using the Aramaic *barnasha* in both cases. Therefore, the Son of Man in v 27 might be a misunderstanding of *barnasha*. This interpretation is confirmed by the examples used by Jesus to defend his non-observance of the Sabbath. David (Mk 2,25), the priests in the temple (Mt 12,5), or any Jew did not observe the Sabbath to save one sheep which had fallen into a hole (Mt. 12,11) because, being men, the Sabbath was made for them. Therefore, Jesus, who came to save many has more reason to work on the Sabbath.[265]

Some authors defend the authenticity of Mk 2,28 because the earlier Q (Mt 12,8; Lk 6,5) does not have the Mk 2,27 saying which subordinates the Sabbath to man in general.[266] But the interpretation of the evangelist in Mk 2,28, namely, that Jesus referred to himself as the Son of Man and not to man in general, can be justified by a double consideration according to the synoptic tradition. To be the Lord of the Sabbath, in the case of Jesus, does not mean a freedom to do the most necessary things on the Sabbath, but the introduction of a new law, which is not only a rabbinic interpretation of the existing law, but a creation of a new one which did not exist before: "You have heard. . . . But I tell you."

Moreover, Jesus worked on the Sabbath not only because it was absolutely necessary, but because he must always work with his Father who works even until "now" (cf Jn 5,17). So once again he made his actions equal to God's activities. On account of this the Jews could have said that he not only broke the Sabbath but he made himself equal to God (Jn 5,18).

e) Sayings Concerning the Son of Man's Human Condition

The Son of Man, made equal with God, is now compared with foxes and wild birds and is found to be less, since he had nowhere to lay his head (Mt 8,20; Lk 9,58). The saying is in consonance with the sayings concerning the Son of Man's suffering and his apostolic mission. He came to serve and seek the least, thus his disciples too, have to leave their homes and everything they have (Mt 8,19.22; Lk 9.57.60; 10,4). It might be that the Church used this saying to stimulate its tired missionaries, but certainly there was no such reason to preserve another saying, which most evidently describes the human condition of the Son of Man: ". . . the Son of Man . . . does eat and drink, and people say, 'Look at him! A glutton and a drinker, the companion of tax collectors and sinners" (Mt 11,19; Lk 7,34). The Church certainly could not have any other reason but the historicity of Jesus' own saying in reminding its members that their divine "Lord" was a glutton and a drinker.

Just as the message "The Kingdom of God is at hand" so also the sayings concerning the Son of Man express the descent of God to man. The clear allusion to the book of Daniel shows that God comes to man in the Son of Man and not vice versa. Moreover by presuming actions exclusively attributed to Yahweh and placing himself at the right hand of Yahweh as his equal, it seems that Jesus did succeed in suggesting the mysterious nature of the supereminent union of God with him as well as the absolutely unique presence of Yahweh in him. The experience of this union in Jesus caused his followers to ask, "Who is this man?"; "Who is this Son of Man?"

The difference between the titles Son of Man and Son of God

therefore does not lie in the fact that one shows Jesus as man and the other as God. Each title reveals the same mystery. The difference is rather that whereas the title Son of Man expresses more directly the mystery of Jesus' relationship to the created world, the title Son of God or Son expresses the mystery of Jesus' relationship to God, the Father, who has complete communion and oneness with him.

C. The Historical Jesus' Sayings Concerning the Son

1) The Faith of the Early Church in Jesus as the Son of God

The Fourth Gospel was written around the year 100 A.D. to show that Jesus Christ is the Son of God (Jn 20,31). It proclaims the divine sonship of Jesus (Jn 10,30; 14,9 ff. etc.). Faith in him as Son of God brings eternal life (Jn 6,40; 20,31).

In the Acts of the Apostles, Luke says that Paul "began to preach that Jesus is the Son of God" (9,20) and that he confounded the Jews in affirming that Jesus was the Christ (9,22). The use of the term "Christ" in v 22 shows that the concept "Son of God" included Messianism in the mentality of the early Christians. Outside of this reference we do not find the title Son of God in Acts. Acts 8,37 is a very ancient gloss containing a baptismal creed, probably not authentic. Paul, preaching in Antioch, applied to Jesus Ps 2 where Yahweh called the Messiah "My Son" (Acts 13,33).

In the various letters of St. Paul the title is found less frequently than other titles such as Christ or Lord. The reason might be that the title Son of God pertains more to terminology for explaining doctrine. It is not the language of cult, or exhortation, or ordinary conversation. V. Taylor expressed it correctly: "The first Christians fervently believed in the 'Son' but they invoked 'the Lord.' "[267]

In his epistle to the Romans (1,3-4) the Son of God is referred to twice. The first deals with the preexistence of the Son who, sent by God (Rom 8,3; Gal 4,4) was descended from the family of David. The second reference concerns the Son of God in his power which was fully manifested in his resurrection. Since these verses express an ancient confession of faith, it seems that Paul originated neither the expression nor the doctrine of Christ as the Son of God. The Son of God as a title of Jesus appears also in the second epistle to the Corinthians (1,19), and in the epistles to the Galatians (2,20), to the Ephesians (4,13), and to the Hebrews (4,14 etc.). In the first epistle to the Thessalonians, written in the year 51, Paul admonishes the Thessalonians to be converted to God from idolatry, and to await his Son from heaven (1,10). The name Son of God is found in a passage proclaiming a monotheistic Christianity. Jesus' unique monotheistic sonship is radically distinct from the hellenistic concept of the son of gods. From here we can conclude that the faith of the early Church in Jesus as the Son of God is attested to in an exclusively unique way around the late forties and early fifties.

2) The Son of God in Hellenism and in the Old Testament

There are some authors, v.g. A. Loisy, W. Bousset, R. Bultmann, etc. who suggest that the faith of the early Christians in Jesus as the Son of God originated from hellenistic thought. The Greek mind knew three kinds of sons of God. The first category does not pertain properly to the human race, because these sons of God are begotten by other gods, thus, e.g. Dionysus is the son of Jove and Semel. The second category includes kings, pharaohs (who are considered to be the sons of the sun god Re), and Roman emperors like Augustus, Caligula, Domitian, etc. The third category applies to those men who enjoyed the power of miraculous prophecy.

Since the Son of God was used as a title not only by the hellenistic community but even earlier by the Palestinian Church, W. Bousset guessed that the title Son of God was used in the Palestinian community only in a messianic sense, and that afterwards the Hellenists developed the properly transcendent sense of the Son of God.

We have seen that the title Son of Man, used in the Palestinian community, involved such degrees of mystery that it could fit God alone. Therefore, it cannot be said that Jesus was raised to the divine order first by attributing to him the title "Son of God." Moreover, there is a radical difference between the sonship of Jesus, as we have it in the NT, and the hellenistic notion of sons of gods. The hellenistic concept occurred in polytheistic thought and did not have the connotation of uniqueness and radical exclusivity of Jesus' sonship. Furthermore, Jesus' sonship is rooted not in his work of miracles, but rather in his obedient fulfillment of the tasks and sufferings which God the Father asked of him. This kind of sonship is evidently not Greek but Hebrew and corresponds to Old Testament thought.[268]

In the Old Testament there are different groups and personalities who are called sons of God. There are some passages where angelic beings are called sons of God $B^e ne$ '$Elohim$, who, as in the Greek myths, were attracted by the beauty of the daughters of men, had intercourse with them and fathered giants and heroes (Gen 6,1-4). Here the author evidently copies mythological ideas, and it is hard to know whom he had in mind when he wrote about the sons of God. $B^e ne$ '$Elohim$ is also the name of those heavenly beings who form the divine assembly in Job (1,6; 2,1; 38,7) and in Ps 29,1. In Ps 82,1 the same beings are called gods 'el, in the midst of whom God '$Elohim$ is revered by all of them and (Ps 89,6-8) gives his judgment. According to Deut 32,8-9 the Most High assigned the nations to these sons of God, or gods, while he kept Israel as his own portion. In the most recent books of the Old Testament these celestial beings are called "holy ones" or "saints" (Zech 14,5; Job 5,1; Wis 5,5; Dan 4,13) or angels $mal'ak$ $Yahweh$ or $mal'ak$ '$Elohim$ (Judg 6,22, etc.), messengers of God. These heavenly beings are always under God's rule, and if they fail in their mission, they are punished by Yahweh (Is 24,21; 34,4; Dan 10,13; 12,1; Gen 6,3.5-7).

The same term is applied to the people of Israel who are the sons of the living God (Deut 14,1; Hos 1,10). Yahweh called Israel "My first-born" (Ex 4,22; Ps 89,26-27; Jer 31,9), "precious son" (Jer 31,20), or simply "My son" (Hos 11,1), or sons (Is 1,2; 43,6). In the sapiential books the just man, who lives according to the Law, is a son of God (Wis 2,13.18; 5,5; Sir 4,10). The kings of the Davidic house are called again by Yahweh "My son" (2 Sam 7,14; 1 Chron 22,10; Ps 2,7; Ps 89,26-27) for whom Yahweh will be Father in a special way.

Furthermore, there is one passage in the Old Testament where wicked judges are addressed as "sons of God" or "gods" (Ps 82,6). The parallel usage of $b^e ne$ '$Elohim$ with '$Elohim$ where both are applied to wicked human persons, indicates the real meaning of the sons of God in the Old Testament. It does not include any polytheistic sense. The sons of God are not gods, but rather emissaries or representatives of Yahweh who act in the name and person of Yahweh and exercise some perogatives and powers of Yahweh. This moral identity between sender and emissary is expressed by the Jewish term *šālîah* with its fundamental meaning of sending a word or message. According to a proverb of the Talmud, "A man's *šālîah* is as it were himself." [269] Similarly, the emissary or representative of Yahweh had to be considered as if he were Yahweh, and sometimes he was called by the name of *'Elohim*. Notice, however, that unlike *b^ene 'Elohim*, the expression *b^ene Yahweh* never occurs in Old Testament.

To be a son of God, therefore, according to the Old Testament, did not mean being a son of god in the properly hellenistic sense, i.e. that one was constituted a member of the species of deity by virtue of divine conception. Rather it meant being God's obedient servant and representative who by execution of a particular commission of God, acted in his name and in his person.

The Jewish concept of Jesus' divine sonship is reflected in the usage of early Christianity. In Acts 3,13 26 and 4,27.30, Jesus is called not *υἱός* but *παῖς* pointing to the obedient *ebed Yahweh* of Isaiah. From this consideration of the Old Testament's usage of the term sons of God, it follows that Jesus could not use this title if he knew that he was more than a son of God in the common sense of the term.

3) The Titles "Son of God" and "Son" in the Synoptic Gospels and their Authenticity

In the synoptic gospels the term "Son of God" is never used by Jesus in speaking of himself. [270] Generally, Jesus speaks of himself as the Son (8 times: Mk 13,32; Mt 11,27[3]; Mt 28,19; Lk 10,22[3]) [271] and the Father calls him "My Son" (Mk 1,11; Mt 3,17; Lk 3,22; Mk 9,7; Mt 17,5; Lk 9,35; Mt 2,15). The frequent use by others of the term "Son of God" when they are speaking of Jesus (21 times in the synoptic gospels) [272] might suggest that the title "Son of God" was not used by Jesus himself and is, therefore, not one of his genuine sayings. Following the indication of the synoptic gospels, we can admit that Jesus did not reveal his unique sonship and his personal self-consciousness of it by using the title Son of God, but rather by the title "Son," the authenticity of which we have to further investigate. [273]

4) Reflection on the Meaning and Authenticity of the Synoptic Sayings Concerning the "Son"

a) Son

The name "Son" without any further determination is not found either in the Old Testament or in the judaic writings before Christ or during his time. Now in Mk 13,32 Jesus speaks of himself as the Son and calls God simply Father.

The main teaching of the saying is not the relationship between God and Jesus but the date of the Parousia. In this saying Jesus as Son confesses his ignorance: ". . . about that day and hour no one knows, not even the angels in heaven, nor the Son, only the Father." The historicity of the passage is assured since the early Church was not freely inclined to attribute ignorance to the Lord. Indeed, because of its scandalous character, the later tradition ignored the text completely. Several Mss. left it out or kept it only in a milder form: ". . . of that day and hour no one knows, not even the angels of heaven, but the Father only" (Mt 24,36 Vulg.). The expression "not even the Son" is alien to the kerygmatical teaching of the Christian community, and it can be found only in another saying of Jesus without the title "Son" (Mk 10,40; Mt 20,23).

In Mk 13,32, therefore, we may have an authentic saying of Jesus which indicates that Jesus was conscious of Sonship to God in a sense which is not applicable to men or to angels of heaven. He is less than the Father, yet he is more than man and angels, as the enumeration shows: no one knows, not even the angels. The nature of angels is more precisely marked: they are in heaven, or of heaven (cf Mt 24,36). Thus the Sonship of Jesus to the Father is exclusively unique and can be described as "supracreatural."[274]

b) Abba - my Father, your Father

The correlative term of "Son" is "Father." It is remarkable that the Christian community usually called God the Father (75 times outside the gospels), however in the synoptic gospels[275] only Jesus designated God as Father (44 times in Mt, 5 times in Mk, 17 times in Lk). Since Matthew put the term Father on Jesus' lips in many passages where, according to Mark and Luke, he did not utter the name Father (e.g. Mt 12,50 versus Mk 3,35 and Lk 8,21; Mt 20,23 versus Mk 10,40; Mt 26,29 versus Mk 14,25 and Lk

22,18; Mt 6,26 versus Lk 12,24; Mt 10,20.29 versus Lk 12,6.8; Mt 10,32-33 versus Lk 12,8-9, etc.) we must admit that not all Jesus' Father-sayings in Matthew are genuine utterances of Jesus. Thus, e.g. the Father in Mt 7,21; 13,43; 15,13; 16,17; 18,10.35, etc. might be editorial usage introduced by the evangelist.

The evangelist's editorial usage, however, can be excluded from those passages which are found in the triple tradition in the early sources of the synoptic gospels. According to the triple tradition, Jesus in his prayer in the garden of Gethsemani addressed God as Abba, Father (Mk 14,36; Mt 26,39; Lk 22,42). The humiliating fear of death, and an absence of any reference to resurrection emphasizes the historicity of this saying. In an eschatological saying of the same triple tradition, the Son of Man calls God simply Father (Mk 8,38; Mt 16,27; Lk 9,26). In Mk 13,32 and Mt 24,36 the Son designates God as Father. In the Q there is the hymn of jubilation, where Jesus again directs himself to God as his Father (Mt 11,25-27; Lk 10,21). We find the same in the materials peculiar to Mt (26,42), to Lk (23,34.46), and to Jn (11,41; 12,27.28; 17,1.5.11.21.24.25). Therefore, Jesus' addressing God simply as his Father is witnessed by five different gospel traditions.

We must observe also that the gospels show eight prayers which Jesus directed to God: hymns of jubilation (Mt 11,25-27; Lk 10,21), the invocation before the resurrection of Lazarus (Jn 12,27-28), the high priestly prayer (Jn 17,1-26), the prayer in the garden of Gethsemani (Mk 14,36 and parallel), the prayer for his crucifiers (Lk 23,34), the cry of abandonment (Mk 15,34; Mt 27,46), and the last dying invocation (Lk 23,46). Now in each of these Jesus addresses God by the name, Father. There is only one exception, namely the cry of abandonment in which Jesus prays with the words of Ps 22: "My God, my God, why have you forsaken me."

It is a remarkable fact that the way of addressing God simply as Father is not found in Jewish literature before Christ. Even the Jew of the first century did not dare to speak of God as Father. They called God *Abinu* (Hebrew), *Abuna* (Aramaic), i.e. Our Father, or rarely *"abi"* My Father, or O Father. Therefore, they always added to this word some suffix. According to a tradition related in Jn (5,18) the "Jews were all the more eager to kill Jesus, because he not only broke the Sabbath, but actually by calling

God his Father, he put himself on an equality with God." Jesus' addressing God as Abba without any suffix, testified by five different gospel traditions, is unique and it does not have any parallel in the whole of Jewish literature. The use of "Father" by Jesus is distinguished from the use of contemporary religious language and, therefore, we can admit it as *ipsissima verba* of Jesus.[276]

It seems that *Abba* could signify either father with an article, i.e. a father who was mentioned before, or a father adding a familiar meaning, as Dad or Daddy. The first Christians dared to call God *Abba* (Rom 8,15; Gal 4,1-6) because they must have received this prayer from Jesus. With the spirit of adoption God sent the Spirit of his Son into their hearts crying out, "Abba, Father."

In Jesus' sayings we find expressions such as Father, my Father, your Father, their Father. True, he taught his disciples to say "our Father," but when he himself speaks of the Father he never uses this term. This is more startling since, according to the judaic use, that is what we should have expected (e.g. Mt 11,27; Mk 11,25; Mt 5,45; Lk 6,36; Mt 6,32; Lk 12,30; Mt 6,1; cf. Lk 12,32; Mt 5,16; 7,11). From this interesting and constant use it seems that Jesus attributed an entirely singular sonship to himself. This distinction, furthermore, would suggest more than a superior degree of the same sonship. The sonship of Jesus is of a superior order and somehow the principle of the divine sonship of others. The divine sonship of others depends on Jesus (Mk 8,34-38; Mt 16,24-27; Lk 9,23-26; Mt 5,11; Lk 6,22; Mt 10,32-33; Lk 12,8-9; Mt 10,40; Lk 10,16; Mt 25,40-45) which is indicated again in the parable of the vinedressers.

c) The Son in the Parable of the Vinedressers

The parable is narrated in the triple tradition (Mk 12,1-11; Lk 20,9-18; Mt 21,33-46). By removing the particular elements added by Matthew, Mark and Luke we can find the earliest form of the allegorical parable. According to this early parable, there was a man who once planted a vineyard, lent it out to the vinedressers and went abroad. At the proper time he sent a servant to the vinedressers to receive some of the fruit of the vineyard. But they seized him, and beat him, and sent him away empty-handed. He sent another servant whom they wounded and treated shamefully.

And he sent another, and him they killed. Last of all he sent to them his son, saying: "They will respect my son." But the vine-dressers, on seeing the son, said among themselves: "This is the heir; let us kill him and the inheritance will be ours". So they seized him and killed him, and cast him out of the vineyard. What can the owner of the vineyard do after this? He will come and destroy the vinedressers and will give the vineyard to others.

This original parable still has some elements which correspond very much to the kerygmatical preaching of the primitive Church. Thus the attitude of the vinedressers towards the son is much like that of the leaders in Jerusalem narrated in Acts 13,27 and Jn 1,11. The idea of the Father sending his son to reach a just solution is present in Jn 3,17. Jerusalem, the killer of the proph-ets, is a frequent topic in the books of the New Testament (Mt 23,37; Lk 13,34; Lk 11,47-51; Acts 7,51-52; Heb 11, 32-38).

There are other elements, nevertheless, in this parable which indicate its archaic nature. [277] First the idea that not the Son, but the Father comes to judge is absolutely foreign to the post-paschal catechism. Likewise the reasoning that by killing the Jews might become the heirs of Yahweh's vineyard was unthinkable for the early Church as well as for the contemporary Jews. It supposed, on the one hand, the recognition of Jesus as the only Son sent by the Father, and, on the other hand, that someone can become the heir of God's kingdom without accepting Jesus. The first was inadmissible for the Jews, the second for the early Church. The sequence of ideas is conceivable only in the mind of the historical Jesus, who was aware of both: that he is the only son of the Father, and how foolishly behave those who want to kill him.

Moreover, the allegorical form of the parable is not against its historicity as A. Jülicher, W. Bousset, and R. Bultmann thought. [278] First, because we also find allegorical parables in the Old Testament, e.g. the allegory which Nathan directed to King David (2 Sam 12,1-14) and the Song of the Vineyard of Isaiah (5,1-7). Secondly, because a very important element of the parable (Mk 12,7) is not allegorical at all.

The close similarity with another less disputed parable of the wedding feast (Mt 22,1-14; Lk 14,15-24) confirms its authenticity. A further sign of authenticity is that, without direct reference to the resurrection Jesus speaks of it in a discreet and veiled way which compels reflection. Jesus often employed this obscure way of teaching in his lifetime, avoiding a direct revelation of his personal mystery (cf Mt 11,3, etc.).

In spite of its veiled form of expression the doctrine of the parable is clear enough. Jesus is represented as the Son of the owner of the vineyard while the prophets are only servants. Mark's text explicitly insists on the uniqueness of the Son (12,6). Luke has "my own dear Son" and Matthew, "my Son." The uniqueness of the son is at the core of the parable, since it explains the reason for killing the son. Yet Jesus is not only the unique son of the owner, but also the single heir. The possession of inheritance depends upon man's attitude towards him, which in turn determines man's attitude towards God (e.g. Mt 10,34, etc.). By uttering this parable Jesus could have manifested the awareness of his unique sonship on which the sonship of others would depend. But did Jesus really attribute to himself the divine sonship in a way which would not be fitting to a created person? The question would seem to demand an affirmative answer in view of Mt 11,27 (Lk 10,22).

d) Son's Equality with the Father in the Hymn of Jubilation

The hymn has three parts in Matthew (11,25-30) and only two in Luke (10,21-22). The first part is thanksgiving to God the Father, for the gift of revelation and of faith given to the poor. The second part treats of the relationship between the Son and the Father, and the third part of Jesus' invitation to comfort and happiness through believing and to put on his yoke.

Matthew:

"I thank you, Father, Lord of heaven and earth, for hiding all this from the learned and wise and revealing it to the simple. Yes I thank you, Father for such was your choice.

Everything has been entrusted to me by my Father; and no one understands the Son except the Father, nor does anyone understand the Father except the Son and anyone to whom the Son wishes to reveal him.

Luke:

"I thank you, Father, Lord of heaven and earth, for hiding all this from the learned and wise and revealing it to the simple. Yes I thank you, Father, for such was your choice.

Everything has been entrusted to me by my Father, and no one knows who the Son is except the Father, nor who the Father is except the Son, and anyone to whom the Son wishes to reveal him."

Come to me, all of you who labor and
are burdened, and I will let you rest.
Take my yoke upon you . . . for my
yoke is easy, and my burden is light."

(1) *Textual Criticism*

According to Harnack, whom W. Grundmann, T. W. Manson
and P. Winter [279] have followed, the text has been altered. Here is
the history of the text according to Harnack. The original text was
this:

No one knew (aorist in place of present tense) the Father
except the Son; (the Father's knowledge concerning the Son is
omitted) and to whom the Son has wished to reveal him.

To express the idea of intimate and exclusive relationship between
Father and Son the first interpolation was made:

No one knew the Father except the Son; neither does anyone
know the Son except the Father and he to whom the Son
wishes to reveal him.

But since the sentence concerning the knowledge of the Son by
the Father does not correspond well with the following sentence
where the Son is again the subject, and not the Father as in the
second sentence, a new change was made, which is the actual text:

No one knows the Son except the Father; and neither does
anyone know the Father except the Son and he to whom the
Son wishes to reveal him.

However, regarding the aorist use, there is the fact that all the
codices use the present tense. No codex, neither Matthew nor
Luke, contain the aorist which Harnack proposed. [280] The absence
of any hesitation in the codices is persuasive in indicating the
present tense as the original one. The hesitation of the Fathers and
the early writers signifies that they often cite the texts from
memory using the aorist in the present sense. P. Winter admits too
that the difference between the two readings does not affect the
meaning of the texts. Since the Aramaic word *Ydc* would have
been unpointed, we cannot know which one of the translators was
correct: the one who rendered it with γινώσκει pres. part. Aramaic *yodal,* or the other who translated it by ἔγνω reading perf.
$y^e dac.$ [281]

Regarding the omission we notice that no Greek codex omits
the Father's knowledge concerning the Son. P. Winter admits that
"Out of many thousands of gospel codices, Greek and Latin, it is

only Codex Vercellensis from which these words are absent." [282]
And that is only in Luke's codex. Five codices give the mutual
knowledge of Father for Son and Son for Father in inverse order.
Sometimes the Fathers of the Church change the order; however,
elsewhere the same writers have the text without any inversion. It
is easy to understand that citing from memory one begins rather
with the Father than with the Son as it is in the text. Therefore,
the omission is not favored either through the tradition of the
codices or through the ecclesiastical writings.

P. Winter suggests that the inversion and interpolation is indicated, not as much by the sources, but rather by "the cold scalpel
of logic" since the verse implies a contradiction which cannot be
attributed to the text of the evangelical writings. For if, P. Winter
says, no one knows the Son except the Father, no mortal can
receive any revelation from him. The "logical flaw" becomes more
evident if we substitute the cipher X and Y for the Father and
Son:

  No one has any knowledge of X except Y, and no one has any
  knowledge of Y expect X and those to whom Y gives information.
If no one except X knows Y, Y will not be able to reveal
anything to persons other than X, i.e. persons who do not know
him.

  However, there is no logical flaw in the text. Jesus did not say
that no one has any knowledge of the Father and of him, but only
that no one knows the true nature and intimate life of the Father
and vice versa that of the Son, except those to whom he wants to
reveal it. The text as we have it can be critically admitted as
original.

(2) *The Authenticity of the Hymn of Jubilation*
  Its poetic form, its resemblance to Johannine thought, and its
uniqueness in the synoptic gospels raise a serious question about
the authenticity of the hymn of jubilation. Is this an authentic
saying of Jesus about himself, or rather a saying of the Church
about Jesus?

  W. Bousset thought that Jesus could not utter this saying since
it contains mystical ideas of the hermetic literature. Bousset cited
a Hermes-prayer which has as its theme the mutual knowledge of

God and man: "I know thee, Hermes, and thou me. I am thou, and thou art I." Moreover, according to the text, the mysterious knowledge unites the mind with God and makes him "son of God." But this knowledge can be communicated only to the worthy ones. [283]

But the context of the Hermes is different. There is a theurgist who by different names calls upon Hermes that by a theurgic formula he might exercise force upon gods for human purposes. It seems to be a case of occultism with pantheistic syncretism, [284] which is absolutely absent from the evangelical text. Shortly after W. Bousset's book appeared, Ch. Fox Bourney pointed out the Semitic character of the hymn of jubilation. [285] It is indeed difficult to place our text under the direct influence of hellenistic gnosticism, for in all three strophes the Aramaic thought is clear. In Mt 11,26 instead of the vocative without an article, there is the nominative with an article (δ $\pi\alpha\tau\dot{\eta}\rho$) which corresponds with the Aramaic expression. "Little ones" is not a hellensitic term but connected with the Old Testament (cf Is 61,1 which is cited in Mt 11,5). "For such was your choice" is again a Semitic expression which stands for "so you wanted it to be." "Everything has been entrusted to me by my Father" is indicated in Dan 7,14, according to which power, honor and rule is given to the Son of Man. Parallels, like "no one . . . except, nor anyone . . . except" occur frequently in biblical writings. "No one knows the Son except the Father" corresponds to Ps 2,7 and the "Nor does anyone know the Father except the Son" alludes to Ex 33,11 and Num 12,8 or Deut 34,10.

"To whom . . . wished to reveal him" follows the apocalpytical terminology. Finally, "Take my yoke upon you" and "you will find rest" are common expressions in the judaic tradition. The words "come to me" are from Sir 24,19 and "you will find rest for your souls" is a citation from Jeremiah (6,16). "I am meek and humble of heart" recalls to mind the description of Yahweh's servant in Is 42,2-3.

The hymn of jubilation, indeed, does not come from hellenism. It shows far more similarity and connection with the Old Testament and it belongs to Aramaic tradition. There is great similarity with the Old Testament not only in ideas but also in literary form.

On account of a great similarity in literary form of our text to chapter 51 of the book of Sirach, Loisy believed that the hymn of jubilation cannot be attributed to Jesus but to some member of the Christian community. He compared the two texts in the following way:

Chap. 51 Sirach	*Hymn of Jubilation*
a. giving thanks on account of the divine assistance in time of great peril, with the invocation, my God.	a. giving thanks about the privilege of little ones, which leads to the acquisition of faith in the gospel, with the "my Father."
b. the acquisition of wisdom by the author.	b. the intimate relationship and mutual knowledge of Father and Son.
c. the invitation of the author to accept that very teaching of wisdom with the expressions: Come to me and learn . . . put your neck under the yoke . . . , I have labored . . . I found rest.	c. the invitation to receive the gospel: come to me all you who labor. . . Take my yoke upon you . . . you will find rest for your souls.

From the comparison he concluded that such an exact imitation should not be attributed to Jesus and consequently neither should the text. [286]

However, the similarity is not as exact as it seems. There is a great difference between each of these texts. Chapter 51 of Sirach is indeed a single appendix, but contains two canticles. The second and third part form another autonomous alphabetical poem. Regarding the first part, there are different objects of thanksgiving: in the first text, for liberation from danger and in the second, for the revelation of the Father and the Son. Only a variant Hebraic text has "God, my Father." Other earlier texts have "God, my Savior," or "God of my father," or "God, king." This single variant cannot be a sign of literary imitation. Since the chapter of Sirach has some 30 verses and the hymn of jubilation only six we can conclude at least some reminiscence of expressions but not to an exact imitation of the literary form of Sirach.

E. Norden [287] insisted on Loisy's view by pointing out other texts from the writings of Judaism and primitive Christianity with a threefold structure: a thanksgiving, a praise of wisdom and an invitation to the study of wisdom or to the study of the knowledge of God. According to E. Norden this was the general structure of the sermons of certain religious propaganda. Consequently, it is very probable that Jesus did not really pronounce the hymn of jubilation as we have it now.

However, it is not impossible that Jesus himself used the rhythmic and common literary forms and mnemonic devices of his time. [288] It could happen also that certain separated sayings of Jesus received a literary unity from the first Christians. But nothing can be drawn from this literary composition against the authenticity of the saying. The saying transcends the Old Testament and evidently forms a creative synthesis about the Son of God in a "supercreatural" sense. But who else could make this synthesis except the one who declared himself to be the Son of Man in a "supercreatural" degree and also the Son of God in a unique sense? Our text, therefore, can hardly be explained without the intervention of Jesus, and as such can be ascribed to him. Even more so, since the saying includes some indications which cannot be ascribed to post-paschal tradition, but rather to the lifetime of Jesus.

The context of this saying was neither given by Matthew or by Luke, nor in Peter's Caesarean profession of faith. The saying, according to van Iersel [289] was most probably an answer to the question of Jesus' own townsfolk in Nazareth (Mt 13,54-56; Mk 6,2-3; cf also Lk 4,22; Jn 6,42; 7,27). Jesus' own townsfolk are first impressed by his doctrine and the miraculous powers he is said to possess. Then they realize that, after all, they know him. His father was the carpenter, his mother's name is Mary, his brothers are named James, Joseph, Simon and Judas, and all his sisters live there among them. If they know him, where did he get the wisdom and power to do such marvelous things? Evidently not from his father who, they know, was a simple carpenter. From whom then? This question must be ascribed to Jesus' time since the later tradition did not care about the sisters of Jesus and the names of his brothers. Indeed, in the later tradition all these disappear, and they are not mentioned any more (cf Lk 4,22; Jn 6,42). The villagers of Nazareth say that they know Jesus because they know his father. Jesus replies to his own townsfolk, that they really do not know him because they do not know his Father: "No one knows the Son except the Father; nor does anyone know the Father except the Son." Thus, in this context, in this *Sitz im Leben,* Mt 11,27 and Lk 10,22 become understandable. Jesus opposed the Fatherhood of his heavenly Father to the carpenter's fatherhood. Consequently Jesus' sonship is not sonship by adoption, but the sonship of the only begotten son of God equal to his Father. Therefore, as "A. Schweitzer has correctly suggested," [290] says O. Cullmann, "one must seriously consider the 'powerful hymn Mt 11,25-30' and v 27 may indeed 'be spoken from the consciousness of preexistence.' " [291]

4. Conclusion: Jesus' Life as Christ Event

In summing up the seventh chapter, we can say that the special feature of Jesus' life is his unique power of making God and man present to each other. For the historian, the striking element in Jesus' life is that he does not lead men to God but rather brings God to men. Because of his mysterious power of raising questions concerning God and God's presence in him, his self-revelation is intimately connected with God, his Father's revelation. His life appears as a constant ratification, extension and communication of God's presence in every moment of his life. His constant effort to make God present among men is the reason that he also works on the Sabbath. He works on the Sabbath like any other day, not because he does not respect the law, but because God his Father is always at work, and he is at work also. His existence is a constant effort to make a place for God who wants to come to men, even on the Sabbath. The realization of God's presence is for him the real, new everlasting Sabbath (Jn 5,16-17.19-24; cf 5,1ff; Mk 3,1ff; Mt 12,1ff; Lk 6,6ff; 14,1ff; 13,10ff).

According to John, Jesus indicated the difference between himself and other men in the fact that while the time for men is always here, his time is not always at hand (Jn 7,6). Man always has his time, because he always does what he wants to do. But Jesus does not have his own time since his time is the time of the Father, i.e. he has to do not what he wants, but what and when the Father wants. When Jesus says that he came to do his Father's will (Jn 4,32-33; 6,38-40; 7,16.28; 8,42; Heb 10,5-7), he does not mean a servile obedience to some commandments, but rather a laborious effort to accomplish the "teleological" presence of the Father in his mind and action. His prayers (Lk 6,12), temptation (Mk 1,12-13; Mt 4,1-11; Lk 4,1-13), agony (Mk 14,32-42; Mt 26,36-46; Lk 22,40-46), questioning (Mk 5,9; Lk 8,30; Mk 6,38; Mt 15,34; Mk 9,21; 11,13; Jn 11, 34; 18,34), and learning experience (Heb 5,8; Lk 2,52) indicate that he could not realize the "teleological" presence of the Father in his human mind and will (cf Mk 13,32; Jn 12,37) without studious inquiry. He had to keep one eye on God and the other on the surrounding events in which God appealed to his human mind, since each moment of his life was judged by a divine "must" ($\delta\epsilon\hat{\iota}$). His whole life, activity and passion were under the 'must' of His Father (Mk 8,31; Mt 16,21; 26,54; Lk 2,49; 4,43; 9,22; 13,33; 17,25; 19,5; 22,7; 24,7.26.44; Jn 3,14; 9,4; 10,16; Acts 3,21, etc.) which he constantly sought to perceive. The world was for Jesus the Father's world, in which the Father's work was to be found and done, so that by accomplishing it the Father might be present and all might be one in him and happy in God's beatitude (Jn 15,11).

Thus Jesus' life seems to be a constant reception of God's presence as well as a constant communication or "translation" of God's presence into human history, extending it in and through himself to the earth. As a result of Jesus' translation of God's presence, a new presence of God takes place which is distinct from the "hypostatical union" of God in Jesus, and might be called the dynamic or teleological presence of God.

The teleological presence of God is based upon Jesus' "hypostatic" union with God, and is nothing else but the further extension of this latter to the whole created world. The complete fulfillment of this new dynamic presence of God in the world will be in the resurrection, the complete communication of God's beatitude, i.e. the plentitude of being in the unity of knowing and loving. This completion, however, is necessarily preceded by death as the only way to the resurrection in this world constituted by God as well as by man.

CHAPTER EIGHT

JESUS' DEATH
AND ITS HISTORICAL REASON

Besides Jesus' self-and-God revelational life there is another theologico-historical event demonstrating the validity of Christian faith, Jesus' death. According to Christian faith, Jesus' death no less than his life is part of the Christ event, i.e. the powerful sign event of raising faith in God's presence in him. Consequently, how and why Jesus died is not irrelevant for faith. Otherwise Jesus' death cannot be seen as an intensification of the one Christ event which began in Jesus' life and progressed through death to the resurrection as to its final realization. The question of the historical possibility of whether Jesus could have died for the reasons that he is believed to have died is not of insignificant importance for the believer.

One of the most puzzling questions about Jesus is the real historical reason for his condemnation. It seems that in the synoptic narrative as well as in the Johannine references there are many confusing statements which indicate historical improbability rather than verisimilitude.

The testimony of the synoptic gospels seems to be unanimous in saying that Jesus was condemned to death because of his profession of messiahship and for his blasphemous sayings concerning the Son of God and Son of Man.

According to Mark, Matthew and Luke, the high priest asked Jesus: "Are you the Christ, the Son of the Blessed" (Mt: the Son of God); (Mk 14,61; Mt 26,63; Lk 22,67.70). In the triple tradition Jesus' answer is the same: "I am; and you will see the Son of Man sitting at the right hand of the Power and coming with the clouds of heaven" (Mk 14,62; Mt 26,64; Lk 22,69-70).[292]

Mark and Matthew say that Jesus' affirmation was blasphemy in the ears of the high priest and that the Sanhedrin condemned him as deserving to be put to death (Mk 14,63-65; Mt 26,65-66). Luke does not use the word "blasphemy." He only says that after Jesus' declaration concerning the Son of Man, the members of the Sanhedrin had sufficient reason to take him to Pilate and to charge him with the claim of being Christ, a king who misleads the nation and forbids the payment of taxes to Caesar (Lk 23,2). According to the Acts of the Apostles the Sanhedrin condemned Stephen to death for almost the same saying. When Stephen mentioned the Son of Man standing at God's right hand, the Sanhedrin uttered a great shout, stopped their ears apparently in order to prevent themselves from hearing Stephen's blasphemous saying, and rushed at him all together (Acts 7,56-57) as at Jesus according to the synoptics (Mk 14,65; Mt 26,67-68; Lk 22,63-65).

There are two questions to be asked. First, which one of the two affirmations of Jesus could have been considered by the Sanhedrin as blasphemous: the saying concerning the Son of Man sitting at the right of God, i.e. the claim to some divine prerogatives; or his confession of messiahship, i.e. that he is the Christ? Second, why did the Sanhedrin take Jesus to Pilate instead of stoning him immediately like Stephen?

There is one opinion which tries to explain the historical reason for Jesus' condemnation as the blasphemy which Jesus might have committed, attributing to himself dignity which the Jews spontaneously thought pertained to God. [293] For similar arrogations Jesus seems to be accused of blasphemy on many occasions narrated in the gospels.

In the triple tradition he is said to blaspheme by attributing to himself the power of forgiving sins (Mk 2,7; Mt 9,3; Lk 5,21). According to John, the Jews accused Jesus of blasphemy because, being a man, he made himself like God (Jn 10,30-33; cf Jn 10,36,39). Such a concept of blasphemy would correspond also to the concept of blasphemy which is found in the rabbinic tradition as well as in the Old Testament. The Talmud and Midrash, which are based upon the Old Testament tradition, distinguish three classes of blasphemy. [294] The first is to curse or revile God (Lev 24,11ff; Ex 22,27; Num 15,30). The man who curses God must die (cf Deut 21,22). The second case of blasphemy punishable by death is idolatry, [295] i.e., infidelity to the covenant. [296] The third case is "stretching out the hand to God," i.e. when somebody scorns not only God's command (as does the idolator who does not want to deny God) but also God himself, by assuming divine prerogatives, since in this way he abases God. In the eyes of the Sanhedrin this third class of blasphemy can be applied to Jesus. Jesus can commit the sin of blasphemy by his declaration that he wanted to sit by himself at the right hand of the Almighty, not by God's power, but by his own [297] grasping divine dignity and prerogative (cf Phil 2,6).

There are many historically valid objections to this opinion. The first is that the messiahship appears meaningless in the whole trial. Now, even according to the gospel narratives it is evident enough that the question of messiahship had an essential role. The second difficulty is that it does not give any reason for taking Jesus to Pilate, since the supposition that the Jews did not have authority to put anyone to death (cf Jn 18,31) is historically invalid. The third difficulty is that the Sanhedrin could not understand Jesus' divine sonship in a transcendental sense. According to the official teaching of the Sanhedrin and rabbis the Messiah was supposed to be a man and only a man. The rabbis did not think that the Messiah would have any divine attributes. They always interpreted in a merely human sense all the passage of the Old Testament which might have suggested some kind of transcendence (e.g. Is. 7,1; 9,6; Ps. 2,7,110,1; Dan 7,13-14, etc.). Though it is true that, besides the official teaching of Judaism, there was also the Messiah of the late Jewish apocalyptical writings (like the Psalms of Solomon, the Book of Enoch, 4. Ezra, etc.) conceived as a supernatural transcendental being with divine prerogatives, [298] this view was neither popular nor official in Jesus' lifetime. Therefore, Caiphas and the Sanhedrin could not, like the primitive Church, understand Jesus' confession in the sense of some consubstantial divine sonship. On account of these difficulties there is another opinion, [299] which holds that Jesus incurred the charge of blasphemy and was condemned to death by the Sanhedrin solely because of his affirmation of his messiahship. The crime of blasphemy, indeed, must be taken in a broader sense. Jesus was imprisoned, helpless, and delivered to the wishes of his judges. In such a miserable situation his claim to be the Messiah and the holder of the greatest divinity which Yahweh was supposed to confer on one of the sons of David, must have appeared to the members of the Sanhedrin as a mockery and blasphemous derision of the Almighty's promises given to Israel.[300]

The difficulty with this opinion is that the profession of messiahship does not seem in itself to be a cause for condemnation. According to Mt 11,3 (cf Lk 7,19) for example, John the Baptist openly asks Jesus if he is the Messiah who is to come. In Jn 10,24 the Jews do the same: "How long will you keep us in suspense? If you are the Christ, tell us plainly." Now if this were cause for condemnation in itself, they would not ask him so clearly, for that would mean questioning him about something illicit.

Furthermore, there were several men who claimed to be the Messiah without having incurred the condemnation of the religious authority. Even more, Bar Kokheba[301] was proclaimed Messiah by the famous Rabbi Aquiba, in the years 132-135 A.D. He was condemned only after his failure against the Romans. In the eyes of the Jews the Messiah could not be defeated, since this was a sign that God was not with him. But at the time of the trial, Jesus was not yet defeated by the Romans, and the falsity of Jesus' messianism could not have been proved definitively. On the other hand, he might have been condemned for pseudo-prophecy but not for blasphemy, as the gospels claim. It is improbable also that Jesus was condemned on account of the crime of pseudo-prophecy.[302] It is true that according to Deut 18, 20 and 13,5 the false prophet must be put to death.[303] It is also true that after his condemnation Jesus had been mocked as a false prophet (Mk 14,65; Mt 26,67; Lk 22,63-65). But this was not a crime of blasphemy. In fact, the Jewish authorities in talking about blasphemy never mention Deut 18,20 and the crime of pseudo-prophecy.

The opinion that Jesus was condemned solely on account of his profession of messiahship has still another general difficulty. Why did the Jews take Jesus to Pilate, and not stone him immediately like Stephen?

The synoptic presentation presupposes, and the fourth gospel explicitly asserts a disputable historical fact, viz. that the Jews did not have authority to put anyone to death (Jn 18,31). R. W.

Husband, J. Klausner, J. Jeremias, O. Cullmann, J. Blinzler [304] believe that the Sanhedrin was indeed deprived of its right to carry out the sentence of death. J. Juster, A. Loisy, H. Lietzmann, M. Goguel, C. Guignebert, T. A. Burkill, P. Winter [305] on the contrary, defend that the Sanhedrin had the *jus gladii* before the year 70 A.D. After the studies of T. A. Burkill and P. Winter it is the prevailing opinion today that the Jews had the authority to pronounce and carry out sentences of death, at least in cases of offences against Jewish religious law. X. Léon-Dufour admits that in the present stage of research it·cannot be affirmed that the Sanhedrin could not carry out sentences of death in Jesus' time. [306]

One of the arguments is taken from the Acts of the Apostles. According to 7,55ff. when Stephen mentioned the name of the Son of Man standing at the right hand, the Sanhedrin executed him without bringing him to the Roman Procurator. Why did they not do the same with Jesus? That the execution of Stephen was not a lynching improvised by the people, but a legal stoning according to. the prescriptions of the law, is evident from Acts 7,58-60, 8,1-3 and 26,10-11. The witnesses themselves, after having laid their garments at the feet of Saul, who approved of Stephen's death, stoned Stephen according to their duties prescribed in *Sanh.* 6,4. In Acts 26,10-11 Paul confesses that having received authority from the chief priest he imprisoned Jesus' followers, tried them for blaspheming and voted in favor of their death (cf Acts 8,1-3; 9,1-2). It cannot be said that the execution of Stephen happened because of the administrative confusion occasioned by the recall of Pontius Pilate to Rome. For there is still the case of Herod Antipas who killed John the Baptist (Mk 6,26-29; Mt 14,9-12) and whose jurisdiction over Jesus was acknowledged by Pilate even in Jerusalem (Lk 23,7). Herod Agrippa killed James in Jerusalem (Acts 12,1-2), as well as the guards after Peter's escape (Acts 12,19).

Moreover, according to Josephus (*Jewish War* 6, 2.4), the Sanhedrin was allowed to execute even Gentile persons, including Roman citizens, who violated the temple. Notices, of which we actually have two copies, were set at the entrance saying: "No Gentile is to pass inside the wall round the temple. If a man is caught doing so it is his own fault, for death follows." Therefore it seems to be certain that the Sanhedrin had the jurisdiction of capital punishment. This jurisdiction of the Sanhedrin is confirmed also by Acts 4,1-22; 6,17-42. We know that the apostles, examined by the Sanhedrin, were also threatened with death, if they continued to preach Christ. The attendants, with their commander of the temple, who arrested the apostles (Acts 5,17ff.) are mentioned in John (Jn 7,32,45-48; 18,3).

According to the fourth gospel, the purpose of bringing Jesus to Pilate was the fulfillment of Jesus' prediction (Jn 12,32-33) that he would be "lifted up." This seems to support Winter's thesis that if Jesus was to be "lifted up," i.e. crucified, the death penalty would have to be inflicted by the Romans because the Jews did not execute their criminals by means of crucifixion. However, it is evident that the Sanhedrin had no special intention of helping to fulfill Jesus' predictions. Thus, if they brought Jesus to Pilate, they must have had other reasons for doing so.

J. Klausner thinks that the priests did not see in Jesus anything more than a rebel against the Romans. Therefore to save the people from Pilate's cruel vengeance, they delivered him to Pilate because it was in the interest of Israel that "one man should die for the people, instead of the whole nation being destroyed" (Jn 11,50).[307]

P. Winter believes that Jesus was never tried by the Sanhedrin but only by the Romans. It is hard to admit that the Sanhedrinists could commit as many irregularities [308] as appear by comparing the synoptic narrative with the trial procedure outlined in the Mishnah. Indeed the synoptic narrative is filled with incoherences and contradictions. Matthew and Mark mention two sessions of the Sanhedrin, while Luke mentions only one in the early morning. As a matter of fact, John mentions only the trial before Pilate. It seems therefore, says P. Winter, that the Romans executed Jesus as a rebel. This happened not because Jesus had really been a rebel, but because some others understood his preaching in that way. And Pilate had sufficient reason for crucifying Jesus if he thought that Jesus' preaching might have excited the people even against the will of the preacher himself.[309]

A serious objection might be raised against P. Winter's supposition. If Jesus would have been tried only by the Romans and not also by the leaders of Jerusalem, as a victim of the hated Romans, especially of the bloody-handed Pilate, he should have become a national hero. However this does not seem to be true historically.

The early rabbinic literature, Talmud, Toledoth Yeshu, try to degrade Jesus [310] rather than to exalt him. Baraita of the Babylonian Talmud (*Sanhedrin* 43a) narrates that Yeshu was hanged on the eve of the Passover because he had practiced sorcery and enticed Israel to apostasy. [311] It seems, therefore, that some kind of disagreement and rivalry must have existed between Jesus and the religious leaders of Jerusalem.

More recently, Haim Cohn, Israel Supreme Court Justice [312] tried to explain the bitter frustration of the Sanhedrin by Jesus' refusal to plead not guilty before the Romans. According to Haim Cohn the Sanhedrin wanted to save Jesus, the prophetic teacher beloved by the people of Jerusalem, in order to regain their popular prestige. The purpose of the trial before the Sanhedrin, therefore, had been not the condemnation of Jesus but rather a last effort to obtain some witness who would testify in favor of Jesus before Pilate. But as a matter of fact they could not find any who would witness in favor of Jesus. Then the members of the Sanhedrin, in a final attempt, tried to convince Jesus to plead not guilty before Pilate. Jesus refused their offer, however, and stubbornly admitted his guilt before the Romans, i.e. that he was a real rebel against the Romans.

A theory so conceived also involves many incoherences. First, it is hard to believe that Jesus, without defending himself, would have admitted that he was a rebel against the Romans, especially when the leaders of his people wished to save him. No real rebel would give up a fight when he knows that the leaders of his people are with him in favor of his cause. Much less would a religious man, such as Jesus is supposed to have been, accept unjust accusation and die for it without manifesting his disagreement. Second, if Jesus had been so popular a teacher in Jerusalem that the Sanhedrin judged it worthwhile to save him for obtaining popularity, it is hard to believe that there was no one in the whole of Jerusalem who would have witnessed in favor of him, especially if it was known that the leaders themselves wanted to save him from the Romans. The friendship and love toward Jesus could not have been jeopardized at all by any kind of fear from their own leaders.

Indeed the case of Jesus and his trial is still far from being solved historically. Since there are many insufficient solutions, all with some weakness, new hypotheses can be proposed again for further discussion, in the search for truth. We would like to propose now a new hypothesis which seems to be reasonable and good enough to embrace all the clues around the trial of Jesus. [313]

We proceed from the supposition that Jesus of Nazareth was not an insignificant figure in the eyes of his contemporaries. Like the other remarkable men of his time, his fame and reputation must have been based on his remarkable feats or achievements. Without this he could not have emerged from his low social class with his obscure Nazarene background. That Jesus was, in fact, well known and that his fame was based on his deeds and feats is seen not only in the gospels (Mk 6,14-16; Mt 14,1-2; Lk 9,7-9; Jn 7,31-46), but also in the Jewish Talmud tradition which accuses Jesus of sorceries and magic (*Sanh* 43a).

On account of his reputation, Jesus' unusual sayings and claims did not appear as simply impossible and ridiculous to the ears of the Jews. Rather they caused suspicion and suspense (cf Jn 10,24).

Having some extraordinary talent and power (cf Jn 8,48), Jesus was an enigma to the Jews (Jn 7,35-36). On the one hand his claim to have a special relationship to Yahweh, as to his Father, considering himself more important than any other of the great men of the people of Israel, sounded sectarian and unorthodox (cf the transcendent Messiah of 1 Enoch). But on the other hand, his faithful observance of the law (his frequent appearance in the temple, zeal for Yahweh, and the lack of association with groups, e.g. Essene, who never visited the temple) might have suggested that Jesus was thinking of messiahship in the current official meaning of the term: real historical salvation of Israel, and not as a spiritual leadership of religious sects.

In this situation, it seems natural that the Jews, especially their leaders, wanted to see more clearly. They repeatedly asked for more indications and signs (Mk 8,11-13; Jn 10,24) but, apparently, Jesus would not give them the sign they were looking for.

According to the historical circumstances, there was only one sign that would prove Jesus' claim in the eyes of the Jews and that God was with him much more than with any of the great men of Israel. This sign was the liberation of the Israel from the mighty Roman empire. If Jesus' claim were true, he would have to save Israel as the great men of Israel had with whom Yahweh had been present. They believed that Yahweh alone was the mighty Savior of Israel. Now if Jesus was equal to God in power, and his claim were true, he could and had to save Israel. For this reason the leaders of Israel would have welcomed any confrontation between Jesus and the Roman authorities (Mk 12,13-17; Mt 22,15-22; Lk 20,20-26; Jn 18,29-32). Jesus, however, had always managed to avoid any direct conflict and thus deprived them of the distinctive, unambiguous sign they demanded.

Since the people were divided in regard to Jesus, and since national unity was at stake, the leaders, after several attempts, had to solve the problem once and for all. They knew well the extent of Jesus' claim to be equal to God in power. They knew also that all those who, like the Prince of Tyre, or the King of Babylon (Ez 28,2-10; Is 14,14-15), wanted to be like God by ascending above the heights of the clouds and taking seat there, were rejected and plunged to Sheol. Jesus' similar claim sounded like an arrogant blasphemy [314] to the Sanhedrin, fully deserving of death according to the scripture. In the case of Jesus, however, they did not immediately apply the law in order to give to Jesus his final chance and to provide an unambiguous yardstick for the whole of Israel. They took Jesus and brought him to Pilate. Here was the definitive opportunity for Jesus to demonstrate his power and the trustworthiness of his claim. It was clear that if Jesus were like the king of Babylon, a haughty blasphemer, he would be rejected by Yahweh to Sheol and his deceit would be manifest to all forever. But were he really what he pretended, the Son of God supported by Yahweh, then the salvation of Israel and the end of the Roman Empire was at hand.

This was their aim in provoking the confrontation and in deliberately preventing any chance for reconciliation between Pilate and Jesus (cf Lk 23,13-18; Jn 18,29-32). One of the two had to perish, with the survivor to stay as the lord of Israel. When Jesus was dying on the cross, not having responded to their expectations, their contempt prompted their final challenge to him: "If you are the king of Israel, come down from the cross now, so that we may see it and believe that you are the Christ" (cf Mk 15,32,36; Mt 27,40-43; 27,48; Lk 23,35-49).

But Jesus, after his constant avoidance of any direct confrontation with the Romans, did not perform the definitive sign. He failed in his final confrontation with the Roman Empire and died. After this the Sanhedrin and the Jews of Jerusalem could not see Jesus as anything but a liar and an imposter (Mt 27,63).

If this was the historical situation, the Sanhedrin could not have committed the sin of deicide. Indeed they did not commit any sin (cf Acts 3,17; Lk 23,34), since they proceeded logically and judged according to their historical religious conviction. They did what anyone would do if a really talented man were to appear with extraordinary claims and divine pretensions. He would be tested according to the need of his time and place (e.g. hunger, overpopulation, war, etc.) as contemporary criteria of what "God" must or should be in that time. The Jews, too, judged Jesus' claim according to the notion of God at their time; viz. the Savior of Israel in the Jewish-Roman hostilities.

But Jesus had to refuse the criterion proposed by men—proving that he was equal to God by delivering Israel (Lk 24,21)—since the salvation he brought was of different nature. He was commissioned with a different plan of salvation and his sign could not be limited or confined to a certain historical moment, i.e. to one short time or place (such as the Jewish-Roman hostilities 2,000 years ago). His sign had to be a sign for the whole of mankind of any time and any place, manifesting God as one God of all times and all places.

Therefore, Jesus died and did not provide the sign which was wanted. However, he gave another sign adapted to all times and to the nature of salvation he brought: he rose from the dead on the third day, and appeared to the apostles and disciples, to the God-chosen witnesses of the great sign of God of all times, i.e. that of the risen Christ.

This interpretation seems to be confirmed by the first kindly attitude of the early Christians toward the people of Jerusalem and their leaders (cf Acts 3,17; Lk 23,34). When later in the kerygmatic preaching sin is imputed to the people of Jerusalem (Acts 5,28; 18,6; Mt 27,24-25; see also Acts 20,26-27), it is the common sin of presumption: creating one's own sign and establishing one's own contemporary criteria as indispensable conditions of belief in God. It is the sin of a man who tries to speed up . the chain of events and lays down his own choice of times and ways which God must follow if he is to be accepted by man as the God of man. This sin of unbelief as disobedience against the "time of Yahweh" had been symbolized and concretized in the Jewish people, who apparently did not want to accept easily the evangelization of the post-paschal community.

There is our hypothesis about the trial of Jesus. It seems to explain all the questions which we asked. It explains the double reason of the tradition about the condemnation of Jesus: viz. blasphemy as well as messiahship. It further explains how the leaders of the Sanhedrin could take Jesus to Pilate as well as the kerygmatic nature of sin attributed to them by the writers of the early Church. Finally, it explains the unity of the death of Jesus and of his resurrection as a sign manifesting God's special union with him.

CHAPTER NINE

THE RESURRECTION OF JESUS

1. JESUS' RESURRECTION IN THE LIFE OF THE EARLY CHURCH

For the first Christians the resurrection of Christ was a central and fundamental event and it meant something more than resurrection in the usual sense of the term. By Jesus' resurrection the early Church believed not only in a simple revival of Jesus' dead body but also in his glorification and enthronement in heaven at the right hand of his Father. The resurrection and ascension seem to be one mystery of redemption. [315] Jesus was taken up into the divine glory and was manifested exteriorly as he always had been interiorly (cf Phil 2,6-11). God gave him a name and made him both Lord and Christ (Acts 2,36). All roads of salvation from now on must pass through him, since there is a new relationship between God and his people, so that there is no salvation but in him (Acts 4,11-12). The risen Christ brings the blessing promised to Abraham (Acts 3,25-26), the forgiveness of sins (Acts 2,38; 10,43) and the gift of the Holy Spirit (Acts 2,33,38) as well as the Holy Spirit himself (Acts 2,17-20). Therefore, the resurrection is not only a visible reappearance but a revelation of Christ made by God (cf Acts 10,40), a theophany in Christophany. As the theophanies of the Old Testament were the revelation of *Yahweh-Kyrios,* given to Yahweh's chosen men, so the resurrection of Jesus is a Christophany, i.e. the revelation of *Jesus-Christ-Kyrios* given to God's elected people.

Moreover, for the first Christian the revelation of Jesus-Christ-Kyrios was not only a manifestation of the glorification of Jesus. It had a universal cosmic dimension. To recognize Jesus as Christ-Kyrios was also to recognize that the general resurrection expected at the end of time had taken place in Jesus and the final eschatological age had begun. The resurrection of Jesus represented the resurrection of God's people. The early Christians believed that what happened in Christ would be consummated in them very soon and would also be consummated in the entire cosmos. Jesus is the first-born from the dead (Col 1,18; 1 Cor 15,23; Rom 8,29; Rev 1,5), the New Adam, the life-giving spirit (1 Cor 15,45; Rom 5,14ff), the first fruit of God's final harvest (1 Cor 15,20). By virtue of the resurrection Jesus became Christ and rules over sin and death (1 Cor 15,55) and any created power. Possessing the keys of Death and Hades (Rev 1,18) he disarmed the principalities and powers (Col 2,15; Eph 1,21), and the new age foreseen by the prophets had begun (cf Ez 37,1-11). The death and resurrection of Jesus, in which all are baptized, is seen as the final manifestion of God's personal entry into human history bringing about the re-creation of the world destroyed by sin and death.

This mystery of the resurrection as the revelation of Jesus' enthronement at the right hand of the Father and the inauguration of the eschatological restoration is interpreted by the apostles as the miracle of the resurrection, i.e. the transition of Jesus from the state of death to the state of a renewed, glorious life. On account of this renewed life Jesus belongs connaturally to this visible and perceptible world but in a new way. The material and spatial conditions of his body are sublimated and accommodated to the supernaturalized soul. The conditions of his unique divine sonship are communicated to his body which is called a "spiritual body" (cf 1 Cor 15,44 ff.), not in the sense of not being in time and space at all, but of not having the imperfections and fetters of a temporal-spatial being. The faithful believed that by rising Jesus was liberated from the restriction of the body to a particular, spatial-temporal existence and became contemporary and coextensive with all bodies in time and space. Through the resurrection as a completion of his temporal existence with all its moments, he became contemporary to all moments of history and communicatively present to all men of all ages. Hence this resurrection is nothing else but the realization of God's infinite charity in Jesus

Christ. In the moment of resurrection his body shares in that unlimited plenitude of God's charity towards all men, which demands the communication of the plentitude of being in the perfect unity of knowing and loving to men of all ages. In other words, by the resurrection of Jesus' body the infinite love of God was translated into a bodily dimension and a spatio-temporal, limited reality assumed trans-temporal and trans-spatial dimensions, and thus, history and the world reached their end.

Therefore, in the case of the apparitions, the faithful knew that Jesus did not come from some hidden place or from "heaven." He just inserted himself freely into the limited spatial-temporal dimension. Though he was always present, nevertheless, because of his free insertion into the hindering limits of our time and space, not everyone could see and perceive him, but only those to whom God made him manifest (Acts 10,40), and to whom the inserting action was directed. Not everyone and not even the chosen could always perceive him simply by the senses and recognize him as the Lord. The disciples of Emmaus see him in Lk 24,15-29, as Magdalene does in Jn 20,14-15 and the disciples at the Sea of Tiberias in Jn 21,4-6, but only later could they recognize him (Lk 24,31, Jn 20,16 and 21,7). The reason for this is that the apparition of Jesus did not imply only his insertion into the dimension of our world, but also the elevation of the "seer" or "believer" into the new dimension of the resurrection. The faithful seeing of Jesus' Christophany is indeed an anticipation of the immortal, eternal life which cannot be given except as a free gift of God. Not only the risen Christ but the "seer," i.e. he to whom Jesus' appearance is directed, reaches in some sense the completion of history ahead of "time."

In spite of this great mystery of Jesus' resurrection, the resurrection as a miracle was already proposed to the world by the primitive Church as a manifest proof of Jesus' Lordship and of its own credibility. In Acts 2 we have the earliest apologetical argument taken from the fact of the resurrection. [316] Peter offered to the people of Jerusalem the fact of the resurrection as a certain "proof" through which "the whole nation of Israel must know beyond doubt that God has made this Jesus whom they crucified both Lord and Christ" (Acts 2,36). By the miracle of the resurrection it became manifest that the prophecies were fulfilled in Jesus (Acts 3,18; 2,16; etc.) and that God had not deserted

Jesus in death, but, by dispelling the scandal of the cross, had vindicated him, making him both Lord and Christ. The apostles tried to reason (διαλεγομαι; Acts 17,2-3) about Christ, showing that Christ had to suffer and rise from the dead. Therefore, the miracle of the resurrection had for the first Christians not only a theologico-catechetical but also apologetico-kerygmatic meaning. It was already considered by the primitive Church as a convincing demonstration which was expected to lead people to conversion and to faith, as in fact occurred at the end of Peter's speech (Acts 2,41).

According to the New Testament the resurrection of Jesus was revealed by God to the apostles in the signs of the empty tomb, the apparitions, and the faith and the preaching witness of the apostles.

In the faith of the apostles all three aspects of the resurrection, i.e. the invisible mystery of revelation, the miracle of the new spiritual bodily life and the signs, imply each other. The empty tomb, the apparitions, the faith and the preaching witness of the apostles are signs of the resurrection as a miracle, which is, in its turn, the sign of the great mystery of the enthronment of Jesus at the right hand of the Father.

Because of these visible phenomena as clues, the resurrection of Jesus is no longer immune to the results of historical investigation and criticism. It is possible that the historian can discover facts which are totally incompatible with this kind of faith in Jesus' resurrection and propose an explanation distinct from that given by the first Christians. The faith confessed by the first Christians, unlike other beliefs, is vulnerable and may be taken as a mistake.

A historian legitimately can ask and investigate whether there are some facts totally incompatible with the faith in Jesus' resurrection, and whether the first Christians were not evidently mistaken in Jesus' bodily resurrection.

In order to investigate this problem we will proceed in reverse order. By beginning with the gospels we will see whether the gospels attest to the true resurrection and, then, whether the gospels agree with the primitive tradition manifested in the formulas of confession and in the kerygmatic sermons of faith in the primitive Church. Finally, we will ask whether the primitive tradition can be considered by the historian as a constituting ground of the later Church's faith in the bodily resurrection of Jesus. Or in other words, whether the bodily resurrection of Jesus can be seen as a progressive product of the Christian consciousness.

2. THE GOSPEL TRADITIONS CONCERNING JESUS' RESURRECTION

First we will summarize what the four gospels relate about Jesus' resurrection and how they bear testimony to the faith of the early Church. Since we have chosen to proceed in reverse order, we will begin with the latest of the four gospels, the one according to John.

A. The Gospel of John on the Resurrection: Chap. 20-21

Although the style and language of the twenty-first chapter is Johannine enough, nevertheless there are sufficient clues to suggest that this chapter was written, or at least retouched, by someone else than the author of the gospel. This is inferred from the first person plural form of "we know," followed by the singular form "I think," and in the account in which the author of the gospel is named in the third person, "it is this disciple who." In two verses 21,24-25 there are, therefore, three variations of the subject: we, I, this disciple.

However, the authorship of this chapter as well as that of the whole fourth gospel is not relevant to our way of proceeding. [317] Our interest is to see to what extent at the end of the first century A.D. the fourth gospel attests to the faith of the Church in the resurrection of Jesus, in the discovery of the empty tomb and in the bodily apparition of Jesus.

Concerning Jesus' death and burial John freely follows the synoptic tradition. But the great cosmic signs of the day of Yahweh, the darkness, earthquake, etc. which accompany Jesus' death in the synoptic tradition, are missing in John. For the fourth gospel there are only two "great evidences" that Yahweh definitively intervened through Jesus in human history, and that the final age had begun: the fact that Jesus' bones were not broken and that his side was opened and blood and water came out.

The unbroken bones with the blood pouring out (Jn 19,34.36) revealed to the author the final passover of Yahweh (Ex 12,46).

Yahweh did not permit that the bones of the just be broken (Ps 34,20) so that whenever he wanted he could breathe into them and cover them with skin, raising them from the grave like the dry bones of Ez 37,1-14. But to the great surprise of the author, Jesus' bones are not dry at all for shortly after having given up his spirit from his side, as from the sanctuary of Ezekiel (Ez 47,1-12), water comes forth. This indicates to John that Yahweh does not want to wait any longer and he is going immediately to begin the messianic age in Jesus.

Through the piercing of Jesus' side it becomes manifest that in the midst of the great mourning in the world (cf Zech 12,10-14) there is a fountain of life opened for the house of David and Yahweh now becomes the unique king of the whole world (cf Zech 13,1; 14,8-9). The blood and unbroken bones reveal the Passover feast. The water indicates that this final Passover became the feast of the Tabernacle (cf Jn 7,37-38), the feast of harvesting all the fruits of the years, when all the Jews rejoice in the presence of Yahweh (Deut 16,13; Lev 23,34).

Thus, for John not the darkness, earthquakes, etc. but the flowing water is the great sign of the messianic age (cf Jn 4,14; 6,35; 7,38). Directly corresponding to Old Testament usage water is, indeed, a symbol of the life, pleasure and happiness of the messianic age (Is 49,10; 55,1; 58,11; cf 48,21; Ps 36,9; Zech 14,8; Ez 47,5), which eludes the snares of death (Prov 13,14; cf Is 58,11), because it means the presence of Yahweh (Ex 17,6). In the presence of Yahweh water will never fail (Is 48,21-22). Yahweh can turn dry ground into a waterspring (Is 41,18) giving unlimited water (Ps 78,15-16), unlimited happiness and life to everyone. As Ezekiel saw the water flowing from the temple bringing life wherever it flowed, so John saw the water flowing from the side of Jesus cleansing sin (cf Zech 13,1), bringing with the presence of God wherever it flows life, happiness and victory over death. The reality of this life is further revealed by the flowing blood which in Johannine theology has not only the power of uniting men and God but also of revealing its truth. Therefore this is the "trust-worthy" evidence concerning Jesus' death which the author of the fourth gospel considered extremely important (Jn 19,35).

In regard to Jesus' tomb he informs us that it was not far from the place of crucifixion, and that Jesus' body was prepared with a great quantity of linen clothes and about a hundred pounds of spices (Jn 19,39-40). The tradition concerning the linen clothes, known, apart from John, only to Luke, suggests the presence of an eyewitness. [318] The author relates that when John and Peter went to check Mary's report on the empty tomb, they found the linen cloth on the ground and the cloth which had been over Jesus' head rolled up in a place by itself (Jn 20,7; Lk 24,12).

The tradition concerning the women at the tomb, the miraculously removed stone and the presence of the angels is common to John and to the synoptics. The difference is that the angels only ask Mary why she is weeping. They do not say one word about Jesus' resurrection. Interestingly enough, the term resurrection occurs only twice in John's Easter narrative, in both cases as the explanation of the evangelist himself (Jn 20,9; 21,14). In contrast to Willi Marxsen's view [319] the resurrection as an interpretation of the empty tomb is decreasing rather than increasing. Mark, Matthew and Luke explicitly stress the fact of the resurrection as the primary moment. The later gospel of John extolls rather the apparitions of Jesus (Jn 20,14.18.19.20.25.26.29; 21,1.14) completed by the recognition tradition. [320] It is remarkable that according to the fourth gospel the recognition of Jesus is not identical with his physical presence. He might be present as a gardener (Jn 20,15) or a man standing on the shore (Jn 21,4), or walking on the road (cf. Lk 24,15), but the disciples who knew him for many years cannot recognize him if he does not want to be recognized.

A final difference between John and the synoptic tradition is that Jesus is not going to Galilee to meet his disciples, but is ascending to his Father (Jn 20,17).

The purpose of the apparitions in John is threefold: to give instructions concerning the future (Jn 20,23; 21,15-19), to fill his disciples with joy (Jn 20,20), peace (Jn 20,21) and with the Holy Spirit, and finally, to remove any doubt in regard to his bodily resurrection (20,17.21-28; 21,12-14). Though the term resurrection occurs only twice, there is no doubt that in the view of the author of the fourth gospel Jesus is risen in his body, his tomb is indeed empty, and his disciples experienced his presence in his own physical body since they could see him but not recognize him, except by his free grace.

B. The Synoptic Gospels on the Resurrection

1) Mark's Tradition (Mk 16,1-20)

In chapter 16 of Mark's gospel where the resurrection of Jesus is related we might distinguish two parts: the first is vv 1-8, and the second is vv 9-20. There is evidence enough that this second part which is called the longer ending of Mark was written by someone other than the one who wrote the rest of the gospel. Several Fathers, v.g. Clement of Alexandria, Origen, Tertullian, Cyprian and Cyril of Jerusalem, do not know this longer ending of Mark. Eusebius of Caesarea in the beginning of the fourth century says that most of the codices do not contain our long conclusion, and Mark's gospel closes with verse 8. [321] Indeed *codex Vaticanus* and *Sinaiticus* do not have the canonical conclusion, while certain Greek and Latin codices have another brief conclusion.[322]

Internal analysis also indicates the non-Markan authorship of the verses 9-20. There is a lack of continuity between verses 8 and 9. According to the words of the angels (v 7) the apparitions in Galilee are to be expected, unlike those (v 9.12.14) which, we know from John and Luke, took place in Jerusalem. Further, persons mentioned in the previous verses are introduced again (e.g. Mary Magdalene from whom Jesus had cast out seven demons, taken probably from Lk 8,2—although she had already appeared a short time before in 16,1 and 15,47 without any other distinctive notes). Some persons, without having been previously mentioned, are supposed to be known from elsewhere (e.g. two of them, sc. disciples walking to Emmaus, v 12 from Lk 24,13-32). Corresponding to this fact, therefore, we have two different traditions of the apostolic age conserved in chapter 16 of Mark's gospel.

a) The Early Markan Tradition on the Resurrection (16,1-8)

The 1-8 verses of Mark's 16th chapter raised many questions during the last hundred years: How could the gospel narrative be ended with verse 8 so abruptly? Why are the personal appearances of the risen Christ omitted? Was indeed Galilee and not Jerusalem the place of the first encounters with the Lord?

To answer these questions there were numerous views proposed by scholars, but none of them could gain a universal acceptance. The reason for this might have been the fact that they did not give serious consideration to the prophetic eschatological impact of the

Markan gospel and particularly of Mark 16,1-8. In the light of the prophetic eschatological horizon, the Markan message seems to be surprisingly consistent and perfectly finished.

A careful reading reveals that the Markan Jesus in his lifetime as well as in his death and resurrection is presented as a man surrounded by cosmic signs which according to the prophetic eschatological tradition accompanied the day of Yahweh. To indicate this more concretely we might proceed from the commonly admitted view that the whole of Mark's gospel is written in the light of Jesus' resurrection. The purpose of the author is not to relate how he appeared to his disciples, as John did, but rather to show who this man, known to be risen, really was, and what he was doing before his resurrection. To this question Mark's answer is very explicit: The Risen One was the Son of God, who being recognized as such in heaven by God the Father (Mk 9,7), on earth by the Roman centurion, representative of the greatest power of that time (Mk 15,39), and in the underworld (Mk 5,7) by the devils (Mk 1,34; 3,11; 5,7), preached and worked miracles, the cosmic signs of the kingdom of God (Mk 1,15.40-45).

The same cosmic signs surrounded Jesus even in his death. When he died, darkness came over the whole land (Mk 15,33; cf. 13,24) as Amos (8,9), Isaiah (13,10), Ezekiel (32,7-8), Joel (2,10; 3,4; 4,15), Zephaniah (1,15) described that great day of Yahweh. (Matthew did add the earthquake—27,51—and the other signs of the day of Yahweh—Am 8,8; Is 2,10; Jer 4,24; Joel 2,10;4,16—).

And finally as in his death, so also in his resurrection, Jesus is surrounded by the signs of the eschatological messianic age. As a matter of fact, four eschatological signs can be detected in Mk 16,1-8.

(1) The Daughters of Israel as Messengers of the Good News

The women of verses 1-8, Mary Magdalene, Mary the Mother of James and Salome, are described as sharers in the role of women in the messianic age. They not only receive back their captive (Zech 9,12) and dead (cf Heb 11,35) and by their joy manifest the happiness of the day of Yahweh (Zech 9,9) but above all they become the first messengers of the good news. According to Joel, at that day Yahweh would pour out his spirit on all mankind, and the daughers of Israel would prophesy (Joel 3,1-13). As a matter of fact, the resurrection narrative is the only place in the whole

Bible where women are sent by the angels of Yahweh to pronounce his message to men (Mk 16,7). It was, indeed, a new,
unheard of task, and it is no wonder that the women were afraid
to carry it out.

Now the same messianic eschatological impact is conveyed
further in the verses 3-8. The great day of Yahweh, as described in
Ez 37,12, has three instances: (a) Yahweh opens the graves of
Israel; (b) then he raises his people from their graves; (c) he leads
them back to the soil of Israel, resettling them on their own soil,
so that they will learn and know that he is Yahweh and that he has
said and done all this. Now precisely these three instances seem to
form the pattern for Mk 16,3-8. (For more common elements in
Ezekiel's and Mark's tradition see Mk 4,32—; Ez 17,23;31,6—; Mk
6,34—; Ez 34,5—; Mk 8,18—; Ez 12,2—; etc.).

(2) Yahweh Opened the Grave of Jesus

The three other gospels follow Mark in relating that the tomb of
Jesus has not been opened by man. It was found open. The stone
which closed the tomb seemed to have been miraculously removed. Matthew says explicitly that the angels descended from
heaven and rolled away the stone (Mt 28,1-3). Now, if, unlike the
stones laid on the tombs of many others, "which are still there"
(cf Jos 7,26; 8,29; 10,27; 1 Mac 13,30; cf also 2 Sam 18,17-18),
the stone of the tomb of Jesus had been removed and lies not
there any longer, this indicates that Yahweh had fulfilled Ez 37,12
and raised Jesus from his grave.

(3) Yahweh Raised Jesus from his Grave

The young man in a white robe seated on the right-hand side
confirms the women that the course of the events is the one
described in Ez 37,12: The grave is open, and Jesus has been raised
by Yahweh. "He has risen, he is not here. See, here is the place
where they laid him" (Mk 16,6). The resurrection as sign of the
day of Yahweh is known also in 2 Mac 7,9.14 and to Dan 12,2 (cf
Is 26,19). It was the fruit of Israel's deep conviction that Yahweh
cared for the life of his friends. Therefore, all who serve him will
live (cf Deut 30,15-20; 11,26-28; Jer 21,8; Prov 8,35,36; Neh
9,29; Ps 1,5; Is 4,3; 1 Sam 25,29; Gen 2,9; Rom 5,17,21; 6,1-
11.20-23; 8,1-2; Gal 6,8-9; Jn 14,6; 17,3, etc.).

(4) Yahweh Leads Jesus Back to the Soil of Galilee

The message of the young man sitting on the tomb of Jesus is
very simple: "He is going before you to Galilee; it is there you will

see him, just as he told you" (Mk 16,7). In other words, Yahweh is going to resettle Jesus with his disciples on their own soil, in order to let them know that he, Yahweh, has said and done this (cf Ez 37,14).

In the light of Ezekiel 37,1-14, Mark's short ending is a very complete description of the paschal event. By leading the disciples back to Galilee the real resurrection of Jesus is powerfully witnessed. Compared with the Easter message found in John (20,17.21-23; 21,15-18) in Matthew (28,18-20), in Luke (24,25-27.45-49) or even in the second tradition of Mark (16,16-18) the Easter message of Mark 16,7 is more relevant for the exegete. Without mentioning the concretized apparitions, the giving of the Holy Spirit or the kerygmatic mission of the apostles, the simple message of Mark 16,7 witnesses to the faith in the bodily appearance of Jesus more convincingly than the detailed descriptions of Luke and John. It is remarkable that the connection between the resurrection and the Holy Spirit is not mentioned in Mark's short ending. It seems therefore that the pouring of Yahweh's spirit (Ez 37,14) was not one of the primary instances of Markan faith in the resurrection, but a possible further development (cf Jn 20,22; Lk 24,49; Acts 1,8; Rom 8,1; Rev 11,11; 20,4-6; see Ez 37,6.9.10.14 and Ps 104,30). This being so, any theory which tries to explain the Easter-faith by some sort of subsequent materialization of an earlier experience of the Spirit, becomes less plausible.

Thus Mark 16,7 seems to suggest that even according to Markan tradition the place of the resurrection was Jerusalem, the place of exile, trial and death for Jesus, *from where* he was resettled by Yahweh on his own soil, Galilee. And in this fact, his disciples did recognize that Yahweh has done all this, and the final messianic age was at hand indeed. Therefore, the problem of the twofold tradition concerning the place of the apparitions (the Galilean in Mark and Matthew, and the Jerusalemian in Luke and John) might become irrelevant since Mark (and with him, Matthew) is definitively for the Jerusalem tradition, explained in detail by John and Luke. [323] The problem of the twofold tradition is based perhaps upon an inadequate understanding of the Markan Easter message.

b) The Later Markan Tradition on the Resurrection (16,9-20)

The later tradition related in Chapter 16 of Mark (9-20) mentions the apparitions of Jesus to Mary, to the two disciples walking on their way into the country, and to the Eleven when Jesus gave them full power to preach and baptize. The Easter event is interpreted here by the evangelist as the resurrection (16,9.14) or as the being alive of Jesus (16,11). Meeting with him is explained as a correlation between Jesus showing himself (v 9.12.14) and being seen (v 11). The message of the risen Christ is a mission given to the Eleven. They are sent to do what Jesus was doing, i.e. to preach and work the signs of the kingdom (Mk 1,14; 16,15-20).

The resurrection as the final glorification of Jesus is shown in the event of the ascension. Jesus taken up into heaven sits at the right hand of the Father.

2) Matthew's Tradition (Mt 28,1-20)

Matthew, like Mark, sees the death and resurrection of Jesus as the great Day of Yahweh, followed by cosmic signs. After the death of Jesus, the sun became dim, the earth quaked, rocks were split, tombs opened, and the bodies of many rose from the dead, entered into the Holy City and appeared to many. Even the veil of the temple was torn in two (27,45-54). The opening of the tombs of the saints is a preparation for the more solemn opening of Jesus' grave, which is described by Matthew as an authentic theophany of the Old Testament. During a violent earthquake, the angel of the Lord descended from heaven and "rolled away the stone and sat on it. His face was like lightning, his robe white as snow" (28,2-3). As a matter of fact, he is described as Jesus is during his transfiguration (17,2).

Again, as in Mark, the Easter event is interpreted by the angel as resurrection (28,6.7). The message that the disciples will see Jesus in Galilee is repeated three times (28,7.10.16). This seems to be most important to the writer in order to emphasize that Yahweh did all that was happening to Jesus.

The final message of the risen Jesus in 28,18-20 concerns the preaching mission of the disciples. As Jesus went about the whole of Galilee teaching (4,23), so the disciples have to go about the world teaching and baptizing. Since the efficacity of their teaching could have been invalidated by the story about the stolen body of Jesus, Matthew refutes it as pure fiction. The teaching activity of the apostles, the main concern of his gospel, is supported by Jesus' resurrection as the mighty deed of Yahweh. The apostles have to teach the Good News, since Jesus is not in his grave. He is alive since God revealed and his disciples verified it by seeing (28,17) and touching him (28.9). For Matthew the cosmic signs accompanying Jesus' death and resurrection, more than any apparitions, demonstrate that Jesus is risen in his body, and his tomb is really empty.

3) Luke's Tradition (Lk 24,1-53)

Luke follows a systematic order by concentrating all events in Jerusalem. The entire gospel is the journey of Jesus to Jerusalem culminating in both the act of salvation history and Luke's gospel. The message of Mark's young man is translated into its real meaning. Since, according to Ezekiel, the resettlement of Israel on their own soil meant that Yahweh reopened the graves and let his Spirit enter into the dry bones in order to raise them, Luke can interpret Mark 16,7 as the resurrection on the third day foretold by Jesus in Galilee (24,6-7). The return of the disciples to Galilee has only symbolic revelational meaning to help them recognize that Jesus was really raised from the dead by Yahweh. However, according to Luke this does not mean that the teaching activity of the apostles must move from Jerusalem back to Galilee. Once the apostles understood the revelation of God and could reasonably believe it by seeing his empty tomb with his cloths in it, by walking with him on the road (24,13-35), by touching his wounds (24,39-40), and eating with him (24,42-43), there was no need to go to Galilee any longer. They had to go forth and preach repentance and forgiveness of sins to all nations. The Holy Spirit, another sign of the final day of Yahweh (Ez 37,6.8.14), is now given to the apostles (24,49) as the revealing sign of the messianic age as well as a comforting force in their preaching ministry.

It is remarkable how close an affinity the Lucan narrative of the resurrection shows to the other two synoptic evangelists, as well as to John [324] and to the ancient tradition which Paul recalls in his confession of faith (1 Cor 15). Luke knows the great Day of Yahweh, of Mark and Matthew as well as the vision, and the Holy Spirit; and he also recognizes traditions very familiar to John. However, he especially concurs with the ancient tradition which Paul recounts. As in Paul's confession of faith, so too does Luke refer to the apparition made to Peter: ". . . he was raised from the dead . . . and . . . he was seen by Cephas" (1 Cor 15,5): "the Master had really risen and had been seen by Simon" (Lk 24,34). Luke refers to the apparition to the eleven apostles immediately after the apparition to Peter (Lk 24,33-36) as the confession of faith also does (1 Cor 15,5). In both texts there is a discourse about the death of Christ for the remission of sin, about his resurrection on the third day and about the scriptures which had foretold these events.

1 Cor 15,3-5	*Luke 24,46-47*
a) that Christ died for our sins	b) it is written
b) in accordance with scriptures	c) that Christ should suffer and rise on the third day
c) . . . and that he was raised on the third day	a) and that repentance and forgiveness of sins should be preached

Moreover, Luke not only reports the apparition of Christ but even the instruction of the Risen Christ in a way which calls to mind a confession of faith. The author, it seems, had seriously studied the different traditions (Lk 1-4).

C. Conclusion of the Gospel Narratives on the Resurrection

The gospels give evidence of faith, not in some kind of survival of Jesus after death, but in a true corporeal resurrection. If our analysis is right, we have to say that the tradition of the great day of Yahweh opening Israel's tomb is an earlier tradition than the traditions concerning the visions, the effusion of the Holy Spirit, or kerygmatical interpretations of the Easter event. The cosmic and consequently bodily dimensions of the Easter event precede its spiritual interpretation. Contrary to the general view, it is the Markan and Matthean tradition which testifies radically to the event of the bodily resurrection of Jesus. It is the spiritual-theological interpretation of the later Lukan and Johannine tradition which demanded a more detailed description of the bodily apparitions of Jesus, a fact completely unnecessary in the perspective of Mark and Matthew.

In all four gospel narratives there is another common, yet striking element mostly overlooked by the authors. Their style when dealing with the resurrection is different from their style in the rest of the gospels and vividly reflects the psychological excitement of the first witnesses. The incoherencies of the text reflect the narrational incoherences of a man excited by unexpected events. It is almost impossible to find out the temporal order of the apparitions. [325] The protagonists were so absorbed by the event that they did not seem to pay special attention to its successive instances.

It is interesting also that, though in general people of the New Testament do not seem to be in a hurry, they are so in the resurrection narrative. The Greek term τρέχω (run) occurs in the gospels only eight times and four of these instances are in the paschal narratives. Those who only "walk" before the happening (Mt 28,1; Mk 16,2; Lk 24,1; Jn 20,1), after the paschal news are said to hurry up and to run. Thus Mary Magdalene ran (Jn 20,2), the women hurried (Mt 28,8) and fled (Mk 16,8), Peter (Lk 24,12) and John both ran (Jn 20,4) and the disciples at Emmaus got up immediately and went back to Jerusalem (Lk 24,33).

This psychological excitement is reflected in the bewildering incoherences found in the resurrection narratives. Though the passion accounts have a common and uniform structure, those on the resurrection, as recorded by the different evangelists, are full of divergences. For example, here are some of them:

a) The names of the women, except that of Mary Magdalene, are different. Why is the name of Salome mentioned in Mk 15,40, and in 16,1, while in 15,47 it is left out? Why is the second Mary called at one time the mother of James (Mk 16,1) and at another time Mary, the mother of Joseph, while at another time again the mother of the younger James and of Joseph (Mk 15,47; 15,40)?

b) The purpose of the women in going to the tomb is not the same. According to Mark they go to anoint the body of Jesus (Mk 16,1), while according to Matthew they go to pay a visit to the tomb (Mt 28,1).

c) According to the synoptics, Joseph does not anoint Jesus' body, he only wraps it in linen (Mt 27,59-60; Mk 15,46; Lk 23,53). However, according to John, Joseph anoints the body and makes the burial complete on Good Friday (Jn 19,39-40).

d) The time of the visit to the tomb is not the same. According to Mark they come when the sun had already risen (Mk 16,2), and according to John they come while it is still dark (Jn 20,1).

e) The number of angels varies. According to Mark and Matthew there was one young man (Mk 16,5) or angel (Mt 28,2-5), but according to Luke there were two men (Lk 24,4).

f) The silence of the women in Mk 16,8 contradicts the affirmation of Matthew and Luke that the women ran and announced what had happened to the disciples (Mt 28,8; Lk 24,9-10).

g) The place of the apparitions: according to Mark and Matthew, Jesus appeared in Galilee. They seem to ignore completely the apparitions in Jerusalem. According to Luke and John, Jesus appeared in Jerusalem. They seem to know nothing of the apparitions in Galilee.

h) The time of the apparitions: Luke in his gospel places them all in one day while in the Acts of the Apostles he stretches them over forty days. John names at least eight days between two apparitions; Matthew puts them at least during the time necessary to go from Jerusalem to Galilee. Because of the incoherences of the narratives, it seems to be almost impossible to reconstruct the temporal order of the paschal events.

In the past Catholic apologists used to solve these problems by reducing the differences to a minimum and emphasizing the agreement and unity of the common schema. [326] Today these differences are not denied. They are, in a way, extolled since they testify to the plurality of resurrection traditions, reflecting the life and theology of each early Christian community. The divergences reflect the human factor, the subjective and objective conditions which necessarily influenced the life of the community. The striking point is not the divergence and difference in accounts, but rather the faithful concentration of these divergences into an attempted synthetical treatment.

Evidently, the evangelists relate the resurrection accounts as received and established by an earlier tradition. The sources of this tradition can be analyzed in the documents of the early Church, considered to have been written many years before the time of the composition of the gospels. Thus, we must examine the documents of the pre-gospel tradition.

3. PRE-GOSPEL TRADITIONS CONCERNING JESUS' RESURRECTION

Written documents of the pre-gospel tradition are above all the formulas of the confessions of faith. The confessions of faith expressed in a very brief way the nucleus of truth which was held by primitive Christians and which were explained at greater length in the preaching to unbelievers (kerygma) or in instructions given to the faithful (catechesis). The formulas of faith are quite ancient and reflect in an original way the belief and public statements of the apostles. The question which now interests us is, what sort of resurrection did the first Christians profess through these formulas of faith?

We can find such formulas of faith concerning the resurrection of Jesus in the Acts of the Apostles (2,38; 8,12; 10,48) and in the letters of Paul (e.g. Rom 10,9a; 1 Cor 15,3b-5). We will analyze mainly the Pauline confession of faith which is in 1 Cor 15,3b-5.

A. The Date of 1 Cor 15,3b-5

The first epistle of Paul to the Corinthians, where this confession is found, was written by Paul around 56-57. However, Paul recalled there his oral teaching to the Corinthians, which he gave in Corinth, while dwelling there for a year and a half, in approximately 50 A.D. (Acts 18,1-11).

Paul refers to this oral teaching as already given ὁ παρέλαβον. Now, the question is, when did Paul himself receive this teaching? He received his first instructions in 36 or 37 A.D. at Damascus after he had been converted. In approximately 38 A.D. he came to Jerusalem to see Peter and James (Gal 1,18-19; Acts 9,28).

In the year 43, he was added to the group of missionaries at Antioch. From this group he probably received more additional instruction (Acts 11,25-26). After a whole year (Acts 11,26) the teachers of Antioch sent him on the missionary work to which the Holy Spirit called him (Acts 13,1-13). From now on Paul journeyed alone, or with some disciple, who was more dependent upon Paul for instruction than Paul on him. Whatever he learned had to be in the years 36-44 A.D. Therefore, this might also be the time when he received the oral teaching contained in the confession of faith.

B. 1 Cor 15,3b-5 is a Confession of Faith

Paul has several ancient formulas of confession of faith in his letters (e.g. Rom 1,3-4; 8,24; 10,9; 2 Tim 2,8). That our text is one of these is evident from Paul's introduction. He says, in v 3, that this is precisely the gospel which he himself received and which he preached together with the others. This gospel is, then, not so much his as is that in 1 Cor 7,40, which he preached alone.

"I handed on ... what I received," in Greek, Παρέδωκα-Παρέλαβον, are expressions used by rabbis to signify the transmission of doctrine in a fixed form (cf 1 Cor 11,23; Lk 1,2).[327]

Verses 3b-5 are clearly distinguished as something alien to the preceding and following verses:

a) Paul treats in Chapter 15 of the resurrection (cf vv 1 and 7-58) but here he takes the beginning to be from the death and burial of Jesus, apparently he was unwilling to break the original literary unity.

b) Verses 3b-5 are in an indirect style and are joined by ὅτι, καὶ ὅτι, καὶ ὅτι, "and since, and since, and since," i.e. with a causal subordinating conjunction hardly fitting in the context. Then the indirect style ceases in verses 6-8 and the connection is made by ἔπειτα, ἔπειτα, εἶτα, ἔσχατον δὲ πάντων "after that, then and finally."

c) Non-Pauline expressions are present: e.g. δώδεκα, Twelve, which Paul does not like and never uses. Nor does Paul use κατὰ τὰς γραφάς, i.e. "according to the scriptures," elsewhere.

Paul himself considers these verses as an index of topics, a compendium of the apostolic tradition: "For whether it was I or they ..., so we preached, and so you believed" (v 11). But the profession of faith more probably concludes in verse 6. The expression "many of whom remain until now" does not seem to belong to this fixed formula.

This is the formula of faith which Paul expanded in greater detail when he spent more than one whole year in Corinth, around 50 A.D.

C. The Doctrine of the Pauline Confession of Faith[328]

Let us see now to what this confession of faith testifies, particularly in regard to faith in the resurrection and its signs, the discovery of the empty tomb, and the apparitions.

1) The Death and Burial of Jesus

"... since Christ died ... that he was buried."

It is evident that faith in the real death and burial of Jesus is central in Paul's theology of the new Christian life. It was also central for the primitive belief, otherwise it would not have been one of the articles of faith expressed in the formulas of confession.[329]

The word ἐτάφη "buried," is appropriate to signify the placing of the body in the sepulcher. The same word is used to describe the placing of David in the sepulcher (Acts 2,29).

2) The Resurrection of Jesus

"... *he was raised on the third day* ... "

The verb ἐγήγερται is passive voice. The conviction of the primitive community about the objective reality of Jesus' resurrection is already indicated by the fact that God is the one who raised Christ from the dead (1 Cor 15,15; Acts 2,32; 10,40; 13,30), not man (cf Nm 23,19). Later on the idea of the self-resurrection of Jesus will be more common (cf Mk 16,9; Lk 24,7. 46; Jn 2,19.21; 10,17-18; 20,9).

It is evident that the resurrection meant by Paul in 1 Cor 15,4 was not only some kind of spiritual resurrection but the corporeal resurrection of Christ.

Paul asserts in his sermon before the Sanhedrin that he is in agreement with the Pharisees concerning the doctrine of resurrection (Acts 23,6). But the Pharisees believed in the bodily resurrection of the dead. In Athens he had already announced bodily resurrection to the Athenians, to whom both the concept of resurrection and that of immortality were so foreign that they were unwilling to hear Paul any more (Acts 17,18.31-32).

In particular, Chapter 15 of the First Epistle to the Corinthians is directed against the error of the Greek Christians who, as Greeks, could not accept the resurrection of the body. Now from Christ's resurrection, Paul wished to prove the resurrection of the Corinthians. If, therefore, their resurrection will be corporeal, as Paul attempted to prove here, then Paul must think of the resurrection of Christ as corporeal otherwise his argument would not prove anything. The Corinthians did not seem to doubt the resurrection of Christ, but only their own bodily resurrection. Therefore, the bodily resurrection of Christ, according to the mind of Paul as well as the faith of the Corinthians, is not deduced from the desire for their bodily resurrection. Rather, from the incontestable fact of the bodily resurrection of Christ the Corinthians are taught to conclude to their own bodily resurrection.

Paul further explains how he understands the bodily resurrection of the dead. He insists very much on the newness of the resurrected body (vv 36-38). But this is a newness of state in the same body (vv 42-44). Flesh and blood indeed cannot possess the kingdom of God, nor can the corruptible possess the incorruptible (cf vv 50), since "flesh and blood" as a biblical expression designates man as having an infirm and mortal condition. After the resurrection, man will no longer be in this weak and infirm mortal state. His "perishable nature must put on the imperishable," and his "mortal nature must put on immortality" (v 53).

If resurrection is such for the Corinthians, it is equally true that Paul, the so-called theologian of spiritualized Christianity, did not regard the resurrection of Christ as a glorification of the soul only, with the body remaining in the tomb. He understood the resurrection of Christ in such a way that it involved the belief in the empty tomb. This was the belief he received from his teacher before his missionary work.

Although Paul does not mention the empty tomb explicitly, nevertheless, he believed that Jesus' tomb was empty. His confession of faith continues by saying that Jesus was raised by God "on the third day in accordance with the scriptures." Since no particular passage in scripture is indicated, it is difficult to determine what the "in accordance with the scriptures" might mean. [330] In the preaching and in the letters of the early Church there are mainly two categories of scriptural texts on the resurrection: those which interpret the resurrection as (a) the mystery of the enthronement of Jesus (Ps 110,1 referred to: in Acts 2,34-35; 1 Cor 15,25-27; - Ps 2,7 in Acts 13,33; Rom 1,4; Heb 1,5; 5,5; - Ps 118,22-24 in Acts 4,11; 1 Pet 2,7) and those which mention (b) the non-corruption of Jesus' body (Ps 16,10 in Acts 2,27; 13,55). These quotations of the Old Testament refer primarily to the resurrection and are cited to show that the resurrection of Jesus is a sign and proclamation of his Lordship.

Concerning the circumstances of the "third day," no quotation of the Old Testament is found in the preaching of the apostles. There is only one quotation of Jonah 2,1, which is found in Mt 12,40, and uttered by Jesus. We have to notice, however, that in the probably more primitive account of the teaching about Jonah which is found in Lk 11,30, there is no mention of the three days. Jonah is proposed as a sign of the Son of Man, because, having been rejected by their own people, both Jonah and the Son of Man had to preach to foreign people. There is only one good text of Hosea which could be applied, in an accommodated sense, to the resurrection on the third day, viz., 6,2-3. But this text of the Old Testament is never quoted in the New Testament.

Now, the phrase "on the third day" either refers to the nature of the resurrection [331] or to the time of the resurrection. [332] In both cases it implies faith in the empty tomb. If it refers to the nature of the resurrection, then it means nothing other than the fact that Jesus' body did not start to decompose, since it was not in the tomb for four days. According to the Talmud, the Jews believed that the soul somehow remained with the body throughout three days and only on the fourth day did the decomposition begin. [333] That is why people mostly visited the tomb on the first three days. This is also the reason why Martha warned Jesus that in Lazarus' tomb "there will be a stench, for he has been dead for four days" (Jn 11,39).

Now some scholars believe that the disciples did not stay in Jerusalem but that they fled immediately from Gethsemani to Galilee. Consequently the first apparitions, as predicted by the angels in Mark's and Matthew's tradition (Mk 16,7; Mt 28,7; 26,32), took place in Galilee many days after Jesus' death. They conclude, therefore, that the disciples could not have checked Jesus' tomb on the third day.

But granted this supposition, the phrase "on the third day" still indicates that the disciples believed that Jesus left his tomb on the third day. This belief was founded on the belief that he did not undergo corruption.

It is, however, more probable that the phrase "on the third day" is to be referred to the time of the resurrection. Therefore, the idea of "third day" is not taken from scripture but from the possible observation of the empty tomb.

In any case, we should notice that in general a quotation from the Old Testament was never used to prove the fact of the resurrection, but only to elucidate its messianic significance. The paschal event was proposed as a fact of which the apostles were witnesses (Acts 1,22; 2,32; 3,15; 4,33; 5,32; 10,39; 13,31). They were less concerned about demonstrating the details of the "third day" with an Old Testament quotation, since the Old Testament contained little information on this. They proposed the resurrection as a fact known by witnesses. The detail of the "third day" is presented in the preaching of Peter and Paul, without any allusion to the proof from sacred scriptures (cf Acts 10,40-41). The relevance of the texts from the Old Testament is more likely to have been seen only after the event. Once the historical event was known, the apostles could find some indications in scripture concerning that time, but not before the actual event.

If "the third day" was considered important enough by the apostles to be expressed in the catechetical summary, this happened only because the disciples observed some event on the day of the Pasch. This event could not have been the resurrection since no one actually saw the resurrection. There are only two possibilities: either they first discovered the empty tomb and afterwards saw the apparitions of the risen Christ, or they first experienced the apparitions and later went to see the tomb. The accurate observation of the third day can be accredited to them either through the discovery of the empty tomb on the third day, or upon an apparition on the third day. This seems all the more necessary since they were the disciples who buried Jesus and who were supposed to visit Jesus' tomb during the first three days in keeping with the Jewish custom. Thus the possible metaphorical meaning of the not very clear sayings of the Old Testament as well as those of Jesus could be understood by the disciples as having been literally fulfilled.[334]

Therefore, it seems that Paul does indicate the belief in the discovery of the empty tomb. His view concerning the corporeal resurrection of Jesus is further manifested by his list of Jesus' apparitions.

3) The Apparitions of Jesus

"... and that he appeared to Cephas, then to the Twelve."

In the confession of faith after the affirmation of the resurrection, witnesses are referred to. To these Jesus appeared after his resurrection. The reason for the enumeration of witnesses who saw the Lord is evidently to argue further for the resurrection of Christ. Jesus rose, since he appeared to the apostles. But how did he appear: spiritually only or bodily?[335]

What Paul wished to demonstrate through this confession of faith is evidently the corporeal resurrection of Christ. This is clear from the context. The Corinthians shall rise again corporeally because Jesus rose corporeally. And Christ did rise from the dead, for he appeared to witnesses. Therefore, at least in the mind of Paul, the report of the witnesses, which he explained to the Corinthians in the year 50, was such that it proved the bodily resurrection of Christ. The witnesses must have seen the body of Christ living again, otherwise, the thesis of Paul was unprovable. Paul, therefore, considered the reports of the witnesses as reports indicating the bodily appearance and not just a spiritual vision of Christ. Consequently, concerning the apparitions, Paul recommends to us the report, which was presented also in the gospels. Moreover, Paul taught this doctrine as one handed on to him, confessing that he learned it after his conversion, when he received his first indoctrination, around the years 36-44.

Using this testimony of Paul for our investigation of the existence of faith in the bodily resurrection of Christ, we can move backwards from the time the gospels were composed to the first years of the fourth decade of the first century. In the years 40-44 the Christian community believed that the witnesses to the apparitions of the risen Christ truly saw and experienced the body of Christ, and not just a mystical vision.

However, we can ask is this last statement not invalidated by the vision of Paul in Damascus, which he also proposed as an argument? This vision was not an objective vision of the body of Christ, but rather a mystical internal revelation. Now, if Paul equated his vision to the appearances of the risen Christ to the apostles, it might follow that, according to Paul, the appearances of Christ to others were only subjective visions, or internal revelations about the resurrection of Christ.

Let us recall first of all the series of witnesses presented in the Pauline confession:
- the first appearance to Peter
- the second appearance to the Twelve
- the third appearance to more than five hundred
- the fourth appearance to James
- the fifth appearance to all the apostles; and
- the last appearance to Paul.

The question is, what sort of vision was Paul's at Damascus and what significance does Paul give to it in 1 Cor 15?

It is evident that Paul clearly distinguishes his experience of Christ at Damascus from the other visions he had. One of these visions certainly was a vision of Christ where he saw Jesus in a subjective mystical vision according to Acts 22,17-21. But it is only the Damascan experience which he adds to the series of appearances of the risen Christ.

When Paul speaks of other visions he excuses himself (2 Cor

12,1) while he often alludes, and without any excuse, to the appearance of Christ on the road to Damascus (1 Cor 1,17; 15,8; Gal 1,15; 2,7; Rom 1,5). Paul is aware that he was made an apostle through his Damascan vision, a fact of greatest importance to him (Acts 26,16).

The appearance of Christ on the road to Damascus is a particular case, distinct from the other apparitions both from the viewpoint of the object of the vision and also from the viewpoint of the subject perceiving it. The vision is referred to in three places in the Acts (9,3-9; 22,6-11; 26,13-18) and it is very different from the Christophanies given to the apostles. In all three cases there is mention made of a most resplendent light, which Paul sees, and of a voice that he hears, but Jesus is not described as actually appearing. Meanwhile, the Twelve and the other witnesses of Jesus' Christophanies did not see a light but Jesus himself. Now Paul saw only a brilliant light and he was struck to the ground. When he "got up from the ground and opened his eyes, he could see nothing" (Acts 9,8). It seems, therefore, that Paul had his eyes closed during the vision. According to the first account his companions could hear only the voice but saw no one (Acts 9,7). According to the second account (Acts 22,9) they saw light but did not hear the voice. According to the third account, they immediately fell to the ground, as Paul did (Acts 26,14). Paul says in 1 Cor 9,1 that he has seen the Lord, but the verb ὁράω might itself mean a mystical vision too (cf Acts 22,17). The Christophany of Paul is called ὀπτασία, a heavenly vision (Acts 26,19) like the other ecstatic visions in 2 Cor 12,1.

The vision of Paul presented in Acts is to be understood in the light of Paul's own statement expressed in Gal 1,12.16. Now according to Gal 1,12ff, Paul's vision was not an encounter with Jesus on the earth as it happened the other apparitions were, but a revelation from heaven accompanied by the light phenomenon as usual. It was a heavenly revelation, an intellectual revelation of the mystery of divine sonship of Jesus (cf Gal 1,16). Therefore, although Paul relied upon his vision of Christ as a general confirmation of the preaching of the apostles on the resurrection of Christ, the primary argument concerning the bodily resurrection of Jesus was for him the testimony of the apostles. He does not equate his vision of Christ with the other appearances of the risen Lord. He considers his vision as distinct from the others, since it did not belong to the confession of faith. For Paul says, "I have handed on to you what I myself have received" as the intermediate minister in the chain of tradition. But he received only the Christophanies given to the witnessing disciples, not his personal vision of Christ. Moreover, he says too, that "whether it is I or they, we all preach alike" (1 Cor 15,11), but the appearance of Christ to Paul on the road to Damascus was not an object of this common preaching. Furthermore, at Antioch, Paul spoke thus: "... God raised him from the dead ... he appeared to those who had come up to Jerusalem with him from Galilee and they are now witnesses for him to the people" (Acts 13,31). Therefore, for Paul the witnesses are those who came up with Jesus from Galilee, among whom Paul himself cannot be included. Paul did not consider himself a witness in the same sense as the disciples who saw the Lord. He was an apostle, but as we will soon see in dealing with early Christian concept of "witness" and 'apostle,' not a witnessing apostle in the full sense like the Twelve.

Therefore, Paul does not seem to affirm his vision of Christ was of the same kind as the apparitions of the risen Christ given to the other apostles. Paul does not want to assert, from the nature of his vision, anything concerning the nature of the Christophanies given to the official witnesses. He could add his vision of Christ to the list of Christophanies given to official witnesses as a personal confirmation of his belief that Jesus is alive since the term ὤφθη could signify both encounter as well as vision. In both cases, according to early Christians, God was the cause of Jesus' appearance. He caused "Jesus-to-be-seen" either plainly (Acts 10,40) or "to-be-speaking-to" his apostles (Acts 22,18; 9,10).

4) Conclusion Concerning the Pauline Confession of Faith

The Pauline confession of faith attests to the faith of the Church in the empty tomb of Jesus and in his true resurrection as well as in his bodily apparitions to the disciples. It seems that concerning the bodily nature of the Christophanies there is an agreement about these events in the accounts of the gospels (for the years 65-100) and in Paul's testimony (for the years 40-60). Moreover, the same confession of faith attests that the testimony of the apostles to the bodily appearance of Christ was proposed as proof for the resurrection of all bodies.

By considering the Christological confessions (1 Cor 15,3b-5;

Eph 5,14; 1 Tim 3,16; Acts 2,36; 2,38; 8,12; 10,48, etc.), we can affirm that between the Christological confession and the paschal event there is always a necessary relationship. The paschal event is the primary fact from which the subsequent confessions of faith are derived. Such a conclusion is confirmed by Paul's censuring Hymenaeus and Philetus. Since the Greeks found the resurrection particularly difficult to accept (cf Acts 17,31; 1 Cor 15,12), Hymenaeus and Philetus denied the future resurrection of the body by restricting resurrection to some mystical form which occurs in baptism (cf Rom 6,4; Eph 2,6; Col 2,12; 3,1). Now Paul rejects such a doctrine. Both of them have made a shipwreck of their faith and consequently Paul had to deliver them to Satan that they may learn not to blaspheme (1 Tim 1,20). They have upset the faith and have gone far away from the truth by claiming that the resurrection is already past (2 Tim 2,18). In the preaching of Paul the bodily resurrection of Christ is central, [336] not as a speculative doctrine but as a central event. Also, it is central in the early kerygmatical sermons of the primitive Church as we shall now see.

D. Primitive Kerygmatic Proclamation Concerning Jesus' Resurrection

The kerygmatic sermons are the primitive preaching which sought to communicate the good news to nonbelievers. Through these sermons the community at Jerusalem wished especially to inform the Jews of Jerusalem of the resurrection. Since they are the earliest sermons, they manifest the very first formulations of the Christian faith in Jerusalem and might answer many interesting questions. How did the Christians speak to these Jews of Jerusalem who were well aware of how Jesus ended his life? What did they tell these Jews about the life of Jesus? Did they first of all announce to them some doctrine concerning the resurrection, or did they announce the very fact of Jesus' resurrection?

The importance of these sermons is further evident from the fact that this method of preaching by Peter and Paul probably offered instructive norms for the early Church. It seems that the tradition, whether oral or written, which Luke used contained the essential themes used by the other principal preachers, who, under the leadership of Peter and Paul, spread the word of God. [337]

The first announcement of the gospel message by the Jerusalem community is found in the Acts of the Apostles and is proposed in the form of speeches of Peter and Paul.

   (a) the sermon of Peter on Pentecost Sunday, 2,14-40

   (b) the sermon of Peter in the temple, 3,12-36

   (c) the sermon of Peter at Caesarea, 10,34-43

   (d) two professions of faith before the Sanhedrin, 4,8-12; 5,29-32[338]

   (e) the sermon of Paul at Antioch, 13,16-41

Although the style and characteristics are evidently colored with a certain hellenistic influence, the early announcing of the gospel message is still obvious in the sermons.

1) The Resurrection of Christ in the Kerygmatic Proclamation in Jerusalem

From a simple reading of the kerygmatic sermons of Peter and Paul it can be established that they proclaim in fact nothing else but this: Jesus has risen. The apostles present themselves as witnesses of the resurrection and they announce it in Jerusalem with unshaken faith, where not long ago Jesus was condemned to death by the Sanhedrin for blasphemy. Christ's resurrection is central in the preaching of the Jerusalem community and is also the central object of the *marturion* of the apostles.[339]

It should also be noted that the apostles do not primarily and directly proclaim the clues for, but rather the fact of the resurrection. They do not want to persuade men by making deductions from the signs of the empty tomb and the apparitions. Perhaps they would have so proceeded had they themselves arrived at their belief in the resurrection by means of some logical deduction. Their method is otherwise. They affirm the fact of the resurrection as primary and principal, and mention somewhat offhandedly as something accidental and secondary, the empty tomb and details of the apparitions. They themselves seem to know from experience the fact that Jesus lives again in his flesh and they ask others to believe in what they themselves know for certain. Such is the argument, generally, of a man who sees an event, but not of the man who deduces his conclusions about the real order from a theoretical beginning. The apostles argue as witnesses and not as historians.

The historian who has not seen the event proceeds in the

opposite way. His task is to judge through his own criticism of the historical veracity of the witness. The clues, sc. the empty tomb, the apparitions, the belief of witnesses will be primary for him. To convince someone he will lead him to the conclusion through the same mental process through which he himself passed. The apostles, however, do not act as historians in demonstrating Jesus' resurrection but give witness to it in the manner of one who sees it. This difference in method strengthens the trustworthiness of the ancient tradition.

2) The Empty Tomb in the Early Kerygmatic Proclamation

An explicit affirmation of Jesus' empty tomb is lacking in the early kerygmatical speeches. There is, however, a clear allusion to it. As is evident in the speeches of Peter and Paul, the first preaching of the gospel message elucidated the resurrection by biblical references. According to Acts 2,27, Peter applies Ps 16,10 to Jesus ". . . nor will you let your Holy One see destruction." According to Peter, David could not have been speaking of himself in this Psalm, since "David's tomb is here among us to this very day" (Acts 2,29). Therefore, David must have been speaking of Jesus, when he declared "Nor will you let your Holy One see corruption." David underwent corruption, for his sepulcher is here to this very day (Acts 2,29). But Jesus did not, for his tomb, unlike David's is no longer in Jerusalem. In this argumentation there is a clear allusion to the fact supposedly admitted by all, that the tomb of Jesus was empty (cf also Acts 13,36-37). On the one hand the apostles had to know before the proclamation that Jesus' tomb was empty, otherwise they would not have dared to talk after the manner of Peter in the city where the tomb of Christ had been. On the other hand, an announcement like that of Peter forced people to verify the fact by checking the tomb.

3) The Apparitions of the Risen Christ in the Early Kerygmatic Proclamation

In the first sermon made at Jerusalem the apparitions are mentioned but no explicit listing offered. In his sermon in Jerusalem Peter says that God raised Jesus from the dead and that he himself, with the other apostles, was a witness to his resurrection (Acts 2,32). Jesus is said to have appeared for many days to those who had come up with him to Jerusalem from Galilee (Acts

13,30-31). At Caesarea, Peter adds that Jesus, after his resurrection, ate and drank with his disciples (Acts 10,41).

The bodily form of the Christophanies is further extolled by frequent repetition that God is the cause of Jesus' resurrection as well as his apparitions (Acts 10,40; 2,32; 13,30). The activity of God upon Jesus indicates the trans-subjective character of the apparitions. That Jesus is risen and has appeared is not due to an imaginative creation of the community but to the almighty power of God.[340]

The early Church's belief in the real resurrection is further confirmed by the different senses of the early Christian concept "apostle" and "witness."[341]

From the list of witnesses presented in the Pauline confession we might guess that besides the Twelve there existed a greater group of the apostles to whom the fifth apparition was given. Although, according to Luke, Jesus himself called these Twelve men apostles (Lk 6,13), from statistical findings in the New Testament it is evident that the Twelve were usually referred to as a group numbering 12 or 11, or by their individual names.[342] They formed a special group of apostles. The basic requirements for membership to the Twelve seems to have been (1) a vocation given by Jesus, (2) the following of Jesus from his baptism by John to his ascension, and (3) a commission by Jesus to be a witness to his resurrection. On this account a man like Paul was not eligible to take the place of Judas, because he had not conversed with Jesus during his earthly life.

Matthias saw Jesus in the flesh, Jesus appeared to him before the coming of the Holy Spirit. Hence he, like the Twelve, could be an apostle and, not like Paul, a witness of the Christian message only, but also a witness of the resurrection. Thus Matthias was eligible to be one of the Twelve (Acts 1, 21, 22), whereas Paul was not. For the first Christians the Twelve alone were the apostles and witnesses in the full sense of the word.

Besides the Twelve there was another group of apostles to whom, perhaps, the fifth apparition was made and to whom the risen Christ himself had given the mandate of evangelization. Their mission was not from man, but immediately from Jesus himself, therefore they enjoyed a great respect among the first Christians. Paul called them his "predecessors in Jerusalem" (Gal 1,17-2,10) or arch-apostles (cf 2 Cor, 11,5; 12,11).

Finally, there was the third category of the apostles, "the minor apostles," those Christians who did not receive their mission directly from Christ, but from "men," i.e. from the arch-apostles. They too took part in the propagation of the gospel (cf Rom 16,7; 1 Cor 9,5; 2 Cor 8,23; 11,5-13; 12,11-12). Since Paul had not seen the Lord, and was introduced by Barnabas (cf Acts 11,25) many wanted to reduce him to the category of a minor apostle. Against this Paul argues persuasively from his vision on the road to Damascus. His apostolate is not from men, since he got his mission from the living Christ. He is not sent by any man but by Jesus Christ (Gal 1,1.12; 1 Cor 1,17); therefore, he is equal to those apostles in Jerusalem (Gal 2,1-2). He is, indeed, the last and least important of them, even if he once persecuted God's Church, but he is arch-apostle, because like his predecessors he is called by Jesus to preach the Good News and to testify to the things he has seen in Jesus (Acts 26,15-18).

Therefore, according to Luke, Paul the great apostle is not a witness in the same sense as the other apostles. The apostles are witnesses of the resurrection of the Lord Jesus, giving testimony to the event with great power (Acts 4,33; 2,32; 3,5; 5,21 ff.; 10,41; 13,31). Paul is a witness to Jesus' message. He is a witness not so much for the life of Jesus, but for all that he has seen in his vision of Jesus (Acts 22,15; 26,16). His witnessing is based upon the witnessing of the apostles, since the central theme of his theology is the salvific death, burial, and resurrection of Jesus, moments not seen in the vision at Damascus.

Besides the great apostles and Paul, only Stephen is called a witness by Luke (Acts 22,20). He, like Paul, is a witness because he testifies to the gospel message. He is not a martyr in the recent meaning of the word, i.e. because he died. Rather he died because he was a "martyr" of the gospel message. Stephen's witness differs from the witness of the Twelve. Both Stephen and Paul are witnesses in a somewhat lesser sense than the Twelve (Acts 13,30-33). In his speech at Antioch Paul calls upon the testimony of those who accompanied Jesus from Galilee, while he and his companions only announced the Good News. In the argumentation of the Christophanies Paul yields to the apparition given to the Twelve. This distinction is even found in Luke, who always favors his hero Paul. Through this distinction and the different descriptions of the categories of apostles and witnesses found in the life of the early Church, we can conclude that the first hierarchical structure of the Church is related to the resurrection of Christ.

The faith of the early Christians in regard to the bodily apparitions is manifested, finally, in their recognition of Jesus as inaugurator of the eschatological age, as the Lord of the restoration and recreation of a world destroyed by sin and death. The early Christian believed that those who have fallen asleep will rise and those who are alive will not be asleep (cf 1 Cor 15,51) but caught up together in the cloud to meet the Lord and be with him always (1 Thess 4,15-17). The great expectation of many Christians that they were not to die (cf Jn 21,23) supposed that Jesus had conquered death precisely by his bodily resurrection.

4) Conclusion of the Kergymatic Proclamation in Jerusalem

As in the gospels and Pauline confession of faith, so too in the early proclamations, the empty tomb is pointed out, and apparitions are proposed as token of the bodily resurrection of Christ, which is proclaimed as the central theme of an unshaken faith.

In these primary sources we could discover the same belief that we find in the gospels themselves. If there is any evolution present, it is not faith in the resurrection but in the more extensive description of signs, namely the empty tomb and the narration of the apparitions assigned to the witnesses. It seems therefore, that at the time of the writing of the New Testament documents, the early Christians did believe in the resurrection of the body of Jesus.

4. THEOLOGICO-HISTORICAL DEMONSTRATION OF THE VALIDITY OF CHRISTIAN FAITH IN JESUS' RESURRECTION

The historian, in authenticating a past event, ought to give first place to ancient testimony, since he himself is no longer able to experience the event himself. Nevertheless, it is the historian's job not only to establish the story narrated by the ancients, but also to make a critical judgment about its validity. A judgment about the historical validity of any document supposes a twofold criticism: literary criticism and historical criticism. [343] Literary criticism studies the literary form of the documents, their sources and the way the sources are used. Such a literary analysis is necessarily presupposed by historical criticism. If the author is using doubtful sources, or if he uses good sources in a sense other than originally intended, it is evident that the historical context of the events has been changed and the original historical context, in which the primordial validity of the events might authentically be unfolded, must be sought somewhere else.

To find this original historical context is the task of historical criticism. Historical criticism is supposed to make a judgment about the validity of the events first in regard to their actual present, which is our past, and then, in regard to their future, which is our actual present as well as our common future. In a way similar to the verification method, historical criticism will test different possible historical contexts in which the intentionalities of the analyzed event can come to their full disclosure.

Consequently, the application of historical criticism to the instance of Christian faith in Jesus' ressurection would mean, above all, a search for its original historical context in which its meaning, as well as its objective convincing power in regard to the past and to the present, will be seen as understandable and even perceptible.

A. The Historical Evidence of Christian Faith in Jesus' Resurrection

Historical evidence in regard to the resurrection of Jesus is identical with the results of literary criticism. It is an indisputable historical fact, that from the early 40's in the first century after Christ, i.e. not fully ten years after the death of Jesus, there existed a faith in the bodily resurrection of Jesus. This faith in Jesus' resurrection was a faith professed by many communities differing in nationalities, and in cultures sufficiently distant from one another. According to literary criticism documents attesting to this faith were not written primarily for the use of libraries. They were rather living expressions of the personal convictions of the different communities built upon this faith.

B. The Complexity of the Faith in Jesus' Resurrection Evades the Usual Ordinary Explanations of Historical Understanding

Historical understanding like any understanding is an effort to grasp a historical event by relating it to a previous situation, mastered and expressed within categories of historical understanding. One of the most obvious categories of historical understanding which might occur to the historian concerning Jesus' resurrection is the category of fiction or legend. After a more careful analysis, however, it will be manifest that in the case of faith in Jesus' resurrection, legend is not an adequate category of historical understanding. The historical evidence is much more complex and wider than that covered by the category of legend.

1) Legend

Anything legendary grows up through a long period of time. But there are less than ten years between the death of Christ and the first written documents on the resurrection, which by showing a concise form and widespread use reveal their origin as more ancient still. In a fable there is always vagueness, vacillation, with long superfluous descriptions. In the documents of the resurrection such vagueness or vacillation is not found. They contain a simple statement rather than an explanation. It is certain that in the most ancient sources of the New Testament the earliest theme is not the nativity, nor the public life of Jesus, nor the passion, but the laconic statement that Jesus rose from the dead and lives. Such instantaneous and unexpected information with no regard for the life before death demands that some event giving rise to that faith intervened after death. The Easter tradition cannot be evaluated simply as a late legend. The legend itself demands some reason.

Such a reason certainly could not be the life of Jesus before his death. Ancient documents and the apostles themselves do not speak primarily about the events of the life of Jesus before his death. The first proclamation does not treat of the nativity (as some biographies do), nor about his parents, nor about the public life of Jesus, nor about the miracles, but about his death and his resurrection. If the foundation of the Easter story were only the public life of Jesus, without any account of his death, this most probably would have been noted in the primitive proclamation. The first proclamation would have been some systematic story of the life of Jesus, as we actually have in the later gospels. But the first announcements, which belong to the most ancient sources, treat of the resurrection and only afterwards do they begin to add the particulars of the Risen Jesus' life. Jesus' former life is considered from the aspect of the resurrection.

2) Hallucination

Another category of historical understanding explaining the faith of the apostles could be the category of hallucination. Hallucination, however, fails to explain properly the belief in the empty tomb which existed in Jerusalem from the early beginning of the Church. A belief in Jesus' empty tomb in Jerusalem required that Jesus' tomb be really empty. If the corpse was still in the tomb, such a faith was impossible. But, then, what happened to the corpse? Who did remove it? [344] The Romans or the Jews? A historian could not find motive for it. Both the Romans and the Jews were glad that the case of Jesus is closed. The disciples? But this makes hallucination rather difficult since the knowledge of the true cause of the event makes hallucination not only more difficult but the existing hierarchical structure of the early community almost unintelligible. Granted the discussion of rivalry among the disciples some one of them would probably have revealed the fraud and spoken of it. Paul himself never used this kind of argument in defending his equality with the great apostles. The removal of the corpse by thieves and vandals would not exclude hallucination as an adequate category to explain the belief of the disciples in the empty tomb. Grave-robbery ($\tau v\mu\beta\omega\rho v\chi\iota a$) was frequent at the time and Jn 20,2 with Mt 27,62-66; 28,11-15 can be considered as basis for speculation. The report about the wrapped grave-clothes found in the tomb (Jn 20,5.7) can be used as con and pro for such an explanation. But grave-robbery makes sense only in the context of hallucination theory. Once the hallucination as a category for historical understanding cannot be accepted, the grave-robbery category loses its strength. The disciples being aware or even suspicious of such an end of the corpse of Jesus were reticent to appeal to the empty tomb as a sign of resurrection. The grave-robbery fails particularly to explain the faith of the apostles in the risen Messiah, unless hallucination is invoked once more.

Now, hallucination does not seem to be an adequate category for the historical understanding of the faith of the apostles in the risen Messiah. After the scandal of the cross they do not seem predisposed to hallucination. That Jesus after his death could be recognized by his followers as the heavenly and glorious risen Messiah is a puzzling enigma. According to the common messianic faith of the time, in which the apostles certainly participated, the

Christ was supposed to come but once. The apostles, however, believed that Christ came once surrendering himself to the infamous cross and would come again in the form he manifested after the resurrection. It is still mysterious to the historian how Jesus' followers could believe that the End of History had appeared in Jesus, and that the resurrection from the dead was imminent. If, at this time, the Jewish messianic expectation seemed to include not only national deliverance and restoration, but also the cosmic transformation of the whole world indicated since the time of Isaiah (26,19) under the image of the resurrection from the dead,[345] the Easter experience of the disciples could not be a simple hallucination. It had to convince the disciples that God's final, self-demonstrating intervention in Jesus' life after his death did, indeed, take place.

The Easter experiences do not correspond to the model of human hallucination. Ill will on the part of the apostles would be a better category than subjective error to explain their faith. As a matter of fact, the first Christians seem sophisticated enough to distinguish dreams, phantasms and spirits from the real existing world. They had their own practical signs and criteria, by which they could easily distinguish when they saw a man and when they saw a spirit. E. Dhanis defined these converging signs in this way: "Among the first Christians it was commonly thought that the visual perception of an extraordinary object was of a real body and not of its appearance only, if that object showed itself fully inserted in the external sensible world."[346] This full insertion includes three marks, of which none can be lacking.

He who perceived may not be half-awake, drowsy, or more or less ecstatic, but must be fully awake, fully conscious of his surroundings and equally observant of the thing appearing and its milieu.

Further, the thing appearing should appear as real as the other external objects.

Finally, the thing appearing should present itself as participating in the same and usually varied connections of sensible things which exist between the other surrounding objects and the perceiving subject. That is, it should have an active connection of the same quality with other objects as the perceiving subject has, independently of the thing appearing, with the rest of the eternal sensible world.

Examples of these criteria are given in the gospels and in the Acts of the Apostles. For example, because as long as Jesus is walking on the waters, the disciples believe they see a phantasm. Only when Jesus has spoken with them and has entered the boat, i.e. has adequately inserted himself into the world in which they are, do they no longer doubt (Mk 6,51; Mt 14,32-33).

We read also that Peter, led out of prison by an angel, realizes for the first time that he has gained his freedom again, when he is left alone by the angel. Seeing himself walking in his accustomed way among the houses, Peter says, as if returning to his senses for the first time: "Now I am certain that the Lord sent his angel. . . ." (Acts 12,11). Likewise, the others at the household of Mary, Mother of John Mark, at first think it is Peter's angel. Only when Peter has entered the house and their external surroundings, do they recognize him as Peter freed from prison (Acts 12,16).

Another example, is the vision of Peter in the house of Simon. Peter was in ecstasy since, "he fell into a trance" (Acts 10,11), and did not see the one speaking. A sheet hung between the sky and earth. Peter himself did not think he saw a true sheet, but a symbol, and so he asks: "what could the vision he had mean?" (Acts 10,17).

On Easter Evening when Jesus appears, at first he does not show himself as fully a part of the external world, for he stands suddenly in their midst, and the disciples think that they see a spirit (Lk 24,36-37). And what does Jesus do to efficaciously lead them to judge that he is appearing to them bodily? He shows them his hands and his feet that they may see that it is really he. When they still do not believe, he asks them for something to eat. We can see very clearly in this example, how full insertion into the surrounding world is considered a criterion of a true bodily manifestation.

Luke's writings explicitly indicate that the early Christians could distinguish the vision from the real (see Acts 12,9) as well as the apparitions of Christ from the vision of Christ (see 9,10; 16,9; 18,9; 23,11; 27,23, etc.)[347]

Among the examples given above are some which are begun and completed in a strange way. Throughout they appear as otherworldly, as for example, the form of a sheet seen by Peter. Another example which begins in a strange way but ends naturally, as inserted into the world, is the walking of Jesus over the sea. The walking over the sea is something strange, but his boarding the ship is completely inserted into the world of the apostles. By this duality, perhaps a certain phenomenon is shown as both other-worldly and at the same time within the world.

Something similar happens in the apparitions of Christ. The appearances of Christ often begin and end in a strange way after they have endured for a short time in a natural way. From such descriptions of the appearance of Christ, it is clear that the apostles well understood the difference between a vision and the perception of a real body and they give testimony to this differ-ence in a conscious way.

3) Lie

Considering the historical situations the category of hallucina-tion does not offer much help in understanding the Easter experi-ence of the first Christians. Similarly, the category of a conscious lie is not of much help. The first Christians appear in the early documents as men of sincere faith. It is almost impossible to reduce the kind of faith in Jesus' resurrection which we know from the documents, to the conscious lies of simple fishermen.

4) Mystical Vision

Since the category of mystical vision is phenomenologically similar to the category of hallucination, it cannot be considered as a further step in solving the puzzling question of the Easter faith of the first Christians. A mystical vision means that God, or one of God's ministers with special power introduces into the imagina-tion, or into the sensitive-intellective apparatus of man, a process of forming images analogous to the process which causes hallucina-tions. In our case a mystical vision would mean that the vision was indeed divinely caused, nevertheless, it would not be a perception of the body of Christ but a perception of the objective phenom-enon of a body which in fact was not really there.

Of itself this is possible in two ways: either God acts directly upon the internal senses and upon the imaginative power of man, or by using some external object, distinct from the body itself, causes in the external senses of man an impression such as a human body produces in reality with its own proper structure and action.

This theory seems to have some foundation in the gospel

stories. For Christ appears otherwise than he did before his death. He appears suddenly, unexpectedly, even through closed doors, and vanishes again before the eyes of the apostles. The apostles actually think, at least in the beginning of the apparitions, that they see a spirit (Lk 24,37). Sometimes Jesus appears in such a way that they do not recognize him. Perhaps then the Easter event could be explained not by the bodily resurrection but by means of a mystical vision, in the same way that Paul and Stephen saw the Lord.

But as faith in the empty tomb argued against a category of hallucination, so does it against the category of mystical vision. Furthermore the choice of the category of mystical vision is not very fortunate as a means of explaining how the apostles came to believe in Jesus as the risen Messiah. If the appearances of Christ were only visions, such visions at most would strengthen the persuasion of the disciples concerning their prophetic mission and the sanctity of Christ (Lk 24,19-21). The contemporary Jews believed that there was some glorification or punishment for spirits even immediately after death and before the final resurrection. The apocalyptic writings of the Jews confirm this. In the second book of the Machabees, Judas related "a dream worthy of belief" in which he sees Onias, a former high priest, and Jeremiah (2 Mach 15,11-16). Nevertheless, no one believed that Onias or Jeremiah rose from the dead.

Such spiritual glorification or non-punishment manifested in dreams scarcely seems to be sufficient to reveal the messianic quality of the crucified man. After the official condemnation of the leaders of the people and of the high priest, the apostles could hardly see Jesus as the Messiah. They must be clearly shown that the judgment of the leaders and of the high priest has been nullified, and that truth was not with the judges but with Jesus by the Father's action. Death condemnation, however, was revealed as rescinded only by the bodily resurrection, as Peter, indeed, presented the resurrection of Christ in his sermons to prove that God rescinded the condemnation of Jesus and introduced him as the heavenly Messiah.

Moreover, Jesus was believed to be not only the Messiah, but conqueror of death, and inaugurator of the eschatological age. How could the apostles come to this faith in virtue of a mystical vision? The process of materialization of a spiritual glorification takes a long time. By the time of the conversion of Paul, less than ten years after his death, Jesus was already and with great conviction proclaimed and believed to be the conqueror of death. Without hesitation and fear they oppose themselves to the judges (Acts 3,12-16; cf Acts 1,8; 2,32; 3,15; 13,31). They resist the Sanhedrin openly and are beaten, but they go about rejoicing to suffer contumely for Christ (Acts 5,29-41).

The fact of the resurrection exercised such great power over their minds that it led them to acknowledge and proclaim the paradox of a crucified Messiah (1 Cor 1,23; Gal 5,11) and compelled them to produce the first synthetic Christology. They changed the preaching about the kingdom of God into a message about the true resurrection of Jesus. They announced the resurrection as a heavenly enthronement (Acts 2,36; 5,30-32.42; 3,20; 10,42; 8,5; 9,22) as well as the beginning of the transformation of the cosmic world. [348] They confess Jesus as the Lord (Acts 2,21.36; 10,36) and Source of Life. They proclaimed (Acts 3,19; 5,31) and declared that there is no salvation but in him (Acts 2,21; 4,12). In the name of Jesus they baptized, ate the eucharistic meal, and enjoyed a new celebration day. [349] They understood at once how the scriptures were fulfilled in Jesus by uniting in himself the work of the Servant of Yahweh with the work of the Messiah (Acts 3,13; 18,26-28; 4,27-30; 8,32-36). They considered the very mystery of divine sonship in the light of the resurrection which gave to the risen Jesus universal dominion (Acts 10,36), something proper to the Son (Acts 13,33; cf 1,3ff; 8,3; 10,9). All these things they proclaimed as a matter of great importance and as an outflow of their faith in the bodily resurrection of Jesus.

Further, if the appearance of Christ were only a mystical vision, it would be hard to understand why Paul considers the other apostles witnesses of the resurrection of Christ, and himself merely Christ's apostle. Paul reaffirms that he has the same gifts and the same vocation as the others, defending his "theory" against the others. Only one thing he does not call into doubt: that the apostles are witnesses of Christ, and that they saw Jesus in his body up to the time of the ascension. Consequently, he admits the superiority of those who in other human endowments and perhaps even in the gift of proclamation itself, are not his equal. If there were some rumor of doubt among the apostles or some disharmony related to the bodily vision of Christ, this could not have remained hidden from Paul, nor from other "innovators" who would certainly have exploited it in their own favor. But such a rumor or uncertainty is absent from the earliest documents.

Finally, if God had given the apostles sight of the body of Christ by a mystical vision only, then God himself would have been obliged to prevent any belief of the apostles in the bodily resurrection of Jesus for this would have involved some form of pretense and divine deceit.

C. The Proper and Original Historical Context of Christian Faith in Jesus' Resurrection

If the previous considerations are valid, we can say that Christian faith in Jesus' resurrection is complex and puzzling enough to evade any easy human answer. It cannot be referred to the usual ordinary contexts of historical understanding without doing injustice to its historical evidence. It breaks through the common categories of historical understanding, imposing its own claim on the historian, demanding that he look further and try the new category of understanding proposed by the faith itself, the only context where the faith's intentionality might fully appear.

The new and proper historical understanding proposed by faith itself, points to Jesus' resurrection from death as a realization of supreme love, the communication of the plenitude of being with its perfect unity of knowing and loving. Faith in the resurrection of Jesus points to the resurrection as a theologico-historical event in which man now liberated from the restriction of body to a particular spatial-temporal existence, becomes contemporary and coextensive with all bodies in time and space and thus communicatively present to all men of all ages. At the moment of resurrection such a horizon of historical understanding becomes concrete reality. The abstract context will be identified with concrete unlimited reality.

In this context indicated by faith, the resurrection becomes not only understandable but also perceptible in its drawing power if the given horizon is accepted as valid, and if the intentionalities of unlimited love present in human existence are not withheld.

Since the proper context of resurrection is supreme love, the validity of the Christian faith in Jesus' resurrection can be recognized only with supreme love as an adequate context of historical understanding. Only in the context of supreme love recognized as a valid context of historical understanding will the historian find in his historical research not only an "evident *nihil obstat*" in regard to Christian faith in Jesus' resurrection, but also perceive the drawing power of the resurrection as a necessary condition of unlimited love in which historical understanding and faith find their final achievement and synthesis.

A further consideration will clarify this. It had been mentioned that the historian not only collects historical data, but critically evaluates them. In his evaluating judgment he relates the collected evidences to a context which, as a historian, he is successively building up in his understanding during his research and study. The context which the historian is building up is not only a context for a given period, but rather a general ultimate context in which he judges the various data of different times. This context makes the judgment of the historian different from the judgment of the average man. The average man judges an event on the ground of what he has been told, whereas the historian judges it on the ground of coherencies which the event has with the context of his own historical understanding.

Each individual datum is judged in the light of the context, but not in the same way. There are some data which have context modifying power or impact on the historian. The more a historian is open, the more easily he recognizes such a context forming force in his evidences; and the less a historian is open the less chance he has to find context modifying evidences which might change or even break down the context he built up during long years of research.

Supposing this, we can say that the historian as historian, after having studied the data concerning the resurrection of Jesus, will never be able to say (1) that Jesus is risen. The reason for this is that he is neither an eyewitness to the event, nor does he have the sufficient context, sc. God's internal life and revealing love in which such an event can be recognized.

But if the historian cannot make a direct statement about the reality of Jesus' bodily resurrection, this does not mean that he cannot make any judgment at all.

He can for example say, (3) that the apostles (here we mean the early disciples who are supposed to have met the risen Jesus) believed that Jesus is risen in his body. Such a statement is historical justification of a previous more simple statement, sc. (2) that the gospels say that the apostles believed in Jesus' bodily resurrection. After having studied the sources of the gospels and the world in which the disciples lived in the time before the gospels, the historian can say that the gospels are right in saying that the apostles believed in the resurrection of Jesus, since that was the context of their life and understanding.

There is, however, a further question (4): Can the historian say not only that the apostles believed in the resurrection, but that they are not evidently mistaken in believing that Jesus is risen? The meaning of an affirmative statement is that there is no evidence that the apostles are evidently wrong. They can be mistaken, but this possibility is not evident, since the historical research could find no data showing their evident mistake.

There is one more question which can be asked (5): Can a historian say that the apostles are right in believing in the bodily resurrection of Jesus, without believing in the same? In other words, can he say that the apostles are right in believing it and he is not wrong in not believing it? In such a case the historian could judge the same historical datum by using two different contexts: one for the apostles, and one for himself, without confronting and judging the two contexts in the light of a single, higher, ultimate context.

Now it seems that the confrontation of two contexts is inevitable, otherwise no definitive judgment can be made by a man. A definitive judgment supposes a general ultimate context. In the case of the resurrection the possibility of surpassing two different contexts and of creating one general ultimate context depends on the possibility of creating a context in which the apostles and the historian could find coherencies, and in which the two, the apostles and the historian can see themselves as one and coherent.

Now such an ultimate context seems to be the context of supreme love in which the resurrection appears as intrinsically coherent. Since the resurrection is coherent with supreme love and at the same time with an assumed context of historical understanding, the historian can recognize the witnessing apostles as persons, who essentially belong to him, since they manifest something which the historian is and which is immanent to the context of his historical understanding, that is, the ongoing realization of supreme love.

In the present case the old question, sc. whether this can happen with or without grace, is improper. We are dealing here not with profane events (like human existence, origin of the universe, etc. the point of departure of the *a priori* methods), but with the Christ event impregnated with special grace, whose drawing power is immediately at work when men turn to it and ask questions about it.

This being the case, if the historian as historian is able to admit supreme love as the context of historical understanding he can conclude his research about Jesus' resurrection by saying that the apostles are not evidently mistaken and furthermore it would be, indeed, bad for everyone if they were mistaken at all. In other words, it is highly desirable that they be right.

The very final judgment (6) whether they are right or not does not come from any research. It comes from God who will reveal in faith that the apostles are right. In the final analysis the believer does not believe in the resurrection of Jesus because the apostles are right, but rather he believes the apostles, because God reveals to him in faith, that the apostles are right since the resurrection is true. In faith the general supreme love is modified, and appears as the personification of supreme love in the trinitarian God with whom the resurrection is seen as perfectly coherent, and on the ground of his witnessing grace, the human witness about it is accepted as right.

The relation between the recognition of the resurrection of Jesus and the acceptance of supreme love as the context of historical understanding as well as the revelation of God as God will be further developed in chapter eleven when we propose some reflections on the meaning of Jesus' life.

CHAPTER TEN

THE RISEN CHRIST'S SACRAMENTAL PRESENCE AMONG MEN: THE CHURCH OF JESUS

Jesus' life as Christ event was seen in chapter seven as a constant effort to make God present among men. The continuation of this effort is the meaning of Jesus' sacramental presence among men called the Church. The description of how the Church is the continuation of Jesus' effort of making God present among men will have three steps: 1) early Christian faith concerning the time after God's entry into human history; 2) the early Christians' recognition of Jesus of Nazareth in the sacramental presence of the risen Christ; 3) the validity of the early Christian's recognition of Jesus of Nazareth in the Church of Christ.

1. EARLY CHRISTIAN FAITH CONCERNING THE TIME AFTER GOD'S ENTRY INTO HUMAN HISTORY

For the early Christians God's entry into the world was definitively disclosed by Jesus' resurrection. Through the death of Jesus, God manifested that he had fully entered into human history by accepting death, the meaning of humanized history. Through the resurrection God manifested that he wanted to stay in human history by keeping the human nature which he had assumed. The entry of God, therefore, was not a great story of the past which ended when Jesus died. The resurrection disclosed that God would remain actively present among men to communicate his happiness to them and unite all humanity in one beatitude.

This being so, Jesus' ascension did not introduce any change in regard to this permanent beatifying presence of the risen Christ among men. According to very early Christian belief, the risen Christ was present equally in the world before and after the ascension, since the resurrection and the ascension were not considered as two different historical events. The time before the ascension and the time after the ascension, meant only two modes of presence for the risen Christ: the presence of the risen Christ directly and the presence of the risen Christ indirectly by its sacramental sign, i.e. the Church. The Church was conceived as the earthly temporal and spatial extension of the body of the Lord, through which Christ became contemporary with all generations.

The first mode of presence occurred in the apparitions before the ascension and will occur again in the second coming at the end of the world. The second mode of presence takes place from the time after the ascension.

It is true that according to Acts 1,1-11, forty days after the resurrection Jesus was taken up into heaven. Two of the synoptics (Mk 16,19; Lk 9,51; 24,50-51) also give testimony to Jesus' ascension. This gives the impression that the personal entry of God into human history was ended by the ascension. God in Jesus came down from heaven and after having finished his divine journey, he returned to heaven, whence he came (cf Jn 3,13-14; 6,32-33.42.62; 7,28.33; 8,14.21-23; 13,33; 14,2.4; 16,5.7.10.28; Acts 2,34; 5,31; Eph 4,8-10; Col 3,1; Eph 1,20; 1 Tim 3,16; Heb 2,7.9; 6,19-20; 8,1; 9,12.24; 1 Pet 3,22). Indeed, Jesus' departure for heaven is a very early and manifold tradition, which doubtlessly reflects the archaic cosmological concept according to which heaven is situated above.

Beyond this archaic imagery, however, a conviction is expressed according to which the ascension of Jesus was not some kind of happy ending to Jesus' life. It was not a temporal retirement until his next coming, but rather the beginning of a new, vivifying presence which is not limited to any particular time. From that time on the presence of God in Jesus is offered to all in all times. According to the faith of the first Christians, Jesus' new active life after the resurrection was not reduced to an interceding activity in heaven (cf Rom 8,34; Heb 8,1-2; 9,12,24), and not even to the outpouring of the Holy Spirit from heaven (Acts 2,33). It was an active life on earth, similar to that which he started immediately after the resurrection until the day of ascension.

As a matter of fact, the scriptural texts do not give clear testimony to a belief that there was a historical event of ascension distinct from the historical event of resurrection. Except for Acts 1,1-9, there is no mention of forty days in the traditions about the ascension. The resurrection of Jesus already meant his exaltation and his taking his seat at the right hand of the Father (Acts 2,32-35; 5,30-31; Rom 8,34; etc.). Resurrection and ascension were not considered as two different historical events, but rather two different kerygmatical confessions of the same historical happening. The faith in Jesus' ascension was rather to point out that his resurrection did not mean merely that he was no longer dead, but that "God exalted him at His right hand as Leader and Savior" (Acts 5,31) of all men, to be able to "fill all things" (cf Eph 4,10).

From the first moment of the resurrection, Jesus' risen body became the transforming power of the world. It brought about a new revelatory configuration in which the visible world was assumed and transformed into the revelatory gesture of the risen Christ. The revelatory signs became a kind of extension of the risen body of Christ in which men could encounter the glorified Jesus. The progressive assumption of the human world into Jesus' beatifying presence was interpreted as the Church itself, wrought by the transformative manifestation of the risen Christ. Indeed the manifestation of the triumphant risen Christ constituted the Church. Where the risen Christ appeared, there was the Church, and where the Church was, there was the risen body of Christ under the sacramental sign of the assumed human reality.

This world-transforming and Church-constituting power of the risen Christ supplies the answer to the objection, "why did Jesus not appear to his enemies?" He did appear to them but his apparition transformed the enemy and constituted him a member of his Church. For example, he appeared to his enemy, Paul, but in the moment of the apparition Paul is no longer an enemy, but a member of the new transformed history, i.e. of the Church. Jesus in his glorified stage is no longer on trial for his claims. His voice is a living, active force piercing through soul and spirit (Heb 4,12) yet still mysterious since man does not know where it comes from or where it goes (cf Jn 3,8).

Since the risen Christ cannot die again, he will be present among men always unto the consummation of the world (Mt 28,20) and nothing will interrupt this presence (Mt 16,18). This permanent presence of the risen Christ on earth guarantees the permanence of the Church. The Church is the historical extension of the risen body of Jesus, who by his life and death and resurrection became definitively embodied in human history and lives with men forever. The existence of the Church is indefectible, first, because the risen Christ will not die again, and second, he will not leave the earth by turning back to the heaven from which he came.

This universal and eternal presence of Jesus' risen body is taken as the basic *raison d'être* of Christ's presence in the eucharist, in the kerygmatic proclaiming of the Church, in the scripture and in all beatifying moments of human life. As it is the risen Christ who addresses man in the kerygma and the scripture[350] so in the sacraments it is the same risen Christ who touches man in saving encounter.

The risen Jesus' permanent beatifying presence became manifest also in the charity, the chastity, and the sacrifices of his followers. Each Christian who with unlimited love, chastity and courage faced suffering and death was looked upon as a sacramental sign of Jesus' resurrection and of his beatifying presence in the world.

Charity seen as something which does not tolerate limits, but which tends to a wholeness,[351] to the plenitude of being with all its knowing and loving, became a possible reality only in virtue of the resurrection. Indeed, unlimited love, i.e. the fearless and endless communication of the plenitude of being to men of all ages in the perfect unity of knowing and loving was possible only for the man in whom God, the perfect unity of knowing and loving in the plenitude of being, was already present.[352]

The active presence of the risen Christ was manifest also in the already anticipated eschatological state of their risen bodies, i.e. in their chastity. In chastity, actuated by the presence of the risen body of Jesus, the coming new world was already anticipated. Chastity was seen as a real anticipation of the final time, when "they will neither marry nor be given in marriage" (Mt 22,30). The chastity of heaven did not mean an abstinence from a good given by God, as in the case of self-made abstinents, but rather a liberation from the restriction of the body to a particular, spatial-temporal existence. As the risen body of Christ, released from the fetters of the spatial-temporal existence, became contemporary and coextensive to all bodies in space and time, so the spatial-temporal human existence, in chastity sustained by the risen body of Christ, it becomes communicatively present to all men of all ages.

Chastity, being an effect of unlimited charity, was seen as a participation of the body in the unlimited plenitude of charity. In charity, in chastity, as well as in the resurrection of Jesus, present time has already reached its end, and the final consummation become present by anticipation. The ultimate horizon became the concrete proximity of absolute presence. Charity, chastity, and resurrection were understood to be one and the same reality.

Finally, the active presence of the risen Christ was seen also in suffering and death accepted in the joy of the resurrection. Here, once again, the present, particular time could reach its final stage and precisely in the moment of decay and death the resurrection could be inaugurated. Because of this faith, the first Christians did not believe in death as defeat. Since they knew that Jesus, by his resurrection, had conquered death definitively they were not afraid of it.

2. THE EARLY CHRISTIANS' RECOGNITION OF JESUS OF NAZARETH IN THE SACRAMENTAL PRESENCE OF THE RISEN CHRIST

In the light of their experience of resurrection-charity-chastity-fearless joy, the first Christians saw Jesus of Nazareth as a man who lived for others, whose only purpose was to serve, to save, to give, in order to make men happy. They recognized him as a man living for others in his kerygma as well as in his deeds.

A. The Recognition of Jesus' Beatifying Kerygma

After the resurrection the early Christians remembered Jesus as saying that he did not come to be served but to serve and to seek and save the lost man by giving his life as ransom for him (Mk

10,45; Lk 19,10). John expressed it with his favored concept of life: Jesus came that men may have life, and have it more abundantly (Jn 10,10; cf 3,16-17). He came to communicate his happiness that the happiness of men may be complete (Jn 15,11), having his happiness fully realized in their own hearts (Jn 17,13). He invited all men to find rest in him because he wanted to refresh everyone (Mt 11,28-30).

All those who saw him were called happy (Jn 16,22) and blessed (Mt 13,16; 5,3-12; Lk 6,20-23). Now according to the Old Testament the blessed man is the one whose sins are forgiven (Ps 32,1), and who lives in fellowship and union with God. [353] Within this context we can understand why Jesus proclaimed with such power the remission of sins committed against God.

Since sin, as offense against God, is a canceling of God's attempt to make men happy [354] the remission of sin proclaimed by Jesus is the restoration of God's men-beatifying activity. The redemption which he brought meant not only man's deliverance from evils, but also his assumption into intimate union with God. Through the redemption man is acquired by God as his most precious and dearest one.[355]

Similarly, the peace which Jesus wanted to give (Mt 10,13; Lk 10,6; Jn 14,27) meant not just an absence of war. It meant everything that serves a man's welfare; a welfare [356] especially constituted by God's gift of himself to man. God revealed by Jesus (cf Mt 11,27; Lk 10,22) is a "God given to us." [357] Therefore, his message was εὐαγγέλιον the good news of the fact that God's kingdom, i.e. God's presence, is at hand. Accordingly, as the best symbol of this kingdom of God he chose the wedding feast, a sign of happiness and of beatitude (Mt 22,1-14; Lk 14,15-14; Mt 25,1-3; Lk 12,35-40; Mk 2,18-22; Mt 9,14-17; Lk 5,33-39).

The images and parables in which Jesus' mission was represented also show that through Jesus men are supposed to have a better life. He was like a doctor who seeks and heals those who are ill (Lk 5,32; Mt 9,12) and like the good shepherd who feeds his sheep and who when he finds the one lost sheep for which he searches, rejoices over it more than over the ninety-nine not lost (Mt 18,12-14; Jn 10). Even more he was ready to give his own life for his sheep that they might not perish but live (Jn 10,11 ff). Pouring out his blood for men, that their sins might be forgiven (Mk 14,24; Mt 26,28; Lk 22,20; 1 Cor 11,23-26), he showed the greatest love as the obedient servant of Yahweh who gave his life for his friends (cf Jn 15,13) to free all of them (Mk 10,45; Mt 20,23).

Since Jesus wanted to heal the whole man, body and soul, he dared to ask for faith, not in God but in himself. He made himself the center of the new religious life, proclaiming that salvation and eternal happiness depend on faith in him (Mk 8,38; Lk 9,26; Mt 10,32-33; Lk 12,8-9; Mk 16,15; Mt 28,18; Jn 3,15). Extreme sacrifices were demanded for his sake (Mk 8,34-35; Lk 9,23; Mt 16,24-27; Mt 5,11-12; Lk 6,22 ff; Lk 14,26-27; Mt 10,37 ff; Mt 8,21-22; Lk 9,59-62; Mk 10,29 ff; Lk 18,28 ff; Mt 19,28 ff, etc.). Apparently the pre-paschal as well as the post-paschal community was founded precisely upon such an absolute faith in Jesus.

Such an absolute demand to follow him at the risk of losing eternal divine happiness, from a man whose whole life and intention was centered upon God the Father and upon the fulfillment of his will to serve man's happiness, was unique and puzzling for early Christians. How could a man like Jesus who sought exclusively, in all circumstances and with every means, the salvation and happiness of men, demand from all men absolute faith in him as an exclusive guarantee of eternal happiness?

If the early Christians accepted this absolute faith, they did so because they recognized that Jesus was indeed the only access to God, the only communicator of divine beatitude. The divine presence was offered to man only in him. They understood that if a man does not accept Jesus, he will not have divine happiness and must blame himself for his refusal to accept (Jn 12,47-48; Jn 3,17-21). The man who is not with Jesus thinks that Jesus' beatifying power is not universal and there is something in the world which transcends Jesus' *exousia*. But for the faithful the truth is that all power in heaven and on earth has been given to Jesus. His power is universal, and by reason of his resurrection nothing can take place in this world apart from his *exousia*. [358] Since Jesus' beatifying power is universal, there is no salvation apart from him. This is the reason why Jesus, unlike the disciples who must consider as their own all those who are not against them (Mt 9,40; Lk 9,50), cannot admit neutrality. All who are not with him are against him (Mt 12,30; Lk 11,23). [359] His absolute demand of acceptance reflects his unlimited love for man, as well as an awareness that without him a perfect and full happiness is not possible for anyone.

B. The Recognition of Jesus' Beatifying Deeds

In the same light of the resurrection the first Christians recognized also Jesus' activities as beatifying deeds of infinite love. In a systematic sketch we will indicate all the mighty deeds of Jesus narrated in the gospel tradition of the Church. All are signs of Jesus' beatifying presence which is inaugurated wherever he appears in the new time of the resurrection.

1) Jesus' Mighty Deeds in General According to the Gospels

Jesus' mighty deeds ($\delta\acute{v}\nu\alpha\mu\iota\varsigma$: Mt 11,20; Lk 10,13; Mt 13,58; Mk 6,2; Lk 19,37; Mt 7,22; Mk 9,39; Acts 2,22; 10,38; $\acute{\epsilon}\rho\gamma o\nu$: Mt 11,2; Jn 5,20.36; 6,28-29; 7,3.21; 9,4; 10,25.37-38; 15,24) rescue men from diseases (healings) and death (raising from the dead), from the menacing forces of nature (miracles of nature) as well as from the dominion of evil (exorcism). These great deeds are marvels ($\vartheta\alpha\nu\mu\acute{\alpha}\sigma\iota\alpha$: Mt 21,15.42; Mk 12,11; Jn 9,30; $\tau\acute{\epsilon}\rho\alpha\varsigma$: Acts 2,22; Jn 4,48; $\pi\alpha\rho\acute{\alpha}\delta o\xi\alpha$: Lk 5,26) which astonish people, and signs ($\sigma\eta\mu\epsilon\~{\iota}o\nu$: Mt 12,38-39; 16,1-4; Lk 11,16-30; Jn 2,18-22; 2,11.23; 3,2; 4,46-54; 6,2.26; 7,31; 9,16; 11,47; 12,18; 20,30; Acts 2,22) since they manifest a new observable reality, the supercreatural beatitude of man brought by Jesus. About thirty of Jesus' great deeds are individually referred to in the gospels, and in all of them men were freed from their miseries and made happy in a new way. A brief conspectus of these individually mentioned miracles demonstrates this convincingly. Considering the different (common, triple, double, particular) traditions of the gospels, we arrive at the following outline of Jesus' miracles.

2) Jesus' Mighty Deeds in Particular According to the Gospels

Conspectus of the miracles	Mk	Mt	Lk	Jn
1. Feeding of the five thousand	6,35ff	14,15ff	9,12ff	6,5ff
2. Healing of Peter's mother-in-law	1,29ff	8,14ff	4,38ff	...
3. Healing of a leper	1,40ff	8,2ff	5,12ff	...
4. Healing of the paralytic at Capharnaum	2,1ff	9,2ff	5,18ff	...

5. Healing of the man with the withered hand	3,1ff	12,9ff	6,6ff	. . .
6. Stilling of the storm	4,35ff	8,23ff	8,22ff	. . .
7. Healing of Gerasene demoniac	5,1ff	8,28ff	8,26ff	. . .
8. Raising of Jairus' daughter	5,22ff	9,18ff	8,41ff	. . .
9. Healing of hemorrhaging woman	5,25ff	9,20ff	8,43ff	. . .
10. Healing of epileptic demoniac	9,14ff	17,14f	9,37ff	. . .
11. Healing of the blind man at Jericho	10,46f	20,29f	18,35f	. . .
12. Healing of the servant of the centurion	. . .	8,5ff	7,1ff	. . .
13. Exorcism of a dumb and blind man	. . .	12,22f	11,14f	. . .
14. Healing of the demoniac at Capharnaum	1,23ff	. . .	4,33ff	. . .
15. Jesus walking on the water	6,46ff	14,22f	. . .	. . .
16. Healing of the daughter of the Syrophoenician woman	7,24ff	15,21ff	. . .	. . .
17. Feeding of the four thousand	8,1ff	15,32f	. . .	. . .
18. Cursing of the fig tree	11,12f	21,18f	. . .	. . .
19. Healing of a deaf-mute	7,31ff	. . .	. . .	. . .
20. Healing of a blind man of Bethsaida	8,22ff	. . .	. . .	. . .
21. Healing of two blind men (see No. 11)	. . .	9,27ff	. . .	. . .
22. Exorcism of a dumb man	. . .	9,32ff	. . .	. . .
23. Shekel in fish's mouth	. . .	17,24f	. . .	. . .
24. Miraculous catch of fish	. . .	. . .	5,1ff	. . .
25. Raising of the youth in Naim	. . .	. . .	7,11f	. . .
26. Healing of stooped woman	. . .	. . .	13,10f	. . .
27. Healing of a man with dropsy	. . .	. . .	14,1ff	. . .
28. Healing of ten lepers	. . .	. . .	17,12f	. . .
29. Healing of Malchus' ear	. . .	. . .	22,49f	. . .
30. Turning water into wine at Cana	. . .	. . .	. . .	2,1ff
31. Healing of the son of a royal official	. . .	. . .	. . .	4,46f
32. Healing of a man sick for 38 years	. . .	. . .	. . .	5,1ff
33. Healing of a man born blind	. . .	. . .	. . .	9,1ff
34. Raising of Lazarus	. . .	. . .	. . .	11,1f
35. Miraculous catch of fish	. . .	. . .	. . .	21,1f

According to their nature, Jesus' miracles can be divided into three classes: the healing miracles, miracles of raising from the dead, and the nature-miracles.[360]

a) The Healing Miracles

We have the following healing miracles narrated in the gospels:

(1) Two Healings of Lepers

The ancient source common to Matthew and to Luke, the Q, gives witness to the healing of lepers (Mt 11,5; Lk 7,22). In particular there are two cases of healing lepers described by the evangelists (cf above No. 3 and No. 28). One is the immediate healing of the leper found in the triple tradition of Matthew, Mark and Luke. Any explanation made in the sense of hypnotical or suggestive treatment of skin diseases is questioned by the unanimous synoptic testimony that when Jesus had spoken, "immediately the leprosy left him and he was made clean" (Mk 1,42; Mt 8,3; Lk 5,13). F. Mussner considers this miracle as *ipsissimum factum* of Jesus.[361]

Its authenticity is suggested by the fact that there is no theological doctrine involved. It is a pure deed of mercy. There is not one word about faith or remission of sin. [362] Not the observation of Mosaic Law, but rather the mercy which moved Jesus to healing, recommended the observation of the law by which the leper can be completely reintegrated into the human society, from which he had been cut off by his leprosy. The other healing (that of ten lepers) is told only in Luke.[363]

(2) Three Immediate Healings of Blind Men

The healing of the blind man which took place near Jericho is told by the three synoptics (cf above nos. 11 and 21). According to Mark, the miracle occurs as Jesus is going out of the city, but according to Luke, whom the Greek Matthew follows, it happens as Jesus is going into Jericho. There was an Old Jericho and a New Jericho extending southwards, in which Herod had built his winter place. Thus the miracle might have happened between the Old and New Jericho. [364] But it is more probable that the difference between Luke and Mark originated for literary reasons. The healing of the blind man was for Luke an introduction to illustrate the story of Zacchaeus at Jericho, who wanted to see Jesus. And his desire was rewarded by Jesus' entry into his house. Mark says that there was one blind man while Matthew speaks of two. But this is the style of Matthew, who speaks also of two demoniacs at Gerasa to suggest that there were other similar healings. He narrates another at Capharnaum (9,27), taken from his own exclusive source. Mark and Luke even know the name of the blind beggar; he was Bartimeus, the son of Timeus.

The healing of the blind man of Bethsaida is told only in Mark (No. 20). Jesus' way of healing here differs from the other healings. Jesus leads the blind man out of the city, puts saliva on his eyes, and only after the second imposition of hands did the blind man receive his sight fully. The realistic mode of narration as well as the lack of theological teaching attached to the story indicates that the story cannot be easily ascribed to late catechetical teaching. There is not a single word about the faith or a doctrinal teaching for the disciples. The way of healing is somewhat similar to the healing in Epidaurus performed by the god Aesculapius, but still very different from those in Epidaurus. [365] It is immediate. The man sees fully in the same hour.

The healing of a man born blind told by John (No. 33) is evidently inserted into a theological teaching. The content and the form show that it is not a simple report of the event.

(3) Three Immediate Healings of Paralytics

The healing of the paralytic in Capharnaum is found in the three synoptics (No. 4). Through this miracle Jesus shows his power of forgiving sins. The Sabbath conflict between Jesus and the Pharisees also characterizes the other two healings of paralytics: one is the man with the withered hand known by the three synoptics (No. 5) and the other is the man sick for 38 years narrated by John (No. 32). The theological structure of the stories does not necessarily invalidate their historicity. Like the blind and the lepers, the lame also had a share in the new beatitude brought by Jesus.

(4) Direct Healings of the Deaf-Mutes

Mark alone speaks of a deaf-mute, or more exactly a deaf-stammerer, according to the meaning of the Greek word μογιλάλος (No. 19). That he was not supposed to have been born mute follows from the v 37 according to which he began to speak correctly. The event is carefully told in detail. Jesus leads the deaf-mute a long way from the crowd and puts his fingers in his ears, puts saliva on his tongue, and he says in Aramaic, *Ephphata,* that is "be opened." The ingenious method of referring to the means Jesus uses suggests the reliability of the narrative. The use of spittle, laying on of hands, etc. are to indicate that Jesus not only by words, but also by his action brings salvation and beatitude. He is the bringer of God's beatifying presence in word and in action.

There are two other healings of dumb men, one common to

Matthew and Luke (No. 13) and the other peculiar to Matthew (No. 22). According to the evangelists these men were both demoniacs. However, Jesus does not seem in his words to make himself a guarantor of the possession in these cases. He does not address the demon at all, as he does in other cases.

(5) Healings of the Possessed

There are three healings in which Jesus directly addresses the demon during his exorcism (Nos. 7, 10 and 14). It is notable that in the cases of demoniacs Jesus never touches the sick man and never uses any "technique" or means of healing. He drives out the unclean spirits by command. Unlike other exorcists of antiquity he does not command them in the name of God, but by his own authority. The healings of these unfortunate sick men are really deeds of great divine mercy. The exorcisms indicate especially the message and aim of Jesus. He came to free men from all evils and to restore them as members of human society to the spiritual and corporal health and happiness which comes from God's presence in Christ.

According to the evangelists, the daughter of the Canaanite woman (No. 16) and the stooped woman (No. 26) were also loosed by Jesus from the bond of Satan. The disease is not specified in either case. The healing of the daughter of the Canaanite woman is described as healing from a distance.

(6) Three Healings of Seriously Sick Persons from a Distance

Besides the daughter of the Gentile woman found in Mark and in Matthew (No. 16) there are two healings at a distance in the gospels. One is the healing of the servant of a centurion of Capharnaum in Matthew and in Luke (No. 12) and that of the son of a royal official found in John (No. 31). This latter is probably different from the healing of the servant of the centurion. There are some apparent differences in place (Capharnaum—Cana), in the persons (pagan centurion—Jewish nobleman, official of Herod; servant—son). Both the sick are at the point of death; from palsy in the one case and from fever in the other.

(7) Four Other Healings of Jesus

The triple tradition attests to the healing of Peter's mother-in-law, who had fever. The healing is instantaneous since she is able to administer to them immediately (No. 2). According to the triple tradition, Jesus also cured a hemorrhaging woman (No. 9). Luke relates from his own particular sources the healing of a man with dropsy (No. 27), and the restoration of Malchus' ear (No. 29).

b) Miracles of Raising from the Dead

The Q, ancient common source for Matthew and Luke, gives witness to the raisings from the dead performed by Jesus (Mt 11,3-6; Lk 7,19-23). By the resurrection-miracles the evangelists did not introduce an absolutely new miracle. Power like this was ascribed to others by Old Testament tradition as well as by the Talmud and pagan literatures.[366]

In the gospels three miracles of raising from the dead are related. The history of the raising of Jairus' daughter (No. 8) is told by the three synoptic gospels. Its more ancient form seems special to Mark. The story has many concrete particulars uncommon to the miracle style. The journey to the house of Jairus is interrupted by the healing of the hemorrhaging woman. Since it rather disturbs the story, its peculiar place in the narrative seems to indicate the way it actually happened. It mentions a none too gracious observation of the disciples about Jesus (Mk 5,31) at whom the crowd also laughed scornfully. The age of the girl is noted by the evangelist at the time when the disciples could have judged of it for themselves, sc. at the moment of her standing up and walking.

The raising of the youth in Naim is known only to Luke (No. 25). The miracle has an analogy with the story of Eliseus, in which he brought back to life the only son of a widow in Serapta (1 Kings 18,17-24) as well with the story of Elias (2 Kings 4,29-37). The fact that Luke knew the story of Eliseus and Elias would not necessarily challenge the trustworthiness of the miracle.

The raising of Lazarus is told only by John (No. 34) who was especially interested in events which took place in the region of Jerusalem. It is strange that this great miracle is not narrated in the synoptics. The story itself fits well into the history of the last days of Jesus. It explains the triumphal entrance of Jesus into Jerusalem. It explains why the authorities became so eager to put Jesus to death, since they feared an upsurge of the dangerous messianic movement (Jn 11,45-53; 12,10-11).

c) The Nature Miracles

There are seven different kinds of nature miracles related by the evangelists. Since two miraculous feedings and two miraculous catches of fish are told, we have nine nature miracles narrated in detail by the evangelists.

(1) The Miraculous Feeding of the People

The miraculous feeding of five thousand people is the only miracle of Jesus which is found in all four gospels (No. 1). The feeding of four thousand is found only in Mark and Matthew (No. 17). The data which suggest the acceptance of two feedings are the numbers of the loaves and fishes, the people present, the baskets full of fragments, the initiative taken in the former by the disciples, and in the latter by Jesus himself. However, it is very probable that the same event formed the basis of the different accounts. Both are multiplication of loaves and fishes. In the second case, it is interesting that not the disciples but Jesus took the initiative. The similarities in the two accounts are many. In Mark as well as in Matthew the feeding of four thousand raises no discussion afterwards. The story stands without introduction and without consequence (Mk 8,14-21 and Mt 16,6-12 recall the episodes in question-answer catechetical form, therefore, they are probably not authentic). The feeding of four thousand is rather an independent source which confirms the trustworthiness of the same event witnessed by an independent source.

The narration of the feeding of five thousand is full of concrete details which might call for eyewitness (cf Mk 6,39-40; green grass, distribution of the people into groups of hundred and fifties over the green field). A. Schweitzer [367] admitted the historicity of the narrative but in the sense of an eschatological sacrament. Jesus and the apostles were carrying with them some loaves of bread and fishes from which all the people received a small portion. Thus they were all consecrated by a figurative meal as companions of future glory. But the whole story of Mark does not suggest a symbolic meal. Mark notes the radical disproportion between the disciples and the five thousand men. The dialogue between the disciples and Jesus also shows the apparently insoluble difficulty. The miraculous feeding, rather, finds its type in the past in the miraculous feeding of Israel in the desert. Jesus did not perform a "Schauwunder" for his glory. It is the saving love of Jesus for man in his totality as well as the will of the Father which seem to be the motives for this mighty deed. He came to minister to other and to do the will of his Father on earth. Therefore, this miracle like the following, is in complete agreement with the humility of Jesus.

(2) The Stilling of the Storm

It is narrated by the threefold tradition (No. 6). We have similar accounts in the first chapter of the book of Jonah, in the Talmud tradition and in the primitive stories of weather magic. [368] Jesus does not pray to God but commands directly to the wind and the sea. Concrete description is not lacking. Jesus sleeps in the boat on a cushion. He is manifested here to his disciples as a redeemer in all circumstances. As master of the forces of nature he will renew nature as well as man by a new presence of God.

(3) The Walking on the Sea

It is found only in Mark and Matthew (No. 15). In Matthew's version, Peter also walks on the water with Jesus. Again, it is a general belief of religious literature that gods, or men with the help of gods, can subdue the elements. In Indian literature there is a legend which tells us that a poet once held back the waters of the Ganges so that groups of soldiers could cross it. [369] The purpose of the gospel narrative is not an ostentatious display of power, but the revelation of the saving nearness of God to everyone who is ready to accept him in Jesus. The reality of God's saving presence is manifested by Peter's anticipation of the renewed cosmos in the post-resurrection era.

(4) Three Other Miracles of Nature

There are two accounts of a miraculous catch of fish. One is in Luke (No. 24) and the other in John (No. 35 [370]). The latter is not necessarily a variant of Luke's accounts. After his sin, Peter might really have needed a new confirmation that in spite of his denial, Jesus still willed him to catch men.

The historicity of the other nature miracles, sc., the shekel in the mouth of the fish (No. 23) is disputed. Jesus' power is most evidently revealed in turning water into wine at Cana (No. 30). John proposes Jesus as the renovator of the world whose power to change the old world into a new one is limited only by the

Father's will. Jesus does his mighty deed when the hour comes to perform it.

(5) The Cursing of the Fig Tree

According to some critics, the story of the cursing of the tree (No. 18) does not seem to be consonant with the benign character of Jesus who came to serve and beatify man. Though in Acts we read that Peter and Paul perform "miracles" of cursing (Acts 5,1ff; 13,10-12), it is not absolutely excluded that the nucleus was a pronouncement or a parable of Jesus. However, since Jesus did not seem to worry about the loss of the swine (according to Mk 5,13) he probably did not worry about a tree either if this might open the mind of men to receive the salvation offered by God's presence. Moreover, the driving of the people, of the sheep, of the cattle etc. out of the temple with a whip of cord (Jn 2,14ff) suggests that Jesus' benign character was sometimes "tempered" by physical and psychical strength particularly impressive in the eyes of illiterate men, as most of Jesus' early followers were.

In addition to the historical setting, the passage has theological meaning. The old tree which caused the fall of the first Adam will be cursed and withered forever and no one ever eat from it, since a new tree, the tree of life, sc. the cross will be raised by the new Adam. If, unlike Adam, man has faith in God (v 22) the tree of death becomes the tree of life and resurrection.

3) The Meaning of Jesus' Mighty Deeds

According to the gospels Jesus himself explicitly invokes all these deeds as signs of his mission (Mk 2,10; Mt 9,6; 11,2-6; Lk 5,18-26; Jn 5,36; 10,38; 11,42; 15,24). He interpreted them as signs of the kingdom of God (Mt 12,28; Lk 11,20; Mt 11,2-7; Lk 7,20-23; 4,14-23), who visited his people by going about doing good, healing and ministering to others. Although it is not certain that all these deeds can be performed only with divine power, nevertheless, they all gave witness to the love of Jesus for men, and to his intention of inaugurating a new visible kingdom for the divine beatitude of man. All miracles proved the meaning as well as the realization of a new era following God's entry into human history.[371]

They were the new creation and realization of a new man in a new society on a renewed earth. As the manifest reality of God's

new kingdom which involves cosmic innovation they were a kind
of participation (or anticipation) and extension of Jesus' resurrection, in which the spatial-temporal conditions of the cosmic world
are sublimated by the powerful communication of the Spirit of
God. Since the miracles indicated the new presence of God in the
world, they had to show a difference from the usual human world.
They had to be extraordinary, unusual [372] and new in the sense of
the Greek, καινός (e.g. Mt 26,29; Lk 22,20; 1 Cor 11,26; 2 Cor
3,6; Heb 8,8-13; 9,15; 12,24), which means a distinction not in
time, but in nature and perfection. As man by his entry into the
cosmic world humanized it, so God by his entry into the human
cosmic world, divinized it. As the human style of life is manifest in
the humanized world, so God's style of life must be manifest in a
world divinized by his personal entry into it. The miracles had to
be somehow outside of the known cosmic order, since God, whose
mode of life they represent, is somehow outside the cosmic
world. Christ's deeds were extraordinary happenings because the
divinized cosmic order must be different from the humanized
cosmic order. It includes a new "element," a new happiness, which
was not there before, i.e. the new beatifying presence of God, a
new nearness of God to the world.

After the resurrection of Jesus, his great deeds, i.e. miracles
were not considered as something exceptional, but as absolutely
required (cf Mk 16,17-20). They were the necessary consequences
of Jesus' resurrection by which the eschatological time had already
begun. In virtue of the inauguration of God's kingdom these deeds
were not the exception but the general common law, since they
were the visible revelation of God's new beatifying presence
among men. They became the "here" and "now" of the eschatological time in which the present is already extended to the "end,"
or in which ordinary history has already reached its end, i.e. in the
complete realization of salvation-history.

C. The Recognition of Jesus' Church as Šālîah-Apostolic

The early Christians realized in the light of the resurrection that
the beatifying presence of the risen Christ was working not only in
Jesus of Nazareth, but also in themselves. The risen Christ was
really in them and through them beatifying the world as he did
before in his earthly life. They became aware that the same Jesus

who had commissioned them before stood behind their works and words. He was displaying the miracles and preaching through them. That is the reason that they began to preach faith in Jesus Christ as the central point of their message. Jesus, they knew had commissioned them, and through them was calling men to himself, thereby continuing his work unto the consummation of the world (cf Mt 28,20).

For this reason they called themselves ἀπόστολος, and their Church, the apostolic Church. [373] The term "apostle" in the New Testament always means a man who is sent and never as in classical Greek the object of sending or the act of sending. The classical Greek writers, with the exception of Herodotus (*Hist* 1,21) did not use this term in the sense of a messenger. Originally it was used as an adjective and meant "transport" as in transport ship or a group sent out on an expedition. Moreover, it is noticeable that the primary element of meaning is not the authority of sending, but the passive character of being sent.

In the Greek Septuagint, in 1 Kings 14,6, *apostolos* was the rendering of the Hebrew *šālîah,* which is probably the closest parallel to the term apostle of the New Testament. Now *šālîah* in the Old Testament means the representative of the man who gives the commission. [374] Besides the priests, Moses, Elias, Eliseus and Ezekiel are called representatives of God. [375] It is interesting that the prophets and the Jewish missionaries were never called *šālîah*. The reason according to K. H. Rengstorf [376] might be that although the prophets spoke in the name of God, they did not, like the priests, perform the actions of Yahweh. Consequently, the idea of *šālîah* of Yahweh did not mean merely that man had to do what Yahweh did, but that somehow Yahweh himself was acting in his *šālîah,* so that the action of *šālîah* was the action of Yahweh.

Now it seems that this is exactly the meaning of the term "apostle" in the New Testament. In Jn 13,20 there is a full identity between apostle and *šālîah*. According to Mark (9,41ff) Matthew (10,40ff) and Luke (10,16), the disciples should be treated like Jesus himself and what is done to them is done to Jesus. In Heb 3,1 Jesus himself is called apostle. It means that he was sent by the Father and that the Father speaks and acts in him and by him.

Now if the followers of Jesus called themselves apostles, they did so because they were convinced that they had to do not only what Jesus did, i.e., beatify men with supreme happiness, but also that the risen Christ was working in them as in his *šalîah*.

3. THE VALIDITY OF THE EARLY CHRISTIANS' RECOGNITION OF JESUS OF NAZARETH IN THE CHURCH OF CHRIST

It cannot be said that the early Christians were evidently mistaken in recognizing the presence of Jesus of Nazareth in the new sacramental presence of the risen Christ. First of all, they did not consciously adulterate Jesus' intention. There are many indications that the historical Jesus had an intention of founding a *šalîah-Church,* a Church he really intended to be the actuation and representation of his beatifying presence among men.

Since the historical Jesus regarded himself as the Son of Man, he had to recognize himself also as being charged with bringing into existence on earth the everlasting kingdom of the saints of the Most High, described in Dan 7,14-18. He could not apply the title of the first part of the vision to himself without also assuming the second part, which is inseparably united to the first.

As a matter of fact, in the Q there is already a saying concerning the eschatological coming of the Son of Man, where Jesus calls his Twelve closest followers, Judges of the twelve tribes of Israel (Mt 19,28; Lk 22,30). There is a clear allusion to the dominion and everlasting kingdom of Dan 7,14-18.

The historical Jesus' intention of forming a Church is further manifested in the election of the twelve apostles. There are many reasons which indicate that this group could not have been developed in the period after Jesus' death and before the conversion of Paul. [377] They must have been trained in the work of Jesus prior to his resurrection. [378]

According to manifold tradition, the primitive Church knew the group of apostles as the Twelve. Apart from their number, there is no completely identical list of their names. Eleven names are identical in the synoptics and in Acts, but the twelfth apostle is called by Mark (3,19) and by Matthew (10,3) Thaddeus, and by Luke Judas, the son of James (6,16). John gives nine names and of these one is unknown to the synoptic tradition: Nathanael (Jn 1,45; 21,2). Thus the names are different, yet the number twelve is used invariably by all different traditions.[379]   Now, it is strange that these Twelve had a special primacy and authority which was not due to personal qualities or talents similar to those which, for example, Paul and some others had, who according to New Testament books seemed to have had a much more active part in strengthening and extending the primitive Church. The names of some of the Twelve were very soon forgotten. There is no passage in the New Testament which would show the great works of the Twelve either in Jerusalem or beyond Jerusalem. They act only in Acts 6,2 in the election of the seven to take care of the Greek-speaking Christians. If we do not admit that the election of the Twelve was made by the historical Jesus, their peculiar position in the early Church is, indeed, quite unintelligible.

Further, the tradition calls the traitor Judas, one of the Twelve (Mt 26,14; Mk 14,10; Lk 22,47, etc.), a fact which indicates that the group of the Twelve goes back to the period prior to the crucifixion. Moreover, during the period between the death of Jesus and the election of Matthias, some traditions speak of the Eleven (Mk 16,14; Mt 28,16; Lk 24,9.33; Acts 1,26). This would again be meaningless, if the Twelve had not been accepted as a group brought into being prior to the death of Jesus. Both traditions, the one about the Twelve as well as the other about the Eleven would be inexplicable without an election made by the historical Jesus.

The existence of the special mission of Jesus' disciples narrated by the synoptics strengthens further the historical Jesus' intention of building a Church. According to the synoptics, Jesus gave his disciples a mission which was very different from the later mission of the Church. They had to preach that the kingdom of heaven was at hand (cf the preaching of the early Church about the resurrection of Jesus), and this exclusively to Israel. Their task was like the task of the prophets of the Old Testament. Their activity is not described in ecclesiastical and liturgical terms such as baptizing, sanctifying or teaching (cf Mt 28,19-20), but rather by the image of fishing (Mk 1,17; Mt 4,19; Lk 5,10; Mt 13,47-50) and of harvesting (Mt 9,37; 13,24-30). Yet these images indicate already that these men were supposed to work in the eschatological kingdom where all nations shall come to the God of Israel (cf the image of fishing in Jer 16,16; or the image of the harvest in Jer 13,24; Joel 4,13; Am 9,13; Is 33,11; 41,16).

It is characteristic that this group seems to be created neither by a special spiritual existence nor by the decision of the members, but only by the free initiative of Jesus. They formed the circle because Jesus elected them and made them participants in his own work: by accepting Jesus' vocation they believed that in Jesus they were with God, preparing a community of God. Their election was not only for one temporal mission, since the creation of the group of the Twelve and their appointment as apostles are not coincident in time according to the synoptics (Mk 3,13-19 and 6,7-13; Lk 6,12-16 and 9,1-6; Mt 10,2-4 and 9,35-37; 10,1.5-42).

The gospels and the Acts make clear that the death of Jesus found the disciples and the Twelve confused and unprepared. It was through the leadership of the risen Christ, the Lord, that this confused group became a community ready for action (Lk 24,36ff). It was only after the resurrection that Jesus gave them their final commission to re-present him, to do the work he must do to beatify men supercreaturally. The act of the risen Lord was the authentication of an election made before his death.

CHAPTER ELEVEN.

REFLECTION ON THE MEANING AND PURPOSE OF GOD'S PERSONAL ENTRY INTO HUMAN HISTORY

According to the description of the object of apologetics we have adopted, God enters into human history for the super-creatural beatitude of man. The purpose of his coming is not the satisfaction of some divine need as the Greeks thought of their gods, but only the beatitude of man. In a mysterious way man becomes the end and meaning of God's personal entry into human history in Jesus.

The meaning of the term supercreatural which we have used here is rather simple. It means that God wished to make man happy not through any created goods, but precisely through his presence. He wished to let man share in his beatitude, so that God and man might be happy through the one divine beatitude.

In the previous chapter we have seen that the purpose of Jesus' šālîah-Church is to continue or rather re-present the meaning of Jesus' resurrection. This resurrection we defined as an act of supreme charity, the communication of the plenitude of being with a perfect unity of knowing and loving. Since the resurrection is the supreme revelation of God's entry into human history in Jesus, the present chapter is nothing else but an explanation based upon existential human experience of the resurrection as the supreme act of love in its relation to supreme happiness and God.

Since we have said that in revelation-faith experience man becomes aware that God entered into human history to beatify him supercreaturally, the question sooner or later will arise, how can man be happy in the presence of God? Why does Jesus, communicating God to him, beatify man supercreaturally and provide the grounds for him to attain the supreme love, fulfillment of life as well as of history?

To answer these questions we can analyze the human experience of infinite longing for happiness and freedom. By doing this we will be able to discover in human experience the proper place of God's self-manifestation and self-communication and to translate the meaning of God's entry into human history into the common human language of happiness and of freedom.[380]

Reflecting on our human existence as infinite longing for happiness we realize that beatitude (supreme happiness) has its necessary conditions and implications immanently present in each experience of happiness. These conditions and implications manifest the beatitude, the fulfillment of happiness, as the perfect unity or "harmony" of knowledge and love with the plenitude of being.

Above all this, perfect happiness must include the plenitude of being having everything which belongs to it. If a subject needs something which he does not have, he cannot be called happy. His desires cause anxiety, envy, fear, insecurity and hatred; hence he cannot have peace and happiness. Resignation to not having the Whole is no solution either, because it is incompatible with beatitude. A man who does not want to have everything cannot be called happy, since he makes only compromises with the unattainable happiness by reducing his wishes to a limited happiness. Now this limitation and resignation is diametrically opposed to happiness. Happiness tends by itself to wholeness, whereas the resignation tends towards the progressive limitation of human existence, which means the beginning of decomposition and decay.

Further, beatitude includes the knowledge of the plenitude of being, since, if someone does not adequately know the plenitude of being that he has, he cannot be really happy.

Finally it includes the perfect love of the adequately known plenitude of being, since he who does not love the known plenitude of being cannot be happy.

Besides these explicit elements, complete happiness has several other implications.

First, the plenitude of being must be knowable and lovable, since no one can love something which is not lovable and knowable.

Secondly, the same plenitude of being must be absolutely and wholly lovable and knowable, otherwise it is not the plenitude of being.

Thirdly, the wholly lovable and knowable plenitude of being requires as its subject a person who knows and loves the wholly lovable and knowable plenitude of being not only to some extent but wholly and completely as the wholly lovable and knowable plenitude of being is, in fact, lovable, knowable and "possessable." This, however, is not possible if the absolutely knowable plenitude of being is not wholly identified with the totally knowing and loving possessor of the absolutely knowable and lovable plenitude of being.

Therefore complete beatitude and the completely happy subject must be absolutely identical without any distinction of a subject-object relation in the beatitude. This perfect identity of "whom" and "what" in complete beatitude is called God. God is therefore the "whole" beatitude.

Thus man is not beatitude for himself. He has to move and tend towards complete beatitude, i.e. to the Someone-Something, commonly called God. Hence as there is no man who does not want beatitude (this statement cannot be denied by anybody without contradicting himself since by denying it he opposes his correct negation to my incorrect affirmation, and so tends already towards the plenitude of being), so there is no man who does not want God, although it might happen that he does not want to call Him or It by that name. Men do not differ in seeking beatitude, God, but they differ in understanding what they call God, i.e. the complete happiness.

Since God and beatitude are the same, the two terms God and beatitude seem to be interchangeable: God is beatitude, beatitude is God. Or in another form, God who is not beatitude, is not God at all, and a beatitude which is not God (i.e. perfect unity of knowing and loving with the plenitude of being) is not beatitude either.

Thus the affirmation of the existence of complete beatitude is necessarily connected with the affirmation of the existence of God. The affirmation of one includes the affirmation of the other. Consequently, whereas the denial of either one is the denial of the most fundamental tendency of man (and the denial of the most fundamental tendency of man is the beginning of the destruction of the possibility of the supreme happiness of human existence), the affirmation of either one is the affirmation of the most fundamental tendency of man (and the affirmation of the most fundamental tendency is the beginning of the attaining of the supreme happiness of human existence).

These are the conditions and implications of supreme happiness immanently present in each experience of happiness. Everyone, who has had a happy moment, can recognize and explicitate them and move closer to that experience which originated this "argument." In that movement towards the supreme happiness the "argument" described above will be understood as true, and logically valid.

If this analysis is correct man appears as essentially transcending himself, since he has an infinite longing for complete happiness, yet he realizes that this complete happiness can only be found in a completely "Other" than himself. The beatitude communicated to him will never appear in man's awareness as exclusively his own human beatitude, but as divinely communicated to him.

The unity of knowing and loving with the plenitude of being which is communicated by God to men will always appear to men as a beatitude which man does not have by himself. The beatitude which Jesus communicates to all men will be the beatitude of man in God and not the beatitude of God in God. Men will be assumed into the divine beatitude of God though they will, in their proper personalities, remain constituted by their own human existence. They will be neither divinized nor annihilated, but will remain human persons, sharing the plenitude of divine beatitude. Their sharing will be a constant possession as well as a constant reception of God. Because they will always remain men they will always need to accept and receive the already possessed divine beatitude. Since the living God communicates himself to living man, the enjoyed and possessed beatitude of God will be endlessly longed for and desired by an indefinitely progressing human existence.

Thus the consummation of time will be nothing else but the consummation of an eternalized time.

The communication of divine happiness is the mystery of the new life in the risen Christ, in which human and divine (i.e. natural and supernatural with their irreducible distinction based upon the difference between man and God) form a mysterious unity. Although man as man has to incessantly advance in knowing and loving, by the communication of the divine beatitude, God's infinite knowing and loving is already present in each moment of human progression. The divine beatitude is fulfilling each moment of human life which is moving toward the consummation of spatial-temporal historical existence, the resurrection. What already happened in Jesus' life must happen also in the life of mankind. The risen Christ, as prototype and principle moves history towards its consummation, towards the complete insertion of divine beatitude into the life of all of mankind.

Now since the main purpose of Jesus' life is to make God present among men and thus to communicate to them infinite beatitude, the only reason for the existence of Jesus' *šalîah*-Church is to make the communication of divine beatitude sacramentally visible. Because divine beatitude implies the plenitude of being, there is no area of life where the Church should not promote the happiness of men, helping them to know and to love everything which belongs to the plenitude of being. In the Church, it is Jesus who wants to assume everything into the presence of God and to fill the whole world with the beatitude of God. He is the only one who brings this unity of beatitude both to those who recognize him as Jesus (the members of the Christian Church) and to those who do not yet recognize him as the sole bestower of infinite beatitude (members of the non-Christian religions and all those who follow the voice of God manifested through their conscience). He is the One who saves and beatifies Hindus, Buddhists, Moslems etc. under the veil of their religion, since as we have seen his beatifying power is unlimited. Because he is the living Kyrios, men do not choose him first, but he invites those whom he wants: Some to meet him in the Church and so to become a sacramental sign of his active beatifying presence on earth; others to recognize him as infinite beatifier only in the final decision of death.

The task of the Church, therefore, as the servant of the living

Christ, is not above all to convert people, as if Christ were dead and unable to save men, but to do what Jesus wants to be done, sc. to find all those who from all the world's peoples have been invited to be sacramental signs of God's incarnated beatifying presence. The Church must proclaim Christ in order that each man, who according to the will of God is called to make a final decision about Christ, can freely accept the role of becoming the visible witness of God's beatifying presence among men.

In re-presenting the communication of the knowing and loving beatitude of full-being, the Church must always seek and find out where and how and by whom the risen Christ wants to communicate divine beatitude to men. To fulfill this duty, it must listen to and learn from the world because the risen Christ is present and speaks to it through the world and in the world. It must receive God even from the world, since Jesus communicates himself to it through the world. Because Jesus is now the really risen Kyrios, and already coextensive and contemporary with all ages, the apostle-Church, learning from the world, learns from Christ about Christ. Engaged in a constant dialogue with the living Christ, the apostolic Church must join knowledge to love, love to knowledge and both to the Wholeness of Reality and conversely, the Wholeness of Reality to the unity of knowledge and love.

A further analysis of human existence as tendency toward infinite independence may lead one to recognize God and his entry into man's lives as the necessary condition of the experience of any sort of independence as well as that of any talk about any form of real independence or freedom.

A meaningful God-language is conditioned not only by an experience of God but also by the active role of language in the same experience. It seems that if we can describe the experience of God as a dimension of human experience and language as the constitutive function in reaching that dimension we can answer two questions at once: Is experience of God a real possibility and is talk about God, indeed, meaningful? This we try to do again beginning with the most common form of human experience, sc. knowing and loving.

Considering knowing and loving, it seems that every act of knowing and loving includes three dimensions of dependence and as many dimensions of independence.

The *first* dimension of dependence and independence is in

regard to the external sensible world. To know and love is always to know and to love a spatio-temporal phenomenon which, being ob-jected to the subject as such, is to be accepted by the subject. Such a dependence of the subject on the object is the proper case of natural sciences and also, partially, of history.

But since the subject becomes conscious as subject precisely in his opposition to the object, the dependence of the subject on the object actuates at the same time his independence from the object and lets him emerge as an object-founding subject with proper object-determining power.

In a *further* dimension, the knowing and loving subject realizes that knowing and loving is not only knowing and loving something but knowing and loving together with other human selves. Without the other selves he could neither accept his dependence on the spatio-temporal world nor exercise his object-founding function. Thus the object-founding subject seems to depend not only on spatio-temporal objects but also on the intersubjective world of human selves.

But again the dependence on other human selves also reveals an independence in regard to the same other selves in the sense that he actuates intersubjectivity as intersubjectivity by founding others as "other selves" differing from him. Since knowing and loving something is founded by knowing and loving together with others, the second dimension of human experience appears as the determination of the first dimension. Or, in other words, human sciences appear as the origin and foundation as well as the purpose of the natural sciences.

In exercising the intersubjective dependence and independence in regard to other selves, a *third* dependence and independence appears. The person-creating subjective independence appears to the subject as a given independence whose existence and conditions are not completely in his power. He recognizes himself as the one who is to be independent and the fact that the pattern of that independence cannot be changed by himself. He is, indeed, "condemned" to be independent. His independence, therefore, is not an independent, but dependent independence.

But again in addition to its dependence the dependent independence includes also a real independence in regard to the independent independence. Being conditioned by the independent independence, in its turn, it conditions the independent independence in the sense that by the actuation of his objectifying independence it makes possible precisely that function by which the independent independence forms dependent independences. Since the independent independence cannot experience any independence differing from itself, any new form of independence cannot but be dependent independence experienced in the dependent independence itself. Thus the possibility of the different forms of independence is conditioned by the dependent independences. Only in their objectifying power can dependent independences be ob-jected as real independences to the independent independence and manifest the latter authentically so. Thus the exercise of any independence is the affirmation of both, that of dependent as well as that of independent independence.

Now if language is conceived as the objectifying power by which, in the recognition of the subject as subject, the object is affirmed as object, language seems to be a necessary condition of the affirmation of any form of independence. It is the condition of the subject's independence not only in regard to the independent dependences (objects) or to the dependent independences (other selves) but also in regard to the independent independence (God). Moreover, if language makes independence possible, according to the different independences there must be different forms of objectifying language. Corresponding to the subject's independence from the independent dependences, dependent independences and independent independence, there must be a language of object, a language of subjects and finally a language of God. Now since the different dependences and independences are interwoven, no independence can be experienced and expressed without experiencing and expressing the other forms of dependences and independences. Thus it seems that the language of God as language of independent independence is the necessary condition not only of the experience of any sort of independence but also that of the expression of the same independence. Therefore talk about God is meaningful in the sense that it is the necessary condition of any talk about any form of real independence.

Being so, even faith cannot be accepted as a new experience unless it provides a new form of experience of independence and dependence. Once we agree that human experience is the actuation of independence aiming at the radicalization of independent independence by the sublation (*Aufhebung*) of dependent independences (see for example language talking about man becoming god), faith-experience as a new form of actuation of independence seems to be aiming at the radicalization of the dependent independence by a certain form of sublation of the independent independence. If this is so a new language (such as God becomes man, or a particular moment of history receives universal value, or again, the body is risen forever etc.) seems to be inevitable for faith.

Within this perspective even the most difficult notions, e.g. God, love, beatitude, freedom, resurrection, Jesus and Church, are brought meaningfully together in a marvelous harmony and simplicity.

In this perspective even the embarrassing fact that deficiency, suffering, misery and evil deluge the world even after 2000 years since God's personal entry in the world does not seem to be frightening for the man of faith. The meaning of this "terrifying" fact is to be sought not so much in some sort of punishment, or in the possibility of God's testing the believer's faith, or in the notion of vicarious redemption by making atonement for others, or in the challenging task of transforming evil into good. [381] Rather it is to be understood as a real condition for man to be able to create the context of supreme love with all its conditions, where the completely free unrestricted self-giving, God's way of existence, is made incarnate.

The presence of suffering may call forth in man different attitudes:
- attitude of humiliation, full of anger when man realizes his own inability to react positively to suffering and consequently tries to wipe it out by denying it;
- attitude of humiliation with fear, when man realizes his inability to react positively to suffering and tries to flee from it;
- attitude of reparation, when man realizes the fact of suffering and tries to restore the loss by attention to both cause and effect of suffering;
- attitude of love-creation, when man faces the situation of suffering in order to make possible the realization of supreme love.

Now man cannot create supreme love as the horizon of his existence unless he recognizes his love as the actualization, the realization, the visible embodiment of God's infinite self-giving love toward man here and now. In other words the creation of supreme love as the final horizon of human existence means that man does not love other men only "because" of God as if he were loving God first, and man after God. Rather man sees himself as the free love of God for other men. This becomes unambiguously evident in the proper attitude to suffering. Thus the final fulfillment of love is not just unselfish in its intentional tendency. It is so even in its origin: it is the love of someone's other (God) for someone other. This is the meaning of the Christian revelation that the love of God is a gift of God which is the specifically unique character of the Christian's love of God.[382]

Thus the actual coexistence of human suffering and of supreme love indicates both the present shortcoming of human rationality in dominating existing reality and the present ability of human love in transcending the existing reality. Suffering as the "human not yet" and the supreme love as the "human already" reveals both: man as becoming and man as reached by the ultimately final.

EPILOGUE

To conclude our study [383] we might say that Christians are evidently not mistaken in believing that God in Jesus personally entered into human history. The testimony of the Holy Spirit is not against the historical evidence, and faith in Jesus Christ is not evidently improbable or unreasonable. As a matter of fact, it is rooted in history since in addition to the Holy Spirit the historical Jesus was the originator of the Christian faith in himself as God's greatest, definitively ultimate beatifying presence to men.

Without being reduced by historical investigation to a merely human dimension, Christian faith in Jesus Christ as in God's personal entry into human history is embodied in historical events which have the power of raising questions in man concerning God and his personal presence in history. The different theologico-historical events, the pre-Christian Jewish tradition concerning Yahweh's special active presence among his people, the historical Jesus' self- and- God's revelation, his death and resurrection as well as his sacramental presence after resurrection (the Church) are complex and puzzling enough to surpass any easy human explanation and are convincing enough to force man to make a decision: either to bypass or to yield to the drawing power of these events. In virtue of being impregnated with God's special presence, they point beyond themselves to the higher goal of human existence, the goal given in Christian faith.

Since these events are meant to provoke in the human mind a question which initiates a dialogue with God, they must have something unusual, critically inexplicable. Their lasting value is to not let human understanding simplify or overlook their complexity. They aim to challenge man and constantly to force him to bring questions concerning Jesus before God and await his answer. A free dialogue between the revealing God and believing man cannot take place unless man wishes freely to bring the question concerning Jesus, raised in him by God himself, before his Questioner and await his response.

The function of these signs, and consequently that of the Church too, is not so much to convince, or to teach, but to raise questions and to rouse man to strive to place his life and everything in the world in the right context, sc. the supreme love, the fullness of being with the perfect unity of knowing and loving, in other words the infinite beatitude of God.

Now, since the fullness of being with the perfect unity of knowing and loving is offered to men not in several but only in the one historical event of the unique historical Jesus, in addition to the unity of men with God, the unity of men with men is realized too in the most perfect way. Since all men are to meet the fullness of being in one man, Jesus, a new unification of men becomes possible expressed by an extended use of "We in Christ". After the unity of men in Christ the statement "We men," "We Christians," "We Jews," "We Arabs," "We Germans," "We black men," etc. gains new dimensions. In Christ, "I, the non-Japanese," "I, the non-Jew," "I, the non-Arab" and so on, can and must recognize myself and pronounce a statement like this, "me a Japanese in Christ," "me a Jew in Christ," "me an Arab in Christ," etc. This new universalization of any singular in Christ might stir up criticism against me and even persecution on the part of those not yet incarnated with me in the one man of God (understand here also apparent Christians). But this is exactly the life of God entering into human history: not "from life to life," but "from life through death to life," which, as we have seen, is the program of divine-human history. Only by sharing in this life of God entered into human history, will the Church of Jesus fulfill its fundamental role of being an instrument for the achievement of intimate union with God and of the unity of all mankind which cannot take place except in the communion of God's infinite happiness offered to man in Christ.

Were the description of faith-experience given in the present book quite adequate, the drawing of the first macro- and micro-flow chart of faith-behavior could follow. But before such a step is taken, the description of faith-experience must be discussed once more. It is a common experience that the inadequately described problem can frustrate all the subsequent efforts in computer-programming, and cause discouraging, tiresome "debugging." To reduce the inevitable initial mistakes the present description of faith is submitted to checking criticism. The professional computer-programmers claim that the theologians, like the artists, have a permanent tendency to escape "understanding." The actual lack of real programs is due perhaps not to the impossibility of the enterprise itself, but rather to the miserable state of analytical criticism and reflection. Unlike what one would expect, the description of the situation which is to be programmed is more difficult than the programming itself. It requires a sharp analytical mind which can recognize within the original problem all the subproblems and their contributions to the central questions. And this was precisely our aim. The "human activity" called faith was broken apart in order to recognize relations betweens parts, and to see the plan of the whole experience. Should the present work be moderately successful in accomplishing this objective, the work put into it would be highly rewarded.

STUDY QUESTIONS

CHAPTER ONE

1) In what sense did the branch of theological science, called apologetics after the book of J. S. Drey (1838), exist from the earliest time of the Church?

2) Why do we add to the self-reflective activity the clause "dialogizing?"

3) In what sense does the challenger condition the self-understanding of the challenged and in what sense does each self-understanding suppose another understanding of himself in someone else?

4) When and how is the internal turmoil within the Church necessary for the growth of the self-understanding of faith?

5) What are the main historical periods which opened new possibilities for the self-reflective dialogizing activity of faith?

6) How is the self-reflective dialogizing activity of faith presented in the synoptic gospels, in John's gospel, and in the Acts of the Apostles?

7) What kind of change in apologetics was brought about by Christianity's leaving Palestine?

8) What is the difference between biblical and non-biblical apologetics?

9) What were the problems which Tertullian and Augustine had to face and how did they solve them?

10) What is the relevance for apologetics of the Great Schism of East and West in the 9th and 11th centuries.

11) How did the solutions given to the 12th and 13th century problems lead to the new challenges of the 16th century?

12) How did Pascal try to show that the venture of faith can be justified from a logical point of view?

CHAPTER TWO

1) What kind of scientific developments raised new problems for faith in the 18th and 19th centuries?

2) Why did man try to free the cradle of Christianity from any religious interpretation?

3) What was the real cradle of Christianity according to Reimarus?

4) Was the faith in Jesus' resurrection of primary or of secondary importance in Reimarus' theory?

5) To what event did Reimarus reduce the mystery of Christianity?

6) To understand and evaluate Reimarus' contribution, try to find reasons which support his view and reasons which make it inadmissible!

7) Is there one among your reasons challenging Reimarus' view, which is identical with the one for which Gottlob Paulus or Strauss rejected his view?

8) On what ground could Schweitzer rightly criticize Harnack's effort to discover the real fact about the origin of Christianity?

9) Why could fideism not accept Schweitzer's view?

10) What is the difference between rationalism and fideism?

11) How did the first Vatican Council solve the tension between fideism and rationalism?

12) Why did Kähler in 1892 introduce a new distinction between the historical and historic aspect of Christianity?

13) If the discoveries of the 19th century scholarship (e.g. two-fold tradition of apparition, inauthenticity of Mark 16,9-25 and that of John 21 etc.) were right, why could the coming generation not accept its conclusion?

14) What do you think of the solutions of the apologists of the 19th century?

15) Do you appreciate the contribution John Henry Newman and M. Blondel made to the self-reflective dialogizing activity of faith? Was their question mainly historical or speculative? How did they try to answer their questions?

16) What was the basic concern of Modernism?

17) Do you accept the statement that belief cannot rest upon the verification of sensible experience?

18) Do you have two (faith and reason) or one (faith or reason) ultimate context (horizon) of understanding?

19) Which one is playing the definitive role? How do they work together in solving problems and reaching final decisions?

20) Do you think the way Loisy explained the cradle of Christianity is shared by some people you know? In what sense are they right, and in what sense are they not? Why do they think the way they do?

21) What do you think: is the resurrection of Christ a fact in history, or something that the Christian conscience gradually developed from other facts, e.g. Jesus' glorification in heaven?

22) Is it true that the belief of the early Christians was in the immortal life of Christ with God rather than in his actual resurrection? Why?

23) Is the resurrection of Christ historical in the sense that it is real or also in the sense that it can be the object of the science of history?

24) What was the historical event which the rationalistic and the modernistic hypotheses about the origin of Christianity could not explain properly?

25) When was the history-of-religions-school inaugurated and what was its great insight?

26) Did you ever hear of "hellenized Christianity?"

27) What is the difference between the theory of the direct and indirect influence of the Greek mythology upon Christianity?

28) Is there any difficulty in admitting the direct influence of the myth of Attis, Adonis, Osiris, and that of Dionysus-Zagreus upon the belief in Jesus' resurrection?

29) Did you ever meet anyone who talked as if he believed in the direct influence of Greek myth on Christianity?

30) Why was the theory of direct influence abandoned?

31) Is there any difficulty in admitting the theory of an indirect transforming influence, or that of an indirect contributory influence?

32) What is the main problem in admitting the indirect transforming influence?

33) How did the discovery of the scrolls from the Dead Sea renew in the fifties of this century the idea of the history-of-religions-school?

34) What are the great similitudes and substantial differences found between the Qumran community and the early Church?

35) Why was Alegro's book, *The Sacred Mushroom and the Cross* (1970) considered as an ideological setback in academic circles?

36) What do you think about Toynbee's *Dichtung* and *Wahrheit* distinction and of the tables II-VII published in his book, *A Study of History*, vol. 6 (New York, Oxford University Press, 1962) pp. 409-414?

37) What benefit could the self-reflecting dialogizing activity of

faith draw from the discussion with the history-of-religions-school?

38) Do you have any more questions concerning the material discussed above?

39) What is the most important result in the history-of-religions-school for the self-understanding of faith?

40) What is form criticism all about and who are the inventors?

41) How do the static and the dynamic moments of form criticism differ from each other?

42) What is the difference between literary criticism, form criticism and redaction criticism?

43) What are the main literary forms of the gospels according to Dibelius, Bertram, Goguel, and Bultmann?

44) What is Bultmann's demythologizing existential interpretation?

45) Do you realize that at the present time most of us use existential interpretation in regard to faith?

46) Is it not commonplace to talk about the difference existing between the "primitive" mythical man and the modern technical man?

47) What are the different meanings of the term "myth?"

48) What is the essence of Bultmann's demythologized Christianity?

49) What role does the Christ of faith and the historical Jesus play in it?

50) What is the difference between the historical Jesus and the Christ of Kerygma?

51) Can you justify Bultmann's solution as helpful for faith?

52) Why did the disciples of Bultmann not follow their professor?

53) Why was Bultmann criticized?

54) Why did Pannenberg succeed so well in post-Bultmannian theology?

55) Do you agree with Pannenberg on the assumption that the resurrection of Jesus is historically verifiable? How?

56) What are the values of form criticism?

57) What are its weak points?

58) Can we talk about demythologization or rather of trans-mythologization?

CHAPTER THREE

1) In what sense are the years between 1962 and 1973 turning points in the history of the self-reflective dialogizing activity of faith?

2) What are the answers offered by Vatican II?

3) What is Christianity for, according to Vatican II?

4) What are the possible tendencies in apologetics for the years of the seventies?

CHAPTER FOUR

1) What is the consequence of the possibility of the man-computer symbiosis for the self-reflective activity of faith?

2) What do you think of Donald G. Fink's last chapter in his book *Computer and the Human Mind*?

3) Do the conclusions of the historical review of apologetics vindicate faith or not?

4) What is wrong with admitting that early Christian community and not the historical Jesus is the origin of our faith?

5) The traditional self-reflective activity of faith includes the logic that if someone says that he is supercreatural and if such a person after his death can be seen again, he must be God; is there any logical necessity between the two statements?

6) Why does our faith not want to admit that the divinization of

the historical Jesus is the same as the divinization of Gautama Siddhartha?

7) Why is the survey of the history of the problem concerning Jesus useful before we build up our own self-reflective dia-logizing activity of our faith?

CHAPTER FIVE

1) What kind of suggestions have been made more recently concerning the constitution of a new apologetics?

2) What is the involved problem of apologetics?

3) Personally do you prefer the *a priori* or the *a posteriori* way of proceeding in apologetics?

4) Why can it not be admitted that apologetical activity is useless and nonsensical?

5) How do we describe the object of apologetics?

6) What are the reasons for such a description?

7) What kind of notion and structure of fundamental theology do we suppose in our description? Do you agree? Why?

8) Can you place in our outline of fundamental theology the different contributions made by contemporary authors like R. Panikkar, J. Cahill, K. Rahner, H. Bouillard, H. Fries, J. Macquarrie, J. Secundo, L. Gilkey, etc. (cf J. Metz, editor, *The Development of Fundamental Theology,* Concilium 46 1969)?

9) Why is our way of proceeding in apologetics theological, Christological, systematic, vital, effective, ecumenical, appro-priate, catholic and suitable for modern man?

10) What about the phenomenological distinction between "human and divine" religion? Do you like it? Why?

11) What is the value of the notion "supercreatural?"

12) In order to define the method of apologetics, why do we have to describe the nature of faith first?

13) What does it mean that faith is supernatural and ecclesial?

14) Why can faith not be based except upon God? How?

15) How does the supernaturality of faith make it possible that man does not have to believe "because he knows," or "because he sees," or "because he wills?"

16) In what sense does the believer become an "eye witness" to the actually revealing God?

17) Does the believer believe in God on account of the Church, or rather believe the Church on account of God?

18) What does it mean that faith is reasonable?

19) What is the difference between the evidence of truth and the evidence of credibility?

20) What are the internal and external testimonies (or signs), or internal and external revelatory constellations and their role in the different instances of faith?

21) How can we explain that faith, unlike other knowledge, can be absolutely certain and still include the possibility of error?

22) What does it mean that faith is historical?

23) How does an adequate description of the nature of faith affect the method of the demonstration of the validity of Christian faith?

24) What are the functions of apologetics?

25) How can the question-raising function of apologetics bring about a personal dialogue between revealing God and believing man?

26) How do the two processes, the one of recognition of God in faith and the process of the critical recognition of miracles differ from each other?

27) What kind of demonstration is the theologico-historical demonstration?

28) What are the theologico-historical events which form the rest of the book?

29) What is the historical analogy (or context of understanding) used by positivist historiography, by W. Dilthey, E. Troeltsch, O. Cullmann, W. Pannenberg, etc.?

30) What is the most adequate context of understanding in which all the theologico-historical events can perfectly manifest their intentionalities?

31) What is supreme love and its essential implications?

32) What is the threefold operation of the context-creating function of apologetics?

33) What are the three basically Christian insights which can be acknowledged after having accepted supreme love as the proper context of understanding?

CHAPTER SIX

1) What is the quintessence of the pre-Christian Jewish religious belief?

2) In what sense is this religious belief a historical fact, which can be admitted without any belief?

3) What is the twofold value of this datum?

4) Considering the relativity and the historicalness of all human ideas is there anything remarkable?

5) What are the two images of messianism and what is their common foundation?

6) Can the messianic meaning of the Old Testament, defined as the special presence of God among Israel, be seen as "prediction" in the light of modern historical criticism?

7) As believers, will we conclude from the historical truth of Yahweh's previous interventions to the historical truth of the incarnation or rather from the historicity of the personal entry of God in Jesus to the validity of God's interventions as presented in the Old Testament?

8) At the present time do we consider the reality of Yahweh's

interventions prior to Jesus or rather the belief in such interventions?

9) Do the previous interventions merely prepare or also prefigure a final intervention of Yahweh in the messianic age?

10) Which one of the 12 various interventions of God seeking man strikes you the most?

11) What is the difference between Yahweh described in Genesis and the gods presented by the ancient philosophers?

12) How is God's search for man described in the life of Noah, Abraham, Jacob, Moses, Joshua and the Judges, David and in that of the prophets?

13) What is remarkable about the pillar of cloud and the pillar of fire in Ex 13, 21-22; 40,1.34-38?

14) What are the different symbols of Yahweh's special presence in Israel?

15) What is the new symbol of God's search for man in the book of Daniel?

16) Does the Son of Man in Daniel mean an individual or a group?

17) Is the Son of Man in Daniel an ascendent or a descendent figure?

18) Does this question make any difference? Why?

19) In what sense is the Son of Man in Daniel the sign and summation of all that we have said about the activity of God seeking man?

20) Do you see any reason why Jesus chose this title as his symbol?

21) What is the common element to the Old and New Testaments?

22) How does this common element become new in the New Testament?

23) In what sense is Jesus seen by the New Testament writers as the fulfillment and realization of the ultimate intervention of God?

CHAPTER SEVEN

1) What is our objective in describing the different theologico-historical events in the following chapters? (See e.g. whether the historical Jesus can create theologico-historical situations in which man can feel reasonably invited to an affirmation of faith, sc. "My God, You are present here.")

2) Is the historical existence of Jesus disputed among the scholars at the present time?

3) What was the main argument brought up by the rationalists of the 19th century against the historical existence of Jesus?

4) Why did the representatives of the school of historical criticism refute the arguments of the rationalists from the gospels and not from the existent profane and pagan documents?

5) What do the writings of Cornelius Tacitus, G. Suetonius Tranquillus, C. Plinius Secundus Minor and Mara bar Serapion have to say about Jesus of Nazareth?

6) How does Guignebert demonstrate the historical existence of Jesus from the gospels (contradictions and incoherencies!)?

7) How does Paul acknowledge the existence of the historical Jesus?

8) Did the recognition of Jesus' earthly existence help Paul's position among the Twelve or not?

9) How can it be demonstrated from the attitude of the contemporary Jews that Jesus lived?

10) Can a contemporary Jew as Jew recognize the divine origin of Christianity?

11) What is the question historical research asks about faith in the divinity of Jesus?

12) Why do we begin our research with the testimony of John's gospel, followed by the synoptic evangelists?

13) How does John witness to the divinity of Jesus?

14) In what sense does Mt 11, 27 witness to the divinity of Jesus?

15) How can we unearth the testimony of the early Church before the gospels?

16) Why is Tit 2, 13 interesting?

17) Did Paul believe that Jesus was God?

18) To what date does Paul's testimony belong?

19) How can we know that about 40 A.D. the primitive Church already believed that Jesus was God?

20) In what way is Phil 2, 6-11 a confession of faith in the divinity of Christ?

21) How can we demonstrate that Phil 2, 6-11 is pre-Pauline?

22) Can you describe the two Christologies given in Phil 2, 6-11 and 1 Tim 3, 16?

23) What concept of 1 Tim 3, 16 indicates belief in the divinity of Jesus?

24) What can we conclude from these two hymns?

25) Why could Jesus not conceive and express God's relation to him by applying the term "God" to his "I" and pronounce "I am 'God?' "

26) Why could he not say "I am Yahweh," or "I am Elohim?"

27) Why could he not make use of the way of speaking we find in Ex 4, 16?

28) Who are "Elohim" according to the Old Testament?

29) What was that prevailing social view in Jesus' time which specially recommends the consideration of Mt 12, 41-44; 22,43; 5,21; Jn 5,46; 8,56 with 8,58?

30) How is your supposition confirmed by Mt 13, 54-58; Mk 6,1; Lk 4,23-30?

31) Why do we have to say that the way the Church expressed 'Who Jesus was' had to be different from the way the historical Jesus expressed to his followers 'Who he was?'

32) How do we know that the kingdom of God idea is pre-paschal Christology?

33) How do the sayings concerning the kingdom of God outside the synoptic gospels relate to those in the synoptic gospels?

34) What are the different Basileia sayings in the synoptic gospels?

35) Which one of them indicates the actual presence of the kingdom of God and which one the future coming of the kingdom of God?

36) How did the early Church reinterpret the idea of the kingdom of God?

37) Was it the pre-paschal or the post-paschal community that specially lived with the idea of the presence of the kingdom of God?

38) Are we sure that the actual establishing of the kingdom of God was the idea of the historical Jesus?

39) What kind of awareness is involved in the proclamation that "The kingdom of God is at hand?"

40) What is the notion of the kingdom of God in the Old Testament?

41) What understanding of the kingdom of God did the historical Jesus have?

42) How does the notion of the kingdom of God fit into the ideas we have studied in the Old Testament, e.g. fire, cloud, glory, tabernacle, Son of Man?

43) When people were asking about his messianism, why did Jesus always insist upon the fundamental meaning of his messianism?

44) Why could the early Church not use the Christology of the kingdom of God?

45) In what way is the function of Jesus' proclamation of "the kingdom of God is at hand" the same as the function of the proclamation of the early Church's "Kyrios," "Son of God," or *theos?*

46) What is the threefold remarkable fact which suggests that Jesus used the title Son of Man?

47) What are the three points which make improbable the view according to which the saying 'Jesus is the Son of Man' originated in the Church independently of the historical Jesus?

48) Why is the book of Enoch relevant to our present question?

49) How does the fact that the title "Son of Man" is used exclusively on the lips of Jesus and not on those of other men, confirm the authenticity of the title?

50) How can we explain the gradual increase in the use of the title "Christ" and the gradual decrease in the use of the "Son of Man?"

51) What are the five categories under which the Son of Man sayings can be grouped?

52) Are the sayings concerning the Son of Man's eschatological glorification in his equality to God authentic?

53) Where do the sayings "Son of Man seated at the right hand of the Almighty" and "coming upon the clouds of Heaven" come from: apocalyptic literature, Old Testament, or somewhere else?

54) What are the other eschatological sayings concerning the Son of Man present in the triple tradition?

55) What are the indications that the sayings present in Q can be authentic?

56) Could Jesus identify himself with the glorious Son of Man or not? Why?

57) What are the indications that the historical Jesus could think about the temporary suffering followed by his everlasting kingdom?

58) Does it make any difference that Q contains suffering sayings referring to the Son of Man or not?

59) Why is it worthwhile to consider the veiled prediction of Jesus' suffering?

60) What is peculiar about Mk 10,39?

61) Why could the Church not make up the prediction of the passion and resurrection after the event?

62) Can the sayings concerning the Son of Man's kerygmatical apostolic mission be related to the historical Jesus?

63) What is the question about the pre-paschal community which has always puzzled the historian?

64) How does the pre-paschal community differ from other communities known from the history of religions?

65) What is the difference between the adherence of the pre-paschal community to Jesus and the adherence of the post-paschal community to Jesus?

66) How does the soteriological function of the Son of Man presented in the gospels differ from that of the mythical figure of the *Anthropos* of Gnostic writings?

67) What do the sayings concerning the Son of Man's divine power tell us about Jesus?

68) Is there any special difficulty against the historicity of Mk 2,10?

69) How could the Church come to the consciousness of having the right to forgive sins?

70) Can we defend the authenticity of Mk 2,28?

71) Why are the sayings concerning the Son of Man's human conditions admitted without difficulty?

72) How do the message 'the kingdom of God is at hand' and the sayings concerning the Son of Man mutually complete each other?

73) Does the question of the Son of Man form part of the Christ event (i.e. manifesting the power of raising questions about God and his presence in Jesus)?

74) What is the difference between the two titles "Son of Man" and "Son of God?"

75) Did the early Church believe in Jesus as the Son of God?

76) From what time do the documents of the Church witness to faith in Jesus as the Son of God?

77) Is the title "Son of God" language of cult, or of exhortation, or ordinary conversation, or terminology for explaining doctrine?

78) Was this title used only by the Hellenistic community or also by the Palestine Church?

79) What is the difference between the hellenistic and Hebrew notion of the Son of God?

80) Who are the sons of God in the Old Testament?

81) Did Jesus use the title Son of God?

82) Is the title "Son" in Mk 13,52 authentic? Why?

83) What is special about the notion "Abba," "my Father," "your Father?"

84) Is the title "Son" in the Parable of the Vinedressers authentic?

85) What are the elements of the parable which indicate that this parable was uttered by Jesus himself before his resurrection?

86) Is our parable allegorical? What difference does it make?

87) Where is the Hymn of Jubilation found in the New Testament?

88) Can you guess why Harnack proposed a threefold development in the history of the text?

89) Do you remember which one is first?

90) Why was it important for Harnack to suppose a past tense instead of a present one in the sentence; "No one knows. . . "?

91) Do the early codices and writers support Harnack's theory?

92) Why is the omission of the Father's knowledge concerning the Son relevant according to some critics?

93) What do you think about Winter's theory?

94) Can we say that the Hymn of Jubilation is authentic? Why?

95) Does it come from Hellenism?

96) What are the Semitic characters of the Hymn of Jubilation?

97) Is there any similitude and dissimilitude between chap. 51 of Sirach and the Hymn of Jubilation?

98) What is the most probable historical context in which this saying took place?

99) How can we sum up the seventh chapter?

100) What is the striking element in Jesus' life?

101) How do we understand the idea of the "teleological presence" of the Father in Jesus' mind and will and how did Jesus progressively realize this presence?

102) How does he translate God's presence into human history?

103) What is the relation between the hypostatic union, the telelogical presence and the resurrection?

104) How can we say that whenever we communicate God's beatitude to the world, we follow Jesus in his "translating" dynamic union with God?

CHAPTER EIGHT

1) In addition to Jesus' self-and-God revelation life are there any theologico-historical events demonstrating the validity of Christian faith?

2) In what sense could the historical reason for Jesus' condemnation challenge the validity of Christian faith?

3) What is the unanimous testimony of the synoptic gospels concerning the reason for Jesus' condemnation?

4) What are the reasons pro and con for the opinion which claims that Jesus had been condemned for blasphemy?

5) What are the three classes of blasphemy according to the Old Testament tradition?

6) What objections are there against the opinion which holds that Jesus was condemned because of his affirmation of his messiahship?

7) Was Jesus condemned on account of the crime of pseudo-prophecy?

8) Did the Jews have authority to put anyone to death in the time of Jesus?

9) Why did the Sanhedrin take Jesus to Pilate instead of stoning him immediately as they stoned Stephen?

10) Do we have documents which confirm that the Jews had the *jus gladii* before the year 70 A.D.?

11) What is your objection to P. Winter's supposition?

12) What is your objection to Haim Cohn's theory?

13) How do you explain the trial of Jesus?

14) What is the sin which the early Christian saw symbolized in the attitude of the people of Jerusalem?

CHAPTER NINE

1) Did the resurrection of Christ mean for the first Christians more than a simple revival of Jesus' dead body?

2) Can you describe Jesus' resurrection and its meaning for the early Church?

3) What is the mystery of the resurrection?

4) Why could only the believer see the appearance of the risen Lord?

5) What is the threefold aspect of the resurrection?

6) How does John present the threefold aspect of the resurrection:
   (a) the invisible mystery of revelation,
   (b) the miracles of the new spiritual body life (apparitions),
   (c) and the historical signs (empty tomb, faith and preaching witness of the apostles)?

7) Why do we have to distinguish two parts in Mark's tradition concerning the resurrection of Jesus?

8) How do you explain the Markan tradition in the light of Ez. 37,12?

9) Does the Markan tradition support the Galilean or Jerusalemian tradition?

10) What is special in Matthew's tradition concerning the resurrection narrative?

11) What is the Lukan tradition?

12) Is there something remarkable about style in the gospel narratives of the resurrection?

13) Are the divergencies found in the resurrection narratives to be extolled rather than denied? Why?

14) What is the difference between *kerygma* and *catechesis*?

15) Is there more than one confession of faith concerning the resurrection of Jesus in the New Testament?

16) What is the date of 1 Cor 15,3b-5?

17) What are the indications that 1 Cor 15,3b-5 is a confession of faith?

18) Does 1 Cor 15,3b-5 teach spiritual or bodily resurrection? Why?

19) Does our confession of faith say something about the belief in the empty tomb?

20) Does the "third day" refer to the nature of the resurrection or to the time of the resurrection?

21) Does the "third day" come from the scripture or from the discovery of the tomb being empty?

22) How did Paul conceive the apparitions of Jesus: spiritually or bodily? Why?

23) Does Paul equate his vision at Damascus to the appearances of the risen Lord to the apostles?

24) What is the difference between Paul's witnessing and the witnessing of the Twelve?

25) Where are the most evident primitive kerygmatic proclamations concerning Jesus' resurrection recorded in the New Testament?

26) What does the early kerygmatic proclamation say about the empty tomb and the apparitions of Christ?

27) How do the different meanings of the concepts "apostle" and "witness" confirm the early Church's belief in the real resurrection?

28) What is the twofold job of the historian in authenticating a past event?

29) What is the difference between literary criticism and historical criticism?

30) What are the historical evidences of Christian faith in Jesus' resurrection?

31) Does the complexity of the faith in Jesus' resurrection evade the usual explanations of historical understanding?

32) How does it evade the following obvious categories of historical understanding: fiction, legend, hallucination, conscious lie and mystical vision?

33) Did the first Christians have criteria by which they could distinguish the difference between a man and a spirit? Is there any application in the resurrection narrative?

34) What is the only proper historical category or context in which Christian faith in Jesus' resurrection makes sense?

CHAPTER TEN

1) Can you summarize the early Christian faith concerning the time after God's entry into human history?

2) What is the difference between the time before the ascension

and the time after the ascension according to the early Christian belief?

3) What is the meaning of Acts 1, 1-11?

4) What is the relation between the mystery of the resurrection and the mystery of Jesus' presence in the Church, in the eucharistic meal, in kerygmatic proclamation, in scriptures, in charity, in chastity, in sacrifice and death?

5) How did the early Christian recognize Jesus of Nazareth as risen Christ in his beatifying kerygma about happiness, sin and remission of sin, peace, the absolute demand to follow him at the risk of losing eternal happiness, his unlimited beatifying ἐξουσία?

6) How could the early Christians recognize Jesus of Nazareth in Christ's beatifying deeds?

7) Why do we consider Jesus' miracles after his resurrection and not before his resurrection?

8) What is the meaning of the Greek terms used in the New Testament for Jesus' mighty deeds?

9) What is the meaning of Jesus' miracles?

10) How many miracles are recorded in the gospel tradition?

11) What is the difference between the threefold-, Q-, particular-, and the outside of the gospels tradition concerning the miracles?

12) What are the different types of healing miracles?

13) How many miracles of raising from the dead are recorded in the gospels?

14) What is the meaning of the nature miracles?

15) In what sense does the validity of the early Christians' recognition of Jesus of Nazareth in the Church of Christ depend on the historical Jesus' intention of forming a Church?

16) Are there some indications that the historical Jesus had the intention of forming a Church?

17) How does the purpose of Jesus' šāliah-church represent the meaning of Jesus' resurrection?

CHAPTER ELEVEN

1) What does it mean that God entered in the world to beatify men supercreaturally?

2) How does Jesus provide the grounds for men to attain the supreme love, fulfillment of life as well as of history?

3) Analyzing our human existence and infinite longing for happiness, what conditions do we discover immanently present in each experience of happiness?

4) Why does beatitude (supreme happiness) include the plenitude of being, knowledge and love of the same plenitude of being?

5) Why does the wholly lovable and knowable plenitude of being require as its subject a person who knows and loves wholly and completely the wholly lovable and knowable plenitude of being?

6) Why is man not his own beatitude?

7) Why are the two terms "God" and "beatitude" interchangeable?

8) In what do men differ and in what do men not differ?

9) Why is the affirmation of the existence of complete beatitude connected with the affirmation of the existence of God?

10) Why is the risen Christ the prototype and principle of the communication of the divine beatitude?

11) If Christ is the sole beatifier, how does he beatify the non-Christians?

12) In what sense is the resurrection the consummation of the spatial-temporal existence of man?

13) If Jesus is the sole beatifier of men, what is the role of those who are called to be members of his Church?

14) Can we sum up in a few words that Christians are not evidently mistaken in believing that God in Jesus personally entered into human history?

15) If the question No. 14 includes only a negative result of our study, is there a positive result which our historical investigation could discover about the Christ event? What?

16) Does the present description of faith-experience serve as a micro-, or macro-flow chart?

17) What should the next step be?

BIBLIOGRAPHICAL NOTES

[1]DREY's book had been photographically reproduced by Minerva G.M.B.H. Frankfurt A.M., in 1967; for the history of apologetics, see A. DULLES, *A History of Apologetics* (Philadelphia 1971); J.K.S. REID, *Christian Apologetics* (Grand Rapids 1969).

[2]B. LINDARS, *New Testament Apologetics* (London 1960).

[3]*Epistle to Diognetus*, 6, 1; in *The Fathers of the Church,* edited by L. SCHOPP, 1 (New York 1947) p. 360; The Greek text in J. MARROU, *A Diognète, Sources Chrétiennes,* edited by H. de LUBAC, J. DANIELOU, 33 (Paris 1951) p. 65.

[4]TERTULLIAN, *Apology* in *Corpus Christianorum, Series Latina,* 1, 85-171; *The Fathers of the Church* 10 (New York 1950) pp. 2-126.

[5]TERTULLIAN, *De Testimonio animae* 2-6 in *Corpus Christianorum, Series Latina* 1, 178-182; see also *The Fathers of the Church* 10 . . . p. 143.

[6]PRUDENTIUS, *Contra Symmachum,* 2, 609-635; PL 60, 228-230; see also G. B. BOISSIER, *La fin du paganisme, Études sur les dernières luttes religieuses en Occident au quatrième siècle* (Paris 1894) pp. 136, 137.

[7]L. CRISTIANI, *Why we believe* (London 1959) p. 20ff.

[8]J.E.D. ANGERS, *Pascal et ses précurseurs* (Paris 1954); R.E. LACOMBE, *L'apologétique de Pascal* (Paris 1958); J. F. THOMAS, *Les caractères de la démonstration dans l'apologie Pascalienne* (Paris 1942).

[9]L. von RANKE, *Geschichte der romanischen und germanischen Völker* (Leipzig 1874), vol. 33, p. 7.

[10]H.S. REIMARUS, *Apologie oder Schutzschrift für die vernünftigen Verehrer Gottes.* G. LESSING published Reimarus' manuscript in the years 1774-1778 with the title, *Beiträge zur Geschichte und Literatur aus den Schätzen der herzoglichen Bibliothek zu Wolfenbüttel. Fragmente eines Ungennanten.* English translation: *Fragments from Reimarus, Consisting of Brief Critical Remarks on the Object of Jesus and His Disciples*

as Seen in the New Testament (London 1879). For a historical survey see J. H. ELLIOTT, "The Historical Jesus, the Kerygmatic Christ and the Eschatological Community" in *Concordia Theological Monthly* 37 (1966) 470-491.

[11]E. RENAN, *Vie de Jesus* (Paris 1863) English translation: *The Life of Jesus* (New York 1891).

[12]A. SCHWEITZER, *Vom Reimarus zu Wrede, Eine Geschichte der Leben-Jesu-Forschung* (Tübingen 1906); English translation: *The Quest of the Historical Jesus, A Critical Study of its Progress from Reimarus to Wrede* (London 1910).

[13]J. CARMICHAEL, *The Death of Jesus* (New York 1962).

[14]H.E. G. PAULUS, *Philologisch-kritischer Kommentar über das Neue Testament* (Lübeck 1800-1804); id., *Das Leben Jesu als Grundlage einer reinen Geschichte des Urchristentums* (Heidelberg 1828).

[15]W. SAND, *La vérité sur la mort de Jésus Christ* (Paris 1903).

[16]P. CALLUAUD, *Le probléme de la résurrection du Christ* (Paris 1909).

[17]P. DOR, *Solution au problème de Jésus* (Nimes 1935). See also D. JOYCE, *The Jesus Scroll* (New York 1974).

[18]D.F. STRAUSS, *Das Leben Jesu kritisch bearbeitet* (Tübingen 1835-36); English translation: *The Life of Jesus* (London 1846).

[19]G. VOLKMAR, *Jesus Nazarenus und die erste christliche Zeit* (Tübingen 1882); A. HILGENFELD, *Historisch-kritische Einleitung in das Neue Testament* (Leipzig 1875); C. HOLSTEN, *Die drei ursprünglichen, noch ungeschriebenen Evangelien* (Karlsruhe 1883); A. SABATIER, "Jesus Christ" in *Encyclopédie des sciences religieuses* 7 (Paris 1880); J. REVILLE, *Jésus de Nazareth* (Paris 1897); W. WREDE, *Das Messiasgeheimniss in den Evangelien* (Göttingen 1901). These authors were all attached to the Tübingen school. The traditional thesis of this school was that from the beginning there have been in the Church two factions, sc. the Petrine and the Pauline contending with each other. The different books of the New Testament serve at one time one faction, at another time the other.

[20]See Schweitzer's recent follower, F. BURI, "Entmythologizierung oder Entkerygmatisierung der Theologie" in *Kerygma und Mythos* 2, edited by H. W. BARTSCH (Hamburg 1952) 85-101, pp. 85ff.

[21]Cf "The Fideism of L. BAUTAIN and the Traditionalism of A. BONNETTY" in *The Teaching of the Catholic Church* edited by K. RAHNER (Staten Island 1969) no. 1-6, 15-17; H. DENZINGER, A. SCHÖNMETZER, *Enchiridion Symbolorum Definitionum et Declarationum de Rebus Fidei et Morum* (Freiburg 1963) nos. 2751-2756; 2811-2814; see also P. POUPARD "Fideism" in *Sacramentum Mundi* 2 (Montreal 1968) 335-337.

[22]*The Teaching of the Catholic Church* . . . no. 79; H. DENZINGER, A. SCHÖN-METZER, *Enchiridion* . . . no. 3019.

[23]*The Teaching of the Catholic Church* . . . no. 724; H. DENZINGER, A. SCHÖN-METZER, *Enchiridion* . . . no. 3094.

24*The Teaching of the Catholic Church* ... no. 68; H. DENZINGER A. SCHÖN-METZER *Enchiridion* ... no. 3013, cf J. D. MANSI, *Sacrorum conciliorum collectio*, 51 (1951) 235-326.

25M. KÄHLER, *Der sogenannte historische Jesus und der geschichtliche Christus* (Leipzig 1892).

26M. GOGUEL, *The Birth of Christianity* (London 1953) p. 66; see also M. GOGUEL *La foi et la résurrection de Jésus dans le christianisme primitif* (Paris 1931). We mention there M. Goguel as well as C. Guignebert and R. Otto, since their views are insignificant modifications of Renan's theory.

27C. GUIGNEBERT, *Jésus* (Paris 1933).

28R. OTTO, *Aufsätze das Numinose betreffend* (Göttingen 1923) pp. 157-170.

29E. von DOBSCHÜTZ, *Ostern und Pfingsten, Eine Studie zu I Kor 15* (Leipzig 1907); K. LAKE, *The Historical Evidence for the Resurrection of Jesus Christ* (London 1907).

30P. ROHRBACK, *Der Schluss des Markusevangeliums* (Berlin 1894).

31H. HURTER, *Theologia generalis complectens disputationes quattuor* (Innsbruck 1876); C. MAZELLA, *Praelectiones scholastico-dogmaticae de religione et ecclesia*, 3rd edition (Roma 1880); P.W. DEVIVIER *Cours d'apologétique chrétienne* (Paris 1884); C. PESCH, *Praelectiones dogmaticae I, Institutiones pro-paedeuticae ad Sacram Theologiam* (Freiburg 1895); A. TANQUEREY, *De vera religione* (Baltimore 1895); S. SCHIFFINI, *De vera religione, seu de Christi Ecclesia eiusque munere doctrinali* (Siena 1903). For a detailed exposition of the "Classical Method" see M. NICOLAU, "De revelatione christiana sive de vera religione" *Sacrae Theologiae Summa,* (Madrid 1958) *I*, 62-499.

32V. ROSE, *Études sur les Évangiles* (Paris 1903).

33A. ALLINI, *Gli ultimi capi dal tetramorfo e la critica razionalistica* (Roma 1906). H. LESÊTRE, "Jésus résuscité" in *Revue du Clergé Français* 52 (1907) 241-263; F. TILLMANN, "Einige Bemerkungen zur Kritik der Osterbotschaft und der Auferstehungsberichte" in *Theologie und Glaube* 2 (1910) 529-550. For a historical survey see P. de HAES, *La résurrection de Jésus dans l'apologétique des cinquante dernières années* (Roma 1953); C.M. MARTINI, *Il problema storico della risurrezione negli studi recenti* (Roma 1959).

34B. GUNDERSEN, *Cardinal Newman and Apologetics* (Oslo 1952); M. BLONDEL, *L'Action* (1893 Paris); M. BLONDEL, *Exigences Philosophiques du Christianisme* (Paris 1950).

35"Absolutely impossible and absolutely necessary to man; that is what the supernatural really is: the action of man transcends man; and the meaning of all reasoning power is to see that he cannot, must not be satisfied with all he has," H. BLONDEL, *L'action* (Paris 1893) p. 338.

36D. PALMIERI, *Esame d'un opusculo il quale gira intorno ad un piccolo libro* (Rome 1904).

37J.B. DISTELDORF, "Die Auferstehung Jesu Christi, Eine apologetisch-biblische

Studie" in *Festschrift des Priestersseminars zum Bischofsjubiläum* (Trier 1906) pp. 496-572. A. SEEBERG, *Der Katechismus der Christenheit* (Leipzig 1903).

[38]A. HARNACK, *Lukas der Arzt, der Verfasser des dritten Evangeliums und der Apostelgeschichte* (Leipzig 1906).

[39]*The Teaching of the Catholic Church* ... no. 308-309; H. DENZINGER, A. SCHÖN-METZER, *Enchiridion* ... nos. 3436-3437.

[40]See 4th Lateran Council, 2nd Council of Lyons, Council of Florence or the Creed of Leo IX, *The Teaching of the Catholic Church* ... nos. 837c,841; H. DENZINGER, A. SCHÖNMETZER, *Enchiridion* ... nos. 801,854,1338,681.

[41]"La foi à la résurrection, qui, dès l'abord fut la foi à la vie immortelle du crucifié, bien plus qu'au fait initial qui est suggeré à notre esprit par le mot résurrection" - A. LOISY, *Autour d'un petit livre* (Paris 1903) p. 120.

[42]E. POULAT, *Histoire, dogme et critique dans la crise moderniste* (Paris 1962).

[43]R. REITZENSTEIN, *Die hellenistischen Mysterienreligionen, ihre Grundgedanken und Wirkungen* (Leipzig 1910).

[44] LOISY'S Book Review on R. Reitzenstein's work is in *Revue d'Histoire et de Littérature Religieuses* 2 (1911) 588.

[45]A. LOISY, *Les mystères paiens et les mystères chrétiens* (Paris 1919); W. BOUSSET, *Kyrios Christos* (Göttingen 1921, English translation New York, 1970); R. BULTMANN *Theologie des Neuen Testaments* (Tübingen 1948; English translation *Theology of the New Testament* (New York 1951); id., *Das Urchristentum im Rahmen der antiken Religionen* (Zürich 1949). This view supposes that the Gnoticism of 2-4 century known in Syria and Egypt is the same as the Gnosis of 2-1st century B.C.; cf. H. ANDERSON, *Christ and Christian Origins* (New York 1964) p. 48.

[46]M.J. LAGRANGE, "Attis et le christianisme" in *Revue Biblique* 16 (1919) 419-480.

[47]Notice that in the "Correspondence between the story of Jesus and the stories of certain Hellenic saviors with the 'time Machine,' " outlined by A.J. TOYNBEE in his *A Study of History* 6 (Oxford 1939) 377ff., there is no pagan mythological hero who was believed to be risen from the dead (see *op cit.* p. 411). - "This Tyrian festival is referred to as that of resurrection of Hèraklês ... in a Greek work from the pen of a half-hellenized Jewish scholar who lived and wrote in the first century of the Christian era" - A.J. TOYNBEE, *A Study* ... p. 477. See *ibid.* note 2. Thus A. J. TOYNBEE seems to confirm M.J. LAGRANGE'S thesis.

[48]W.W. von BAUDISSIN, *Adonis und Essun, eine Untersuchung zur Geschichte des Glaubens an Auferstehungsgötter und an Heilsgötter* (Leipzig 1911); H.J. LAGRANGE'S Review on *Adonis und Essun* ... in *Revue Biblique* 9 (1912) 117-127.

[49]A. LOISY, *Les mystères paiens* ... p. 134.

[50]According to G. WAGNER the hypothesis of mystical dying and rising god in the hellenistic cults at the time of Paul is ill-founded; see *Das religionsgeschichtliche Problem von Römer* 6, 1-11 (Zürich 1962); cf. also L. COLPE, "Gnosis I. Religionsgeschichtlich" in *Religion in Geschichte und Gegenwart* 3rd edition, 2 (1958) 648-652. L. Colpe thinks

that the Gnostic redeemer myth has risen out of Docetic interpretation of Christ; cf. also E. BEVAN, *Hellenism and Christianity* (London 1921) p. 88; F.C. BURKITT, *Church and Gnosis* (Cambridge 1932). For Marxist specialists see B. KOWALINSKI, "The Genesis of Christianity in the view of contemporary Marxist specialist in religion" *Antonianum* 47 (1972) 541-575.

[51] See H. KRAEMER, *The Christian Message in a Non-Christian World* (New York 1938); D. BONHOEFFER, *Prisoner for God* (New York 1957); M. ELIADE, *The Sacred and the Profane* (New York 1961); D. JENKINS, *Beyond Religion* (London 1962); W.C. SMITH *The Meaning and End of Religion* (New York 1964); R.E. WITT, *Isis in the Greaco-Roman World* (Ithaca 1971) pp. 279-281.

[52] K. PRÜMM, *Der christiliche Glaube und die altheidische Welt* (Leipzig 1935); see also S.G.F. BRANDON, *The Saviour God* (Manchester 1963) p. 19.

[53] E. WILSON, *The Scrolls from the Dead Sea* (New York 1955) p. 77.

[54] C. F. POTTER, *The Lost Years of Jesus revealed* (New York 1958) p. 155.

[55] A. DUPONT-SOMMER, *Aperçues préliminaires sur les manuscripts de la Mer Morte* (Paris 1950); English translation: *The Dead Sea Scrolls: a preliminary survey* (New York 1952) p. 98.

[56] G. GRAYSTONE, *The Dead Sea Scrolls and the Originality of Christ* (New York 1956) p. 97.

[57] E. STAUFFER, *Jesus and die Wüstengemeinde am Toten Meer* (Stuttgart 1957); English translation: *Jesus and the Wilderness Community at Qumran* (Philadelphia 1964) pp. 12-19.

[58] J. COPPENS, *Les documents du Désert de Juda et les Origines du Christianisme* (Louvain 1953) p. 34.

[59] J. COPPENS, *Les documents* . . . p. 39; English translation is taken from G. GRAYSTONE, *The Dead Sea* . . . pp. 79-80. After having reached these conclusions it was not surprising that the book J.M. ALEGRO, *The Sacred Mushroom and the Cross* (Garden City 1970), presenting Jesus as *Amanita Muscaria,* (a certain hallucinatory mushroom, a code for phallic symbols) appeared in some scholarly circles as "the erotic nightmare of a seminatic philologist" based on no evidence whatsoever.

[60] A.J. TOYNBEE, *A Study of History* (London 1939) 6,538; see ibid., pp. 537-539.

[61] See A.J. TOYNBEE, *A Study* . . . 6,411: Table V. Common Scenes . . . A supper (Cleomenes); A bosom friend leaning on the hero's breast (Cleomenes, Gaius Gracchus); The Agony (Gaius Gracchus) . . . A young male fugitive leaving his wrap in the hand of his pursuer (Tiberius Gracchus); A trial at night-time (Agis); The hero arrayed in a royal robe and crown (Tiberius Gracchus); The Via Dolorosa (Agis); The Crucifixion (Cleomenes); The acclamation of a crucified man as the Son of God (a child of God) (Cleomenes) . . . The Descent from the Cross (Agis); the Pietà (Agis). - Notice, however, that A.J. Toynbee could not find any pagan hero, whose life was God's revelation, or who had been risen from the dead. In the problem concerning Jesus these two features are precisely relevant.

[62]A.J. TOYNBEE, *A Study* . . . 5,433-434.

[63]A. OBRIK, "Die epische Gesetze der Volksdichtung" in *Zeitschrift für deutsches Altertum* 51 (1901) 1-12; E. NORDEN, *Die Griechische Kunstprosa* (Leipzig 1909); id., *Agnostos Theos* (Leipzig 1913).

[64]H. GUNKEL, *Genesis* (Göttingen 1901).

[65]M. GOGUEL, *Jésus* (Paris 1932).

[66]E. HIRSCH, *Die Auferstehungsgeschichten und der christliche Glaube* (Tübingen 1940). Hirsch's thesis had been sharply criticized by M. LEHMANN *Synoptische Quellenanalyse und Frage nach dem historischen Jesus* (Berlin 1970).

[67]O. CULLMANN, "La délivrance anticipée du corps human d'aprés le Nouveau Testament" in *Hommage et reconnaissance . . . 60ᵉ anniversaire de K. Barth* (Neuchatel 1946) pp. 31-40; id *Immortality of the Soul or Resurrection of the dead? The Witness of the New Testament* (London 1958).

[68]R.BULTMANN, "New Testament and Mythology" in H.W. BARTSCH, editor, *Kerygma and Myth* (London 1953) pp. 1-44.

[69]R. BULTMANN, "Die christliche Hoffnung und das Problem der Entmythologizierung" in *Glauben und Verstehen* 3 (Tübingen 1962) 81-90, p. 84.

[70]R. BULTMANN, "New Testament and Mythology . . . " p. 10.

[71]R. BULTMANN, "Welchen Sinn hat es von Gott zu reden" in *Glauben und Verstehen* 1 (Tübingen 1961) 26-37, p. 29.

[72]R. BULTMANN, "The Concept of revelation in the New Testament" in *Existence and Faith* (New York 1960) 58-91, pp. 85-86.

[73]R. BULTMANN, "The Concept of Revelation . . ." p. 81.

[74]R. BULTMANN, "The Concept of Revelation . . ." p. 82ff.

[75]R. BULTMANN, "The Concept of Revelation . . ." p. 84.

[76]R. BULTMANN, "The Concept of Revelation . . ." p. 87.

[77]R. BULTMANN, "The primitive Christian Kerygma and the Historical Jesus" in C.E. BRAATEN and R.A. HARRISVILLE ed. *The Historical Jesus and the Kerygmatic Christ* (New York 1964) 15-42, p. 18.

[78]R. BULTMANN, "Die Bedeutung des Alten Testaments für den christlichen Glauben" in *Glauben und Verstehen* 1, 313-336, p. 331; id., "The Christological Confession of the World Council of Churches" in *Essays, Philosophical and Theological* (London, 1955) pp. 273-290.

[79]R. BULTMANN, "The Christological Confession . . ." p, 288.

[80]R. BULTMANN, "The Concept of Revelation . . ." p. 76.

[81]R. BULTMANN, "Die Christologie des Neuen Testaments" in *Glauben und Verstehen* 1 . . . 245-267, p. 265.

[82]R. BULTMANN, "New Testament and Mythology . . ." pp. 37-38.

[83]P. ALTHAUS, *Fact and Faith in the Kerygma of Today* (Philadelphia 1960).

[84]E. KÄSEMANN, "Das Problem des historischen Jesus" in *Zeitschrift für Theologie und Kirche* 51 (1954) 125-153; English translation in W.J. MONTAGUE, *Essays on New Testament Themes* (London 1964) 15-47; G. BORNKAMM, *Jesus von Nazareth* (Stuttgart 1956); English translation: *Jesus of Nazareth* (New York 1960); H. CONZELMANN, "Jesus Christ" in: *Religion in Geschichte und Gegenwart* 3 (Tübingen 1959) 619-653; id., "The Method of the Life of Jesus Research" in C.E. BRAATEN and R.A. HARRISVILLE, *The Historical Jesus* . . . pp. 54-68; E. FUCHS, *Zur Frage nach dem historischen Jesus* (Tübingen 1960) pp. 143-167; English translation: *Studies of the Historical Jesus* (London 1964); E. EBELING, *The Nature of Faith* (Philadelphia 1961); for a general survey see J.H. ELLIOTT, "The Historical Jesus, the Kerygmatic Christ and the Eschatological Community" in *Concordia Theological Monthly* 37 (1965) 470-491, pp. 481-489.

[85]J.M. ROBINSON, *A New Quest of the Historical Jesus* (London 1959).

[86]J. CAHILL, "Rudolf Bultmann and Post-Bultmann Tendencies" in *Catholic Biblical Quarterly* 26 (1964) 153-178. R. BULTMANN, "An Interview with Rudolf Bultmann" in *Christianity and Crisis* 26 (1966) 252-255.

[87]See for example *Constitution on Divine Revelation of Vatican II:* "God speaks (now!) in sacred Scripture through men" (no. 12); "and make the voice of the Holy Spirit resound in the word . . ." (no. 21).

[88]L. MALEVEZ, *The Christian Message and Myth* (London 1958); R. MARLÉ, *Bultmann et l'interprétation du Nouveau Testament* (Paris 1956).

[89]K. JASPERS, "Myth and Religion" in H.W. BARTSCH and R.H. FULLER, *Kerygma and Myth,* 2 (London 1962) pp. 133-180.

[90]T. HORVATH, "L'athéisme contemporaine et le retour a la métaphysique" in *Sciences Ecclésiastiques* 15 (1963) 467-478, pp. 470ff; H.C. WOLF, *Kiergegaard and Bultmann: The Quest of the Historical Jesus* (Minneapolis 1965).

[91]W. PENNENBERG and his circle became the center of a wide theological discussion as the following bibliography might indicate: W. PANNENBERG, *Jesus - God and Man* (Philadelphia 1968); *Revelation as History* (New York 1968); *Grundfragen Systematischer Theologie* (Göttingen, 1964); "Redemptive Event and History" in C. WESTERMANN, *Essays on Old Testament Hermeneutics* (Virginia 1963) pp. 314-335; "Did Jesus Really Rise from the Dead" in *Dialog* 4 (1965) 128-135; "The Revelation of God in Jesus" in J.M. ROBINSON, *Theology as History* (New York 1967) pp. 101-133; "Theology and the Kingdom of God" in *Una Sancta* 24,2 (1967) 3-19; "The Kingdom of God and the Church" in *Una Sancta* 24,4 (1967) 3-27; "The Kingdom of God and the Foundations of Ethics" in *Una Sancta* 25,2 (1968) 6-26; "Appearance and the Arrival of the Future" in *Journal for the American Academy of Religion* 35 (1967) 107-118; "The Quest of God" in *Interpretation* 21 (1967) 284-314; "Hermeneutics and Universal History" in *Journal for Theology and the Church* 4 (R.W. FUNK, editor), *History and Hermeneutic* (New York 1967), pp. 122-152; J. BARR, "Revelation through History in

Modern Theology" in *Interpretation* 17 (1963) 193-205; C.E. BRAATEN, "The Current Controversy on Revelation, Pannenberg and his Critics" in *Journal of Religion* 45 (1965) 225-237; id., "Theology and Historical-Critical Method" in C.E. BRAATEN, *History and Hermeneutics* (Philadelphia 1966) pp. 33-52; J.B. COBB, "A New Trio Arises in Europe" in M.E. MARTY, *New Theology* 2 (New York 1965) 257-263; D.F. FULLER, *Easter Faith and History* (Grand Rapids 1965) pp. 145-187; G.G. O'COLLIN "Revelation as History" in *Heythrop Journal* 7 (1966) 394-406; R.T. OSBORN, "Pannenberg's Programme" in *Canadian Journal of Theology* 13 (1967) 109-122; J.M. ROBINSON, "Revelation as Word and as History" in J.M. ROBINSON, J.B. COBB, *Theology as History* (New York 1967) pp. 1-100; see review: *Heythrop Journal* 9 (1968) 206-207.

[92]D. FULLER, "The resurrection of Jesus and the Historical Jesus" in *The Journal of Bible and Religion* 34 (1966) 18-24.

[93]O. CULLMANN, "La foi à la résurrection et l'espérance de la résurrection dans le Nouveau Testament" in *Études theologiques et religieuses* 18(1943)pp.3ff.

[94]H. DICKMANN, "Die Formgeschichtliche Methode und ihre Anwendung auf die Auferstchungsberichte" in *Scholastik* 1 (1926) 379-399.

[95]VATICAN II, *Constitution on Divine Revelation* no. 19.

[96]D. GUTHRIE, *New Testament Introduction, The Gospels and the Acts* (London 1965) pp. 189-194; see also K. KOCH, *The Growth of Biblical Tradition, The Form Critical Method* (New York 1969); E.V. McKNIGHT, *What is Form Criticism* (Philadelphia 1969); N. PERRIN, *What is Redaction Criticism* (Philadelphia 1969); W.A. BEARDSLEE, *Literary Criticism of the New Testament* (Philadelphia 1970); N. HABEL, *Literary Criticism of the Old Testament* (Philadelphia 1971); G.M. TUCKLER, *Form Criticism of the Old Testament* (Philadelphia 1971).

[97]About "remembering" as an important motive in the life of the early Christians see J. ROLOFF, *Das Kerygma und der irdische Jesus* (Göttingen, 1970); cf. also B. GERHARDSSON, *Memory and Manuscript* (Uppsala 1961).

[98]L. de GRANDMAISON, *Jesus Christ,* I (Paris 1928) p. 199; A. BEA *The Study of the Synoptic Gospels* (New York 1965) pp. 40-44.

[99]H.R. SCHLETTE, *Towards a Theology of Religions* (New York 1966).

[100]D. BONHOEFFER, *Letters and Papers from Prison* (New York 1959) pp. 90-127; R. MARLÉ, *Bonhoeffer, The Man and His Work* (New York 1968) pp. 107-135.

[101]Cf The Death-of-God controversy: T.J.J. ALTIZER, *The Gospel of Christian Atheism* (Philadelphia 1960); W. HAMILTON, *The New Essence of Christianity* (New York 1961); S. OGDEN, *Christ without Myth* (New York 1961) P. van BUREN, *The Secular Meaning of the Gospel* (New York 1963); J.A. ROBINSON, *Honest to God* (London 1963); W. PELZ, *God is No More* (London, 1964); H. COX, *The Secular City* (New York 1965); A. LOEN, *Secularization, Science without God* (London 1965); W. HAMILTON, *Revolt Against Heaven* (Grand Rapids 1965); W. HAMILTON, *God is Dead, The Anatomy of a Slogan* (Grand Rapids 1966); T.J.J. ALTIZER, W. HAMILTON, *Radical Theology and the Death of God* (New York 1966); G. VAHANIAN, *No Other God* (New York 1966); E.L. MASCALL, *The Secularization of Christianity, An Analysis and a Critique* (London 1965); D. CALLAHAN, *The Secular City Debate* (New York 1966);

W.R. COHNSTOCK, "Theology after 'The Death of God', A Survey of Recent Trends in Religious Thought", in *Cross Currents* 16 (1966) 265-304; F.C. COPLESTON, "Dialogue with Humanism" in *The Month,* 36 (1966) 114-120; P.C. HODGSON, "The Death of God and the Crisis in Christology" in *Journal of Religion* 46 (1966) 446-462; Th. OGLETREE, *The Death of God Controversy* (Nashville 1966); R.G. SMITH, *Secular Christianity* (London 1966); A. DULLES, "Notes, Some Recent 'Death-of-God-Theology' Literature" in *Theological Studies* 28 (1967) 111-118; J. CAHILL, *Death of God Theology as Biblical Hermeneutics* in Ephemerides Theologiae Lovanienses 43 (1967) 445-459; M. McDERMOTT - J.A. PATRICK - B.A. WILSON, "A Bibliography of the New Theology, New Theologians" in *Journal of Canadian Theology* 13 (1967) 56-63; 134-138; B. MURCHLAND, *The Meaning of the Death of God* (New York 1967); W. PANNENBERG, "The Quest of God" in *Interpretation* 21 (1967) 284-314; R.L. RICHARD, *Secularization Theology* (New York 1967).

102T.J.J. ALTIZER, *The Gospel of Christian Atheism* . . . pp. 103, 110, 85-86.

103Cf J. MOLTMANN and the debate on his view: J. MOLTMANN, *Theology of Hope* (New York 1967); "An Eschatological Humanism without God" in *Concilium* 10 (1965) 25-40; "Resurrection as Hope" in *Harvard Theological Review* 61 (1968) 129-147; "Hoping and Planning" in *Cross Currents* 18 (1968) 307-318; E. BLOCH, "Man as Possibility" in *Cross Currents* 18 (1968) 273-283; Ernst Bloch in *Herder Correspondence* 5 (1968) 53-56; C.W. BRATTEN, "Toward a Theology of Hope" in *Theology Today* 24 (1967) 208-226; or *Theology Digest* 16 (1968) 151-154; W.H. CAPPS, "The Hope Tendency" in *Cross Currents* 18 (1968) 257-272; "An Assessment of the Theological Side of the School of Hope," *Cross Currents* 18 (1968) 319-335; F.P. FIORENZA, "Dialectical Theology and Hope" in *The Heythrop Journal* 9 (1968) 143-163; Ph. HEFNER, "Questions for Moltmann and Pannenberg" in *Una Sancta* 25,3 (1968) 32-51; W.P. MARSCH, *Diskussion über die 'Theologie der Hoffnung' von Jurgen Moltmann* (München 1967); J.B. METZ, "God before us instead of a Theological Argument" in *Cross Currents* 18 (1968) 296-306; H. MOTTU, "L'espérence chrétienne dans la pensée J. Moltmann" in *Revue de théolgie et de philosophie* (1967) 242-258; G.G. O'COLLINS, "The Principle and Theology of Hope" in *Scottish Journal of Theology* 21 (1968) 129-144; G.G. O'COLLINS, "Spes quaerens intellectum" in *Interpretation* 22 (1968) 36-52; W. PANNENBERG, "The God of Hope" in *Cross Currents* 18 (1968) 284-295.

104C.E. BRAATEN, *The Future of God. The Revolutionary Dynamics of Hope* (London 1969) p. 142.

105J.B. METZ, "Relationship of Church and World in the Light of Political Theology" in L.K. SHOOK, ed. *Theology of Renewal, II* (Montreal 1968) 255-270, p. 263. For further readings see J.B. METZ, ed. *Faith and World of Politics* (New York 1968) Concilium 36; id. *Perspectives of a Political Ecclesiology* (New York 1971) Concilium 66; W. CHRISTIAN, *Christenheit in Angriff; Zur Theologie der Revolution* (Gütersloh 1969); R. WETH, ed. *Diskussion zur "Theologie der Revolution"* (Mainz 1969).

106F. FANON, *Black Skin, White Masks* (New York 1967); J. BALDWIN, al., *The Negro Protest* (Memphis 1970); J.H. CONE *A Black Theology of Liberation* (Philadelphia 1970).

107A. GHEERBRANT, *L'Église rebelle d'Amerique Latine* (Paris 1969).

[108]A.J. AYER, *Language, Truth, and Logic* (London 1936).

[109]F. FERRÉ, *Basic Modern Philosophy of Religion* (New York 1967).

[110]J. MACQUARRIE, *Gold-Talk, an Examination of the Language and Logic of Theology* (New York 1967).

[111]L. GILKEY, *Naming the Whirlwind, The Renewal of God-Language* (New York 1969) p. 422.

[112]L. GILKEY, *Naming the Whirlwind* . . . pp. 446-447, 454.

[113]See J.B. METZ, editor, *The Crisis of Religious Language* (New York 1973) Concilium 85.

[114]VATICAN II, *Pastoral Constitution on the Church in the Modern World* (GS) no. 62.

[115]GS no. 40.

[116]VATICAN II, *Dogmatic Constitution on the Church* (LG) no. 9.

[117]GS no. 53. 63. 77.

[118]GS no. 76; LG no. 13; LG no. 1; GS no. 42.

[119]LG no. 1; GS no. 42.

[120]Some typical examples were, G. BAUM, *Credibility of the Church Today* (New York 1968); L. DEWART, *The Foundations of Belief* (New York 1969); O.A. RABUT, *La verification religieuse*, (Paris 1964); id. *Un christianisme d'incertitude* (Paris 1968) - *L'expérience religieuse fondamentale* (Paris 1969); M. BELLET, *Le Point critique* (Paris 1970).

[121]See E.G.W. ROHRER, *Ist der Mensch konstruierbar?* (Munich 1966).

[122]E.E. DAVID, J.G. TRUXAL, *The Man Made World* (New York 1968) p.v.

[123]D.G. FINK, *Computers and the Human Mind, An Introduction to Artificial Intelligence* (Garden City 1966).

[124]D.G. FINK, *Computers and the Human Mind* . . . pp. 258-259.

[125]D.G. FINK, *Computers and the Human Mind* . . . pp. 278-280.

[126]D.G. FINK, *Computers and the Human Mind* . . . pp. 279-280.

[127]Cf D.M. MACKAY, *Information, Mechanism and Meaning* (London 1969) p. 42.

[128]T.G. EVANS, "Geometric Analogy" in M. MINSKY, ed., *Semantic Information Processing* (Cambridge, Mass. 1968) pp. 271-351.

[129]B. RAPHAEL, "Semantic Information Retrieval" in M. MINSKY, *Semantic Information* . . . pp. 33-132; M.R. QUILLIAN, "Semantic Information Processing" in M. MINSKY, *Semantic Information* . . . pp. 216-255.

[130]K.M. SAYRE. *Recognition: A Study in the Philosophy of Artificial Intelligence* (Notre Dame 1965); id., *Consciousness: A Philosophic Study of Mind and Machines* (New York 1969).

[131]K.M. SAYRE, *Consciousness* . . . p. 145.

[132]J.S. BEZZANT, "Intellectual Objections" in D.M. MACKINNON and al., *Objections to Christian Belief* (London 1963) pp. 79-111.

[133]C.H. ROBERTS, *An Unpublished Fragment of the Fourth Gospel in the John Rylands Library* (Manchester 1935); X. LÉON-DUFOUR, *Les évangiles et l'histoire de Jésus* (Paris 1963) pp. 47-48.

[134]H.J. BELL and T.C. SKEAT, *Fragments of an Unknown Gospel* (London 1935); M.J. LAGRANGE, "Un nouveau papyrus évangélique" in *Revue Biblique* 44 (1935) 327-343; W.C. van UNNIK, "The Gospel of Truth and the New Testament" in F.L. CROSS, ed. *The Jung Codex* (London 1955) pp. 81-119.

[135]A. GARDEIL, *La crédibilité et l'apologetique*, (Paris 1912), p. 203.

[136]J. LEVIE, *Sous les yeux de l'incroyant* (Paris 1946), p. 17; A. LIÉGÉ, "Bulletin d'apologétique" in *Revue des sciences philosophiques et théologiques*, 33 (1949) p. 53.

[137]N. DUNAS, "Les problèmes et le statut de l'apologétique" in *Revue des sciences philosophiques et théologiques* 43 (1959) p. 644; J. SCHMITZ, "Die Fundamentaltheologie im 20. Jahrhundert" in H. VORGRIMLER, R.V. GUCHT, ed., *Bilanz der Theologie im 20. Jahrhundert* (Freiburg, 1969) v. 2, p. 201; C. GEFFRE, "Recent Developments in Fundamental Theology: An Interpretation" in *Concilium* 46 (1969) p. 5, J.K.S. REID, *Christian Apologetics* (Grand Rapids, 1969) p. 210; A. DULLES, *A History of Apologetics*. (Westminister 1971) pp. VIII, 246.

[138]See e.g. J.B. METZ ed. *The Development of Fundamental Theology, Concilium* 46 (1969).

[139]Cf. H. HOLSTEIN, "Le problème de Jésus dans l'enseignement de l'Apologétique depuis le début du XXe siècle" in *Bulletin du comité des études*, 5(1961) pp. 340-341.

[140]H. BOUILLARD, *The Logic of Faith*, New York, 1967; Id., "Human Experience as the Starting Point of Fundamental Theology" in *Concilium* 6 (1965) pp. 79-91; cf also B.B. BAXTER, *I Believe Because* (Grand Rapids 1971).

[141]K. RAHNER, "Way to Faith" in *Sacramentum Mundi* 2 (New York 1968) pp. 310-315.

[142]"When I am told it is precisely its immunity from proof which secures the Christian proclamation from the charge of being mythological, I reply that immunity from proof can secure nothing whatever except immunity from proof, and call nonsense by its name." J.S. BEZZANT, "Intellectual Objections . . . " pp. 90-91.

[143]"The World Council of Churches is a fellowship of Churches which accepts our Lord Jesus Christ as God and Savior" in D.P. GAINES *The World Council of Churches* (Peterborough 1966) pp. 1106-1245.

[144]Although this concept of formal theology of revelation does not coincide completely with K. Rahner's idea of formal and fundamental theology, it is however, very close to it. Cf K. RAHNER, "Formale und Fundamentale Theologie" in *Lexikon für Theologie und Kirche*, 4, (Freiburg, 1960) 205-206; Id., *Theological Investigations*, I, (London,

1961) pp. 19-23; G. SOHNGEN "Fundamentaltheologie" in *Lexikon für Theologie und Kirche,* 4, pp. 452-459.

[145]Fundamental Theology is basically fundamental because it treats of Jesus Christ, the real foundation of our faith, inasmuch as he is the final revelation of God.

[146]Notice that H. Bouillard, K. Rahner propose reverse of this method of procedure.

[147]Cf H. DENZINGER, A. SCHÖNMETZER *Enchiridion . . .* no. 3016-17 *The Teaching of the Catholic Church . . .* no. 43; also Y. CONGAR, *La foi et la Théologie,* (Paris, 1962) pp. 197-206; J.P. TORELL "Chronique de théologie fondamentale" in *Revue thomiste* 64 (1964) 97-127; p. 102.

[148]See J. MACQUARRIE, "Religious Language and Recent Analytical Philosophy" in *Concilium* 46 (1969) 159-172; H. FRIES "From Apologetics to Fundamental Theology" in *Concilium* 46 (1969) 57-68.

[149]See e.g., R. PANIKKAR, "Metatheology or Diacritical Theology as Fundamental Theology" in *Concilium* 46 (1969) 43-55.

[150]See J. CAHILL, "A Fundamental Theology of our Time" in *Concilium* 46 (1969) 93-101; L. GILKEY, "Trends in Protestant Apologetics" in *Concilium* 46 (1969) 127-157; J. SECUNDO, "Fundamental Theology and Dialogue" in *Concilium* 46 (1969) 69-79.

[151]Since λόγος can mean Christ and ἀπο means *from* and *by* whom an act comes or it is done as well as *because* a thing is done (see H.G. LIDDEL, R. SCOTT, *Greek-English Lexikon* (Oxford 1951) 1, pp. 191-192) the real purpose of apologetics can be considered as to refer everything to Christ and see how the event or idea in question is from Christ, through and for Christ, the final explanation of any theological understanding.

[152]Cf S. WEIL, *Intuitions pré-chrétiennes,* (Paris 1951) pp. 9-21; English translation *Intimations of Christianity* (London 1957) p. 1 ff.

[153]A. FEUILLET, "Le Fils de l'Homme de Daniel et la tradition biblique" in *Revue Biblique* 60 (1953) 170-202, 321-346, p. 177; see also E.B. ALLO, *Apocalypse,* 4th edition, (Paris, 1933) p. 16; M.-J. LAGRANGE, *Le judaisme avant Jésus-Christ* (Paris 1931) p. 388 ff.

[154]See Council of Orange, H. DENZINGER A. SCHÖNMETZER *Enchiridion . . .* no. 373-400, *The Teaching of the Catholic Church* no. 218; Council of Trent, H. DENZINGER, A. SCHÖNMETZER *Enchiridion . . .* no. 155 ff.

[155]A.J. HESCHEL, *God in Search of Man* (New York 1955) pp. 425-426; see L. SCHMIDT, *Menschlicher Erfolg und Jahwes Initiative* (Neukirchen 1970).

[156]C.M. BOWRA, *The Greek Experience* (London 1957) pp. 45-47, 61.

[157]C.M. BOWRA, *The Greek Experience . . .* p. 59.

[158]*The Geeta, The Lord Gospel of the Lord Shri Krishna,* translated by SHRI PUROHIT SWAMI (London 1935) p. 16ff.

[159]Ch. GUIGNEBERT, *Jésus* (Paris 1933), p. 74.

160Cf R.E.L. MASTERS AND J. HOUSTON, *The Varieties of Psychedelic Experience* (New York 1969) pp. 312-313; W. BRADEN, *The Private Sea LSD and the Search for God* (Toronto 1968) pp. 14-20.

161*The Teaching of the Catholic Church ... no. 35;* H. DENZINGER, A. SCHÖN-METZER, *Enchiridion ...* no. 3008.

162*The Teaching of the Catholic Church ...* no. 37; H. DENZINGER, A. SCHÖN-METZER, *Enchiridion ...* no. 3010.

163The solution of *Analysis fidei* as proposed, e.gr. by H. HURTER, *Theologiae Dogmaticae Compendium* 1 (Innsbruck 1891); A. KOLPING *Fundamentaltheologie I* (Regensburg 1967), cannot be accepted. According to this view the act of faith is conceived as discursive act of understanding. The fact of revelation is known by a merely scientific process by means of the signs of miracles. The faith is resolved to syllogism, and the absolute certitude of faith is based upon a fallible human knowledge. Indeed there is no need for supernatural faith in the fact of revelation (except for believing propositions of faith) since faith is reduced to natural faith which is inadmissible. Cf G. de BROGLIE, *Revelation and Reason* (London 1965) cf also H. DENZINGER, A. SCHÖNMETZER, *Enchiridion ...* no. 3035; *The Teaching of the Catholic Church ...* no. 57.

164Lugo's solution is also inadequate. In order to avoid the difficulty of the first solution Lugo proposed an immediate intuitive knowledge of God, the Revealer. According to this theory the revealed truth is believed while the fact of revelation, namely, that it is God who reveals, is not believed, but seen by immediate perception. But the question is whether such an intuition of God exists? The supernaturalness of faith was not properly understood by Lugo. See J. LUGO, *De virtute fidei divinae* (Paris 1868).

165The so-called *fides auctoritatis,* "authoritarian faith" had been defended by L. BILLOT, *De virtutibus infusis,* (Rome 1905), C. PESCH *De Virtutibus in genere, De Virtutibus theologicis* (Freiburg 1922), H. LENNERZ *De Virtutibus theologicis* (Rome 1947) etc.

166Cf J. ALFARO, "Motive of Faith, Preambles of Faith" in *Sacramentum Mundi 2,* (London 1968) pp. 322-326; K. RAHNER, "Analysis fidei" in *Theological Dictionary* (New York 1965) p. 19.

167*The Teaching of the Catholic Church ...* no. 57; H. DENZINGER, A. SCHÖN-METZER, *Enchiridion ...* no. 3035.

168*The Teaching of the Catholic Church ...* no. 42-48; H. DENZINGER, A. SCHÖN-METZER, *Enchiridion ...* no. 3015-3020.

169*The Teaching of the Catholic Church ...* no. 37; H. DENZINGER, A. SCHÖN-METZER, *Enchiridion ...* no. 3010.

170*The Teaching of the Catholic Church ...* no. 56; H. DENZINGER, A. SCHÖN-METZER, *Enchiridion ...* no. 3034.

171*The Teaching of the Catholic Church ...* no. 46; H. DENZINGER, A. SCHÖN-METZER, *Enchiridion ...* no. 3019.

[172]*The Teaching of the Catholic Church* ... no. 44; H. DENZINGER, A. SCHÖN-METZER, *Enchiridion* ... no. 3017.

[173]*The Teaching of the Catholic Church* ... no. 46; H. DENZINGER, A. SCHÖN-METZER, *Enchiridion* ... no. 3019.

[174]*The Teaching of the Catholic Church* ... no. 36; H. DENZINGER, A. SCHÖN-METZER, *Enchiridion* ... no. 3009.

[175]*The Teaching of the Catholic Church* ... no. 356; H. DENZINGER, A. SCHÖN-METZER, *Enchiridion* ... no. 3013 "evidentem.... credibilitatem ..."

[176]See MANSI, *Conciliorum Collectio* 5, 235, 326.

[177]Although, as Pius XII in *Humani Generis* taught, it is possible in itself to recognize the evident credibility of Christian faith by natural reason alone, without any special grace, in fact it occurs always under the light of the helping grace of God, see H. DENZINGER, A. SCHÖNMETZER *Enchiridion* ... no. 3875-76; *The Teaching of the Catholic Church* ... no. 74a. But this grace will not change the act of understanding into an act of faith. Therefore the recognition of evident credibility of Christian belief—with or without grace—is always an act of understanding about faith and not an act of believing about faith.

[178]*The Teaching of the Catholic Church* ... no. 36; H. DENZINGER, A. SCHÖN-METZER, *Enchiridion* ... no. 3009.

[179]Cf VATICAN II, *Dogmatic Constitution on Divine Revelation* no. 21 and 7. Notice the preposition "in" as opposed to the preposition "through" as the specific character-istic of knowing God by faith and not only by natural knowledge.

[180]*The Teaching of the Catholic Church* ... no. 57; H. DENZINGER, A. SCHÖN-METZER, *Enchiridion* ... no. 3035.

[181]The role of apologetics is, therefore, not just to show that reason cannot raise straight objections against faith—see P. KNAUER, *Verantwortung des Glaubens* (Frankfurt 1969); id., "Hermeneutische Fundamentaltheologie" in H. WOLTER, ed. *Testimonium veritati* (Frankfurt 1971) pp. 169-180; W. KERN, P. KNAUER, "Zur Frage der Glaubwürdigkeit der Christlichen Offenbarung" in *Zeitschrift für katholische Theologie* 93 (1971) 478-491)—but to let prevail the Christ event's attractive power of raising questions about God.

[182]"... Wie es eigentlich gewesen," see L. von RANKE, *Geschichte der romanischen und germanischen Völker,* ... vol 33, p. 7; see more recently R. PESCH, *Jesu ureigene Taten?* (Freiburg 1970) p. 16.

[183]The sacred history notion has many difficulties: on the one hand it removes the sacred events from the real ordinary events of the world history and on the other hand it supposes that the event of the history of salvation can be grasped by a historian. It separates salvation history from the world history suggesting a notion of time and history which is not necessarily taught by the biblical writers, Cf J. BARR, *Biblical Words for Time* (London 1962).

[184]Cf T. HORVATH, *Caritas est in ratione, Die Lehre des hl. Thomas über die Einheit der intellektiven und affektiven Begnadung des Menschen* (Münster 1966) pp. 242-255.

[185]Cf J. WALGRAVE, "The Essence of Modern Fundamental Theology" in *Concilium* 46 (1969) p. 81-91.

[186]Cf E.O. DOHERTY, "The Organic Development of Messianic Revelation" in *Catholic Biblical Quarterly* 19 (1957) 16-24; J.L. MCKENZIE, "Royal Messianism," *Catholic Biblical Quarterly*, pp. 25-52; R.E. MURPHY, "Notes on New Testament and Apologetics," *Catholic Biblical Quarterly* . . . pp. 5-15; R.E. BROWN, "The Messianism of Qumran," *Catholic Biblical Quarterly* . . . pp. 53-82.

[187]An inadequately defined concept of messianism might presuppose meanings which could not be seen by the human authors of the Old Testament and might indicate texts as messianic which do not have any reference to the Messiah at all. See the critique on this way of arguing from prophecy, B. VAWTER, "Messianic Prophecies in Apologetics" in *Proceedings of the 14th Annual Convention of the Catholic Theological Society of America* 14 (1959) 97-119.

[188]Cf M.D. HOOKER, *The Son of Man in Mark* (London 1967) pp. 91ff.

[189]O. PLÖGER, *Das Buch Daniel* (Gütersloh 1965) pp. 110-114; N.W. PORTEOUS, *Daniel* (London 1965) p. 110.

[190]Cf T.W. MANSON, *Studies in the Gospels and Epistles* (Manchester 1962) p. 126; E. SCHWEITZER, "The Son of Man Again" in *New Testament Studies* 9 (1963) p. 256-261; E.W. HEATON, The Book of Daniel (London 1964) p. 183; H.M. TEEPLE, "The Origin of the Son of Man Christology" in *Journal of Biblical Literature* 84 (1965) p. 213-250.

[191]E. DHANIS, "De Filio hominis in Vetere Testamento et in judaismo" in *Gregorianum* 45 (1964) 10ff.

[192]A. FEUILLET, "Le Fils de l'homme du Daniel et la tradition biblique" in *Revue Biblique* 60 (1953) 170-202; 321-346, pp. 187-189.

[193]R. BULTMANN, *Jesus and the Word* (New York 1958) p. 13. See also, "Soviet Historians Admit Real Existence of Christ" in *Herder Correspondence* 3 (1966) 227-228.

[194]C.F. VOLNEY, *Les ruines ou méditations sur les révolutions des empires* (Paris 1791).

[195]Ch. F. DUPUIS, *Origine de tous les cultes ou la religion universelle* (Paris 1794).

[196]J.M. ROBERTSON, *Christianity and Mythology* (London 1900).

[197]A. DREWS, *Die Christusmythe* (Jena 1909).

[198]W. ERBT, *Das Markusevangelium* (Leipzig 1911).

[199]P. JENSEN, *Das Gilgamesch-epos in der Weltliteratur* (Strassbourg 1906); id. *Hat Jesus der Evangelien wirklich gelebt?* (Frankfurt a.M.1910).

[200]B. BAUER, *Christus und die Caesaren* (Berlin 1877).

[201]A. KALTHOFF, *Das Christusproblem, Grundlinien zu einer Sozialtheologie* (Leipzig 1902).

[202]P.L. COUCHOUD, *Le mystère de Jésus* (Paris 1924); A. BAYET, *Les morales de Jésus* (Paris 1928).

[203]W.B. SMITH, *Der vorchristliche Jesus nebst weiteren Vorstudien zur Entwicklungs-geschichte des Urchristentums* (Jena 1906).

[204]Ch. GUIGNEBERT, *Jésus* (Paris 1950) 2nd ed. pp. 59-60; M. GOGUEL, from the same school, suggested that it were "piquant" to refute them by opposing one opinion to the other, see his *Jésus* (Paris 1950) 2nd ed. p. 42.

[205]Namely, that he, Nero, ordered the fire, which occurred in the summer of A.D. 64. The English translation is taken from D.J. THERON, *Evidence of Tradition* (London 1957) pp. 11-13, 15.

[206]D.J. THERON, *Evidence of Tradition* ... p. 21; W. CURETON, *Spicilegium-Syriacum* (London 1855) p. 73.

[207]C. GUIGNEBERT, *Jésus* ... pp. 16-17.

[208]C. GUIGNEBERT, *Jésus* ... pp 71-73.

[209]Cf H.L. STRACK, P. BILLERBECK, *Kommentar zum neuen Testament aus Talmud und Midrasch* (Munich 1922) 1, 36-43.

[210]It is remarkable that contrary to the ancient Jewish tradition, which made Jesus responsible for persecutions and miseries which happened to the Jews during their history, the modern tendency (at least among the progressive Jews) is to consider Jesus a national hero, a classical Jew—see M. de JONDE, *Jeschuah der klassische jüdischer Mann, Zerstörung des kirchlichen, Enthüllung des jüdischen Jesusbildes* (Berlin 1904)—who belongs to the Jewish messianic movement of the first century but has nothing in common with Jesus Christ of the Christian dogmas. Moreover, beginning with S. FORMSTECHER, *Religion des Geistes* (Leipzig 1841), S. L. STEINHEIM, *Die Offenbarung nach dem Lehrbegriff der Synagogue* (Leipzig 1835-1865), the Jewish-Christian attitude has undergone a fundamental change and a Judaeo-Christian dialogue has been made possible. F. ROSENZWEIG, *Briefe* (Berlin 1935), N.N. GLATZER, F. ROSEN-ZWEIG, *His Life and Thought* (New York 1953), M. BUBER, *Die Stunde und die Erkenntnis*, "The Time and the Perception" (Berlin 1936) and H.J. SCHOEPS, *The Jewish-Christian Argument,* 3rd ed. (London 1963) state that "the Jewish side recognizes the divine origin of Christianity and its revelation as the way of salvation for the Gentile world outside of Israel" (H.J. SCHOEPS, *The Jewish-Christian* ... pp. 159-160). The Church as well as the Synagogue might consider each other (Islam not excluded) as a transitory representative of the true religion of the Spirit and thus have motives leading to dialogue, since both are united by one common expectation: "The messianism of Israel is directed toward that which is to come, the eschatology of the universal Gentile Church toward the return of Him who has come. Both are united by one common expectation, that the truth which we do not know, which we can only guess, is yet to come, in that hour when the beginning is swallowed up in the end. At this point all Judaeo-Christian dialogue ends in the ancient petition of the Pater Noster; 'Thy kingdom come to us' " (H.J. SCHOEPS, *The Jewish-Christian* ... p. 172).

[211]Cf X. LÉON-DUFOUR, "Passion- Sources non-chrétiennes" in *Dictionnaire de la Bible Supplément* 6 (Paris 1960) 1421-1923; C.M. MARTINI, "Il silenzio dei testimoni non christiani su Gesu" in *la Civilta Cattolica* 1132 (1962) 346-348; F. SCHEIDWEILER, "Das Testimonium Flavium" in *Zeitschrift für die neutestamentliche Wissenschaft.* 45 (1954) 230-243.

212For historical reflection on Jesus' self-consciousness see G. BORNKAMM, *Jesus of Nazareth* (New York 1960); E. FUCHS, *Studies of the Historical Jesus* (London 1964); M.C. VANHENGEL, J. PETERS, "This Same Jesus" in *Concilium* 20 (1967) 161-173; R.E. BROWN, *Jesus God and Man* (London 1968): F. HAHN, ed. *What Can We Know About Jesus* (Edinburgh 1969). For dogmatic reflection on the same question see K. RAHNER, "Dogmatic Reflections on the Knowledge and Self-Consciousness of Christ" in *Theological Investigation* 5 (London 1966) pp. 193-215; E. GUTWENGER "The Problem of Christ's Knowledge" in *Concilium* 11 (1966) 91-128; H. RIEDLINGER, *Geschichtlickeit und Vollendung des Wissens Christi* (Freiburg 1966); J. GALOT, *Vers une nouvelle Christologie* (Gembloux 1971).

213D. MOLLAT, "The Divinity of Christ in Saint John" in A. GELIN, ed., *Son and Saviour* (Baltimore 1967) pp. 125-151; French original in *Lumière et Vie* 9 (1953) 101-134; R.E. BROWN, "Does the New Testament call Jesus God?" *Theological Studies* 26 (1965) 545-573.

214Cf C. HEADLAM, *The Fourth Gospel as History* (Oxford 1948) pp. 11-13.

215Cf F. FUNK, ed. *Patres Apostolici*, I (Tübingen 1901) p. 640.

216D. GUTHRIE, *New Testament Introduction, The Gospels and Acts* (London 1965) pp. 43-44, 68-72, 104-109; A. WIKENHAUSER, *New Testament Introduction* (New York 1958) pp. 170-171, 196-198, 220-221.

217P. BENOIT, "The Divinity of Jesus in the Synoptic Gospels" in A. GELIN, *Son and Saviour . . .* pp. 50-85; Ch. P. CEROKE, "The Divinity of Christ in the Gospels" in *The Catholic Biblical Quarterly* 24 (1962) 125-139.

218Cf O. CULLMANN, *The Christology of the New Testament* (London 1963) pp. 234-237, 197-233; A. GEORGE, "Jésus Fils de Dieu dans Saint Luc" in *Revue Biblique* 72 (1965) 185-209.

219J.M. VOSTÉ, "The Title 'Son of God' in the Synoptic Gospels" in *The American Ecclesiastical Review* 121 (1949) pp. 26-28.

220B.M.F. Van IERSEL, '*Der Sohn' in den synoptischen Jesusworten* (Leiden 1961) pp. 160-161; O. CULLMANN, *The Christology . . .* pp. 287-289.

221J. DUPONT, "La révélation du Fils de Dieu en faveur de Pierre (Mt 16-17) et de Paul (Gal 1,16) in *Recherches de science réligieuse* 52 (1964) pp. 411-420; Th. de KRUIJF, *Der Sohn des lebendigen Gottes* (Roma 1962).

222M.E. BOISMARD, "The Divinity of Christ in Saint Paul" in A. GELIN, *Son and Saviour . . .* pp. 86-112.

223Cf 1 Cor 16, 22; 1 Thess 1, 9-10; 5, 2; see P.E. LANGEVIN, *Jesus, Seigneur et Eschatologie, Exégèse des textes Prépauliniens* (Paris 1967). About the Christology of Q see D. LÜHRMANN, *Die Redaktion der Logienquelle* (Neukirchen 1969). The relation between Q and Mk proposed by Lührmann is doubtful: J.T. SANDERS, *The New Testament Christological Hymns* (Cambridge 1971) 58-74.

224D.M. STANLEY, "The Divinity of Christ in Hymns of the New Testament" in *Proceedings of the Fourth Annual Convention of the Catholic College Teachers of*

Sacred Doctrine 4 (1958) p. 22 ff.; L. CERFAUX, *Christ in the Theology of St. Paul* (New York 1959) pp. 374-375.

225A. FEUILLET, "L'hymne christologique de l'Épitre aux Philippiens (11, 6-11)" in *Revue biblique* 72 (1965) 352-380, 481-507; pp. 483ff.

226J.B. LIGHTFOOT, *Saint Paul's Epistle to the Philippians* (London 1881) p. 133.

227See A. FEUILLET, L'hymne christologique ... " pp. 352-380, 481-507. A reply from J. COPPENS, "Les affinités littéraires de Philosophie 2, 6-11" in *Ephemerides Theologicae Lovanienses* 42 (1966) 238-241; see also F.C. SYNGE, *Philippians and Colossians, Introduction and Commentary* (London 1958) pp. 29-35; R.P. MARTIN, *The Epistle of Paul to the Philippians* (London 1960) pp. 100-101. J.J. BEHM, " μορφη " in J. KITTEL ed. *Theological Dictionary of the New Testament,* 4 (Grand Rapids 1967) 742-752; J. SCHNEIDER, "σχῆμα" in G. FRIEDRICH ed. *Theological Dictionary of the New Testament* 7 (Grand Rapids 1971) 954-956.

228J. CARMIGNAC, "L'Importance de la place d'une negation: οὐχ ἁρπαγμὸν ἡγήσατο (Philippians II.6)" in *New Testament Studies* 18 (1972) 131-166.

229C. SPICQ, *L'Épitre aux Hebreux* 2 (Paris 1953) p. 23.

230D.M. STANLEY, "The Divinity of Christ ..." p. 24; L. CERFAUX, *Christ in the Theology of St. Paul* ... pp. 372-374.

231J. SCHMITT, "Christ Jesus in the Apostolic Church" in A. GELIN, *Son and Saviour* ... pp. 35-55; D.M. STANLEY, *The Apostolic Church in the New Testament* (Westminister 1965) pp. 95-118; J.N. D. KELLY, *Early Christian Creeds* (London 1950) pp. 1-29; M.E. BOISMARD, *Quatre hymns baptismales dans la premiere épitre de Pierre* (Paris 1961).

232Since Jesus came to fulfill the covenant, he could not use the name El-Shaddai, the pre-mosaic name of Yahweh (cf Ex 17,1; 6,2-3; Gen 28,13; 35,11; 43,14; 48,3; 49,25). The use would have suggested some kind of return to Israelites' pre-covenant relation to God.

233In the following sections we will employ the criteria accepted by scholars for distinguishing authentic texts referable to Jesus from the text of the early Church's tradition. See D.G.A. CALVERT, "An Examination of the Criteria for Distinguishing the Authentic Words of Jesus" in *New Testament Studies* 18 (1972) 209-219. The authenticity of a text can be tested by the following criteria:
   1) The text can be referred neither to the early Church nor to the political, social, historical and religious circumstances of contemporary Judaism. And at the same time it can easily be explained through Jesus' own historical situation; cf J. DUPONT, "L'origine du récit des tentations de Jésus au désert" in *Revue Biblique* 73 (1966) 30-76; D.E. NINEHAM, *The Gospel of St. Mark* (London 1963); R.H. FULLER, *A Critical Introduction to the New Testament* (London 1966); H.E.W. TURNER, *Historicity and the Gospels* (London 1963); M. LEHMANN, *Synoptische Quellenanalyse und die Frage nach dem historischen Jesus* (Berlin 1970) pp. 178-186.
   2) The meaning of the text contradicts the tendencies and interest of the early Church e.g., Jesus' confession of ignorance concerning the time of the *parousia,* see O. CULLMANN, *The Christology of the New Testament* (London 1963) p. 295; The words

of Jesus about John the Baptist in Mt. 11, 12f. are opposed to the early tradition of the Church which tried to reduce John the Baptist to the position of a forerunner: see D.G.A. CALVERT, "An Examination of the Criteria for Distinguishing"... p. 215; the embarrassment to missionary activity of obstructive facts, like baptism received from John the Baptist, death on the cross; see W. TRILLING, *Fragen zur Geschichtlichkeit Jesu* (Düsseldorf 1969); M. LEHMANN, *Synoptische Quellenanalyse* ... pp. 174-178.

3) The same saying or event is witnessed by several different traditions, and it does not serve the theological purpose of the redactor: see H.K. McARTHUR "Basic Issues, A Survey of Recent Gospel Research. Interpretation" in *A Journal of Bible and Theology* 18 (1964) 39-55; C.H. DODD, *The Parables of the Kingdom* (London 1961); D.G.A. CALVERT, *An Examination* ... p. 219; M. LEHMANN, *Synoptische Quellenanalyse* ... p. 163-174; G.B. GERHARDSSON, *Memory and Manuscript* (Uppsala 1961); id. *Tradition and Transmission in the Early Church* (Lund 1964).

4) Ideas, parables, words "Abba," "Amen," "But I say to you," expressions, style (Aramaism), dialectical tension between the present existence and the future (Kingdom is here and Kingdom is to come) which point to a real religious genius who would be an anonymous person unknown to the early Church if Jesus were discounted: J.M. ROBINSON, *A New Quest of the Historical Jesus* (London 1959); M. LEHMANN, *Synoptische Quellenanalyse* ... p. 186-195; M. BLACK, *An Aramaic Approach to the Gospels and Acts* (Oxford 1946); J. JEREMIAS, "Kennzeichen der 'ipsissima vox Jesu' " in *Synoptische Studien, Alfred Wikenhauser* ... *dargebracht* (Munich 1953) pp. 86-93; id., "Der gegenwärtige Stand der Debatte um das Problem des historischen Jesus" in H. RISTOW, K. MATTHIAE ed., *Der historische Jesus und der kerygmatische Christus* (Berlin 1960) pp. 12-21; id. *The Parables of Jesus* (New York 1963).

5) Some features of Jesus which could not have been invented by the authors of the gospels: e.g. a man dedicated to God, and a man who claims to have full power of making the greatest demands and is at the same time ready to forgive: see P. ALTHAUS, *The So-called Kerygma and the Historical Jesus* (London 1959); M. LEHMANN, *Synoptische Quellenanalyse* ... pp. 200-202.

6) Texts which fit into the total context of Jesus' message: see M. LEHMANN, *Synoptische Quellenanalyse* .... pp. 195-199.

Though the method we follow is similar, our objective is different. To find out and know exactly what and how much Jesus did know is extremely difficult if not entirely impossible since the historian supposes that Jesus could not differ from an ordinary man, who is the only "analogy" available to the historian. Therefore instead of establishing what the historical Jesus did think of himself and what he actually did, we will ask rather whether it is historically possible that Jesus did evoke faith in himself.

[234]Mt 3,2 is probably a term introduced by the early Church who had the tendency to harmonize the doctrine of John the Baptist with that of Jesus for kerygmatic purposes. Mt. 3,2 contradicts Mt. 11,12 and Lk 16,16.

[235]There are twenty other instances where basileia means either the kingdom on earth in general (Mt 4,8; 12,25; 24,7; Mk 6,23; 11,10; 13,8; Lk 11,17; 19,12.15; 21,10; Acts 1,6; Heb 11,38; Rev 16,10) or that of the Satan (Mt 12,26; Mk 3,24; Lk 4,5; 11,18; Rev 17,18). We do not count here Rev 11,15 which says that the kingdom of the world has become the kingdom of the Lord.

[236]A. ROBERT, A. FEUILLET, *Introduction to the New Testament* (New York 1965)

p. 757. K.L. SCHMIDT, "βασιλεία" in G. KITTEL, *Theological Dictionary* 1 (London 1964) pp. 588-590; 591-593.

[237]The Son-of-David-Theology might be considered as second stage of The Son-of-God-Theology (Rom 1,3; 2 Tim 2,8): see C. BURGER, *Jesus als Davidsson, Eine traditions-geschichtliche Untersuchung* (Göttingen 1970); G. RUGGIERI, *Il Figlio di Dio davidico* (Rome 1968).

[238]See e.g. R. BULTMANN, "The Primitive Christian Kerygma and the Historical Jesus" in C.E. BRAATEN AND R.A. HARRISVILLE, ed. *The Historical Jesus and the Keryg-matic Christ* (New York 1964) p. 23; id., "The Study of the Synoptic Gospels" in R. BULTMANN, K. KUNDSIN, *Form Criticism, Two Essays on New Testament Research* (New York 1962) 11-76, pp. 61-63. R. Bultmann however did not analyze all the *Sitz im Leben* implications of his statement: ". . . he doubtless appeared in the consciousness of being commissioned by God to preach the eschatological message of the breaking-in of the kingdom of God . . ." R. BULTMANN, "The Primitive Christian Kerygma . . ." p. 23.

[239]R. SCHNACKENBURG, *God's rule and Kingdom* (New York 1963); N. PERRIN, *The Kingdom of God in the Teaching of Jesus* (Philadelphia 1963); W. PANNENBERG, "The Kingdom of God . . ." in *Una Sancta* 24, 2 (1967) 3-19; 24, 4 (1967) 3-27; 25, 2 (1968) 6-26; R.H. HIERS, *The Kingdom of God in the Synoptic Tradition* (Gainesville 1970).

[240]P. FIEBIG, *Der Menschensohn* (Tübingen 1901); T.W. MANSON, "The Meaning of 'Son of Man' " in *Journal of Biblical Literature* 60 (1941) 151-157; H.B. SHARMAN, *Son of Man and Kingdom of God* (New York 1943); G.S. DUNCAN, *Jesus, Son of Man* (London 1947); J. BOWMAN, "The Background of the Term 'Son of Man' " in *Expository Times* 59 (1947-48) 283-288; J.Y. CAMPBELL, "The Origin and Meaning of the Term 'Son of Man' " in *Journal of Theological Studies* 48 (1947) 145-155; C.C. McCOWN, "Jesus, Son of Man: A Survey of Recent Discussion" in *Journal of Religion* 28 (1948) 1-12; M. BLACK, "The 'Son of Man' in the Teaching of Jesus" in *Expository Times* 60 (1948) 11-14, 32-36; A. FEUILLET, "Le Fils de l'homme de Daniel et la tradition biblique" in *Revue Biblique* 60 (1953) 170-202, 321-346; V. TAYLOR, *The Names of Jesus* (London 1953) pp. 23-35; A. FEUILLET, "L'Exousia du Fils de l'homme" in *Recherches de Science Religieuse* 42 (1954) 161-192; E. SJOBERG, *Der verborgene Menschensohn in den Evangelien* (Lund 1955); S. MOWINCKEL, *He that cometh* (Oxford 1956); E. STAUFFER, "Messias oder Menschensohn?" in *Novum Testamentum* I (1956) 81-102; O. CULLMANN, *Die Christologie des Neuen Testaments* (Tübingen 1957); English translation: *The Christology of the New Testament* (London 1959) pp. 137-192; P. VIELHAUSER, "Gottesreich und Menschensohn in der Verkündi-gung Jesu" in W. SCHNEEMELCHER, ed., *Festschrift für Günther Dehn* (Neukirchen 1957) pp. 51-79; A. RICHARDSON, *An Introduction to the Theology of the New Testament* (London 1958) pp. 125-46; A.J.B. HIGGINS, "The Son of Man-Forschung since the Teaching of Jesus" in *New Testament Essays in Memory of* T.W. MANSON (Manchester 1959) pp. 119-135; H.E. TÖDT, *Der Menschensohn in der Synoptischen Überlieferung* (Gütershof 1959): English translation: *The Son of Man in the Synoptic Tradition* (Philadelphia 1965); see its Review in *Expository Times* 77 (1966) 257-258; H. CONZELMANN, "Jesus Christus" in *Religion in Geschichte und Gegenwart 3*

(Tübingen 1959) 630-631; J. MUILENBURG, "The Son of Man and the Ethiopic Apocalypse of Henoch" in *Journal of Biblical Literature* 79 (1960) 197-209; L. DE-QUEKER, "Daniel VII et les Saints du Très-Haut" in *Ephemerides Theologicae Lovanienses* 36 (1960) 353-392; A. ASHLY, "The Coming of the Son of Man" in *Expository Times* 72 (1960-61) 360-363; G.H.P. THOMPSON, "The Son of Man - Some further Considerations" in *Journal of Theological Studies* 12 (1961) 203-209; P. BENOIT, *Exégése et Théologie* 1 (Paris 1961) pp. 133-140; J.A. EMERTON, A. FARMER etc., *The Communication of the Gospel in New Testament Times* (London 1961) pp. 35-36; J. COPPENS, "Le Fils de l'homme daniélique et les relectures de Dan. VII, 13, dans les apocryphes et les écrites de Nouveau Testament" in *Ephemerides Theologicae Lovanienses* 37 (1961) 5-51; J. MORGENSTERN, "The Son of Man of Daniel 7,13; A New Interpretation" in *Journal of Biblical Literature* 53 (1961) 65-77; A. VOGTLE, "Der Menschensohn" in *Lexikon für Theologie und Kirche* 7 (Freiburg 1962) 297-300; M. BLACK, "The Son of Man Problem in Recent Research and Debate" in *Bulletin of the John Rylands Library* 45 (1963) 315-318; F.H. BORSCH, "The Son of Man" in *Anglican Theological Review* 45 (1963) 174-190; M. CAMBE, "Le Fils de L'Homme dans les Évangiles Synoptiques" in *Lumière et Vie* 12 (1963) no. 62, pp. 32-64; L.M. ORRIEUX, "Le Problème du Fils de l'Homme dans la Littérature Apocalyptique" in *Lumière et Vie* 12 (1963) no. 62, pp. 9-31; Y.B. TREMEL, "Le Fils de l'Homme selon Saint Jean" in *Lumière et Vie* 12 (1963) no. 62, pp. 65-92; E. SCHWEITZER, "The Son of Man Again" in *New Testament Studies* 9 (1963) 256-261; id. "The Son of Man" in *Journal of Biblical Literature* 79 (1960) pp. 119-129; id. "Der Menschensohn" in *Zeitschrift für die neutestamentliche Wissenschaft* 50 (1959) 185-209 E. DHANIS, "De Filio Hominis in Vetere Testamento et in Iudaismo" in *Gregorianum* 45 (1964) 5-59; A.J.B. HIGGINS, *Jesus and the Son of Man* (London 1964); see its review, G.B. CAERD, "Jesus and the End" in *Expository Times* 77 (1965) p. 78; H.M. TEEPLE, "The Origin of the Son of Man Christology" in *Journal of Biblical Literature* 84 (1965) 213-250; E.G. JAY, *Son of Man, Son of God,* (London 1965) pp. 32-43; R. MARLOW, " 'The Son of Man' in Recent Journal Literature" in *Catholic Biblical Quarterly* 28 (1966) 12-30; I.H. MARSHALL, "The Synoptic Son of Man Saving in Recent Discussion" in *New Testament Studies* 12 (1966) 327-351. M.D. HOOKER, *The Son of Man in Mark* (London) 1967; F.H. BORSCH, *The Son of Man in Myth and History* (London) 1967); R. MADDOX, "The Function of the Son of Man According to the Synoptic Gospels" in *New Testament Studies* 15 (1968) 45-74; N. PERRIN, "The Synoptic Son of Man" in *Biblical Research*, 13 (1968) 3-25; F.H. BORSCH, *The Christian and Gnostic Man* (London 1970; K. MÜLLER "Menschensohn und Messias" in *Biblische Zeitschrift* 16 (1972) 161-187; 17 (1973) 52-66; B. VAWTER, *"This Man Jesus"* (New York 1973).

241Mk 2,10; 2,28; 8,31.38; 9,9.12.31; 10,33.45; 13,26; 14,21. 21. 41. 62.

242Mt 8,20; 9,6; 10,23; 11,19; 12,8.32.40; 13,37.41; 16,13. 27. 28; 17,9. 12.22; 19,28; 20,18.28; 24. 27. 20. 30. 37. 39. 44; 25,31; 26,2. 24. 24. 45. 64. - Notice, Mt 18,11 is a gloss introduced here from Lk 19,10, and therefore must be discounted.

243Lk 5,24; 6,5.22; 7,34; 9,22.26.44.58; 11,30; 12,8.10.40; 17,22.24.26.30; 18,8.31; 19,10; 21,27.36; 22,22.48.69; 24,7. - Notice, Lk 9,56 is an addition in the Vulgate.

244Jn 1,51; 3,13.14; 6,27.53.62; 8,28; 9,35 (Greek Text); 12,23.34.34; 13,31. In 5,27 the *tou* article is missing, therefore it is not counted.

245Even if the opportunity offers itself, e.g. the comparison of Christ with Adam, Paul does not speak of the "Son of Man" but of one man (Adam) and of a second man (Christ) Rom 5,12-21; 1 Cor 15,21. 45-49.

246For example, H.M. TEEPLE, "The Origin of the Son of Man Christology" in *Journal of Biblical Literature* 84 (1965) 213-250.

247The nature of preexistence attributed to the Son of Man by the Ethiopic version is not very clear: "And for this reason has he been chosen and hidden before him, before the creation of the world and for evermore." (Chapter 48,6.) See E. DHANIS, "De Filio hominis in Vetere Testamento. . . ." p. 18 and footnotes 9-10.

248In Mark's gospel the word "Christ" is used 7 times, in Matthew's 17 times, in Luke's 12 and in John's 20 times.

249Cf Mk 9,41; Mt 16,20; 23,10; 24,4; Lk 24,26.46; Jn 4,(25).26; 17,3.

250Cf. P. BILLERBECK, "Der 110 Psalm in der Altrabbinischen Literatur" in H.L. STRACK, P. BILLERBECK, *Kommentar zum Neuen Testament* 4,1 . . . (München 1928) pp. 451-452; 458-460.

251A.J.B. HIGGINS, *Jesus and the Son of Man* (London 1964) p. 199.

252H.E. TÖDT, *The Son of Man in the Synoptic Tradition* (Philadelphia 1965).

253R. BULTMANN, *Theologie des Neuen Testaments* (Tübingen 1948) pp. 29-31; English translation *Theology of the New Testament* . . . pp. 30-31.

254W. BOUSSET, *Kyrios Christos* (Göttingen 1921) pp. 5-10.

255W. BOUSSET, *Kyrios* . . . p. 10.

256A.J.B. HIGGINS, *Jesus and the Son of Man* . . . pp. 119, 132-133.

257R. BULTMANN, *Theology of the New Testament* . . . pp. 30-31.

258J. JEREMIAS, "Der gegenwärtige Stand der Debatte um das Problem des historischen Jesus" in H. RISTOW, K. MATTHIAE, *Der historische Jesus and der kerygmatische Christus* (Berlin 1962) pp. 23ff; also, E. FUCHS, *Die Frage nach dem historischen Jesus* . . . pp. 152ff.; M. HENGEL, *Nachfolge und Charisma, Eine exegetisch-religionsgeschichtliche Studie zu Mt 8,21f und Jesu Ruf in die Nachfolge* (Berlin 1968).

259X. LÉON-DUFOUR, *Les Évangiles et l'Histoire de Jesus* . . . pp. 301-314; H. SCHURMANN, "Die vorösterliche Anfänge der Logion-tradition, Versuch eines formgeschichtlichen Zugangs zum Leben Jesus" in H. RISTOW and K. MATTHIAE, *Der historische* . . . pp. 342-370.

260E. KÄSEMANN, "Das Problem des historischen Jesus" in *Exegetische Versuche und Besinnungen I* (Gottingen 1954) pp. 187-214.

261A. FRIDRICHSEN, "Le péché contre le Saint-Esprit", in *Revue d'Histoire et de Philosophie Religieuses* 3 (1923) 367ff.

262R. REITZENSTEIN, *Das iranische Erlösungsmysterium* (Bonn 1921); W. BOUSSET, *Die Religion des Judentums im späthellenistischen Zeitalter* (Tübingen 1926) p. 267, tried to show that the notion of the Son of Man comes from the ancient oriental myth, the Anthropos. Since the myth (known only from Christian writings) was spread in diverse forms, they conjure to the existence of the same myth in much older times. M.J. LAGRANGE, *Le judaisme avant Jésus-Christ* (Paris 1931); L. CERFAUX, *Christ in the Theology of St. Paul...*, A. FEUILLET, "Le Fils de l'homme et la tradition biblique ...," demonstrated that the Son of Man's eschatology cannot be explained by Hellenism.

263Ch. P. CEROKE, "Is Mk 2,10 a Saying of Jesus?" in *The Catholic Biblical Quarterly* 22 (1960) 369-390.

264H.E. TÖDT, *The Son of Man* ... p. 130.

265Cf O. CULLMANN, *The Christology of the New Testament* ... pp. 152-153.

266F. GILS, "Le Sabbat a été fait pour l'Homme et non l'Homme pour le Sabbat" in *Revue Biblique* 69 (1962) 506-523; A. FEUILLET, "*L'Exousia du Fils de l'Homme* ... " pp. 181-192.

267V. TAYLOR, *The Names of Jesus* ... p. 57.

268O. CULLMANN, *The Christology of the New Testament* ... pp. 271-275; V. TAYLOR, *The Names* ... pp. 52-55; E.G. JAY, *The Son of Man, Son of God* ... pp. 44-50.

269Cf *Mishnah, Berakoth,* 5,5; H. DANBY, *The Mishnah* (London 1958) p. 6.

270In John there are three instances: 5,25; 10,36; 11,4.

271In John, Jesus speaks of himself as Son 14 times.

272Nine times in Mt (4,3.6; 8,29; 14,33; 16,16; 26,63; 27,40.43.54); 5 times in Mk (1,1; 3,11; 5,7; 15,39; 14,61); 7 times in Lk (1,31; 1,35; 4,3.9.41; 8,28; 22,70).

273Worthy of notice: the title Son of Man is never applied to the Christians though they are several times called sons of God: υἱοὶ Θεοῦ (Mt 5,9; Lk 20,36; Rom 8,14.19; 9,26; Gal 3,26); υἱοὶ τοῦ πατρὸς ὑμῶν (Mt 5,45); υἱοὶ ὑψίστου (Lk 6,35); τέκνα Θεοῦ (Children of God, Jn 1,12; 11,52; 1 Jn 3,1.2.10; 5,2; Rom 8,16.21; 9,8; Phil 2,15) or simply υἱοὶ (Gal 4,6; Heb 12,7).

274Cf B.M.F. van IERSEL, *Der Sohn in der synoptischen Jesusworten* (Leiden 1961) pp. 117-123.

275In general this is the same in John's Gospel where, aside from the Evangelist himself (1,14.18; 3,35; 5,17; 8,27; 13,1.3), only Jesus speaks of God as Father. In 8,19.41 and 14,8. in dialogue with Jesus, the Jews and Philip repeat what Jesus said.

276J. JEREMIAS, "Kennzeichen der ipsissima vox Jesu ..." pp. 86-89; B.M.F. van IERSEL, *Der Sohn* ... pp. 104-116.

277B.M.F. van IERSEL, *Der Sohn* ... pp 132-145.

278A. JÜLICHER, *Die Gleichnisreden Jesu* (Tübingen 1910) 2, 385-406; W. BOUSSET, *Kyrios Christos* ... pp. 50-51; R. BULTMANN, *Die Geschichte der synoptischen Tradition* ... pp. 191ff; W.G. KÜMMEL, "Das Gleichnis von den bösen Weingartnern" in *Mélanges Goguel* (Neuchatel 1950) pp. 120-131.

279A.˙ HARNACK, *Die Sprüche und Reden Jesus* (Leipzig 1907) pp. 189-216; W. GRUNDMANN, *Jesus der Galiläer und das Judentum* (Leipzig 1941) pp. 221-223; T.W. MANSON, *The Sayings of Jesus* (London 1949) p. 80; P. WINTER "Matthew XI 27 and Luke X 22 from the first to the fifth century" in *Novum Testamentum* 1 (1956) 112-148.

280The versions differ a little. *Codices Vercellensis* and *Veronensis* render Luke's text as *novit*, contrary to the Latin Vulgate which has *scit*. The Latin Vulgate, however, has the past tense in Matthew's text. *Cognovit* and *novit* often might have the meaning of perfect present and mean *scit*, i.e. having known. The Fathers of the Church cite the text in different ways. Fathers and early writers who have the *aorist* ἔγνω have also elsewhere the present ἐπιγινώσκει. Thus JUSTIN, in I *Apol* 63 (PG 6, 424) has ἔγνω but in *Dial. with Trypho* (PG 6, 709) he gives the text with γινώσκει. In opposition to Irenaeus who reads the present tense, the Gnostic reads in its place the aorist in the sense that, before the coming of our Lord the true God was known by no one. After his coming however, Jesus' knowledge of the Father is no longer exclusive. IRENAEUS, *Adv. Haeres.* 2,6.1 (PG 7, 724); 4,6.1 (PG 7, 986); cf P. WINTER, "Matthew XI 27 ... " pp. 131 ff. Similarly ORIGEN has ἔγνω in his *Contra Celsum* (e.g. 2,71 PG 11, 908) but in *Comm. on Romans* (PG 14,949) again the present tense.

281P. WINTER, "Matthew XI 27 ... " p. 140.

282P. WINTER, "Matthew XI 27 ... " pp. 131-132.

283W. BOUSSET, *"Kyrios Christos ... "* p. 48.

284A.J. FESTUGIÈRE, *La révélation d'Hermès Trismégiste* (Paris 1950) 1, 290-291.

285Ch. F. BURNEY, *The Poetry of Our Lord, An Examination of the Formal Elements of Hebrew Poetry in the Discourses of Jesus Christ* (Oxford 1925) pp. 171-172.

286A. LOISY, *Les Évangiles Synoptiques* (Ceffonde 1907) 1, 905-915.

287E. NORDEN, *Agnostos Theos* (Berlin 1913) pp. 277-308.

288B. GERHARDSSON, *Memory and Manuscript, Oral Tradition and Written Transmission in Rabbinic Judaism and Early Christianity* (Uppsala 1961).

289B.M.F. van IERSEL, *Der Sohn ...* pp. 151-157.

290A. SCHWEITZER, *Geschichte der Leben-Jesu-Forschung* (Tübingen 1913) p. 310.

291O. CULLMANN, *The Christology of the New Testament ...* p. 288.

292G. AICHER, *Der Prozess Jesu* (Bonn 1929) pp. 58-75, and O. CULLMANN suggests that Jesus' answer was rather negative. "The corresponding Aramaic to the Greek expression 'You said so' (Mt 26,64; Lk 22,70) might mean 'You say so, not I.' " See *The Christology of the New Testament* (London 1963) p. 118. In Mk, however, Jesus' answer is certainly "Yes" (Mk 14,62). Moreover, Jesus' answer in Mt 16,13ff. is also affirmative. Therefore, there is no reason why it should not also be affirmative in Mt's culminating point of the sayings concerning the Son of God. For an overall view of the various solutions see R.C. CATCHPOLE, *The Trial of Jesus, A Study in the Gospels and Jewish Historiography from 1770 to the Present Day* (Leiden 1971).

293E.J. BELSER, M.J. LAGRANGE, J.M. VOSTE, D.J. SAUNDERS, J. BIENECK, etc. Cf J. BLINZLER, *The Trial of Jesus* (Westminister 1959) pp. 127-134.

294H.L. STRACK, P. BILLERBECK, *Kommentar zum Neuen Testament aus Talmud und Midrash* . . . 1, 1003-1019.

295H.L. STRACK, P. BILLERBECK, *Kommentar zum Neuen Testament aus Talmud und Midrash* . . . I, 1011-1012, 1016-1017.

296R. Jischmael and R. Eleazar demonstrate the penalty of death for idolatry from Num 15,30.

297H.L. STRACK, P. BILLERBECK, *Kommentar* . . . 1, 1016-1019.

298J. BONSIRVEN, "Judaisme, Le Messianisme" in *Dictionnaire de la Bible Suppl.* 4 (1949), 1239-1242; W. BOUSSET, *Die Religion des Judentums* . . . pp. 228-232, 259-268; P. VOLZ, *Jüdische Eschatologie von Daniel bis Akiba* (Tübingen 1903) pp. 216-219. About 300 A.D., Rabbi Aquiba said: "If someone tells you 'I am God' then he lies, or 'I am the Son of Man' he will that regret." in H.L. STRACK P. BILLERBECK, *Kommentar* . . . 1, 486.

299J. SCHMID, *Des Evangelium nach Markus* (Regensburg 1954) pp. 283-284; J. BLINZLER, *The Trial of Jesus* (Westminister 1959) pp. 90-112; 125-134.

300J. BLINZLER, *The Trial of Jesus* . . . pp. 104-108, 132-134.

301A Letter from Bar Kokheba, see J.T. MILIK, "Une lettre de Siméon Bar Kokheba" in *Revue Biblique* 60 (1953) 276-294.

302J. WEISS, *Das älteste Evangelium* (Göttingen 1903) p. 312; J. JEREMIAS, *The Eucharistic Word of Jesus* (London 1966) p. 79.

303*Mishnah Sanh.* 11, 1 prescribes strangulation for the crime of pseudo-prophecy but probably in the time of Jesus it was punishable also by stoning. H. DANBY, *The Mishnah* . . . p. 399.

304R.W. HUSBAND, *The Persecution of Jesus* (Princeton 1966) p. 173; J. KLAUSNER, *Jesus of Nazareth* (London 1929) p. 333; J. JEREMIAS, "Zur Geschichtlichkeit des Verhörs Jesu vor dem Hohen Rat" in *Zeitschrift für die Neutestamentliche Wissenschaft* 43 (1950-51) pp. 145-150; O. CULLMANN, *The State in the New Testament* (New York (1956) pp. 41ff; J. BLINZLER, *The Trial of Jesus* . . . pp. 157-163.

305J. JUSTER, *Les Juifs dans l'Empire Romain* (Paris 1914) 2,133; H. LIETZMANN, "Bemerkungen zum Prozess Jesu" in *Zeitschrift für die neutestamentliche Wissenschaft* 30 (1931) 193-201; 31 (1932) 78-84; A LOISY, *Les Actes des Apôtres* (Paris 1920) p. 309; M. GOGUEL, "A Propos du Procès de Jésus" in *Zeitschrift für die Neutestamentliche Wissenschaft* 31 (1932) 289-301; Ch. GUIGNEBERT, *Jésus* (Paris 1933) p. 567; T.A. BURKILL, "The Competence of the Sanhedrin" in *Vigiliae Christianae* 10 (1961) 80-96; P. WINTER, *On the Trial of Jesus* (Berlin 1961) pp. 63-74.

306X. LÉON-DUFOUR, "Passion" in *Dictionnaire de la Bible Suppl.* 6 (Paris 1960) p. 1487.

307J. KLAUSNER, *Jesus of Nazareth* . . . p. 345.

[308]J. BLINZLER, *The Trial of Jesus* ... p. 134-145.

[309]P. WINTER, *On the Trial of Jesus* ... pp. 138-148.

[310]H.L. STRACK, P. BILLERBECK, *Kommentar* ... 1, 36.43.

[311]On the date of the text and the discussion about the identity of Ieshu see J. BLINZLER, *The Trial of Jesus* ... pp. 24-28.

[312]H. COHN, *Trial and Death of Jesus* (New York 1967).

[313]In a letter written six days before his death (October 9, 1969) P. Winter expressed his view on our solution with these words: "I was interested in reading your paper 'Why was Jesus Brought to Pilate?' in the recent issue of *Novum Testamentum*...... Appreciating your frank and open article with a *Köszönöm szépen* (Thank you very much), Yours sincerely. ..."

[314]See H.L. STRACK, P. BILLERBECK, *Kommentar* ... 2, 462ff. Notice that the application of the name El or Elohim to man was not necessarily considered as blasphemous (e.g. Ex 4,16; 7,1; Gen 33,30; Ps 82,1.6; Ps 50,7—more probable reading is "O my people ... gods, your God I am"; Ex. 22,27—the name "gods" was applied in early times to the rulers of Israel and only after the rabbi Aquiba was the text understood as a form of blasphemy against God; Jn 10,34, etc.). In rabbinical exegesis the name "gods" also applied to men on several occasions. Therefore, not the term, but the meaning was important. If, however, one applied this name to himself, he was regarded as an arrogant blasphemer.

[315]See V. LARRAÑAGA, *L'Ascensión del Señor en el Neuvo Testamento* (Madrid 1943); P. BENOIT, "L'Ascension" in *Revue Biblique* 56 (1944) 161-203; J.G. DAVIES, *He ascended into Heaven* (London 1958); P.A. VAN STEMPSVOORT, "The Interpretation of the Ascension in Luke and Acts" in *New Testament Studies* 5 (1958-59) pp. 30-42. F.X. DURRWELL, *The Resurrection* (New York 1960); N. CLARK, *Interpreting The Resurrection* (London 1967); D.M. STANLEY, *Christ's Resurrection in Pauline Soteriology* (Rome 1961); C.F. EVANS, *Resurrection and the New Testament* (London 1970); for the meaning of the resurrection-experience see K. RAHNER and W. THÜSING, *Christologie systematisch und exegetisch* (Freiburg 1972) pp. 36-50.

[316]B. LINDARS, *A New Testament Apologetics* (London 1961) pp. 32-74.

[317]The authorship of the fourth gospel in relation to the historicity of Jesus' resurrection is defended by E. GUTWENGER, "Zur Geschichtlichkeit der Auferstehung Jesu" in *Zeitschrift für Katholische Theologie* 88 (1966) 263-273, 280-282.

[318]M. BALAGUE, "La prueba de la resurrección (Jn 20,2-7)" in *Estudios Biblicos* 25 (1966) 169-192.

[319]W. MARXSEN, *The Resurrection of Jesus of Nazareth* (New York 1970); id. "The Resurrection of Jesus as a Historical and Theological Problem" in C.F.D. MOULE ed. *The Significance of the Resurrection of Jesus for Faith in Jesus Christ* (London, 1968) pp. 15-20.

[320]For the function of language in the explanation of the Paschal Message see X. LÉON-DUFOUR, *Résurrection de Jésus et message Paschal* (Paris 1971).

321EUSEBIUS OF CAESAREA, *Gospel Questions to Marinus,* 1, 1; PG 22, 937.

322The brief conclusion runs so: "They reported briefly to Peter and his companions what they had been told. And then Jesus himself, through their agency, broadcasted from the east to the west the sacred and incorruptible message of eternal salvation" *The Jerusalem Bible* (London 1966), *The New Testament,* p. 89.

323"... Der Galiläa-These der Boden, d. h. die exegetische Basis entzogen." B. STEIN-SEIFER, "Der Ort der Erscheinungen des Auferstandenen" in *Zeitschrift für die Neutestamentliche Wissenschaft* 62 (1971) 232-265 p. 264.

324F. LAMAR CRIBBS, "St. Luke and the Johannine Tradition" in *Journal of Biblical Literature* 90 (1971) 422-450.

325There might be conceived a possible order like the following: After the death (Mt 27,50; Mk 15,37; Lk 23,46b; Jn 30b-37) and the burial of Jesus (Mt 27,57-60; Mk 15,42-46; Lk 23,50-54; Jn 19, 38-42), on the first day of the week, at early dawn Mary Magdalene and the other women went to the tomb and they found it empty (Mt 28,1; Mk 16,2-4; Lk 24,1-2; 24,22-24; Jn 20,1). Mary ran back to the disciples with the message that "they have taken the Master out of the tomb and we do not know where they have put him" (Jn 20,2), but she does not mention the angels. While Magdalene was on the way, the angels are supposed to announce to the women that Jesus has risen (Mt 28,2b-7, Mk 16,5-7; Lk 24,3-8; 24,22-24). The women hurried away and ran to tell the news to his disciples (Mt 24,8; Mk 16,8; Lk 24,9-11) that they had actually seen a vision of angels who said that he was alive, but the women apparently did not see Jesus yet (Lk 24,33). After this second message Peter and John both ran to the tomb and found things as the women had said, but they did not see either Jesus nor angels (Lk 24,12; Jn 20,3-10). After the return of Peter and John from the tomb, two disciples left Jerusalem for Emmaus since they did not know anything about Mary Magdalene's Christophany (Lk 24,22-24). After her first message Mary went back to the tomb again without knowing about the angel's message given to the women. She is weeping and asks the gardener to tell her where he put him (Jn 20,13-15). After recognizing the Master (Jn 20,16-18; Mt 28,9-10; Mk 16,9) she ran back again to the disciples with her second message: "I have seen the Lord and he said this to me" (Jn 20,18; Mk 16,10-11). The apostles, however, did not believe it (Mk 16,11). The message of Mary Magdalene was followed by the christophany of Peter (Lk 24,33; 1 Cor 15,5), that of the disciples of Emmaus (Lk 24,13-33; Mk 16,12-13), of the apostles without Thomas (Mt 16,14; Lk 24,36-43; Jn 20,19-23; 1 Cor 15,5).

After eight days Jesus appeared to the apostles with Thomas in Jerusalem (Jn 20,24-29). Later he appeared again in Galilee (Jn 21,1-20; Mt 28,16-20; Mk 1,15-18). He was also seen by more than five hundred brothers (1 Cor 15,6). by James (1 Cor 15,7), by all apostles again in Jerusalem (1 Cor 15,7; Lk 24,44-49, Acts 1,3-8) and finally he departed into heaven from Jerusalem (Mk 16,19; Lk 24,50,51; Acts 1,9-11).

326The difference in the names of the women is explained by the two different traditions. One tradition enumerates the two sons of Mary and even adds Salome, while the other (in Mk 15,47) only mentions one son, Joseph, and leaves out Salome. The full names of Mary, Mary the mother of younger James and the mother of Joseph (in Mk 15,40) is varied so that in two places (Mk 15,47; 16,1) they are only abbreviations by naming only one of the two sons. One tradition prefers the one, the other prefers the other name. Cf V. TAYLOR, *The Gospel according to St. Mark* (London 1952) p. 51.

In regard to the visit to the tomb, there are redactional differences. Mark speaks of the sun because for him the sun is the symbol of Christ. John speaks of darkness which was present after Christ's death, and remains in the soul of Magdalene a symbol of man seeking Jesus. Cf E. DHANIS, "L'ensevelissement de Jésus et la visite au tombeau dans l'évangile de Saint Marc" in *Gregorianum* 39 (1958) 364-410; E.L. BODÉ, *The First Easter Morning: The Gospel Accounts of the Women's Visit to the Tomb of Jesus* (Rome 1970).

The number of angels as well as their introduction into the Easter event is to be explained again by tradition. Their significance comes from the belief that the knowledge of Jesus' resurrection is communicated finally not by a woman's message, but by God himself. It is remarkable finally that according to Luke the women found the tomb empty without having seen the angels. The apostles never did see angels in the empty tomb.

As to the silence of the women, R. KNOX, guesses in his *The Holy Bible* (London 1953), *New Testament*, p. 52, that they did not tell anything to those whom they met on their way, but spoke only to the apostles.

But the incoherencies about the place of apparitions reveal the redactional properties of the four gospels much more than any other divergencies.

The reason Luke does not mention apparitions in Galilee, stems from his systematic order: salvation comes from Galilee to Jerusalem whence it spreads throughout Judea, to Samaria and to Rome. The high point is found in Jerusalem where the apostles accept the mission of bearing witness to the resurrection of the crucified Jesus (Lk 24,48; Acts 1,8,22). The gospel narration is directed to this point and from this point begins the narration of the Acts of the Apostles.

Similarly, John even in his gospel account prior to the passion selects and narrates with preference events which happened in Jerusalem. If therefore he is silent about the Galilean Christophanies it is because of his literary form.

Mark could consider the Galilean apparitions as the only ones worth mentioning. In comparison to Christ's manifestations in Galilee, the christophanies in Jerusalem are neglected by Mark all the more because he is concerned in his whole gospel with Galilee even to the extent of neglecting Christ's journeys to Jerusalem which nevertheless were known in the early tradition (cf Mt 23,37). Mark emphasizes this position when twice he repeated the words of Jesus that they will see him in Galilee (Mk 14,28; 16,7) while Matthew does it three times (Mt 26,32; 28,7,10). This shows how Markan tradition endured and preserved those words of Jesus which seem to extol Galilee in other places.

Also, Matthew in narrating the public ministry of Jesus limits himself to the Galilean ministry. His topographical order reflects the emphasis of his thought. According to Matthew the apostles are sent to spread the words of Christ (Mt 28,19), but this command for the most part was given to the apostles in Galilee, while according to Luke the command was given in Jerusalem. The appearance of Jesus in Galilee was necessary for Matthew. The insertion into the Galilean environment had to confirm the identity of the resurrected Christ with historical Galilean man known to the disciples as well as to reassure the validity of the Galilean teaching given before Jesus' death.

[327]H.L. STRACK, P. BILLERBECK, *Kommentar* . . . 3rd ed. (Munich 1961) 3,444.

[328]See E. DHANIS, *Miracula et Resurrectio Jesu* (Rome 1965) pp. 76-86, 90-121; P.

BENOIT, *The Passion and Resurrection of Jesus Christ* (New York 1966); J. KREMER, *Das älteste Zeugnis von der Auferstehung Christi* (Stuttgart 1967); R.H. FULLER, *The Formation of the Resurrection Narratives* (New York 1971); R.E. BROWN, *The Virginal Conception and Bodily Resurrection of Jesus* (New York 1973) pp. 69-129.

329Some critics, such as Loisy and Guignebert, thought that the body of Jesus was not buried, but had to be left in a ditch by the soldiers because he had been condemned to the cross. But in the *Digest* of Ulpianus, the Roman jurist, we read: "The bodies of those executed must be given for burial to anyone whomsoever who asks" (48,1). The same Ulpianus affirms that this custom existed in the time of Augustus. Suetonius confirms Ulpianus' views in his *Augustus* (13,1ff).

330J. DUPONT, "Resuscité 'le troisième jour' " in *Studia Biblica et Orientalia* 2 (Rome 1959) pp. 179-192; B. LINDARS, *New Testament Apologetics* . . . pp. 59-72.

331K. LEHMANN, *Auferweckt am dritten Tag nach der Schrift* (Freiburg 1968) pp. 80-82; 262-290.

332J. BLANK, *Paulus und Jesus* (Munich 1969).

333H.S. STRACK, P. BILLERBECK, *Kommentar*. . . . . 2, 544-545 and 1, 747. Notice, however, that "On the third day" and "After three days" in the Bible can mean the same thing. Cf the book of Esther: ". . . neither eat nor drink for three days or three nights . . . on the third day . . . " (4,16-17; 5,1). In the gospel both expressions are found together. ". . . The imposter said . . . after three days I will rise again . . . Give orders therefore to have the tomb closely guarded until the third day . . ." (Mt 27,63-64).

334J. Jeremias sees the "third day" (1 Cor 15,4; Lk 24,21; Mt 16,21 with Lk 9,22; Mt 20,19 with Lk 18,33; Mt 17,33; Lk 13,32) as the post-paschal determination of the pre-paschal "three days." See Mk 8,31; 9,31; 10,33 against the third day of the Q; J. JEREMIAS, "Les paroles des trois jours dans les Evangiles" in E. CASTELLI, ed. *Herméneutique et Eschatologie* (Rome 1971) pp. 187-195). It seems, however, the "on the third day" and "after three days" in the Bible means the same (cf footnote 333). The discovery of the empty tomb, nevertheless, cannot be dismissed too easily by the exegetes: see X. LÉON-DUFOUR, *Résurrection de Jésus et message pascal* (Paris 1971) pp. 269-270. See also the importance of the new celebration day, (footnote 349) and the common tradition according to which Jesus was raised on the first day of the week (Mk 16,2; Mt 28,1; Lk 24,1; Jn 20,1).

335See W. MICHAELIS, "ὁράω" in G. KITTEL, *Theological Dictionary* . . 5 (Grand Rapids 1967) 315-382, J. JEREMIAS, *The Eucharistic Word of Jesus* . . . pp. 102-103.

336D.M. STANLEY, *Christ's Resurrection* . . . pp. 84 and 39-50.

337L. CERFAUX, *Les Actes des Apôtres* (Paris 1954) pp. 22-23.

338Cf H.N. RIDDERBOS, *The Speeches of Peter in the Acts of the Apostles* (London 1962).

339F.X. DURRWELL, *The Resurrection* . . . pp. 10-13, 33-34.

340J. SINT, "Die Auferstehung Jesu in der Verkündigung der Urgemeinde' in *Zeitschrift für Katholische Theologie* 84 (1962) 129-151; English summary "The Resurrection in the Primitive Community" in *Theology Digest* 12 (1964), 33-39; cf K.H. RENGSTORF, *Die Auferstehung Jesu* (Witten 1960) 4th ed. 113-114.

341L. CERFAUX, "Pour l'histoire du titre 'apostolos' dans le Nouveau Testament" in *Recherches de Science Religieuse* 48 (1960) 76-92; K.H. RENGSTORF "ἀπόςτολος" in G. KITTEL, *Theological Dictionary* . . . 1, 424-445; L. CERFAUX, "Témoins du Christ d'après le Livre des Actes" in *Recueil Lucien Cerfaux* 2 (Gembloux 1954) pp. 157-174; H. STRATHMANN, "μάρτυς" in G. KITTEL *Theological Dictionary* . . . 4 (Grand Rapids 1967) 474-509.

342In the gospels they are designated by number 30 times (Mt 10,1.2.5; 11,1; 19,28; 26,14.20.47; Mk 3,14; 4,10; 6,7; 9,34; 10,32; 11,11; 14,10; 14,17.20.43; Lk 6,13; 8,1; 9,1.12; 18,31; 22,14.30.47; Jn 6,67.71.72; 20,24). They are called apostles in the gospels only six times (Mt 10,2; Mk 6,30; Lk 6,13; 9,1.10; 22,14). In the other books of the New Testament they are called by names or by number three times (Acts 6,2; 1 Cor 15,5; Rev 21,14). The term "apostle" in the epistles means generally any man sent by God or by the communities.

343C.E. BRAATEN, *New Direction in Theology Today II, History and Hermeneutics* (Philadelphia 1966) 91-102; G. LOHFINK, "Die Auferstehung Jesu und die historische Kritik" in *Bibel und Leben* 9 (1968) 37-53.

344F. MORISON, *Who Moved the Stone?* (London 1945); D. WHITAKER, "What Happened to the Body of Jesus? A Speculation" in *Expository Times* 31 (1969-70) 307-310.

345N. CLARK, *Interpreting the Resurrection* . . . pp. 14-26; W. PANNENBERG, "The Revelation of God in Jesus of Nazareth" in J.M. ROBINSON, J.B. COBB, Jr., *New Frontiers in Theology*, Vol. III, *Theology as History* (New York 1967) pp. 101-133; see pp. 118-125.

346E. DHANIS. *Miracula et Resurrectio* . . . p. 95.

347W. MICHAELIS, "ὁράω" in G. KITTEL *Theological Dictionary* . . . 5, pp. 356-357, 350-355.

348G. FRIEDRICH, "Die Bedeutung der Auferstehung Jesu" in *Theologische Zeitschrift* 27 (1971) 305-324.

349J. Van GOUDOEVER, "The Celebration of the Resurrection in the New Testament" in *Studia Evangelica* 3 (1964) 254-259; P. DELHAYE, J.L. DECAT, "Dimanche et Sabbat" in *Mélanges de Science Religieuse* 23 (1966) 3-14; D. BOTTE, et al. *Le Dimanche,* Lex Orandi 39 (Paris 1965); W. RORDORF, "La célébration dominicale de la Sainte Cène dans l'Eglise Ancienne" in *Revue de Théolgie et de Philosophie* 99 (1966) 25-37; F. HAHN, "Der urchristliche Gottesdienst" in *Jahrbuch für Liturgik und Hymnologie* 12 (1967) 1-44.

350J. FEINER, "Die Vergegenwärtigung der Offenbarung durch die Kirche" in J. FEINER, M. LOHRER, *Mysterium Salutis* 1 (Einsiedeln 1965) pp. 497-541; J. HAAG, "Die Buchwerdung des Wortes Gottes in der heiligen Schrift" in *Mysterium Salutis* 1, 289-428.

351C. QUELL, "ἀγαπάω" in G. KITTEL, *Theological Dictionary of the New Testa-*

ment, 1 . . . pp. 28-29; V. WARNACH, "Agape" in *Lexikon für Theologie und Kirche* 1 (Freiburg 1957) 178-180.

[352]This is the reason why the Church of charity will be always χαθογικ\'η "catholic," i.e. tending to the plenitude of being by affirming its "also and also," its *"etiam et etiam"*; and opposing herself to any kind of heresy which tries to ignore the wholeness of being by proclaiming its "nothing else but" and its *"solum"* which indeed absolutizes or idolizes the particular. God the plenitude of being is visible in the plenitude of charity of the "catholic" Church of the risen Christ.

[353]See C.R. SMITH, *The Bible Doctrine of Grace* (London 1956) pp. 28-29, 15-16.

[354]S. LYONNET, *De Peccato et Redemptione I. De Notione peccati* (Roma 1957) p. 60.

[355]S. LYONNET, *De Peccato et Redemptione II De Vocabulario redemptionis* (Roma 1960) pp. 65-66.

[356]C.R. SMITH, *The Bible Doctrine* . . . p. 29.

[357]Notice that from 100 cases of New Testament where God is said to give something to men, there are 27 explicit instances according to which God gives himself to men. In the remaining 73 cases God is said to be given only indirectly sc. in his gifts, like eternal life, peace, etc.

[358]L.W. FOESTER, "ἐξουσία" in G. KITTEL, *Theological Dictionary* . . . 2 (Grand Rapids 1964) pp. 568-575.

[359]ἡμῶν in the Greek text of Mk. 9,40 is more probably not authentic. The ὑμῶν of Luke 9,50 seems to be closer to the authentic saying of Jesus. The reason is the singular fact that speaking about his redemptive work Jesus never included himself with the disciples in a grammatical plural "we." He did it only in purely human activity: for example; "let us cross over" (Mk 4,55; Lk 8,22), or "let us go" (Mk 14,22; Mt 26,46). From the codices and versions, the *AD it vg sype* have indeed "you" instead of "us." Cf S. THOMAS, *Super Evangelium S. Matthaei* (Torino 1951) No. 1022; C.E.B. GRANFIELD, *The Gospel according to Saint Mark* (Cambridge 1959) pp. 310-311; T. HORVATH, "Is hémôn in Mk 9,40 authentic?" in *Journal of Ecumenical Studies* 8 (1971) 385-386.

[360]Concerning the history of the meaning of the miracles in light of the Protestant theology see E. and M-L. KELLER, *Der Streit um die Wunder, Kritik und Auslegung des Übernatürlichen in der Neuzeit* (Gütersloh 1968); in the light of the Catholic theology see L. MONDEN, *Signs and Wonders* (New York 1966); the historicity of the miracles in particular is discussed by X. LÉON-DUFOUR, *Les évangiles et l'histoire de Jésus* (Paris 1963) pp. 309-310; H. VAN DER LOOS, *The Miracles of Jesus* (Leiden 1965) pp. 339-698; F. MUSSNER, *The Miracles of Jesus* (Notre Dame 1968), R. LATOURELLE "Authenticité historique des miracles de Jesus; essai de criteriologie" *Gregorianum* 54 (1973) 225-262.

[361]F. MUSSNER, *The Miracles of Jesus* (Notre Dame 1968); R. PESCH in his book *Jesu ureigene Taten?* (Freiburg 1968) unconvincingly tried to challenge Mussner's thesis. For the Markan use of the miracles material see K. KERTELGE, *Wunder Jesu im Markusevangelium* (München 1970).

[362]Cf H.D. BETZ, "The Cleansing of the Lepers (Lk 17, 11-19)" in *Journal of Biblical Literature* 90 (1971) 314-328.

[363]For J. Roloff, however, the simple story of the miracles is rather characteristic of the post-paschal community's way of seeing the miracles. The pre-paschal community understood the miracles exclusively in their faith-creating function. See J. ROLOFF, *Das Kerygma und der irdische Jesus* (Göttingen 1970).

[364]P. KETTER, "Zur Lokalisierung der Blindenheilung bei Jericho" in *Biblica* 15 (1934) 411-418.

[365]P. HERZOG, *Die Wunderheilungen von Epidauros, Ein Beitrag zur Geschichte der Medizin und der Religion* (Leipzig 1931) p. 95.

[366]H. VAN DER LOOS, *The Miracles* . . . pp. 641-646.

[367]A. SCHWEITZER, *Geschichte der Leben-Jesu-Forschung* (Tübingen 1913) pp. 421-424; Q. QUESNELL, *The Mind of Mark, Interpretation and Method through the Exegesis of Mark 6,52* (Rome 1969).

[368]H. VAN DER LOOS, *The Miracles* . . . pp. 641ff.

[369]P. SAINTYVES, *Essais de Folklore Biblique. Magie, Mythes et Miracles dans l'Ancien and le Nouveau Testament* (Paris 1922) pp. 338-340.

[370]R. PESCH, *Der reiche Fischfang Lk 5, 1-11, Jn 21,1-14* (Düsseldorf 1969); cf G. SCHNEIDER'S review in *Biblische Zeitschrift* 15 (1971) 286-288.

[371]C. DUMONT, "Unité et diversité des signes de la Révélation" in *Nouvelle Revue Théologique* 90 (1958) 135-158; F.H. LEPARGNEUR, "La nature fonctionelle du miracle" in *Nouvelle Revue Theologique* 94 (1962) 283-295.

[372]The critical recognition of the inexplicability of the new revelatory configuration (miracles) does not imply the exact knowledge of the limits of natural powers. In previous times many authors used to consider these deeds as exclusive actions of God which could not be performed by any power of nature. These deeds seemed to be, therefore, credentials which God the Father gave to his Son to prove his divinity.

   This argument, however, could incur many difficulties. According to the New Testament not only Jesus but Satan himself can perform marvelous deeds. The false prophets show signs and wonders successfully misleading many people (Mk 13,22; Mt 24,24; Lk 23,8; 2 Thess 2,9; Rev 13,13; 16,14; 19,20). Jesus himself does not like to extol his deeds, but rather he praises the faith of the beneficiaries (Mk 5,34; Mt 9,22; Lk 8,48; Mk 10,22; Lk 18,42; Mt 15,28; Mk 7,29; Mt 8,13; Lk 7,9; Lk 7,50; 17,19). In cases of lack of faith he does not perform his mighty deeds (Mk 6,5; Mt 13,58; cf Mk 8,13; Mt 16,4; Mt 15,39; Lk 11,29; Mt 17,19-20). Frequently he does not perform his miracles before the crowd, but privately, charging men to tell no one (Mk 7,36; Mk 1,44; Mt 8,4; Lk 5,14; cf Mk 8,30; Mt 16,20; Lk 9,36; Mk 9,9; Mt 17,9; Lk 9,36). All these indicate that his deeds are directed more to seek the betterment of men rather than his reputation.

   Moreover, we realize more and more in our days that the forces of nature are exceedingly grandiose and we do not have any adequate knowledge of their limits. The case of a resurrection from real death might be a conspicuous one. However the acceptance of these resurrection-narratives depends ultimately upon one's belief in the resurrection of Jesus. There is another difficulty which comes also from comparative religion. As a matter of fact, the comparative study of religions shows that miracles, resurrection-narratives, and sorcery play a great part in non-Christian religions too.

All these facts, which might pose difficulties only for an inadequate understanding of miracles, indeed help us to understand and appreciate the exact meaning and the right way of recognition of the events of the cosmos divinized by Jesus' resurrection. It is not the exception or irregularity which manifest the presence of God in the world but rather *the regularity of the irregularities and exceptions.* The unpredictably constant lifting out of the infinitesimal possibilities around the Kingdom of Jesus indicates the permanent presence of the always "other" God among men. The exception might find its explanation in the statistical fluctuation of the physical laws, but what is ultimately inexplicable according to the critical consideration of the normal course of nature, is not the extraordinary happening but the historically constant repetition of the extraordinary happenings around the same religious phenomenon, sc. Jesus.

Consequently, the miracles of today as well as those of Jesus must be inexplicable according to the normal course of nature as we know it today. Since the miracles must be a sign of the presence of a new force, of a new reality, the result of this new force must be visible, otherwise it cannot be assumed critically that there is something else than the common force of nature. The critical recognition of the departure from the habitual course of nature does not include a definitive knowledge of the absolute limits of that nature, but only the recognition of the infinitesimal possibility of the happening in this circumstance. This is the first step in the critical scientific recognition of miracles.

The next step is the recognition of a constant lifting out of the infinitesimal possibilities in a special configuration of elements which points out to a constant factor (e.g. many different miracles around the same religious phenomenon). A further step is a search after the cause of the unpredictable constant lifting out of the infinitesimal possibilities in spite of the statistical fluctuation of natural forces. Now if the critical scientist, not as scientist but as thinking philosopher, does not ask about the particular object of a particular scientific investigation, but about the total complex reality, which surpasses the domain of each particular science as particular, the search after the cause of the unpredictable constant lifting out of the infinitesimal possibilities might lead him to perceive the constant religious factor as the only cause of the observed special configuration of elements.

The final step of the process is when someone, not as scientist, or thinking philosopher, but as man (under the influence of grace) perceives these mighty deeds as an invitation of God to which he might respond in the dialogue of faith: "My God you are here, indeed to beatify us in body and soul with your presence." Thus the complete sense of miracle is grasped only in faith, its puzzling lifting out of the infinitesimal possibilities, however, can be and must be observed by scientific method.

The miracles, therefore, should be defined as revelatory configurations, i.e. extraordinary happenings perceived in the context of the Kingdom of God, definitively established by Jesus' resurrection, which are unexplainable according to the critical consideration of the normal course of nature, but which through an exclusive inductive process indicate the beatifying active presence of God as their only explanation. To recognize the presence of God in a miraculous event therefore, we need many miracles, different in nature, time and place and persons, etc. otherwise we cannot exclude by means of induction the numerous surrounding cosmic possibilities. The mighty deeds must be unable to be restricted to any other force but to the two thousand years old unpredictable constancy of the same religious phenomenon, i.e. faith in God's personal presence by Jesus in the world. Therefore the miracles of Lourdes as well as all the miracles of the canonized and uncanonized saints together with the miracles of the apostles (Acts 3,1 ff; 5-12-16; 9,32-43; 6,8; 7,6-7; 14,3; 14,8-10; 16,16-18; 19,11-12; 20,9-10; 28,7-10) are in some sense the spatial and temporal extension of Jesus' mighty deeds, and ultimately of his resurrection.

Thus the mighty deeds of Jesus are continually recognizable in the miracles of today. They establish "here and now" the divinized cosmos in the humanized world of history, inaugurated with his resurrection.

By the miracles of today, the mighty deeds of Jesus and his resurrection are made accessible to the critical consideration of our generation. The miracle of today (e.g. the healings approved by the Medical Bureau of Lourdes or the heroic self-giving for the happiness of others performed in the spirit of Jesus) and the mighty deed of the historical Jesus are mutually supplementing each other.

From the one side the critically investigated miracles of today, (cf e.g.A. OLIVIERI, *Y a-t-il encore des Miracles à Lourdes?* 18 dossiers de guérisons (1950-1969) (Paris 1969) dispose us to admit that Jesus' deeds are possible, and from the other side the miracles of the historical Jesus dispose us to accept and understand the full meaning of the extraordinary happenings of our days. In both of them God is establishing his Kingdom in which he wants to be present to man and through the free acceptance to communicate his divine beatitude to him.

[373]The term "apostle" occurs in the New Testament 79 times. It is found once in Mk, Mt and Jn; 34 times in Lk and 29 times in Paul. Once in Heb, 1 Peter, Jd, 2 Peter and 3 times in Revelation.

[374]H.L. STRACK, P. BILLERBECK, *Kommentar* . . . . 3,2ff.

[375]H.L. STRACK, P. BILLERBECK, *Kommentar* . . . 3,5ff.

[376]K.H. RENGSTORF, "ἀπόστολος" . . . 420.

[377]Like J. WEISS, *Die Predigt Jesu vom Reiche Gottes* (Göttingen 1900) p. 24f, and R. SCHUTZ, *Apostel und Junger* (Giessen 1921) p. 76.

[378]K.H. RENGSTORF, "δώδεκα in G. KITTEL, *Theological Dictionary* . . . 2, pp. 321-328; B. RIGAUX, "Die 'Zwölf'" in Geschichte und Kerygma" in H. RISTOW and K. MATTHIAE *Der historische Jesus* . . . pp. 468-486; R. SCHNACKENBURG, *God's Rule and Kingdom* (New York 1963) pp. 215-234; X. LÉON-DUFOUR, *Les évangiles et l'histoire de Jesus* . . . pp. 430-433; A. MALVY, "Saint Jacques de Jerusalem était-il un des douze?" in *Recherches de Science Religieuse* 9 (1918) 122-131; S. LYONNET, "Témoignes de Saint Jean Chrysostomus et de Saint Jerome sur Jacques, le frère de Seigneur" in *Recherches de Science Religieuse* 29 (1939) 325-351; U. HOLZMEISTER, "Nathanael fuitne idem ac S. Bartholmeus Apostolus?" in *Biblica* 21 (1940) 28-39.

[379]R.H. RENGSTORF, "ἀπόςτολος" 407-445; J. DUPONT, "Le nom d'apôtres a-t-il été donné aux .Douze par Jésus?" in *L'Orient syrien* 1, (1956) 266-290, 425-444; E.M. KREDEL, "Der Apostelbegriff in der neueren Exegese" in *Zeitschrift für Katholische Theologie* 78 (1956) 169-195, 257-305.

[380]Since the analysis of human existence as inifinite longing for happiness can be understood as an "argument" for the existence of God, let us see the meaning the term

"argument" in the case of the "existence of God" might have. Each argument for the existence of God is like a piece of art. It is a good or bad embodying of a human experience exclusively constructed with the intention of reproducing that experience which originated it, in someone. Its trueness does not consist, therefore, in its logical construction, but in its power of being able to reproduce the experience which brought it about. The argument for the existence of God, like the great axioms and maxims, discovered for the first time, are the fruit of an experience which led its discoverer to formulate and to express it in the way we possess it now. Thus the syllogism itself is nothing else than the systematic description of a way which tends to revive the understanding experience that gave rise to the expressing process.

The general defect of most syllogisms is that they fall short of satisfying the soul's longing after complete knowledge and happiness. During the formulating process the original experience of the knowing and loving person slowly disappears to such a degree that nothing is left in the conclusion but a cognitive summary of the starting reality. Therefore, the arguments are wrong in the sense that they lose the completeness of reality and fail to lead men to the origin of the systematizing process. Instead of reality they retain only the mere idea of reality.

Now the "argument," we propose, in our view can satisfy the soul's longing after infinite knowledge as well as after infinite happiness. It does not lose the reality from which it started and also satisfies logic. It unites logic with happiness, and it leads not to an idea of God, but, by surpassing the subject-object distinction, leads to the living God, the complete happiness of man.

381Cf J. BOWKER, *Problem of Suffering in Religions of the World* (Cambridge, Mass. 1970).

382T. OHM, *Die Liebe zu Gott in den nichchtistlichen Religionen* (Freiburg 1957) pp. 447-449.

383Evidently we could not analyse the Christ event with equal thoroughness on each stratum, sc. that of science, philosophy, history, psychology, sociology, ethics, art and religion. Such a complete scrutiny would demand seven more volumes like the present one. Nevertheless, the analysis we pursued in this book makes sufficiently manifest the question-raising and faith-initiating power of the Christ event.

Subject Index

aesthetic experience, 100
Antiochian Christology, 140-141
apologetics
  a priori way of proceeding, 80
  a posteriori procedure, 80-81
  arguments from etymology, 9
  general principle of, 7-8
  missionary function and, 3
  nonbiblical, 8ff
  question raising and context
    creating function, 96-105
  philosophical, 10ff
  self-reflective dialogizing activ-
    ity, 1ff., 96ff
apostles
  arch-apostle, 227-228
  mission, 227
  šēlîah, 142-143, 258-260
  the Twelve, 227, 260-261
  witness, 228-229
apparent death
  theory of, 15, 21
areligious, 89-91
artist, 97
  (see also: aesthetic experience)

Bhagavad-Gita, 88

challenge, 1-3, 7, 10, 15ff
Christ-event, 96-105, 186-187
  its question raising power,
    101-102, 273-275
  (see also: apologetics)
Church
  its first hierarchy based on reli-
    gious experience, 227-229
  historical Jesus' intention of
    forming, 260-262
  purpose of, 59 f., 104-105,
    258ff. 267-268

computer
  C. engineer, 64ff.
  C. engineer and apologist 69-71
  higher-than-human set of ab-
    straction, 66-67
  inspiration, 64, 67
  man-believer-computer sym-
    biosis, 65-67
  (see also: macro-flow chart,
    micro-flow chart)
convergent probability, 11

demonstration, 96
  theologico-historical, 96ff.

Easter fact and Easter message,
  16, 26
entry of God into human history,
  81, 109ff.
eschatological school, 14, 16
esprit de finesse, 11
ethical consideration, 100
ethician, 97
El, Elohim and its meaning, 142-
  143

Faith, 91ff.
  analysis of, 92-93, 311
  belief and unbelief, 94
  evidence of credibility, 93-94
  freedom of, 94
  as "eye-witness" to God who
    reveals, 92, 96-97, 201
  infallible certitude and the pos-
    sibility of error, 94
  reasonableness of, 16-17, 93-95
  ultimate motive of, 92
  (see also: revelation-faith
    experience)
fideism, 16-17, 74-75

Name Index